D1571525

How the French Learned to Vote

How the French Learned to Vote

A History of Electoral Practice in France

MALCOLM CROOK

OXFORD
UNIVERSITY PRESS

OXFORD
UNIVERSITY PRESS

Great Clarendon Street, Oxford, OX2 6DP,
United Kingdom

Oxford University Press is a department of the University of Oxford.
It furthers the University's objective of excellence in research, scholarship,
and education by publishing worldwide. Oxford is a registered trade mark of
Oxford University Press in the UK and in certain other countries

© Malcolm Crook 2021

The moral rights of the author have been asserted

First Edition published in 2021

Impression: 1

Published in the United States of America by Oxford University Press
198 Madison Avenue, New York, NY 10016, United States of America

British Library Cataloguing in Publication Data
Data available

Library of Congress Control Number: 2020945712

ISBN 978-0-19-289478-6

DOI: 10.1093/oso/9780192894786.001.0001

Printed and bound by
CPI Group (UK) Ltd, Croydon, CR0 4YY

To Marcus, Mathilde, Leo, and Stefan,
dearest grandchildren, for whom I wish
a world of democracy, justice, and peace

Foreword and Acknowledgements

Some years ago, as I was preparing to set off to witness the counting of votes for a local election, in which I was standing as the Labour candidate, my wife called out, only half joking, 'If you do get in, don't come back!' In the event, I was a dozen votes short of a majority but, having spurned the offer of a recount, I was able to return home later that evening. I decided that in future it would be safer to write about the history of the vote rather than seeking office, though I continue to take part in electioneering. Indeed, I care deeply about who is elected in my own country and elsewhere, but my concern in this book is with the process rather than its outcome, set in a French context, where elections have been subject to a great deal of experimentation over a long period of time. It also the country in which I have specialized throughout my career as a historian. My object is to seek fresh insights into the universal practice of voting, with a case study of France, whose rich history of elections will throw its principal characteristics and major developments into especially sharp relief. The resulting analysis will, I hope, also assist our understanding of current electoral behaviour.

Of course, part of the fascination lies in seeing how they do things differently, if not better across the Channel, but this can prove perplexing as well as revealing. A pertinent example is furnished by an election for the administrative committee of a French historical society to which I belong. There were twelve places to be filled and a similar number of candidates on the ballot paper, so I politely inquired why a poll was being taken, only to be met with incomprehension. I therefore elaborated, explaining that it was a redundant exercise, since all twelve aspirants were bound to be chosen. The response was even firmer: 'We are holding an election!' I discovered that this has always been true in France, with a solitary candidate always subject to polling, whereas in Britain such an individual would be declared 'elected unopposed' (the way I have usually succeeded). However, the outcome of the contest I have mentioned was equally instructive, because not all candidates received all of the votes cast; some of my colleagues evidently refused to endorse the full slate of names. As I would discover, the French like to use their vote as a means of protest as well as making a choice.

I have long been drawn to France, though I struggled with the language at school (and still do), but I enjoy every excuse I can muster to spend more time in the hexagon. Indeed, I have been generously supported by Keele University in taking some of the essential research trips for this book. The increasing availability of digital resources is a helpful supplement in this regard, but not one that will ever supplant the need to reserve a regular passage on Eurostar. In any case, this project was based on a huge amount of archival work, conducted in the provinces as well as at Paris. It was preceded by one on electoral practice in the Revolution, a decade of much trial and error, which naturally occupies an important place here, though I intend to give the *Ancien Régime* its due, besides awarding pride of place to what followed in the nineteenth and twentieth centuries. Numerous articles and essays have appeared along the way, charting my gentle progress, and much of that material has been absorbed into this study, albeit always inserted into a broader context and significantly amended as my understanding has developed. Needless to say, there is a vast corpus of published work, produced by political scientists and sociologists as well as historians, on which I have drawn heavily. I owe an enormous debt to those who have tilled the field before me, in particular to those authors who have kindly lent me their assistance, as well as inviting me to participate in numerous *colloques*, collective works, and *soutenances de thèse*. Éric Anceau, Yves Déloye, Natalie Dompnier, Maud Harivel, Raymond Huard, Christophe Le Digol, Frank O'Gorman, Siân Reynolds, Hedwig Richter, Philippe Tanchoux, Vincent Villette, and Christophe Voilliot are foremost among them. My *amis robespierristes* must also be mentioned, for they, like Stephen Clay, Mel Edelstein, and Jeff Horn, have been constant *compagnons de route*.

The personal and the academic intersect especially closely in the case of our son Tom, with whom I have written several comparative studies of voting, and on whose superior historical sensitivities I have drawn deeply in revising the manuscript for this book. To share with him the finer, not to say arcane, aspects surrounding the technicalities of voter registration, or casting a ballot paper, has been a real joy as well as extremely salutary. I must also thank John Dunne, longtime friend and fellow postgraduate in London, with whom I collaborate on the investigation of Napoleonic elections and meet as often as I can to pursue our rewarding discussions. I am also very grateful to Shan and Pierre, for frequent hospitality in Montmorency (at the 'Hôtel Amusan') and in Enghien, and likewise to Claude and Christiane Petitfrère in Joué-les-Tours. Finally, I managed to see off more than one editor at Oxford University Press before this research eventually came to fruition, but their encouragement has proved unwavering and their skills have brought it to a successful conclusion. I should equally like to acknowledge the two anonymous readers of my manuscript for their helpful suggestions. At Keele, Andy Lawrence has once more excelled with the cartography (and resolutely refused to send me a bill), while other colleagues have proved tremendously supportive and I am delighted to have remained in touch with them since retirement. I have not been able to mention everyone who has helped me during the lengthy gestation of this book, but I trust they will excuse me and, perhaps, find some belated recognition in what follows. I am so pleased to have shared their company on this long but, I trust, continuing journey.

Malcolm Crook, Crewe, 2020

Contents

List of Figures, Maps, and Tables

Figures

Maps

Tables

List of Abbreviations

AD	Archives départementales
AhRf	*Annales historiques de la Révolution française*
AN	Archives nationales
AP	*Archives parlementaires*
ARSS	*Actes de la Recherche en Sciences Sociales*
BL	British Library
BNF	Bibliothèque nationale de France
ChesRf	*Commission d'histoire économique et sociale de la Rèvolution française*
EHR	*English Historical Review*
FH	*French History*
FHS	*French Historical Studies*
JO	*Journal officiel de la République*
Moniteur	*Gazette nationale ou le Moniteur universel* (*Le Moniteur universel* from 1811 onwards)
Politix	*Revue des sciences sociales du politique*
PR	proportional representation
PV	procès-verbal
Rfsp	*Revue française de science politique*
Rh	*Revue historique*
Rh19	*Revue d'histoire du XIXe siècle*
Rhmc	*Revue d'histoire moderne et contemporaine*

PRE-REVOLUTIONARY FRANCE

FLANDERS

ARTOIS

Rouen

NORMANDY

Paris
ÎLE DE
FRANCE

LORRAINE
Strasbourg
Nancy

CHAMPAGNE

ALSACE

Rennes

BRITTANY

ANJOU
MAINE
and
TOURAINE

ORLÉANAIS

Nantes

Tours

BERRY

BURGUNDY

Dijon

FRANCHE
COMTÉ

POITOU

BOURBONNAIS

La Rochelle

AUNIS and
SAINTONGE

LIMOUSIN

AUVERGNE

LYON-
NAIS
Lyon

Grenoble

Bordeaux

DAUPHINÉ

GUYENNE

GASCONY

Toulouse

LANGUEDOC

Avignon
PROVENCE
Aix

BÉARN

Mont-pellier
Marseille
Toulon

Perpignan

CORSICA

0   kms.   150
0   miles   100

ROUSSILLON

Map 1 Pre-revolutionary France

THE DEPARTMENTS
OF FRANCE IN 1790

Pas-de-Calais
Nord
Somme
Seine-Inf.
Rouen
Oise
Aisne
Ardennes
Seine
Moselle
Manche
Calvados
Eure
Paris
Marne
Meuse
Bas-Rhin
Orne
Seine-et-Oise
Meurthe
Finistère
Côtes-du-Nord
Rennes
Seine-et-Marne
Aube
Haute-Marne
Vosges
Morbihan
Ille-et-Vilaine
Mayenne
Eure-et-Loir
Haut-Rhin
Sarthe
Loiret
Haute-Saône
Loire-Inf.
Maine-et-Loire
Yonne
Nantes
Loir-et-Cher
Côte-d'Or
Doubs
Indre-et-Loire
Cher
Nièvre
Vendée
Vienne
Indre
Saône-et-Loire
Jura
Deux-Sèvres
Allier
Ain
Charente-Inf.
Creuse
Rhône-et-Loire
Charente
Hte.-Vienne
Puy-de-Dôme
Lyon
Corrèze
Isère
Dordogne
Cantal
Haute-Loire
Bordeaux
Ardèche
Hautes-Alpes
Gironde
Lot-et-Garonne
Lot
Lozère
Drôme
Aveyron
Basses-Alpes
Landes
Gard
Vaucluse (1791)
Gers
Toulouse
Tarn
Bouches-du-Rhône
Var
Basses-Pyrénées
Hte.-Garonne
Hérault
Marseille
Toulon
Hautes-Pyrénées
Aude
Ariège
Pyrénées-Orientales
Corse

0   kms.   150
0   miles   100

Map 2 The departments of France in 1790

THE DEPARTMENTS OF FRANCE IN 1870

Pas-de-Calais
Nord
Somme
Seine-Inf.
Rouen
Oise
Aisne
Ardennes
Seine
Moselle
Manche
Calvados
Eure
Marne
Meuse
Meurthe
Bas-Rhin
Orne
Paris
Seine
-et-
Marne
Finistère
Côtes-du-Nord
Rennes
Ille-et-Vilaine
Morbihan
Mayenne
Sarthe
Eure-et-Loir
Loiret
Aube
Haute-Marne
Vosges
Haute-Saône
Haut-Rhin
Loire-Inf.
Nantes
Maine-et-Loire
Loir-et-Cher
Indre-et-Loire
Cher
Nièvre
Yonne
Côte-d'Or
Doubs
Vendée
Vienne
Indre
Saône-et-Loire
Jura
Deux-Sèvres
Creuse
Allier
Ain
Haute-Savoie
Charente-Inf.
Hte.-Vienne
Charente
Puy-de-Dôme
Rhône
Lyon
Savoie
Corrèze
Loire
Isère
Dordogne
Bordeaux
Cantal
Haute-Loire
Ardèche
Drôme
Hautes-Alpes
Gironde
Lot-et-Garonne
Lot
Aveyron
Lozère
Basses-Alpes
Alpes Maritimes
Landes
Tarn-et-Garonne
Toulouse
Tarn
Gard
Vaucluse
Gers
Hte.-Garonne
Hérault
Bouches-du-Rhône
Marseille
Var
Toulon
Basses-Pyrénées
Hautes-Pyrénées
Aude
Ariège
Pyrénées-Orientales

Corse

0   kms.   150
0   miles   100

Map 3 The departments of France in 1870

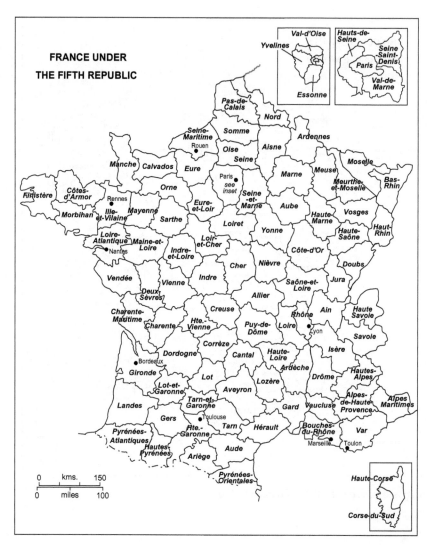

Map 4 France under the Fifth Republic

Introduction

Why France?

Voting? People go into my classroom on a Sunday, hide behind a curtain, then put an envelope into a box with a hole in it.

Paul, aged seven.[1]

Voting constitutes a familiar civic ritual for most adults, albeit one that is infrequently exercised and rapidly accomplished today. Yet the connection between one's daily life and a piece of paper placed in a box is by no means self-evident, as the comment above, from a French child, suggests. Voting did not emerge spontaneously, and it is easy to forget that it represents the outcome of a long, complex, and contested history, which reflects the nature of the society that has constructed it. Far from being a natural gesture it took some time to assimilate, besides requiring the development of the technology to facilitate it. Over the years the vote has evolved from a wholly public to a largely private act, employing ballot papers, pulling levers or, more lately, tapping a screen. In fact, many scholars today are concerned to understand the practice of voting itself, rather than con-centrate their attention exclusively on analysing the political outcome of elections, or their sociology and geography, subjects at which the French have excelled.[2] Inspired by such research into the *acte de vote*, the study that follows does not consider who was elected, nor why, but instead explores the process rather than the product. It examines how voting has been organized and practised in France from the early modern period onwards and, above all, how ordinary French men and women learned to vote.

The social, cultural, and material perspectives on the act of voting that inform my work emanate largely from recent authors, but there were forerunners who pioneered these currently fruitful approaches. For example, members of the 'Chicago school' in the 1920s, like Charles Merriam and Harold Gosnell, sought

---

[1] Cited in Michel Offerlé, *Un Homme, une voix? Histoire du suffrage universel* (Paris, 1993), 101.

[2] This tradition, which began with the ground-breaking study by André Siegfried, *Tableau politique de la France de l'Ouest sous la Troisième République* (Paris, 1913), is exemplified by François Goguel, *Géographie des élections françaises de 1870 à 1951* (Paris, 1951) and the series of departmental mono-graphs he supervised.

How the French Learned to Vote: A History of Electoral Practice in France. Malcolm Crook, Oxford University Press (2021).
© Malcolm Crook. DOI: 10.1093/oso/9780192894786.003.0001

to comprehend why electors turned out to vote or, in many cases, failed to do so.[3] On the other side of the Atlantic, Alexandre Pilenco was simultaneously author-ing two books on electoral culture in France, which went largely unnoticed at the time—both were re-published in 2018.[4] Meanwhile, in interwar Britain, Mass-Observation, an organization devoted to social research, was beginning to employ the sort of public opinion surveys that would routinely accompany much investigation into electoral behaviour after the Second World War.[5] Indeed, the term 'psephology' was coined to describe the branch of political science that analysed electoral statistics, though it was little used in France. Its practitioners continued to explore the outcome of elections rather than the act of voting, but there were studies which considered why people participated or abstained. Alain Lancelot's L'Abstentionnisme électoral en France, which combined statistical, geographical, and sociological approaches to excellent effect, offers an outstanding example of the latter.[6]

The closing decades of the twentieth century witnessed a decisive turning point in the history of voting, marked by the appearance of a collective work entitled Explication du vote, in 1985.[7] It was based on a conference that brought together French historians, political scientists, and sociologists, who sought to take stock of the question and propose new directions for research into electoral behaviour. Contributors to that volume were among those who proceeded to produce a number of path-breaking studies devoted to the history of the vote in France dur-ing the following decade. Raymond Huard paved the way in 1991, with a Histoire du suffrage universel, which explored the practice of voting as well as the exten-sion of the franchise.[8] A year later, Alain Garrigou published Comment les Français sont devenus électeurs, which examined voting in its social context and the emergence of the modern citizen as an independent voter, while Pierre Rosanvallon produced Le Sacre du citoyen, the first instalment of a magnificent trilogy on the 'archaeology of democracy', which analysed the intellectual history of the suffrage in France.[9] The following year, Michel Offerlé published a brief,

[3] Charles Edward Merriam and Harold Foote Gosnell, Non-Voting: Causes and Methods of Control (Chicago, IL, 1924) and Harold Foote Gosnell, Why Europe Votes (Chicago, IL, 1930).

[4] Alexandre Pilenco, Les Moeurs électorales en France: régime censitaire (Paris, 1928) and Les Moeurs électorales du suffrage universel en France (1848–1930) (Paris, 1930). Both volumes can be accessed on Bibliothèque nationale de France (hereafter BNF) Gallica.

[5] Nick Hubble, Mass Observation and Everyday Life (Basingstoke, 2006).

[6] Alain Lancelot, L'Abstentionnisme électoral en France (Paris, 1968).

[7] Daniel Gaxie (ed.), Explication du vote. Un bilan des études électorales en France (Paris, 1985).

[8] Raymond Huard, Le Suffrage universel en France 1848–1946 (Paris, 1991).

[9] Alain Garrigou, Le Vote et la vertu. Comment les Français sont devenus électeurs (Paris, 1992), which was published in a revised version as Histoire sociale du suffrage universel en France 1848–2000 (Paris, 2002), and Pierre Rosanvallon, Le Sacre du citoyen. Histoire du suffrage universel en France (Paris, 1992), followed by Le Peuple introuvable. Histoire de la représentation démocratique en France (Paris, 1998) and La Démocratie inachevée. Histoire de la souveraineté du peuple en France (Paris, 2000).

but lavishly illustrated, *Histoire du suffrage universel,* aimed at a wider readership, which reflected his particular interest in the iconography of voting, though he has written widely on the subject.[10]

Meanwhile, jointly as well as individually, Yves Déloye and Olivier Ihl were exploring the material history of the vote, including the technology of elections such as ballot papers (*bulletins*) and ballot boxes (*urnes*). They subsequently gathered a series of their articles into a single volume entitled *L'Acte de vote.*[11] It was left to jurist Philippe Tanchoux to trace the increasingly regulated transition of the vote in France from its less formal, collective expression in the corporations of the *Ancien Régime* to the more disciplined, abstract choice of an individual citizen in the twentieth century.[12] In fact, by the time these two books appeared, a flourishing academic enterprise had culminated in 2001 with the publication of a splendid, and monumental, *Dictionnaire du vote.* It represented a great, comprehensive, team effort, with almost 400 entries, on a wide variety of relevant topics, compiled by many of the individuals just listed, along with numerous other authors to be found in the footnotes to this book.[13]

French scholars tended to focus their original research into the 'social history' of voting in France on the years after 1848, when direct, universal male suffrage had been introduced under the Second Republic, but earlier periods were also coming under investigation. This was particularly true of the French Revolution, when an initial experiment was conducted with a mass franchise, yet without hitherto attracting great interest from historians. However, the bicentennial commemoration of 1989, plus a shift towards researching political culture, helped turn the elections of the revolutionary decade into something of a minor industry.[14] Yet voting had certainly not been invented in 1789 and, more recently, Olivier Christin has demonstrated its importance under the *Ancien Régime* in a study of the early modern period, which examines polling in corporate bodies such as municipalities and trade guilds.[15] This neglected activity repays careful

---

[10] Offerlé, *Un Homme, une voix?* See also Michel Offerlé, 'Les figures du vote. Pour une iconographie du suffrage universel', *Sociétés & Représentations,* 12 (2001/2), 108–30, an engrossing subject which has not been pursued in this study.

[11] Yves Déloye and Olivier Ihl, *L'Acte de vote* (Paris, 2008).

[12] Philippe Tanchoux, *Les Procédures électorales en France de la fin de l'Ancien Régime à la Première Guerre mondiale* (Paris, 2004).

[13] Pascal Perrineau and Dominique Reynié (eds), *Dictionnaire du vote* (Paris, 2001). See, in particular, the entry by Michel Offerlé, 'Socio-histoire', 850–6.

[14] Patrice Gueniffey, *Le Nombre et la raison. La Révolution française et les élections* (Paris, 1993); Malcolm Crook, *Elections in the French Revolution: An Apprenticeship in Democracy, 1789–1799* (Cambridge, 1996); and Melvin Edelstein, *The French Revolution and the Birth of Electoral Democracy* (Farnham, 2014). See also Serge Aberdam et al. (eds), *Voter, élire pendant la Révolution française 1789–1799. Guide pour la recherche,* 2nd edn (Paris, 2006).

[15] Olivier Christin, *Vox populi. Une histoire du vote avant le suffrage universel* (Paris, 2014).

analysis at a time when parliamentary elections were generally in abeyance.[16] By now the study of electoral culture had been taken up elsewhere, with some significant contributions emanating from anglophone countries, such as Britain, the United States, and Australia, where there is a long history of representative regimes.[17] A flourishing group of electoral historians has emerged in Germany too, under the aegis of Hubertus Buchstein, ranging broadly and probing elections in authoritarian regimes, which employ the vote in their own fashion.[18] The Latin American experience of voting in the nineteenth century has also been attracting some attention of late.[19]

Indeed, in recent years, not simply a comparative history of the vote, but a transnational one has come to the fore. It has roots in the studies conducted by policy-makers and scholars more than a century ago, into how the world was voting, to adapt the title of an overarching survey published by the Americans Charles Seymour and Donald Frary, at the end of the First World War. Indeed, this pair of authors posited a triumphant prospect: 'It is both foolish and futile to retard the progress of democracy in elections', they concluded.[20] Convinced that the principle of electoral liberty was no longer in doubt, they thought its worldwide endorsement inevitable in the near future, only to be cruelly disabused by the dictatorial turn of the subsequent interwar period. In fact, the international development and dissemination of electoral reform was as uneven as it had been within different states, and far from uniform. Yet, from the mid-nineteenth century onwards, such previously overlooked endeavours played a vital role in the unfolding process of democratization. They demonstrate that learning to vote was a genuinely global enterprise, which offers fertile terrain for further research.[21]

---

[16] See Christophe Le Digol et al. (eds), *Histoires d'élections. Représentations et usages du vote de l'Antiquité à nos jours* (Paris, 2018) and Maud Harivel, *Les Élections politiques dans la République de Venise (XVIᵉ–XVIIIᵉsiècle). Entre justice distributive et corruption* (Paris, 2019) for further examples.

[17] Frank O'Gorman, *Voters, Patrons and Parties: The Unreformed Electorate of Hanoverian England, 1734–1832* (Oxford, 1989), has paved the way in Britain, but has few emulators, save for Jon Lawrence, *Electing our Masters: The Hustings from Hogarth to Blair* (Oxford, 2009) and 'The culture of elections in modern Britain', *History*, 96 (2011), 459–76. Richard Franklin Bensel, *The American Ballot Box in the Mid-Nineteenth Century* (Cambridge, 2004), offers a good example from across the Atlantic. See also Graeme Orr, *Ritual and Rhythm in Electoral Systems: A Comparative Legal Account* (Abingdon, 2015), which draws on Britain, the United States, and Australia for a lively thematic survey.

[18] There is a significant school of German scholars working on the history of the ballot, led by Hubertus Buchstein, *Öffentliche und geheime Stimmabgabe. Eine wahlrechtshistorische und ideengeschichtliche Studie* (Baden-Baden, 2000). See also, Ralph Jessen and Hedwig Richter (eds), *Voting for Hitler and Stalin: Elections under 20th Century Dictatorships* (Frankfurt, 2011).

[19] Eduardo Posada-Carbó (ed.), *Elections before Democracy: The History of Elections in Europe and Latin America* (Basingstoke, 1996).

[20] Charles Seymour and Donald Paige Frary, *How the World Votes: The Story of Democratic Development in Elections*, 2 vols (Springfield, MA, 1918), ii, 310.

[21] Malcolm Crook and Tom Crook, 'Reforming voting practices in a global age: the making and remaking of the modern secret ballot in Britain, France and the United States, c. 1600–c. 1950', *Past & Present*, 212 (2011), 199–237.

France as Exemplar and Exception

Today, most countries hold elections on an equivalent basis and in a similar fashion, so it is tempting to assume that their past experience has been essentially the same. Yet, despite the eventual, widespread adoption of a universal franchise and the secret ballot, each state has pursued its own path in this direction and its electoral system has retained a number of specific features. In the quest to incorporate the mass of the people into the process of government, France offers an especially fascinating case study, both exemplary and exceptional in many regards. The issue of voting has occupied a major place in its history since 1789 and deposited vast quantities of documentation as a result. Revolution and military defeat have produced a series of profound ruptures in French history and, in their wake, prompted a succession of debates about the vote, leading to a range of electoral experiments that have no equal elsewhere. Over the last two centuries, successive monarchies, republics, and empires have promulgated two dozen constitutions, while making twenty changes in the legislative electoral system and a dozen major amendments to the franchise (see Appendix 1). By contrast, until very recently, Britain has stuck rigidly to an electoral procedure known as first-past-the-post and made only gradual reforms to the suffrage. In France, in the absence of any incremental development, there was no inexorable progress towards free and fair elections for all, with advances repeatedly followed by reversals which, under the Vichy regime, after the *débâcle* of 1940, resulted in no polling whatsoever.

As a consequence, the country has constituted a veritable laboratory for the vote, on a vast scale, with an unparalleled electorate of roughly five million French men in the 1790s and almost ten million in 1848; in Britain, until 1918, it remained less than seven million. Yet the franchise was extremely slow to follow for French women, who only acceded to the suffrage in 1944, almost a century after French males, a contradiction that has preoccupied a number of contemporary historians. Innovations in the electoral domain have often been pioneered in relatively small polities, the female vote being a good case in point, but the French have launched some unprecedented schemes in a sweeping fashion.[22] Inexperienced voters were summoned to the polls to participate in a multiplicity of elections under the Revolution which, besides national deputies and local administrators, included selecting officers in the national guard militia, justices of the peace, judges, and even bishops and priests. These latter categories have since been removed from the electoral agenda, but of late elections to the presidency, regional councils, and the European parliament have been added to those for

---

[22] John Markoff, 'From centre to periphery and back again: reflections on the geography of democratic innovation', in Michael P. Hanagan and Charles Tilly (eds), *Extending Citizenship, Reconfiguring States* (Lanham, MD, 1999), 229–46.

legislators and local councillors. It is unusual for a year to pass without an election of some sort and 1988 was an *annus mirabilis*, with no less than four separate polls involving seven rounds of voting.[23] Moreover, the number of posts to be filled has always been enormous. Today, the total of *élus* in France stands at over 500,000, so more than one in every one hundred electors is an elected office-holder (overwhelmingly at the municipal level), compared to roughly one in 350 in Britain, for example.[24]

The French Revolution, that decisive moment in modern French history, swept away the great diversity of practice that had characterized the *Ancien Régime*, and instead imposed uniformity from top to bottom of the electoral process. This approach has, with very few exceptions, been maintained ever since, whereas voting laws are still largely determined at state level in the United States, and in Britain a variety of franchises persisted until as late as 1948, while different electoral systems have recently been introduced at the regional and local level.[25] In revolutionary France, widespread illiteracy notwithstanding, written paper ballots were immediately prescribed for all elections. The desire for equality extended to electoral representation, which was partly determined on the basis of departmental population, linking democracy to demography. Indeed, it was stipulated in the Constitution of 1793 that there should be a separately elected national deputy for every 39,000–41,000 inhabitants but, like the document itself, this rather unrealistic provision was still-born. Local government was transformed in a similarly standard fashion in 1789, when all communes (municipalities, large and small) were awarded a mayor and a council, the size of which still depends on the number of inhabitants. The contrast with the patchwork that exists in contemporary Britain could not be starker (see Maps 1 and 2).

Unlike many other countries, the French experience of voting has always been an intensive as well as an extensive one. For although the electoral system has chopped and changed, most famously oscillating between departmental lists and single-member constituencies (*scrutin de liste* and *scrutin d'arrondissement*), not to mention experiments with different forms of proportional representation, a second-ballot provision has lasted longer than any of the alternatives, and is currently in operation for presidential, legislative, and local elections (see Appendix 1).[26] It allows time for reflection between the two rounds of voting today, but the aim of producing an absolute majority for the winner, when only two contestants remain in contention at the *ballottage*, was firmly established in

---

[23] Presidential elections were followed by legislative polls, then 'cantonal' elections to renew half of the departmental councillors and, finally, a referendum. Unlike Britain or the United States, the French have very rarely held more than one election at the same time.

[24] Élus locaux, 2018, http://www.collectivites-locales.gouv.fr/elus-locaux (accessed 20/03/20).

[25] Colin Rallings and Michael Thrasher, *British Political Facts 1832–2006* (Aldershot, 2007), 104.

[26] Peter Campbell (with Alistair Cole), *French Electoral Systems and Elections since 1789* (Aldershot, 1989), 3–4, focuses on successive systems, which will not receive great attention in this study, save in so far as they affected the act of voting.

the Revolution, when a third round was often employed for this purpose. Exhaustive balloting was a deeply entrenched tradition during the *Ancien Régime*, and the same was true of the practice of voting in an assembly, which was retained for public elections in France until 1848, when the huge size of the electorate finally rendered it impractical. It naturally encouraged a collective rather than individual approach to the vote, facilitating deliberation as well as polling; debating and voting had always been inextricably intertwined.

During the early years of the Revolution, meeting in assemblies, many voters insisted on passing resolutions and gathering for the purpose of discussion outside of regular elections, as well as requesting the right to mandate and recall deputies.[27] The practice of 'direct democracy' is especially associated with the Parisian *sans-culottes*, but it was far more widespread. The abortive Constitution of 1793 actually made provision for the ratification of legislation by the electorate, if demand was sufficient, but it remained a dead letter. The idea of representative democracy, which was invented in the late eighteenth century, came to prevail instead.[28] In the novel context of mass voting, most writers and political actors argued that a division of labour was necessary between those chosen to wield authority, on the one hand, and franchise-holders who were to elect them, on the other. Yet this was also a means of balancing 'numbers with reason', creating an elite of office-holders and effectively limiting the rights of ordinary voters, many of whom were regarded with misgivings.[29] Indeed, indirect elections were employed in France during the 1790s and early 1800s, which reserved the choice of legislators to the mostly wealthy members of small, second-degree, departmental assemblies; significantly, they were awarded the title 'electors'.[30] This procedure was only abandoned under the Bourbon Restoration when the suffrage was reduced so drastically that the device was no longer required, though since 1875 members of an upper parliamentary chamber, the Senate, have been chosen by means of electoral colleges.

When universal manhood suffrage was established in 1848, on the basis of direct election to the legislature, the sovereignty of the people was still to be expressed in a representative regime, a stipulation which has proved to be an enduring source of tension in modern French political culture.[31] In 1789, the

[27] Maurice Genty, *Paris 1789-1795. L'apprentissage de la citoyenneté* (Paris, 1987) and R.B. Rose, *The Making of the* Sans-Culottes: *Democratic Ideas and Institutions in Paris, 1789-1792* (Manchester, 1983).

[28] John Keane, *The Life and Death of Democracy* (London, 2009), 159ff. He refers to the preceding era as 'assembly democracy'.

[29] Bernard Manin, *The Principles of Representative Government*, trans. (Cambridge, 1997).

[30] The emergent United States created an electoral college for its presidency, which remains in being today.

[31] Rosanvallon, *La Démocratie inachevée*, 9-38, and *Le Peuple introuvable*, 74ff; Marcel Gauchet, *La Révolution des pouvoirs. La souveraineté, le peuple et la représentation 1789-1799* (Paris, 1995), 7-18 and Jeremy Jennings, *Revolution and the Republic: A History of Political Thought in France since the Eighteenth Century* (Oxford, 2010).

Declaration of the Rights of Man and the Citizen, stated that 'The principle of all sovereignty resides essentially in the Nation', an axiom more explicitly reiterated in all the republican constitutions that have followed, from 1793 to 1958.[32] However, the original Declaration went on to say that 'Law is the expression of the general will. All citizens have a right to participate in its formation, *either in person, or through their representatives*' (my emphasis). Despite the equivocation, and the experimentation with direct democracy that followed, representation prevailed, but the question of how it was to be determined by means of the electoral system remained an extremely thorny issue, the source of endless debate. Would the election of deputies by a simple majority at the ballot box accurately represent the sovereign will of people, and could the electorate be sure that representatives would faithfully fulfil the task with which they had been entrusted?

The Constitution of the Fifth Republic, the current regime, maintains that 'sovereignty belongs to the people', before clearly stating that this authority is 'exercised through its representatives'. Yet representation continues to sit uneasily with this unambiguous assertion, for the same article proceeds to add that popular sovereignty may also be expressed via referendums. Frequently used under the Fifth Republic, which proceeded to re-introduce direct election to the presidency (it had been tried once before, in 1848), consultations of this sort have a long, if episodic history, dating back once more to the French Revolution when they were instituted to obtain approval for the Constitutions of 1793 and 1795 (see Appendix 4). In twentieth-century France, referendums have constituted an adjunct to the representative system, whereas Napoleon Bonaparte employed popular votes at the beginning of the nineteenth century to endorse an authoritarian form of government. Plebiscites, as they became known, were subsequently revived by his nephew Louis-Napoleon as a means of manufacturing assent for his regime, but he justified them as a way of transcending representation by appealing directly to the people.[33] Bonapartism thus provided an early demonstration that mass suffrage should not be automatically equated with democracy, a lesson not lost on later dictatorships.

The sovereignty of the French people may sometimes have been traduced, but it has been underpinned by a strong sense of citizenship, another significant product of 1789.[34] The revolutionaries rejected the social order of the *Ancien Régime* along with its political system, and mass, male suffrage was regarded as being egalitarian as well as democratic; numbers had no respect for rank. Like the achievement of a universal franchise, the embodiment of this somewhat abstract

[32] Jacques Godechot (ed.), *Les Constitutions de la France depuis 1789* (Paris, 1970), for convenient reference.
[33] Rosanvallon, *La Démocratie inachevée*, 183–93.
[34] Raymonde Monnier (ed.), *Citoyens et citoyenneté sous la Révolution française* (Paris, 2006).

construct was a lengthy process, but citizenship in France was conceived as uniform and prescriptive, on account of the priority accorded to institutions of national scope.[35] Although the inculcation of republican values via universal schooling would not commence until a century later, civic instruction was high on the French educational agenda from the very outset of the Revolution. One of the citizens' core responsibilities lies in the elaboration of the general will, through exercising the vote, and engagement in elections constitutes a binding duty as well as an inalienable right.[36] Compulsory voting, the most draconian antidote to the scourge of abstention, has accordingly been a constant source of debate, though it has never been enacted. The deeply ingrained French ideal of the sovereign citizen thus informs many aspects of the electoral practice to be explored in the pages that follow.

What Makes this Study Different?

Besides bringing a British perspective to bear on the subject, and being written in English, this book offers a far more comprehensive investigation of the act of voting than anyone has so far attempted, in terms of its range across time and regime, type of election, and the whole array of associated activity. The general studies that already exist are confined to chronological spans of varying lengths, but this study relates to the *longue durée*, beginning with the early modern period and proceeding to the present day, in order to highlight continuity as well as change in the practice of voting in France. Political scientists are apt to begin in 1848, with the first elections by direct, universal male suffrage, while historians are more likely to go back to the Revolution of 1789. Yet the latter was no year zero where elections were concerned. Taking the *Ancien Régime* into account reveals its legacy to modern elections, to be found, for example, in the reluctance to adopt declared candidatures, or abandon a multi-ballot system. An inclusive approach also means that different forms of government can be accommodated in this history of the vote, whereas French scholars have been inclined to focus exclusively on the contribution of republican regimes at the expense of their rivals. In fact, as a result of frequent polling on the basis of universal male suffrage, the Second Empire deeply embedded the habit of voting, despite the open interference of its administrative personnel in the conduct of elections.

A second key feature, in contrast to similar accounts, resides in the reference made in this book to the full range of polls that involved the entire electorate.

---

[35] Pierre Rosanvallon, *Le Modèle politique français. La société civile contre le jacobinisme de 1789 à nos jours* (Paris, 2004).

[36] Cécile Laborde, 'La citoyenneté', in Vincent Duclert and Christophe Prochasson (eds), *Dictionnaire critique de la République* (Paris, 2007), 116–23.

Legislative elections have always taken pride of place on account of their political importance, though their primacy has been eclipsed under the Fifth Republic by the institution of direct elections to the presidency. Referendums, reinstated under this regime as an additional means of consulting the public, like their avatars, have usually been ignored in general histories of the vote but, like elections, they afford further insight into the practice of voting and they have been incorporated here. Meanwhile, local polls for municipalities and arrondissement and departmental councils have always been a poor relation of electoral research and historical studies of them often concentrate on a single community or circumscription. They are rather more difficult to research in general terms, because the relevant material is located in the provincial *archives départementales*, and data relating to them has only been consistently collected by the central government since the Second World War. Yet both before and after 1789 the majority of elections were concerned with the choice of personnel at this level. It was uniquely in this context that most voters acquired electoral experience under the *Ancien Régime* and during the Revolution. Even after 1848, when direct elections to a national assembly were introduced, polling for local authorities offered far more frequent opportunities to learn how to vote.

Finally, a comparative dimension informs this study, not least because research into the history of voting in another country draws attention to contrasting electoral practices, in the case of this author on either side of the English Channel. Such a perspective can inhibit understanding, since the outsider's view may take an uncomprehending turn when encountering what seem to be odd procedures, such as French elections with a single candidate. Yet it also serves as a critical yardstick for appreciating specificities which may be less apparent to a native observer. Such inherent comparison has also brought to light contemporary investigations into the practice of voting elsewhere that were pursued by policymakers and academics in France, Britain, and other states from the nineteenth century onwards. When they embarked upon their electoral apprenticeship, the French initially had few models to follow beyond classical ones and their own inherited practices, though Britain invariably supplied a negative point of reference, not least in terms of its corrupt practices, which were routinely condemned in France. However, during the latter part of the nineteenth century, the French began to look abroad for inspiration in their quest for freer and fairer elections.

This study thus aims to be comprehensive, but there are perforce limits, because voting is practised in such a variety of different contexts that we scarcely notice it in many different walks of life, where it often serves as the conclusion to collective discussion, not least in parliamentary and local assemblies. As René Rémond puts it, in his introduction to the *Dictionnaire du vote*, its universality, over time and space, is quite remarkable; we do indeed inhabit a civilization that is based on voting.[37] Besides the political domain, where it attracts more participants

---

[37] René Rémond, Préface, in Perrineau and Reynié (eds), *Dictionnaire du vote*, vii–ix.

than any other activity, it ranges from the professional and associational, to the academic and the judicial which both employ juries, and it even extends to the recreational sphere in game shows. The narrower focus here is on public votes, which involve all members of the registered electorate in the whole country or a specific community. This excludes those polls in France which have been employed to elect members of industrial relations tribunals and trades councils, for example. These certainly had an important role to play in the electoral learning process, not least where females were concerned, for women were able to vote in this context long before they could do so in local or national elections.

However, the reach of this book was already sufficiently challenging and this has led to a further omission, which concerns the unusual, if not unique, French practice of extending electoral participation outside the mainland, far beyond the 'metropole'. During the Revolution of 1789, and likewise after 1848, the vote was given to some inhabitants in the colonies acquired by France, who despatched deputies to the French legislature and elected their own local authorities. In the early twentieth century a significant debate began about the degree to which indigenous people should be awarded the franchise, until the issue was overtaken by the end of empire in the wake of the Second World War. Yet the process of decolonization left France with a number of *départements et territoires d'Outre-Mer*, habitually called DOM-TOMs.[38] All their citizens have the right to participate in presidential elections, send deputies to the French and European parliaments, and elect local councils, on the same basis and at the same time as their counterparts in the metropole. More recently, the opportunity for French citizens who reside abroad to vote in legislative elections has been enhanced by the creation of distinct constituencies to represent them. Nonetheless, only the act of voting in the metropolitan departments will be considered here, with one or two minor exceptions, though the particular character of colonial and overseas elections offers another fruitful topic for future investigation.

The Issues to be Explored

Rather than adopting a narrative approach, which might have obscured the salient features of voting practices in France, this book is organized on a thematic basis. The overall aim is not simply to explain how the French learned to vote, but also to problematize the process and to challenge received wisdom, not least by bringing to light contradictory developments and the role of contingency. Besides raising questions, this study will also provide a critical appraisal of what is sometimes regarded as a successfully completed apprenticeship in voting. Such a re-assessment is especially pertinent in the light of current trends which suggest

---

[38] Since 2003 they have officially become the *Départements ou régions français d'Outre-Mer* (DROM) and the *Collectivités d'Outre-Mer* (COM).

that the habit of regular voting, which was established at the turn of the twentieth century, has become an intermittent activity for increasing numbers of citizens. There have been losses as well as gains for the expanding electorate along the way, as the business of voting was more closely regulated, as well as reformed. While the objective of this study is analytical rather than descriptive, each chapter proceeds in an essentially chronological fashion, so that a rudimentary knowledge of French history should suffice to render it accessible to non-specialists. Nonetheless, to assist the reader in following the rapid succession of changes across these chapters, a chronological list of the major legislation relating to regime change and elections since 1789 has been included in Appendix 1.

The investigation begins in Chapter 1 by asking exactly who was able to vote, first of all among men. Much has been written about the male franchise, yet the establishment in France of one man, one vote, let alone universal suffrage proper, was far more problematic than is often realized. The idea that the vote should be awarded on the basis of certain criteria, such as tax payment or property owner-ship, was widely accepted for much of the nineteenth century in France, as else-where. Universal male suffrage may have been proclaimed in the Constitution of 1793, but it was not implemented, and its establishment in 1848 was completely unanticipated. There were moments of reversal as well as advance, notably under the restored monarchy after 1814, while disenfranchisement also occurred during the First and Second Republics. Even at the beginning of the Third Republic, in the early 1870s, the principle was still being forcefully contested by conservatives and its imminent triumph was by no means preordained.

Universal male suffrage thus took nearly one hundred years to achieve, but the process for women would prove still more protracted. Historians highlight the fact that the advent of mass suffrage for males and females in France was separated by almost a century, from 1848 to 1944. Yet this conundrum can be partly explained by the precocious arrival of universal manhood suffrage (invariably referred to as 'universal suffrage' by contemporaries) because, almost everywhere, there was an interval between the award of votes to men and women, usually shorter where full male suffrage arrived later. The frequently invoked 'delay' in France is thus more apparent than real. Not surprisingly, the campaign for a female franchise, which was launched in France towards the end of the nineteenth century, has been the subject of much scrutiny of late, though it has attracted more attention outside than inside the hexagon. Women themselves were rather more inventive in demanding the suffrage than is often supposed and Chapter 2 will highlight their involvement in elections before they could vote, emphasizing political factors in the frustration of their demands for the franchise, before con-cluding with their rapidly accomplished electoral apprenticeship in post-war France.

Candidates and campaigns, which are examined in Chapters 3 and 4, respect-ively, are part and parcel of contemporary elections, but this has not always been the case. An exploration of how individuals offered themselves to the electorate in the past and sought to influence the voter's choice is thus essential to an understanding of how voting developed. Today the term 'candidate' carries a clear meaning: it describes individuals (or a list of individuals) who have registered their intention to stand in an electoral contest. It is therefore a surprise to discover that in France it was only from 1889 onwards that a declaration of candidature was demanded from those seeking election to the Chamber of Deputies. During the early modern period, and beyond, the term 'candidate' did not convey its current meaning, leaving voters free to nominate whom they wished among those who were eligible for election. The practice of supporting 'official' candidates, which was employed by all nineteenth-century French regimes, not just the Second Empire, only served to discredit the idea of formal candidatures. Dogged French resistance in this respect was more than simply deference to tradition; after 1789 it was also an assertion of the right of the sovereign people to make its own, unfettered choices.

So how did voters decide? Just as declared candidatures were resisted, so overt campaigning was condemned by custom. Actively seeking election to office was regarded as self-defeating, and voters were urged to look instead to those who allowed their talents and virtues to speak for themselves. Of course, electioneering had always gone on, but in a discreet fashion, by word of mouth, within small groups. The advent of mass suffrage would eventually change the rules of this game, though the promotion of particular candidates, like the resources expended on their campaigns, was still regarded unfavourably. The lines between simply canvassing for votes and using corrupt means to secure them were frequently blurred. Though the rise of democracy is often equated with a reduction in electoral malpractice, the French case suggests a rather more complicated relationship, since a much larger electorate offered opportunities for bribery and intimidation on a larger scale. The demand for electoral integrity, together with greater security for the ballot, did begin to curb familiar forms of malpractice at the turn of the twentieth century, but fresh means of manipulating the will of the people have emerged in the age of the Internet.

The bitterly disputed question of precisely how votes were to be cast is the subject of Chapter 5. The global development of voting over the past two centuries has been marked by a shift from public to private polling, and the secret ballot has now been generally adopted. A pioneering proposal for a fully secure vote, delivered in a compartment, was made in France during the 1790s, but a measure of this sort was not implemented there until the introduction of an envelope and the polling booth (isoloir) on the eve of the First World War. To be sure, over the intervening hundred years or so, the French had insisted on the employment of a hand-written or printed ballot paper, but they were unable to make it wholly secret on account of widespread illiteracy and the retention of a traditional assembly mechanism, where voters met to conduct their electoral business together. Even after the abolition of assemblies, in 1848, the elector's choice remained something of an 'open secret' until 1914. A century later paper balloting is threatened by the technology of electronic voting, which is currently employed in many countries, but in only a small number of French communes.

After 1789, it soon became evident that awarding the franchise did not automatically lead to its employment. It was necessary to enable, encourage, and educate electors to use their vote, for exhortations usually fell on deaf ears and voter fatigue quickly took its toll, as Chapter 6 will demonstrate. Despite the unprecedented turnout recorded in the spring of 1848, when almost seven million Frenchmen voted, mobilizing the mass male electorate remained a significant challenge and the subject of much concern. Electoral acculturation was a protracted and uneven process, geographically as well as chronologically, with a differentiated response according to the type of election and, briefly after 1945, by gender. Yet the Second Empire marked a significant turning point and, for men at least, the long apprenticeship finally seemed to have come to fruition by the turn of the twentieth century, after which high levels of turnout increasingly became the norm. An overall synthesis and interpretation will be offered here, which emphasizes the importance of local elections in creating the habit of voting.

However, by no means all participants cast a legitimate ballot. Attention will thus turn in Chapter 7 to a deeply entrenched, but hidden aspect of voting in France, called 'civic abstention', which is now becoming more visible. In 2017, some four million French citizens went to the polls, but voted for neither of the two, remaining candidates in the second round of the presidential election. This record number should be related to a long tradition of spoiling papers in France. Voting blank, or annotating the ballot paper, both offer an alternative to non-voting, though neither counts towards the electoral outcome. Indeed, this particular practice is much maligned, even feared by politicians, who have so far refused to make blank papers available at the polling station, or to consider annotated ballots as legitimate forms of electoral expression. The gesture clearly indicates disaffection and represents a form of protest but, unlike abstention, it still involves casting a ballot. The French have learned to subvert as well as support their culture of elections in order to express an objection, or an opinion, and the development of this important yet long-ignored phenomenon comes under close examination in this penultimate chapter.

Last but not least, the subject of abstention itself will be addressed (Chapter 8), in order to add a historical dimension to current preoccupations with the widespread increase in non-voting. Towards the end of the nineteenth century, when a relatively small number of French electors persisted in shunning the polls, there were many advocates of compulsory voting. From our perspective, dismay over a regular turnout of some 75 per cent of the electorate, for both parliamentary and municipal elections, appears an overreaction. Such misgivings had scarcely been evident during the initial experience of mass voting in the 1790s, when non-voters were often more numerous than voters, but abstention was perceived as much more problematic after direct, universal male suffrage was introduced in 1848. Indeed, something of an obsession with *abstentionnisme* would endure for much of the following century, despite persistently high levels of turnout. Yet electoral participation remains a voluntary act, and the duty to vote has been emphasized instead, though more citizens are now choosing to abstain or, as the French put it, 'go fishing'.

1

One Man, One Vote

The Long March towards Universal Male Suffrage

> According to the sovereignty of the people, every French man has the
> right to a say in the laws by which he is governed and in the choice of
> the administration which belongs to him. Otherwise it is not true to
> say that all men are equal in rights, that all men are citizens.
>
> Maximilien Robespierre, 22 October 1789.[1]

We may take it for granted today that all resident adults, with only a few
exceptions such as those serving lengthy prison sentences, should exercise the
franchise. Yet this was simply not the case in the relatively recent past even for
males, who have historically been awarded the vote before women. The principle
that the suffrage constituted a basic right, rather than a function, only awarded
after certain qualifications had been fulfilled, was vigorously contested and it
took a long time to achieve general assent. As a result, those who were deemed
to lack a stake in society, or sufficient independence, were long denied the vote.
The process of recognition for French men took almost one hundred years to
complete after the Revolution of 1789, and another half-century for women,
who will be treated separately, in Chapter 2. Moreover, there were periods of
regression as well as advance in what was a far from linear trajectory (see
Appendix 2). The dramatic enfranchisement of almost ten million adult males
in 1848 by no means settled the issue in a definitive fashion. Even under the
Third Republic, the triumph of a universal male franchise remained a matter of
regret in elite circles, while plural voting was energetically advocated after the
First World War, and the Vichy regime (drawing on reactionary critiques of
democracy) would later suspend elections entirely. The forward march of one
man, one vote, was thus a halting one, and only as debate over the full extent of
male suffrage approached some consensus would the focus shift to the female
franchise.

---

[1] *Archives parlementaires* (hereafter *AP*), 1ere série, IX, 22 Oct. 1789, 479.

How the French Learned to Vote: A History of Electoral Practice in France. Malcolm Crook, Oxford University Press (2021).

The Revolutionary Origins of Universal Male Suffrage

The Second Republic is generally regarded as founding universal male suffrage in France and many scholars begin their exploration of the vote at this point, treating the Revolution of 1789 as no more than its pre-history or 'an important precursor', in the words of Raymond Huard.[2] To be sure, only local elections in the 1790s were 'immediate', as contemporaries put it, because intermediate electoral colleges were responsible for electing national deputies. The advent of 'direct' universal suffrage in 1848, to appoint all elected officials from municipal councillor to president did, therefore, constitute a watershed. Indeed, all adult males were now given the franchise, without exception, whereas some of them had always been excluded during the 1790s. However, if the term 'mass suffrage' is employed, then the enfranchisement of some five million male citizens during the Revolution must serve as a better starting point for the French apprenticeship in electoral democracy. Nor should the disparate opportunities to vote under the old regime, which were manifest in a variety of local contexts, from villages to trade guilds, confraternities, and provincial estates, be discounted. On the contrary, traditional electoral culture would exert a good deal of influence over subsequent developments, though earlier polls were no match for the unprecedented and audacious electoral experiment inaugurated in 1789, that was to continue under Napoleon, albeit in much altered circumstances.[3]

At the beginning of the Revolution the National Assembly had certainly introduced an infamous distinction between those adults who could vote and those who could not, in terms of 'active' and 'passive' citizenship, based on the criteria of gender, age, residence, and tax payment. Nonetheless, its electoral legislation enfranchised over four million Frenchmen and summoned them to vote on numerous occasions. In 1792, when the First Republic replaced the constitutional monarchy, the fiscal requirement was abolished, while the age of voting was lowered from twenty-five to twenty-one. This did not herald the advent of universal male suffrage *stricto sensu*, since those lacking financial or personal independence were still denied the vote, but it did potentially admit roughly another million Frenchmen to the suffrage, paving the way for the enfranchisement of all adult males in the Constitution of 1793, even though, like the document itself, this further extension was never implemented. The Directory re-introduced a minimal fiscal barrier: the liability to pay something in direct tax. It was less exclusive than many historians have assumed and the enlarged electorate was probably maintained at around five million. Under the Consulate and Empire, after 1799, this residual requirement was abolished, leaving only domestic

[2] Huard, *Le Suffrage universel*, 14.
[3] Crook, *Elections*, chapters 1 and 2 for much of what follows.

servants and those of no fixed abode without the vote. At this point perhaps six million Frenchmen were entitled to vote.[4]

The revolutionary franchise was thus extremely broad and its limitations provoked little immediate opposition. The abbé Sieyès, author of the celebrated pamphlet 'What is the Third Estate?' published on the eve of the upheaval, coined the expression 'active citizen' to define those who were to be given the vote, and 'passive citizens' for those who were not, but the terminology evidently caused some embarrassment. Historians have employed the antonym far more readily than contemporaries, who preferred to use the words 'non-actif' and 'inactif', or simply talk about voters and citizens, without specifically designating those who were disenfranchised. This was because in Rousseauian terms a citizen who could not vote was a contradiction in terms, a veritable oxymoron.[5] The Declaration of the Rights of Man and the Citizen had unambiguously proclaimed all men equal and a determined democrat like Maximilien Robespierre quickly drew attention to the discrepancy between principle and practice, when the Comité de Constitution published its proposals for elections to the Legislature in October 1789. Indeed, as far as he was concerned, all citizens should be eligible for office, as well as given the vote, 'without any distinction of fortune'.[6]

Yet, apart from Robespierre, all-out dissenters were initially thin on the ground, as little evident in the burgeoning political press and clubs as they were in the National Assembly. Among the deputies, the abbé Grégoire defended the rights of the poor and suggested that full citizenship required only 'sound judgement and a patriotic heart', while Jacques Defermon warned against creating 'an aristocracy of wealth'.[7] By contrast, the physiocrat Duport de Nemours argued that property ownership was more important in determining electoral participation than the payment of taxes, but the original proposal prevailed; it offered the opportunity and gave every incentive to those excluded to become better off and cross the fiscal threshold. Later proponents of universal male suffrage raised no objection to the limitations incurred by basic franchise restrictions, the so-called *cens*, at this point for, as Jérôme Pétion put it, 'the people are steeped in tradition and corruption' and education was required for citizenship. In fact, Bertrand Barère argued strongly in favour of excluding domestic servants, who would long remain on the electoral margins, because they lacked the 'free, untrammelled and independent will' deemed essential to be entrusted with the franchise.[8]

[4] All these figures, save one for 1790, are approximations and, as always, what happened 'on the ground' was another matter. Other historians have arrived at different estimates.
[5] William H. Sewell Jr, 'Le citoyen/la citoyenne: activity, passivity, and the revolutionary concept of citizenship', in Keith M. Baker et al. (eds), *The French Revolution and the Creation of Modern Political Culture*, 4 vols (Oxford, 1987–94), ii, 107–8 and *A Rhetoric of Bourgeois Revolution: The Abbé Sieyes and What is the Third Estate?* (Durham, NC, 1994).
[6] *AP*, 1ᵉʳᵉ série, IX, 22 Oct. 1789, 479.   [7] *AP*, 1ᵉʳᵉ série, IX, 22 Oct. 1789, 479.
[8] *AP*, 1ᵉʳᵉ série, IX, 27 Oct. 1789, 590.

The general acceptance of limitations on the suffrage at the outset of the Revolution has been largely overlooked; more widespread criticism and popular condemnation only began to grow, with a vengeance, after the new regime was established. The initial demand for a 'contribution' to society (the term now employed for taxation, in the vain hope it would prove more palatable than the old-regime 'imposition'), was taken for granted. It would inform the later decision to award the vote to anyone who had fought for the *patrie*, regardless of their fiscal status. Conversely, the limitations imposed by the payment in direct taxation to the local value of three days' wage labour have often been exaggerated. After all, corporate distinctions were now abolished and, unlike the infinite variety of pre-revolutionary arrangements, the ability to vote was set on a uniform basis. Protestants and Jews, even free men of colour, were brought within the pale, provided they complied with the other requirements. Not least, the restricted suffrage was relatively generous by contemporary standards, for roughly 60 per cent of adult French males were given the vote. In proportional terms this was substantially wider than the franchise in unreformed Britain, and at least comparable with most states in the revolutionary United States.[9] In absolute terms, far more adult males could vote in France at the end of the eighteenth century than anywhere else in the world.

This great experiment with mass voting is all too frequently ignored by political scientists, who have pioneered a new history of voting, but rarely examine the ground-breaking nature of the French Revolution on account of its complex and rapidly changing electoral metrics. Needless to say, the shift from the *Ancien Régime* was a huge one, not least in overturning huge inequalities and vast disparities where the suffrage had been concerned. To be sure, the franchise for elections to the Estates General of 1789, a curtain-raiser for what was to follow, was a broad one for members of the third estate, who constituted the vast majority of the electorate. Regulations stipulated that all native or naturalized French commoners aged over twenty-five years old, who were listed on the tax rolls, could vote at the preliminary assemblies. This dispensation afforded considerable scope for popular participation, but voting remained organized on a corporate basis, by order (there was separate provision for clergy and nobles) and community. In the countryside non-taxpayers were by definition excluded, but in towns the numbers ruled out were far greater, since only masters could vote in the artisan corporations. Whole groups might be excluded, like the dockyard workers of Toulon, though their violent protests would secure belated admission to the town's electoral assembly. Paris, as so often, was treated separately and the franchise was limited to 'university graduates, government office-holders, master craftsmen and all who

[9] Robert R. Palmer, *The Age of the Democratic Revolution*, 2 vols (Princeton, NJ, 1959–64), i, 525–7.

paid six *livres* in the *capitation* (or poll tax)'; at best 50,000 Parisians could vote in a population estimated at 550,000.

Prior to 1789 most city councils were oligarchic and the sale of offices had often ended elections altogether. Nantes was a rare exception to the general rule in permitting in excess of a thousand rather than a few hundred voters to take part, despite repeated efforts to narrow the suffrage on account of alleged rowdiness.[10] In small towns like Aubusson, situated in the centre of France, general assemblies had indeed been curtailed 'because the fear of disorder keeps the leading inhabitants away'.[11] The tradition of summoning heads of household to elect syndics and councillors, or to discuss local issues (two inextricably intertwined activities), had been progressively eroded in most rural areas too, though Peter Jones has questioned whether a '"mythic past" of fully representative village institutions ever existed in reality'.[12] In the countryside of Normandy, the Franche-Comté, or Gascony, a broad swathe of *chefs de famille* continued to enjoy the opportunity to meet on an annual basis to elect village officials or conduct debate.[13] Elsewhere, attendance was often restricted to wealthier members of the community, usually the case in Provence, while in some parts of Brittany existing personnel simply nominated their successors.[14]

In 1765, as the royal administration began to embark on the reform of municipal government, Controller-General Laverdy was criticized for giving too much weight to representatives of the artisan corporations and he was obliged to reduce their numbers in supplementary legislation issued the following year.[15] By contrast, on the eve of the Revolution a further attempt at change, albeit one restricted to smaller communities, awarded a vote to those paying over ten *livres* in direct taxes. This measure only enfranchised about 50 per cent of householders, but the use of a fiscal criterion was to herald developments after 1789.[16] The revolutionaries thus had solid precedents on which to build when they instituted a more inclusive franchise on this 'censitary' basis, yet within a few years, as the constitutional monarchy was overturned by a 'second revolution' and replaced by a republic, their initial legislation was extended still further. On 10 August 1792, the tax

---

[10] Guy Saupin, *Les Villes en France à l'époque moderne (XVIe–XVIIIe siècles)* (Paris, 2002), 227–31.

[11] Nora Temple, 'Municipal elections and municipal oligarchies in eighteenth-century France', in J. F. Bosher (ed.), *French Government and Society, 1500–1850: Essays in Honour of Alfred Cobban* (London, 1973), 76.

[12] Peter Jones, *Liberty and Locality in the French Revolution: Six Villages Compared, 1760–1820* (Cambridge, 2003), 54.

[13] Antoine Follain, *Le Village sous l'ancien régime* (Paris, 2008), 215–43 draws on a host of local studies too numerous to list here.

[14] Michel Derlange, *Les Communautés d'habitants en Provence au dernier siècle de l'ancien régime* (Toulouse, 1987), 344–9 and Christian Kermoal, *Les Notables du Trégor: éveil à la culture politique et évolution dans les paroisses rurales, 1770–1850* (Rennes, 2002), 25–30.

[15] Maurice Bordes, *La Réforme municipale du Contrôleur général Laverdy et son application, 1764–1771* (Toulouse, 1968).

[16] Maurice Bordes, *L'Administration provinciale et municipale au dix-huitième siècle* (Paris, 1973), 334–6.

requirement was abolished, but it remained necessary 'to be living from one's unearned income or the proceeds of one's labour, and not to be a domestic servant'.[17] It is difficult to assess how far these changes expanded the electorate in real terms, since there was little time to draw up new registers for the elections that were hastily convened to create a fresh constituent assembly, the National Convention. Some rare evidence from Paris where, as in most towns, the numbers previously enfranchised were lower than in the countryside—a reflection of urban poverty and the lower incidence of direct (as opposed to indirect) taxation before 1789—suggests an increase of over 50 per cent.[18] This was doubtless exceptional and in practice earlier regulations may have remained in force at the grassroots until the new franchise could be more effectively implemented.

In any event, this 'quasi-universal' franchise (a term later used in the 1840s) seemed destined to serve as no more than an interim measure. When a new, republican constitution was drafted in the spring of 1793, there was virtual unanimity, and pressure from below, in favour of further enlargement that even encompassed servants. The Declaration of Rights which prefaced the document stated that 'each citizen—simply defined as every Frenchman domiciled in in a commune for six months who was twenty-one years old—has an equal right to participate in the formulation of laws and the election of representatives.'[19] Subsequent efforts to gauge the extent of this radical change, which also aimed to institute a direct vote to the national legislature in single-member constituencies— as opposed to the prevailing departmental lists at second-degree assemblies— suggest that the size of this electorate might reach seven million (one quarter of the overall population). Yet, as historian Serge Aberdam cautions, 'the suffrage still cannot be considered "universal" at this point. What one observes resembles instead a difficult and incomplete transition from a limited right to vote … towards an extended right to vote which would tend to encompass the immense majority of adult males.'[20] In any event, though the Constitution of 1793 was overwhelmingly endorsed in a popular vote held that July, the crises the Republic was facing, both internally and externally, precluded its application.

By the time a fresh constitutional draft was similarly submitted for approval in 1795, the tide had turned against such latitude. The much more pragmatic approach that ensued after a period of 'revolutionary government' left dogged defenders of the recent franchise extension such as the Anglo-American radical, Tom Paine (elected to the National Convention in 1792 along with other 'friends

---

[17] AP, 1ere série, XLVIII, 12 Aug. 1792, 29–30.

[18] Isser Woloch, The New Regime: Transformations of the French Civic Order, 1789-1820s (New York, 1994), 82.

[19] Godechot (ed.), Les Constitutions, 83–4.

[20] Serge Aberdam, Démographes et démocrates. L'œuvre du comité de division de la Convention nationale (Paris, 2004), 297.

of humanity'), in a very small minority.[21] Despite suffering from typhus as a result of imprisonment during the Terror, his commitment to the universal vote was unwavering and he argued in vain, like Robespierre before him, that limitations on the suffrage were contrary to the Declaration of the Rights of Man which prefaced the new Constitution. Merlin de Douai riposted that affairs of state should not be entrusted to 'the man who has nothing and produces nothing'. This view was supported by Jean Denis Lanjuinais: 'Are we going to award the franchise to men who, possessing nothing, will be at the mercy of whoever pays them to vote? The time for toadying to the people is past...which of us wants to witness for a second time the spectacle of political assemblies given over to crass ignorance, to contemptible greed or vile drunkenness...which was the sort of thing we recently had to endure....'[22] The abbé Grégoire gamely suggested that deputies should 'guard against corrupters as well as the corruptible', but to no avail. This time, the Parisians who invaded the Convention demanding implementation of the democratic Constitution of 1793 were firmly repressed. In fact, even though a fiscal criterion was reinstated, the franchise remained a little more generous than the early years of the Revolution. The adult male who paid any amount of direct tax whatsoever was eligible for registration as a voter, as opposed to the earlier equivalent of three days' labour, while the infamous notion of passive citizenship disappeared from the discourse.

However, opposition to the idea of voting as an inalienable right was underlined by an additional stipulation in the Constitution of 1795. Besides paying the requisite tax, after 1804 only those who could prove they were literate would be allowed onto the electoral register when they came of age.[23] As the deputy Boissy d'Anglas remarked: 'The illiterate individual lacks the plenitude of resources necessary for the exercise of political rights...he needs help to vote and may easily be misled as a result.' It was intended that the ability to write a ballot paper would be supplied by an emergent system of public education. In the event, like the promised schools, this 'cens culturel' did not come into being. Although the Constitution of 1795 lasted for all of four years—longer than either of its predecessors in the 1790s—it was overturned, along with its suffrage requirements, when Napoleon came to power in the coup d'état of Brumaire (November) 1799. The idea of a literacy test was revived in 1849, when an electoral law was discussed under the Second Republic. Édouard Charton, an educationist, suggested that adolescents should be told they would be denied the vote at twenty-one unless they could read and write, 'albeit imperfectly'.[24] His initiative was not endorsed, but the sentiment survived and informed later suggestions that ballot

---

[21] Crook, *Elections*, 116–17.

[22] *Gazette nationale ou le Moniteur universel* (hereafter Moniteur), 25 messidor III (13 July 1795), 1188.

[23] Godechot (ed.), *Les Constitutions*, 105 and see Bronislaw Baczko, *Comment sortir de la Terreur. Thermidor et la Révolution* (Paris, 1989), 345–9.

[24] *Moniteur*, 16 Feb. 1849, 515–16.

papers should be hand-written by voters as proof they were fit to qualify for the franchise. Indeed, this measure of electoral aptitude remained popular, among liberals as well as conservatives, prompting further proposals of a similar sort until the provision of universal primary education resolved the issue.[25]

To judge by its text, the Constitution of the Year VIII (1799), rapidly introduced after the Brumaire coup in the absence of any public discussion, completely removed remaining restrictions on the franchise and gave all adult French males the vote, apart from domestic servants.[26] In practice, the mobile poor (difficult to register under any circumstances) remained beyond the electoral pale. Even so, the mass electorate reached its maximum extent of perhaps six million males in the 'old' France of the early 1790s, and it was still more extensive if the annexed departments of an expanding Empire are taken into account, for adult males in those adjacent areas were given exactly the same right to vote. However, neither Napoleon, nor his close collaborators at this point, who included the seasoned politicians Sieyès and Pierre-Louis Roederer, were anxious to give these electors much real say. Pierre Rosanvallon is correct, in his study of the suffrage in France, to characterize the system as 'citizenship without democracy', for this Bonapartist regime, like its later successor, carefully managed the electoral process.[27] The opportunity to vote in a closely regulated procedure was offered just once every five years and many posts were now filled by appointment. It should also be emphasized that after 1802 the election of municipal councillors (in larger towns), justices of the peace, and members of the legislative body, like the earlier creation of lists of 'notables' in 1801, was designed to furnish no more than 'candidates' for office, among whom the regime made the final choice.[28] Still, the overwhelming majority of adult Frenchmen continued to enjoy the franchise during the Napoleonic period, and substantial numbers employed it, something that is not widely appreciated (Table 1.1).

Table 1.1 The franchise during the Revolution

Year	No. of electors	Age	No. eligible	Age	% of electorate	Age of deputies
1790	4,298,360	25	c.3,000,000	25	c.70	25
1792	c.5,000,000	21	c.4,500,000	25	c.90	25
1793	c.6,000,000	21	c.6,000,000	21	100	25
1795	c.5,000,000	21	c.1,000,000	25	c.20	30/40
1799	c.6,000,000	21	c.6,000,000	21	100	25/30
1802	c.6,000,000	21	c.600,000	21	c.10	25/30

Note: It should be emphasized that these are estimated and approximate figures for the most part, designed to offer an order of magnitude, not scientific precision.

---

[25] Journal officiel de la République (hereafter JO), Annexe 769, 26 Apr. 1871, 768–9.
[26] Godechot (ed.), Les Constitutions, 151.   [27] Rosanvallon, Le Sacre du citoyen, 195–205.
[28] Jean-Yves Coppolani, Les Élections en France à l'époque napoléonienne (Paris, 1980).

It was at this precise moment that the term 'universal suffrage' made its first appearance in France, though it only became more common currency in the 1830s and 1840s.[29] Its English provenance (the first attested use across the Channel occurred in 1798) is reflected in its employment by the exiled journalist Mallet du Pan, who was publishing his *Mercure britannique* in London. Commenting on the Constitution of the Year VIII, Mallet remarked early in 1800 that despite concerns on the part of property and property-holders, 'the modest limitations on the right to vote enforced by the constitutions of 1791 and 1795' had now been suppressed and 'universal suffrage' established, 'in the absence of any pecuniary or political requirement'.[30] The abolition of restrictions on the male franchise was somewhat surprising, since most of those who supported the new regime were anticipating their reinforcement.[31] Speculation regarding a substantial rise in the tax threshold for voters was confounded, in Mallet's view, because the incoming rulers wished to render homage to equality while dethroning liberty, a policy which led him to denounce the loss of any real power for the electorate in this constitution: 'The sovereignty of the people is inscribed on its frontispiece, then confiscated in what follows.'[32] Indeed, 'by abolishing all distinctions in favour of the wealthy where eligibility to public office was concerned', access to authority was likewise open to all, at least in theory, a short-lived development at variance with the preceding regime and most of the revolutionary decade.

From Indirect Elections to Restricted Franchise, 1790–1848

The broad, male electorate of the Revolution had been given a direct vote at local level, in elections for mayors, municipal council members, justices of the peace, and national-guard officers. This constituted an important role, with great scope for regular voting, all too often ignored.[33] However, historians do rightly stress that, as a result of the retention of an indirect, two-tier system, mass participation during this period was limited to the initial, cantonal stage of polling when it came to the choice of departmental personnel and national deputies.[34] This

---

[29] Huard, *Le Suffrage universel*, 26–30. The phrase 'the universality of citizens' had, however, made its way into the Constitution of 1793.

[30] *Mercure britannique*, IV, 10 Jan. 1800, 492.   [31] Rosanvallon, *Le Sacre du citoyen*, 197–8.

[32] *Mercure britannique*, IV, 10 Jan. 1800, 475.

[33] Rosanvallon, was evidently unaware of this when he wrote, in a foreword to Christine Guionnet, *L'Apprentissage de la politique moderne. Les élections municipales sous la monarchie de Juillet* (Paris, 1997), i, that these were the 'first mass, direct elections in France', while the municipal electorate of the 1830s and 1840s was actually smaller than in the 1790s.

[34] The still-born Constitution of 1793 made provision for direct legislative elections, initially retained in proposals for its replacement in 1795, but subsequently jettisoned in favour of the two-tier model.

specific task was entrusted to some 30,000–50,000 second-degree electors, who were selected at 'primary' assemblies in a proportion that varied across the decade from one in one hundred to one in two hundred registered voters, and they met in departmental electoral colleges to discharge it (see Appendix 3).

Under the constitutional monarchy, from 1790 to 1791, college membership demanded payment of ten days' labour in tax. However, the number of second-degree electors who actually served in a particular year is often confused with the much larger pool from which they were drawn, for this was a fiscal threshold that most active citizens could cross. Some three million out of four million of them qualified and, like the graduated procedure itself, this requirement initially encountered little dissent. Yet, to borrow historian Patrice Gueniffey's striking phrase, the two-tier process was an effective means of balancing 'numbers and reason', allowing a wide distribution of the suffrage in the knowledge that the choice of personnel for the more elevated posts would mostly lie in the hands of better-off citizens.[35] As such, it would remain the preferred option for nineteenth-century conservatives seeking to reduce the risks they regarded as inherent in the arithmetic of universal male suffrage, especially once they came to accept it as unavoidable. Moreover, after 1875, as part of the price paid for establishing a democratic Third Republic, electoral colleges were re-established for elections to an upper chamber, the Senate. They remain in being today, currently involving some 150,000 *grands électeurs*, most of them municipal councillors.

Eligibility for local office was also limited between 1789 and 1791, with municipal officers subject to the ten days' wages tax requirement, a barrier which again prompted little or no criticism. By contrast, what did provoke widespread ire in 1789 was the proposed tax payment, equivalent to some fifty days' wages in labour, which was to be demanded of national deputies. It was estimated that this qualification would have severely reduced the ranks from which deputies might be recruited to perhaps 250,000 Frenchmen, but it was the prospect of excluding the likes of Jean-Jacques Rousseau—not to mention themselves—that especially exercised journalists and members of the National Assembly.[36] Such was the fury this emblematic 'marc d'argent' aroused that it was withdrawn in 1791, when the first revolutionary constitution underwent a final revision before its promulgation. In theory, any citizen could now serve as a deputy, but abolition of the silver mark was a trade-off for the last-minute imposition of more stringent thresholds for eligibility to membership of the electoral colleges. This amendment simply shifted a much more exclusive hurdle down to this level, though it was not to be introduced immediately. In the event, the Constitution of 1791 in which it was included lasted less than a year before being overturned.

---

[35] Gueniffey, *Le Nombre et la raison*.
[36] L. G. Wickham-Legg (ed.), *Select Documents Illustrative of the History of the French Revolution*, 2 vols (Oxford, 1905), i, 171–5, for a range of comments in the press.

A two-tier process was retained for election to higher office in 1792, but restrictions on eligibility were abolished, save for the requirement that post-holders still had to be at least twenty-five years old, while the age of voting was reduced to twenty-one. This change made little practical difference to the occupational composition of the electoral colleges, save for delegations from the larger towns and, above all, at Paris. Despite the award of reimbursement for travel and subsistence, attendance at a departmental assembly in a distant location, for several days on end, was sufficient to deter most poorer citizens from becoming second-degree electors. It was thus the urban middle classes and wealthier inhabitants from the countryside who dominated the electoral colleges throughout the 1790s. Notwithstanding, after Thermidor, as part of the general reaction against 'democratic excess', their membership was once again restricted to the better-off, or 'the best', as Boissy d'Anglas put it when he presented a new constitution in 1795.[37] In essence, the untried revisions of 1791 (belatedly inserted into the Constitution of that year) were resurrected and now put into operation. Property-ownership, which many eighteenth-century authors had deemed vital for citizenship, now explicitly entered the equation, since second-degree electors had to own, or at least rent a substantial amount, with revenues ranging from the equivalent of one hundred to two hundred local days' labour, depending on the nature and size of the community.

A fundamental line was thus drawn, after 1795 as before 1792, between second-degree electors and primary voters, rather than between voters and non-voters, the former representing a division of electoral labour approved by most leaders of the Revolution. As Bernard Manin has remarked, 'the debate over how popular government (in France) should be did not center on who could vote. Rather, it centered on who could be voted for.'[38] The total of potential participants at the secondary level of the electoral process fell below one million in the later 1790s. Yet, overall, this was still more than the 600,000 biggest taxpayers among whom life-members of the departmental colleges were chosen after 1802, for the abolition of eligibility criteria in the Constitution of 1799 proved short-lived. Napoleon quickly came to the conclusion that the three-tier lists of notables conjured up by Sieyès, from which office-holders would be chosen by the regime, were much too complicated; he ordained a reversion to electoral colleges in the newly created arrondissements as well as departments.[39] The task of the primary assemblies was to periodically top up these electoral colleges, which maintained some significant electoral practice for the notables, who proposed candidates for the Legislative Body and the Senate, among whom Napoleon made the final choice. A wealthy

---

[37] Crook, *Elections*, 117–19.
[38] Manin, *The Principles of Representative Government*, 99. Significantly, it was the latter who were referred to as 'electors' in the relevant legislation.
[39] Coppolani, *Les Élections*, 60 et seq.

elite of this sort would, in fact, constitute the entire electorate after 1814, its sole task the election of a Chamber of Deputies.

The restored Bourbon monarchy, under Louis XVIII, drastically reduced the parliamentary suffrage to just over 90,000 substantial property-owners and dispensed altogether with elections for any other levels of office-holding, departmental or municipal. Even the surviving electors in this stripped-down polling system declined in number after 1820, before recovering later in the decade as a result of improved voter registration.[40] The Charter (the term 'Constitution' was studiously avoided) issued by the crown in 1814 demanded a payment of 300 francs in direct taxation and stipulated that electors should be at least thirty years old. Eligibility for a seat meant crossing a still higher fiscal hurdle, set at 1,000 francs, and to be aged over forty; in 1817, just 16,000 individuals were listed as potential deputies.[41] When a department was unable to furnish a minimum number of electors or eligible candidates, the case of Corsica for instance, recourse was made to individuals who fell below the fiscal threshold.[42] There was little opportunity for public discussion of this extremely restrictive *cens* during the period following Napoleon's abdication, when the Charter was composed. However, in the wake of Bonaparte's unexpected return and then defeat at Waterloo, in 1815, the definitive, second restoration of the monarchy witnessed a lengthy debate over details in a new electoral law, which once again raised some fundamental questions regarding the right to vote.[43] According to the parliamentarian Charles de Rémusat, the ensuing argument captured the public's attention and inaugurated 'a live course in constitutional politics', while some historians regard the outcome as one of the most important decisions taken under the Restoration.[44]

The franchise became far narrower than at any point since 1789, but more individuals were now able to select national deputies at a single assembly in each department than ever before. Indeed, one way of justifying the new arrangement was to argue, as many liberals did (no democrats they), that it was preferable to give a greater number of wealthy and educated Frenchmen a direct vote for the Chamber of Deputies, rather than to offer the illusion of participation to millions of citizens who could only choose the members of electoral colleges. Thus the politically engaged writer, Benjamin Constant, observed: 'It is better to give 100,000 men a direct, active and real participation... instead of giving 4,000,000 of them an indirect, passive and chimerical involvement, which is always limited

[40] *AP*, 2ᵉ série, XVIII, 3 Jan. 1817, 30–1, Annexe au PV. Sherman Kent, *The Election of 1827 in France* (Cambridge, MA, 1975), puts the numbers slightly higher, but they follow the same trajectory.
[41] Godechot (ed.), *Les Constitutions*, 221 and Archives nationales (hereafter AN) F1cII 55, Les éligibles à la Chambre des Députés, 1839, with earlier comparisons.
[42] *AP*, 2ᵉ serie, XVIII, 30–1, 3 Jan. 1817 and AN F1cII 50, Liste des éligibles, 1820.
[43] Rosanvallon, *Le Sacre du citoyen*, 209–30. From the Restoration onwards, French electoral laws would be separated from the Constitution.
[44] Charles de Rémusat, *Mémoires de ma vie*, 5 vols (Paris, 1958–67), i, 316 and Emmanuel de Waresquiel and Benoît Yvert, *Histoire de la Restauration 1814–1830* (Paris, 2002), 208.

to an empty ritual.'[45] A number of correspondents also saw fit to inform the ministry of the interior that they approved of the new system, because in the past 'popular assemblies' at the cantonal level had only generated unruly passions and produced disorder.[46] Moreover, this system was certainly more palatable for many deputies than the return to corporate representation that some dyed-in-the-wool reactionaries were proposing. The baron de Vitrolles, for example, had advocated resurrecting a modified version of elections to the Estates General of 1789, while others were soon denouncing procedures that they claimed owed more to British than French tradition.[47]

Ironically it was left to conservatives, indeed ultra-royalists, to argue in favour of a broader suffrage. The reactionary comte de La Bourdonnaye contended that:

> The proposed electoral law (the so-called 'loi Lainé', after the minister who introduced the bill) divides the immense majority of the nation into two classes: on the one hand those property-owners paying 300 francs in taxation to whom is reserved the right to participate in the election of deputies...and, on the other, those deprived of this right by the modesty of the tax they pay. You are thus forcing the whole country to bow down before the golden calf, before the aristocracy of wealth, the harshest and most unyielding of all aristocracies...[48]

Yet his diatribe was predicated on a two-tier electoral system that was far from 'democratic' (as some commentators have mistakenly concluded). As the comte de Castelbajac frankly admitted in the course of debate: 'The indirect method was not so bad, since it was at once more popular and also more aristocratic than what is proposed...the people were able to exercise their rights, but there was a guarantee against them abusing it.'[49]

It should be emphasized that liberals were certainly not advocates of universal male suffrage, in Restoration France or elsewhere, a stance they maintained late into the nineteenth century. As historian Alan Kahan has convincingly argued, their hallmark was the limitation of the franchise to those who had the 'capacité', defined in terms of wealth and education, to exercise it in a responsible fashion.[50] Some of them did regard the electoral *cens* of 300 francs as too high, but it was enshrined in the Bourbon Charter and thus not readily negotiable. Moreover, they enjoyed some signal success under the provisions of the new dispensation, with the election of deputies like Lafayette, a veteran of the American War of

---

[45] Benjamin Constant, 'Loi sur les élections', *Mercure de France*, 18 Jan. 1817.

[46] AN F1cII 48, Plusieurs particuliers présentent leurs réflexions sur le système des élections, 1816.

[47] Eugène François de Vitrolles, *Mémoires*, 2 vols, ed. Pierre Farel (Paris, 1950–2), ii, 50–3. Others proposed cantonal assemblies based on a *cens* of 50 *francs*: *AP* 2ème série, XVI, 29 Feb. 1816, 331–6.

[48] *AP*, 2e série, XVII, 28 Dec. 1816, 737.   [49] *AP*, 2e série, XVII, 26 Dec. 1816, 705.

[50] Alan S. Kahan, *Liberalism in Nineteenth-Century Europe: The Political Culture of Limited Suffrage* (Basingstoke, 2003), 5–11.

Independence and moderate leader of the French Revolution, in the annual polls that took place from 1817 onwards. However, a growing backlash among disaffected ultra-royalists was brought to a head by the election of a former revolutionary and alleged regicide, the abbé Grégoire, in 1819. Revision of the electoral system was already under consideration when, amidst the reaction that followed the assassination in 1820 of the duc de Berry, a future heir to the throne, Louis XVIII was persuaded to introduce the law of the 'double vote'.[51] This alteration to the suffrage gave the wealthiest 25 per cent of the already limited electorate an opportunity to vote for deputies twice, first at revived arrondissement assemblies, along with other voters, and then again, on their own, at the departmental colleges, where these 18,000 'double voters' chose two-fifths of the deputies.[52] Liberals were profoundly dismayed by this regressive legislation, which was specifically designed to work to their disadvantage, but the campaign to ensure registration of their sympathizers (by no means a simple process), and to mobilize their vote, would begin to bear fruit in the late 1820s.[53]

Their revival prompted panic on the part of the regime, headed since 1824 by the rather more reactionary Charles X. Partial renewal of the Chamber each year had been abandoned just before he acceded to the throne, in order to obviate the annual disruption which critics regarded as encouraging. Yet neither of the septennial parliaments that followed were allowed to run for even half their due distance. The result of the general election of 1827 had already caused concern, but that of 1830 was still more favourable to the liberal opposition.[54] As a result, this Chamber was immediately dissolved and the Ordinances of Saint-Cloud were issued on 25 July, which included a series of reactionary measures, notably the provision that at fresh elections, the departmental assemblies, where the propertied aristocracy of double voters held sway, would effectively control the overall outcome. According to this modification, electors in the arrondissement colleges were limited to simply nominating candidates among whom their departmental counterparts had the final say, as well as selecting other deputies themselves.

The already limited suffrage would, in effect, be concentrated among the 20,000 extremely wealthy electors, when they used their second vote, but these edicts proved completely counter-productive. They provoked the July Revolution of 1830, as widespread protest erupted across the country, not merely at Paris, though events in the capital were to prove crucial. Lower-class involvement was prompted by economic distress, but it also reflected the fact that elections during this period had witnessed the noisy, indirect participation of ordinary people on the streets of towns where they the electoral assemblies were held (see Chapter 6).

---

[51] *AP*, 2e série, XXIII, 20 Feb. 1819, 85 and Alan B. Spitzer, 'Restoration political theory and the debate over the law of the double vote', *Journal of Modern History*, 55 (1983), 57–8.
[52] AN F1cII 50, Loi du 29 June 1820.   [53] Kent, *The Election of 1827*, 112–20.
[54] Bertrand Goujon, *Monarchies postrévolutionnaires, 1814–1848* (Paris, 2012), 221–2.

Indeed, protests against the law of the double vote in 1820 had attracted thousands of signatures from non-electors on petitions organized by the opposition.[55] Yet the 'Trois Glorieuses', the three days of Parisian insurrection at the end of July 1830 that forced Charles X to flee, and brought down the Bourbon Restoration, did not benefit those who were hoping for radical change. Rather, they produced another monarchy, courtesy of the Orleanist branch of the French royal family, in the person of Louis-Philippe.

It was thus no surprise that this 'confiscated' revolution produced only a slight extension of the franchise, despite demands from some quarters that the *cens* should be cut to 50 francs, if not entirely abolished.[56] Other, more modest proposals notwithstanding, in the absence of a general election, let alone the creation of a constituent assembly or a popular vote, the result was a revised charter, which lowered the age for voting and eligibility to twenty-five and thirty, respectively, while deferring a decision on the fiscal criteria to be applied to both. In the event, the threshold for the former was reduced from 300 to 200 francs in direct tax per annum. This only increased the electorate by a paltry 50 per cent to some 160,000, though by the late 1840s rising prosperity and demographic growth had gradually raised it to almost 250,000 (see Appendix 2).[57] Meanwhile, the fiscal requirement for deputies was halved to 500 francs, suggesting that some 50,000 notables were now eligible for election to the legislature.[58]

Yet another substantial, and instructive, discussion over the principles and nature of the suffrage took place and it culminated in the law of April 1831, which regulated triennial elections to the Chamber of Deputies. Its opening section was entitled 'electoral capacity', terminology which reflected the dominant liberal belief in a restricted franchise on the basis of property-ownership, but also sought the inclusion of less wealthy groups endowed with intellectual and professional expertise. Numerous deputies argued that the tax threshold was a blunt instrument for determining who was fit to vote and that educational attainment or occupational experience should also be taken into account. Yet, in 1831, the addition of members and corresponding members of the National Institute, as well as retired military officers, who were all still obliged to pay 100 francs in taxation, only increased the electorate by a small amount. Many liberals had demanded greater scope for such 'capacités', but conservatives were condescending in their critique: 'Is the possession of a university degree or a public qualification a sure guarantee of anything?'[59] However, it could be unwise to leave well-educated

---

[55] See AN F7 6740 and 6741, Rapports des préfets et de la police concernant les élections, 1817–30.
[56] Pierre Rosanvallon, *La Monarchie impossible. Les Chartes de 1814 et de 1830* (Paris, 1994), 306.
[57] AN F1cII 55, Listes des électeurs, 1830–47.
[58] AN F1cII 55, Liste des éligibles, 1839. However, Sherman Kent, *Electoral Procedure under Louis Philippe* (New Haven, CT, 1937), 54–6, suggests a number half this size, on the grounds that not all taxpayers in this bracket were eligible.
[59] Cited in Kahan, *Liberalism*, 43.

individuals without a vote, for intellectuals lacking a good deal of wealth might pose a subversive threat. Meanwhile, legitimists, who supported the deposed Bourbon dynasty, vainly continued to demand a universal male franchise, albeit on the basis of indirect election, while republicans sought a rather more generous extension of the vote, likewise without success.

This debate was combined with a simultaneous discussion of the suffrage for municipal elections, which the revised Charter had promised to reinstate. Similar arguments were inevitably made in the course of considering a local franchise and an overwhelming majority remained in favour of limitations. However, in the case of municipalities a rather lower fiscal threshold was agreed, while the adjunctions according to 'capacity' were much more numerous. Such differentiation at the local level constitutes a rare exception to the general French rule of a uniform suffrage and it was justified on the grounds that even modest tax-payers had a personal stake in municipal administration and could be safely entrusted with making a choice of councillors. As one conservative deputy had put it immediately after the July Revolution, when it was decided to re-establish these elections: 'the farmer and the artisan may struggle to judge complicated broader issues, but they are capable of weighing up the interests of their own communities...'.[60]

The municipal law of 1831 thus instituted triennial elections and awarded the franchise to almost three million adult males, including 'adjunct' voters drawn from national-guard officers, members of the liberal professions and retired servants of the state, who were to elect some 400,000 councillors (among whom mayors and *adjoints* would be nominated by the government).[61] Paris was subject to a specific and highly restricted regime, since the capital was considered too politically volatile to be granted the same electoral status. In fact, quite deliberately, and understandably for a regime that faced great hostility in many of the bigger cities, this municipal suffrage had a much more dramatic impact in smaller communes. There, up to half the adult males over twenty-five years old might be enfranchised, whereas in the largest towns it was nearer one in ten. Nonetheless, during a period when France and Britain shared a common political system, the former exceeded the latter in terms of the breadth of its municipal franchise, while the British parliamentary electorate was somewhat larger than its French counterpart.

Elections were also re-introduced for departmental and arrondissement councils in 1833.[62] In keeping with the notion that a wider purview was required for the choice of personnel at a higher level, this vote was initially restricted to some 200,000 of the wealthiest citizens. It was slightly broader than the parliamentary

---

[60] *AP* 2ᵉ série, LXIII, 30 Aug. 1830, 307–8.
[61] AN F1bI 258, Élections municipales, 1834 and Guionnet, *L'Apprentissage de la politique moderne*, 9–11.
[62] *Moniteur*, 26 June 1833, 1761.

suffrage, as a result of adding those liable to serve on juries. By contrast, a far more generous franchise had been granted in 1831 for the election of officers in a reconstituted national guard in which service was compulsory for nearly all adult males. It offered voting rights to over three million militia-men and its impact in cities was far more extensive than the municipal dispensation, not least in the capital, where large numbers of guards were soon employing their newly conferred right to vote every three years.[63] More immediately, this broad suffrage, which 'came the closest to popular sovereignty' and offered 'a great electoral education', prompted the demand that 'every guard should be a parliamentary voter'. This cry was taken up by radicals who, in 1839 and 1840, mounted a concerted campaign for electoral reform that was backed by more than two thousand petitions, bearing almost 200,000 signatures, and eventuated in another extensive debate on the franchise in the Chamber of Deputies in February 1842.[64] Yet liberals who led the discussion were only proposing to encompass more of the 'capacités' ruled out in 1831, and to increase the minimum number of electors in every parliamentary constituency to 400 by recruiting below the current fiscal threshold where necessary.[65] 'The aristocracy of wealth...pales before the aristocracy of intelligence and genius', asserted the deputy Théodore Ducos, but that was as far as he was prepared to go.[66]

It was reckoned that the adoption of a measure of this sort would merely double the number of parliamentary electors to some 400,000. However, Guizot, then minister of Foreign Affairs, flatly refused to countenance change, because in his opinion there was no pressing need for franchise reform. Moreover, proclaiming himself a staunch enemy of universal suffrage, 'opposed to any tendency in this direction', he seemed to be dismissing future prospects for progress as well.[67] Undaunted, proponents of reform resumed their campaign and, in 1847, they staged another major debate in the Chamber of Deputies, this time with the prominent liberal politician, Prosper Duvergier de Hauranne, leading the charge. He demanded the franchise for all who possessed 'a free and enlightened judgement' and proposed was to reduce the *cens* to 100 francs, as well as increasing the number of adjunct voters.[68] In response, Guizot, now prime minister, reiterated his implacable opposition to any change, either now or later. He should have known better than to tempt providence by declaring: 'The principle of universal

[63] Mathilde Larrère, *L'Urne et le fusil. La garde nationale parisienne de 1830 à 1848* (Paris, 2016), 270.
[64] AN C2169-72, Pétitions, Chambre des Députés, 1838-9; A. Gourvitch, 'Le mouvement pour la réforme électorale (1838-1841)', *La Révolution de 1848. Bulletin de la Société d'histoire de la Révolution de 1848* (1914-17), 11-13; and Benoît Agnès, *L'Appel au pouvoir. Les pétitions au Parlements en France et au Royaume-Uni (1814-1848)* (Rennes, 2018), 201.
[65] Kahan, *Liberalism*, 46.   [66] *Moniteur*, 15 Feb. 1842, 306-7.
[67] *Moniteur*, 15 Feb. 1842, 321-2.
[68] *Moniteur*, 23 Mar.1847, 574-6. See also Prosper Duvergier de Hauranne, *De la réforme parlementaire et de la réforme électorale* (Paris, 1847).

suffrage is so absurd that none of its partisans dare accept or support it completely. The day of universal suffrage will never dawn. There will never be a time when all human beings, whoever they are, will be called upon to exercise political rights.'[69] The prospect of franchise reform was deferred once again yet, less than a year later, confounding every expectation, France began a second experiment with mass voting.

The Unexpected Advent of Direct Universal Male Suffrage in 1848

There was little debate about the suffrage in the immediate wake of the Parisian uprising at the end of February 1848, for the sudden collapse of the July Monarchy had taken everyone by surprise and urgent action was required to restore order. Organizers of the banquet campaign for franchise reform (a means of bypassing the ban on public meetings), which began the chain of events leading to another change of regime, were seeking an extension of the male suffrage rather than the removal of all restrictions on the adult vote, while republicans had been anticipating no more than gradual movement towards a fuller franchise. However, under severe pressure from crowds in the capital, a hastily and haphazardly established Provisional Government promised to give the French people a direct say in the election of a Constituent Assembly. Women were to be excluded, not without demur (see Chapter 2), but all males aged twenty-one and over were enfranchised and twenty-five-year-olds were eligible to serve as deputies. Even servants and members of the armed forces were now awarded a vote in what was correctly described as 'an unprecedented step on a global scale'.

It was also a huge leap in the dark. As the jurist Louis Cormenin, who was among those responsible for it, remarked to the writer and deputy, Alexis de Tocqueville, 'Has the world ever seen anything like what the world is seeing today'?, before adding, 'it will be very curious to see what comes of all this'.[70] Some radicals baulked at the prospect of an untried mass electorate deciding the fate of the new republic and sought to postpone the elections so as to conduct a rapid campaign of political education. In order for the gamble to proceed, let alone succeed, it would be necessary to facilitate the participation of more than eight million citizens at the polls (a subject to be explored in Chapter 5).[71] For the advent of universal male suffrage was, as Rosanvallon suggests, a matter of social as well as political inclusion. The new government proclaimed: 'There will not be one citizen

[69] *Moniteur*, 26 Mar. 1847, 616.
[70] Alexis de Tocqueville, *Recollections: The French Revolution of 1848 and its Aftermath*, ed. Olivier Zunz (Charlottesville, VA, 2016), 131.
[71] Vincent Villette, *Apprendre à voter sous la IIe République. Le suffrage de masse dans le département de la Seine (1848–1851)* (Paris, 2013), 27ff.

who can say to another "I am more sovereign than you", before concluding, 'there will no longer be any proletarians in France'.[72] The question of personal dignity and civic integration, albeit exclusively gendered, was neatly encapsulated in a popular song, 'Vote universel', which began: Every Frenchman is an elector, what a delight! I, a tailor, you a gilder, he a paver, yet here we are recognized as men...'.[73]

When the Constituent Assembly met, in May 1848, there was little debate over the franchise. Its Comité de Constitution brushed aside any suggestion that the right to vote should depend on literacy and maintained the unalloyed dispensation granted by the Provisional Government, the final document underlining that the suffrage was 'sans condition de cens'. Many erstwhile monarchists (the so-called *républicains du lendemain*) had somewhat unexpectedly found themselves returned as deputies, an outcome which temporarily assuaged their profound misgivings about the all-inclusive male franchise. Yet the precocious triumph of one man, one vote would prove extremely short-lived in practice. Electoral surprises continued when Louis-Napoleon was the overwhelming choice as the Second Republic's first (and last) president in December 1848. A further shock was to follow when the polls of May 1849 for a Legislative Assembly produced a sizable minority of deputies affiliated to the left-wing *démocrate-socialiste* group, despite the victory of a substantial conservative majority. Subsequent by-elections, above all the triumph of Eugène Sue, the radical novelist, at Paris the following year, only increased right-wing alarm and prompted a rapid re-examination of the Second Republic's suffrage legislation.[74]

For some reactionaries it was an opportunity to dust down their dearly held project of indirect voting, but such a radical change would be tantamount to constitutional revision and demand a majority of 75 per cent in a parliamentary vote, while there were fears of a popular backlash if the process went too far. As a result, the changes made in the electoral law of 31 May 1850 were presented as 'technical' modifications, which circumvented but did not abrogate the principle of universal male suffrage.[75] The imposition of a three-year residence requirement, like disqualification as a consequence of criminal and political convictions, aimed to prevent the 'dangerous' classes from voting. As Adolphe Thiers explained, it was not the poor whom the proposed law sought to disenfranchise, but 'vagabonds' or, as he infamously put it, 'the vile multitude that has dragged down republican regimes in the past'. Yet no one was sure what the precise effect would be.[76] A mass franchise remained, broad by contemporary standards, but roughly a third

[72]   Rosanvallon, *Le Sacre du citoyen*, 284ff.
[73]   Pierre Barbier and France Vernillat, *Histoire de France par les chansons*, 8 vols (Paris, 1956–61), vii, 35–7. The author was Eugène Pottier, who later penned the celebrated *Internationale*.
[74]   Villette, *Apprendre à voter*, 155–7.
[75]   R. Balland, 'De l'organisation à la restriction du suffrage universel en France (1848–1850)', in Jacques Droz (ed.), *Réaction et suffrage universel en France et en Allemagne* (Paris, 1963), 67–180.
[76]   *Moniteur*, 24 May 1850, 1805.

of the overall electorate of 1848 was removed from the electoral registers as a result. The reduction was over 60 per cent at Paris and still more in industrial towns like Lille or Roubaix.[77]

The attachment of many ordinary people to their voting rights was demonstrated in the 'barricade of paper' built by extensive petitioning against the bill, which attracted over 500,000 signatures.[78] Yet the greatest beneficiary of this imbroglio was Louis-Napoleon, who shrewdly exploited the situation with a proposal to rescind the restrictive legislation, which was defeated by just seven votes on 4 November 1851. Liberals led the opposition to his opportunism and quickly came up with an alternative for reducing the residence requirement, which would apply to municipal elections in the first instance, but might then be extended to legislative polls.[79] This ploy did not succeed either and Louis-Napoleon immediately declared that, were he given the power to do so (though his single term of presidential office was drawing to a close), he would reinstate universal male suffrage immediately. A coup d'état, carried out on 2 December 1851, soon put him in a position of supreme authority as Prince President and, a year later he became Emperor, both events ratified by plebiscite. He kept his word on the restoration of voting rights, but the dream of democracy died once more in France. Universal manhood suffrage was used to consolidate another authoritarian regime, just as some critics had warned, though the Second Empire was to provide a good deal of voting practice for the mass male electorate over the next two decades.

Historians have recently, in some cases reluctantly, begun to acknowledge Louis-Napoleon's contribution to the process of electoral acculturation in France.[80] Polling during most of the period from 1852 to 1870 was semi-competitive, with 'official' candidates overtly sponsored by the government, so for much of the period the outcome can be largely dismissed as a foregone conclusion. However, all adult males over the age of twenty-one were offered the opportunity to vote in recurrent legislative and local elections, plus a further plebiscite, and most of them acquired significant experience in voting as a result. The regime was obliged to allow the electoral process to operate with increasing latitude in the 1860s, despite the fact that government officials were already warning of the risks involved in accustoming people to the exercise of this 'capricious' institution.[81] The academic rector at Aix-en-Provence had frankly admitted in 1858 that

---

[77] Huard, *Le Suffrage universel*, 55–7. No general election was held on this basis, but there were a number of by-elections at the legislative and local level.

[78] François Jarrige, 'Une "barricade de papiers": le pétitionnement contre la restriction du suffrage universel masculin en mai 1850', *Rh19*, 29 (2004), 53–70.

[79] Kahan, *Liberalism*, 102–6.

[80] See Patrick Lagoueyte, 'Élections', in Jean Tulard (ed.), *Dictionnaire du Deuxième Empire* (Paris, 1995), 228, for a brief statement of this positive interpretation which has since become commonplace. See also Sudhir Hazareesingh, *From Subject to Citizen: The Second Empire and the Emergence of Modern French Democracy* (Princeton, NJ, 1998), 26.

[81] Cited in Patrick Lagoueyte, *La Vie politique en France au XIXe siècle* (Gap, 1990), 54.

'universal suffrage frightens me as it frightens every honest man. It carries within it the seeds of a social revolution which will break out one day, if we persist with it.'[82]

Meanwhile, republicans struggled to come to terms with what they regarded as the perversion of one man, one vote. Like Karl Marx they were prone to blame the supposedly benighted peasants, whom they recognized as the 'masters of our destiny'. Some hesitated over their commitment to universal suffrage as a consequence but, having asked, 'are inhabitants of the countryside incapable of understanding the price of liberty?', the radical journalist Eugène Ténot for one sought an answer in their enlightenment. Education would have to succeed rather than precede their accession to the franchise.[83] Liberals were moving towards a similar conclusion, accepting that there could be no return to a limited franchise, especially after a degree of freedom was restored by the regime, which permitted more competitive elections, but few anticipated its rapid demise.

The Entrenchment of Universal Male Suffrage under the Third Republic

The Second Empire collapsed dramatically in September 1870 when, following crushing military defeat at the hands of Prussia and its German allies, demonstrators in Paris secured its overthrow and the declaration of a Republic. However, the new regime's survival was soon thrown into doubt by continuing military reverses, and the success of resurgent royalists in the provinces, as soon as fresh elections were held. Offering reassurance at a moment of profound disarray caused by war, occupation, and upheaval, they won a solid parliamentary majority and sought a monarchical restoration instead. Yet their victory at the polls in February 1871 was something of a mirage, the product of exceptional circumstances. This was effectively a 'plebiscite for peace', which attracted a relatively low turnout, mostly on account of disruption accompanying the conflict and the fact that so many men were still under arms. Republicans won most of the ensuing by-elections in the early 1870s, a large number of them necessitated by deputies being returned in more than one department.[84] The reactionaries' grip was thus gradually loosened, most spectacularly with the victory of the radical, Désiré Barodet, at Paris in 1873.[85]

Yet, while the uncertain, piecemeal foundations of what proved to be a long-lasting republican regime are widely recognized, the existential threat to the universal male suffrage on which the National Assembly had been elected is all too

---

[82] Cited in Roger Price, *The French Second Empire: An Anatomy of Political Power* (Cambridge, 2001), 105.

[83] Eugène Ténot, *Le Suffrage universel et les paysans* (Paris, 1865), 9 and 26.

[84] Jacques Gouault, *Comment la France est devenue républicaine, 1870–1875* (Paris, 1954).

[85] Jean-Claude Wartelle, 'L'élection Barodet (avril 1873)', *Rhmc*, 27 (1980), 601–30.

rarely acknowledged.[86] A protracted and wide-ranging debate on the franchise took place, which the commission appointed to receive proposals, and then make recommendations, regarded as 'the most important matter' that the deputies had to decide.[87] It certainly occupied more of their time than other constitutional issues and produced a huge variety of inventive suggestions. The eventual democratic outcome, a reassertion of direct, universal male suffrage, was by no means a foregone conclusion.

Republicans were defending the inclusive franchise employed in the general election of 1871 and went to great lengths to justify it as a means of preserving order, on the basis that a reaffirmation of the popular vote would remove any further pretext for insurrection. It was left to conservatives to propose a series of alternatives. Of course, there were those like the writer Flaubert, who suggested that, in view of the Paris Commune of spring 1871, which had resulted from a further spasm of upheaval in the capital, by far the best thing to do was 'finish with universal suffrage altogether'.[88] It was generally agreed by right-wingers that an unalloyed mass franchise inexorably led to disorder or despotism, but they sought to radically recast it rather than remove it altogether. The historian Hippolyte Taine was among those who resurrected the familiar idea of departmental electoral colleges, in an effort to offset the limited horizons of most voters with the wisdom of second-degree electors, who would choose deputies in a better informed and more responsible fashion. 'It is not universal suffrage which is the problem', he concluded, 'but direct election…'.[89]

Other propositions that had been aired in the past also re-surfaced in a myriad of pamphlets and parliamentary interventions over the next few years.[90] They included the re-imposition of a tax threshold so that the interests of property-owners would be safeguarded; a substantial residence requirement, in order to once more exclude 'nomadic' elements in the population; and literacy tests; not to mention compulsory voting, in the widely held belief that moderates were failing to participate in elections (see Chapter 8). The Prussian model that split the electorate into three categories and gave them a different parliamentary weighting was also advocated, besides proposals for plural voting, which would award additional votes to those with greater wealth, more educational qualifications, or large families. Indeed, regarding the *père de famille* as a bulwark of order in a society of anarchic individuals, Charles Pernolet, the former mayor of a Parisian arrondissement,

[86] See David A. Bateman, *Disenfranchising Democracy: Constructing the Electorate in the United States, the United Kingdom, and France* (Cambridge, 2018), 303–22 and Stephen E. Hanson, 'The founding of the Third Republic', *Comparative Political Studies*, 43 (2010), 1023–8, for two recent exceptions.
[87] Anselme Batbie, *Rapport fait au nom de la commission chargée d'examiner les lois constitutionnelles sur le projet de loi électorale* (Versailles, 1874).
[88] Cited in Huard, *Le Suffrage universel*, 107.
[89] Hippolyte Taine, *Du Suffrage universel et de la manière de voter* (Paris, 1872), 40.
[90] See Bateman, *Disenfranchising Democracy*, 304–16, for numerous references.

suggested a single vote for bachelors, two for married men, and a third for those with more than two children.[91]

Yet when the conservative deputy Anselme Batbie reported to the Assembly in March 1874, on behalf of the commission responsible for determining the electoral law, he ruled out most of these alternatives to the existing universal male suffrage.[92] Having listed objections to all of them, he instead proposed a couple of vital 'guarantees', which involved raising the voting age to twenty-five and re-introducing more stringent residence criteria, like those imposed in 1850. This reluctance to call the principle of one man, one vote into question for the parliamentary suffrage was reflected in a simultaneous debate on the municipal electorate. The draft bill in this regard proposed a similar age for voting and restricted access to the franchise for those not born in the *commune*, but it was substantially amended by deputies to lower the voting age and reduce the residence requirement for non-natives before it passed into law in July 1874.[93] Similar legislation for elections to the Chamber of Deputies, which awarded the vote to all males over twenty-one years of age, after just six months' residence in the *commune*, was subsequently passed in November 1875, despite concerted attempts to alter it.[94] Its proponents had intoned, 'Universal (male) suffrage is the very foundation of our public law, on which rests and reigns the sovereignty of our nation.'[95] Rightly discerning these two victories as defining moments, republicans were exultant. After the passage of the municipal law in 1874 one sympathetic newspaper had already declared: 'Universal suffrage has been preserved. It remains the basis of French society', then in November 1875 it added, 'Universal suffrage, that fundamental institution, is no longer at risk...'.[96] However, there was a small difference between the lower numbers able to vote at the local level and the larger ones participating in legislative elections, which was ironed out in 1884, after republicans had taken complete charge of the new regime.[97]

Universal male suffrage may have triumphed, but only after a long, hard struggle, and some significant concessions, specifically designed to limit its scope and ensure that the Third Republic would not be too radical. One man, one vote was to be counter-balanced by the creation of a second chamber (the Senate, to be chosen indirectly, by means of electoral colleges), the indirect election of the president of

---

[91]   *JO*, 7 and 8 July 1874, 4711–35. For more on the family vote, see Chapter 2.

[92]   *JO*, Annexe 2320, 1874.

[93]   *Annales de l'Assemblée nationale*, 46 vols (Paris, 1871–6), XXX, Annexe 2268, 7 Mar. 1874, 71ff. and XXXII, 17 June 1874, 277ff.

[94]   It should be noted, however, that the withdrawal of the vote and eligibility for office from those serving in the armed forces, after 1872, effectively negated lowering the voting age to twenty-one, on account of compulsory military service, though conscripts remained listed on the electoral registers. Only in 1945 were the rights of active military personnel restored.

[95]   *Annales de l'Assemblée nationale*, XLI, Annexe 3240, 22 July 1875, 17ff.

[96]   *La République française*, 3 July 1874 and 11 Nov. 1875, cited in Rosanvallon, *Le Sacre du citoyen*, 329 and 330.

[97]   *Annales de l'Assemblée nationale*, XLII, 8 Nov. 1875, 55. The discrepancy was put at 362,000 fewer electors at the municipal level.

the republic by members of the two houses of parliament combined, and the re-establishment of single-member constituencies (*scrutin d'arrondissement*), which were reckoned to favour the rural notables. Even so, severe misgivings persisted in many quarters and there was a great deal of equivocation. A preoccupation with electoral aptitude was still quite evident: Edmond Scherer, a liberal, declared in 1883 that lower-class voters were 'so backward, so ignorant, so egotistical and often so corrupt, as to be incapable of choosing a government'.[98] A year later the academic Alfred Fouillée published a celebrated essay entitled 'The philosophy of universal suffrage', which underlined the contradiction between 'the right to vote, given to all, and the ability to exercise it, which really only belongs to a certain number'.[99] He was unsure whether primary education offered a sufficient safe-guard and expressed some sympathy for a political literacy test; in 1910 he was still bemoaning 'the intellectual and moral incapacity of the masses'.[100]

Many conservatives had eventually resigned themselves to universal male suffrage, but only in the belief that it could no longer be resisted.[101] By contrast, staunch royalists were rather less restrained and remained largely un-reconciled. In 1883 one of them was still denouncing the 'tyranny of number': 'Is it not absurd that that the votes of learned members of the Institut de France have no more value than those of provincial road-sweepers...?'[102] During the next decade others continued to assert that universal suffrage had vitiated the moral and intellectual basis of government, because there were 'too many electors' and one of them proposed raising the voting age to thirty, while those over fifty years old should be given an additional ballot.[103] Proposals for plural voting would indeed be resurrected during the interwar years of the following century. Right-wing nationalists like Charles Maurras sought to abolish elections altogether, an objective achieved after 1940 when the authoritarian Vichy regime repudiated an egalitarian, arithmetically based suffrage that was incompatible with its traditional, organic conception of society (though proposals for a different sort of electoral system were drafted).[104] Equally revealing were surveys conducted by female suffragists on the eve of the First World War, to gauge support for their cause, which incidentally demonstrated continuing opposition to universal male suffrage among some 'eminent men'.[105] A major objection to enfranchising women was that it would only exacerbate the existing drawbacks of the mass male electorate.

[98]   Edmond Scherer, *La Démocratie et la France: études* (Paris, 1883), 20.
[99]   Alfred Fouillée, 'La philosophie du suffrage universel', *Revue des Deux Mondes*, 65 (1884), 108.
[100]   Alfred Fouillée, *La Démocratie politique et sociale en France* (Paris, 1910), 5.
[101]   Paul Ribot, *Du Suffrage universel et de la souveraineté du peuple* (Paris, 1874), xiii–xiv.
[102]   Anon., *L'Instruction civique à l'école laïque des sans Dieu expliquée par un homme de bon sens* (Paris, 1883).
[103]   Aloïs Burger, *Le Suffrage universel coordonné, vote plural* (Paris, 1893), 4 and 8–9.
[104]   Huard, *Le Suffrage universel*, 355–61.
[105]   Helen Chenut, 'Attitudes towards French women's suffrage on the eve of World War I', *FHS*, 41 (2018), 721. The military officer and novelist Jean Reibrach opined that the vote for women would only 'increase the immense sum of foolishness that we owe to universal (male) suffrage'.

The franchise was in fact far from equal in terms of the number of votes necessary to elect a deputy because, once the system of departmental *scrutin de liste* was abandoned, the rough equation between population and representation was lost. Paris was set to suffer especially badly when the department of the Seine, which had been awarded a slate of forty-three deputies at the National Assembly of 1871, was subsequently allocated just twenty-five, while the diminutive Basses-Alpes received no less than five.[106] The re-establishment of single-member constituencies under the Third Republic thus re-introduced significant variations across the country. In 1881, for example, there were fewer than 4,000 electors at Barcelonette (Basses-Alpes), while at Marmande (Lot-et-Garonne) the total was over 31,000. Because each administrative arrondissement was awarded at least one deputy, these disparities had scarcely altered half a century later, when Briançon (Hautes-Alpes) mustered just 7,000 registered voters, compared to Corbeil (Seine-et-Oise) with over 40,000. Following the brief post-Second World War experiment with proportional representation (PR), from 1947 to 1958, the return of uninominal seats had familiar consequences: in the 1980s, one constituency in the Lozère inscribed only 26,000 electors whereas, at the opposite extreme, another in the Essonne contained 185,000. This uneven allocation, which was also true of the electoral colleges that elected the Senate, gave greater weight to often-conservative rural voters to the detriment of their urban counterparts, despite the continuing exodus from the countryside.[107]

Discrepancies of this sort have since been significantly reduced, not least because the Constitutional Council now determines the distribution of seats, not the legislature. However, despite the belated advent of the female franchise, which will be examined in Chapter 2, the project of universal suffrage remains incomplete. There are justified concerns about the significant number of potential voters who escape registration, mostly because they have no fixed address, or have moved and fail to inform the authorities.[108] Persistent social inequalities, in terms of housing, income, or education, also continue to inhibit access to, and exercise of, the franchise.[109] On the other hand, the suffrage was awarded to eighteen-year-olds in 1974 and in 2011 they became eligible for office at any level; more recently there has been debate over a further reduction to enable sixteen-year-olds to vote.[110] Conversely, a critique of universal suffrage, reminiscent of nineteenth-century arguments in favour of 'capacity', has emerged, as many voters have shifted their

---

[106]   Huard, *Le Suffrage universel*, 117–18ff.

[107]   Jean-Marie Cotteret et al., *Lois électorales et inégalités de représentation en France, 1936–1960* (Paris, 1960).

[108]   Jean-Louis Hérin, 'Les exclus du vote', *Pouvoirs*, 120 (2007), 95–107.

[109]   Daniel Gaxie, *Le Cens caché. Inégalités culturelles et ségrégation politique* (Paris, 1978).

[110]   It might be added that the electorate for local and European elections has been expanded by the right of resident citizens of the European Union to participate in these polls: Sue Collard, 'French municipal democracy: cradle of European citizenship?', *Journal of Contemporary European Studies*, 18 (2010), 91–116.

allegiance to populist movements and aroused misgivings about their electoral aptitude among the educated elite. Yet the contemporary case for 'epistocracy', or rule of the knowledgeable, which has found proponents in Anglo-Saxon countries, has achieved little or no traction in France.[111] One commentator did post an isolated message on Mediapart, an independent online journal, contending that 'most of the time voters are completely ignorant regarding the problems on which they are invited to pronounce', and recommending 'the institution of a conditional, progressive and enlightened suffrage', but he failed to elicit any response.[112]

Conclusion

The revival of a restricted franchise seems most unlikely, not least in France, where a precocious and precipitous process of trial and error with mass voting for males, accompanied by successive political upheavals, finally concluded in the late nineteenth century. Monarchy meant indirect elections or a limited franchise, but the republic could not simply be equated with its converse, for not only in the 1790s but also in 1850, under the Second as under the First Republic, restrictions had been applied. It was ironic that Louis-Napoleon's authoritarian Second Empire should prove the most effective progenitor of one man, one vote and bequeath a substantial legacy to the democratic Third Republic. Gradual reform proved difficult to implement after the sovereignty of the people had been enunciated in 1789 and universal manhood suffrage remained a bone of contention for almost one hundred years. Due to the emphasis on national uniformity, there has been little room for innovation at the local level in France, unlike other countries. Instead, the general electorate has expanded and contracted in concertina fashion, offering the opportunity for greater or lesser numbers to learn to vote, for limited or lengthier periods. Numerous criteria, including age, family status, tax payment, property ownership, residence, and criminal record, have all been employed to determine who should vote, as the clash of ideals and partisan advantage yielded a huge range of options. There was just one, vital area in which this propensity for experimentation was conspicuous by its absence, to which we now turn: the female franchise.

---

[111] Jason Brennan, *Against Democracy* (Princeton, NJ, 2017).

[112] Jean-Paul Yves Le Goff, 'Pourquoi je suis contre le suffrage universel', 23 Jan. 2009. https://blogs.mediapart.fr/jeanpaulyveslegoff/blog/230109/pourquoi-je-suis-contre-le-suffrage-universel (accessed 07/08/19).

2

Women Had to Wait

A Stubbornly Resisted Female Franchise

Women's hands were made to be kissed, not for casting a ballot paper.
Alexandre Bérard, 3 October 1919.[1]

The award of a universal franchise to males and females in France was separated
by almost a century, from 1848 to 1944. Yet this notorious disparity can be partly
explained by the extremely early acquisition of the vote by all adult Frenchmen,
habitually, if erroneously, referred to as 'universal suffrage' by contemporaries and
some historians. The jurist Charles Turgeon offered the necessary corrective when
he wrote early in the twentieth century, 'Our so-called universal suffrage is in fact
a restricted franchise, a male privilege and a masculine monopoly.'[2] Yet, in most
Western countries some, if not all, men obtained the vote long before any women,
and the time-span was usually shorter where universal male suffrage arrived
later.[3] The undue 'delay' in France must therefore be put into perspective, since
most European women only obtained a legislative vote between the First and
Second World Wars, so their French counterparts were not lagging too far behind
in this regard.[4] Indeed, even in 1950, a few European countries with a universal
male suffrage had still not extended the right to women; it is only since then that
the global adoption of mass voting has usually been accompanied by similar
access to the franchise for both sexes. Nonetheless, French women's especially
protracted struggle for the suffrage requires some explanation. This chapter
investigates the obstacles that stood in its way, as well exploring suffragists' efforts
to secure it, before concluding with the female electoral apprenticeship that commenced in France after 1945.

Pierre Rosanvallon has suggested that in France 'the block on female suffrage
was much more philosophical than political... it was not due to an anti-feminism
that was more pronounced than elsewhere. Instead, it stemmed from a conception,

---

[1] *JO*, Annexe 564, Rapport sur le suffrage féminin, 3 Oct. 1919.
[2] Charles Turgeon, *Le Féminisme français*, 2 vols, 2nd edn (Paris, 1907), ii, 26.
[3] Dawn Langan Teele, *Forging the Franchise: The Political Origins of the Women's Vote* (Princeton,
NJ, 2018), 1–6.
[4] Siân Reynolds, 'Lateness, amnesia and unfinished business: gender and democracy in twentieth-
century Europe', *European History Quarterly*, 32 (2002), 87–91.

How the French Learned to Vote: A History of Electoral Practice in France. Malcolm Crook, Oxford University Press (2021).

as restrictive as it was demanding, of the citizen as an individual.'[5] In other words, the autonomy required for political participation was erected into a universal principle, which deprived women of the vote on account of their genetic nature and social situation, traditionally subordinate to males. According to this view, appeals to represent their separate interests, when made by women (and men), were ill-conceived, just as attempts to enfranchise them solely at the local level, and thus on a different basis, were ill-founded. Yet, the contradiction between universalism and particularism in women's demands for the suffrage, also underlined by historian Joan Scott ('in order to protest women's exclusion...they invoked the very difference they sought to deny'), may be more apparent than real.[6] For fellow historian Anne-Sarah Bouglé-Moalic, 'in practice, the distinction between universalist and particularist arguments was never clearly drawn'.[7] In any event, the appeal to be 'different but equal' was unavoidable in the prevailing circumstances, where full citizenship was associated with masculinity. Difference could be presented as complementary, for women did not need to abandon their family role in order to vote, and supportive male politicians, far from finding the female franchise 'unthinkable', also employed utilitarian language in favour of comparable voting rights for women.[8]

In fact, as suggested in Chapter 1, the universal male franchise, an unexpected and fortuitous arrival in 1848, by no means implied the end of debate over the exclusion of men who failed to comply with the French model of personal autonomy. Indeed, it might be argued that the granting of voting rights to dependent males was achieved at the expense of women, whose enfranchisement would present further difficulties in determining the limits of the electorate. As some deputies pointed out when making a case for restrictions on manhood suffrage, universality could never be interpreted literally; there must always be limits and, in debating votes for women, their misgivings about certain categories of male electors frequently surfaced. Down to 1848 and long after, the franchise was not invariably regarded as an individual right; indeed, under the constitutional monarchy female property could be counted towards a male's fiscal qualification to vote.[9] The collective identity of family or household thus endured beyond the *Ancien Régime*; there were proposals in the Revolution to deny mature bachelors the franchise, while the idea of a plural vote for the paterfamilias was first mooted during the Second Republic. To borrow a phrase from Peter Jones, the political

[5] Rosanvallon, *Le Sacre du citoyen*, 409–10.

[6] Joan Scott, *Only Paradoxes to Offer: French Feminists and the Rights of Man* (Cambridge, MA, 1996), x–xi.

[7] Anne-Sarah Bouglé-Moalic, *Le Vote des Françaises. Cent ans de débats 1848–1944* (Rennes, 2012), 45ff.

[8] Siân Reynolds, 'Le sacre de la citoyenne? Réflexions sur le retard français', in Yolande Cohen and Françoise Thébaud (eds), *Féminismes et identités nationales. Les processus d'intégration des femmes au politique* (Lyon, 1998), 77–8.

[9] Anne Verjus, *Le Cens de la famille. Les femmes et le vote, 1789–1848* (Paris, 2002).

system in nineteenth-century France constituted 'an improbable democracy' in a country that was, and would for some time to come, remain overwhelmingly rural in character, a social factor that surely deserves greater consideration in discussions of suffrage extension.[10] In short, Rosanvallon's interpretation, like other stimulating examinations of the issue, omits a number of important dimensions to women's lengthy quest for the vote in France, besides failing to acknowledge female agency in finally breaking the impasse.

The arrival of universal suffrage in France, for women as for men, was abrupt rather than gradual. All adult females, like their male counterparts before them, were enfranchised at a stroke, a development also instituted by the decree of a provisional government rather than parliamentary legislation. Just as revolution brought the downfall of the July Monarchy in 1848, and ushered in universal male suffrage, so war and occupation caused the collapse of the Third Republic and broke the stalemate which had hitherto thwarted the female franchise. As the future of liberated France was adumbrated, the momentous decision has sometimes been attributed to the recognition of women's role in the Resistance, but such an interpretation ignores the preceding efforts of suffragists in turning public opinion in their favour and, above all, a desire to re-found the Republic rather than return to the political immobility of preceding years.[11] General Charles de Gaulle played a part when this step was taken in 1944, following his earlier commitment to enact the female vote as soon as the conflict drew to a close. Yet it was the Communist delegate, Fernand Grenier, who successfully proposed that 'women will vote and be eligible under the same conditions as men'. His bold proposition encountered some acrimonious discussion and raised familiar misgivings at both the preparatory commission and a Consultative Assembly, based in Algeria, which plotted the path towards a new regime. There was no grand, accompanying declaration of women's rights and historians, like jurists, have been loath to regard the measure as a great landmark, which brought almost half a century of legislative endeavour to fruition.[12]

The thoroughly reactionary Vichy government had in fact made some provision for female suffrage, so 'the fall of the Republic in summer 1940 did not bring the history of French suffragism to a halt', as Bouglé-Moalic suggests.[13] Article 21 of its draft constitution, issued in 1943, began by stating that French men and women, born of a French father and aged over twenty-one, were both to vote for members of the proposed national assemblies (a Chamber of Deputies and a Senate,

---

[10] Peter (P.M.) Jones, 'An improbable democracy: nineteenth-century elections in the Massif Central', *English Historical Review*, XCVII (1982), 530–57, and Huard, *Le Suffrage universel*, 406.

[11] Siân Reynolds, *France between the Wars: Gender and Politics* (London, 1996), 215–16.

[12] Noëlle Lenoir, 'The representation of women in politics: from quotas to parity', *The International and Comparative Law Quarterly*, 50 (2001), 229–31.

[13] Bouglé-Moalic, *Le Vote des Françaises*, 303.

as under the Third Republic).[14] However, women were not eligible for election to these bodies, though they could be chosen, as well as vote, for provincial, departmental, and municipal councils if, like men, they were twenty-five years old. At first sight this might seem a liberal proposition but, besides its limitation of women's political rights at the parliamentary level, it was vitiated by the accompanying family franchise (a right-wing hobbyhorse). This accorded an additional vote to heads of family (fathers in the first instance, mothers in their absence) and reflected the reactionary ethos of the *État français*. Indeed, women had been removed from all public positions in 1940 and generally restricted to the private sphere, though this proved impractical in a situation of war and occupation which had removed so many males from contention. Their subsequent nomination as local councillors was mainly intended to give females a specific role as mothers rather than as individual citizens.[15] Nonetheless, it was an indication of the possibilities that political breakdown presented, especially since other projects were submitted under Vichy that envisaged offering the suffrage to men and women on a more equitable basis.

Framing an Issue and an Agenda, 1789–1848

Securing female enfranchisement proved an extremely long haul, since the first demands for women's right to vote were made during the Revolution of 1789, when just putting such proposals on the table was more significant than their rejection. The historian Joan Landes has claimed that, in so far as 'the Republic was constructed against women, not just without them', the revolutionaries effectively removed the political participation they had enjoyed under the *Ancien Régime*.[16] In fact, relatively few women had been able to vote then, and they did so, like males, as members of corporate bodies, on the basis of customary practice and privilege, not as equal individuals. These exceptions existed for single female property-owners, widowed householders or women practising a trade, often after the demise of their artisan or shopkeeper husbands. In elections to the Estates General of 1789, they were able to take part in preliminary assemblies of the third estate, while female religious were represented at assemblies of their order by male clerics, and the wives and daughters of enfeoffed nobles could vote by

[14] Projet de Constitution du gouvernement de Révolution nationale, 12 Nov. 1943, in Léon Duguit et al. (eds), *Les Constitutions et les principales lois politiques de la France depuis 1789*, 7th edn (Paris, 1952), 386ff.

[15] Michèle Cointet-Labrousse, *Le Conseil national de Vichy. Vie politique et réforme de l'État en régime autoritaire (1940–1944)* (Paris, 1989) and Simone Verdeau, *L'Accession des femmes aux fonctions publiques* (Toulouse, 1942), 149–53.

[16] Joan B. Landes, *Women and the Public Sphere in the Age of the French Revolution* (Ithaca, NY, 1988), 12 and 106–7.

proxy.[17] Condorcet was surely making a tongue-in-cheek remark with his suggestion that some members of what became the National Assembly owed their position to female voters.[18] When the new suffrage was subsequently established, it was thus a matter of not including women in the new regime rather than curtailing a long-held right.

Some groups of women had drawn up their own *cahiers de doléances* in 1789, albeit without making any overtly political demands, while one or two bolder individuals had requested general access to the accompanying elections and also eligibility. However, after the Revolution, when a uniform definition of the franchise was enacted, one of the criteria was gender, which automatically ruled out some 50 per cent of the adult population. This was quite explicit in the Constitutions of 1793 and 1795, if not that of 1791, for the former stipulated 'hommes' as opposed to 'Français' (a designation unsuccessfully contested during the following century on the grounds that it was gender-inclusive). Yet, during the 1790s, women were not alone in being refused a right to vote that was initially limited to 'active citizens', since those adult males who failed to cross a certain tax threshold, or worked as domestic servants, were also denied the franchise on the grounds that they lacked sufficient independence to exercise it (see Chapter 1). However, these masculine exclusions, which could be overcome by a change in financial or occupational circumstances, were strongly challenged and most men were subsequently accorded the suffrage (all of them, in fact, in the abortive Constitution of 1793). By contrast, there was absolutely no legislative change for women, save the very specific award of a vote to female householders in the division of common land, granted that same year.

Yet, in January 1789, in his famous pamphlet 'What is the Third Estate?', Sieyès had alluded to full citizenship for women when he stated that they were everywhere, 'rightly or wrongly', excluded from the electorate and eligibility for office. In his *Observations* on the detailed franchise proposals of the Constitutional Committee, published in October, he went further and suggested that it was 'a bizarre contradiction' that women might wear a crown, yet nowhere exercised the vote. He actually described the obligation to constrain half the population as a matter of 'prejudice', despite otherwise deferring to the dominant view.[19] It was the marquis de Condorcet, liberal aristocrat and *philosophe*, who first took up the case for female enfranchisement, having already raised the issue in some comments he had made on constitutional arrangements in the United States, and on the provincial assemblies set up in France on the eve of the Revolution.[20] In his

[17] Christine Fauré, 'Doléances, déclarations et pétitions, trois formes de la parole publique des femmes sous la Révolution', *AhRf*, 344 (2006), 6–15.
[18] Jean-Antoine-Nicolas de Condorcet, 'Sur l'admission des femmes au droit de cité', in *Œuvres de Condorcet*, eds A. Condorcet O'Connor and M.F. Arago, 12 vols (Paris, 1847), x, 130.
[19] Sewell, *A Rhetoric of Bourgeois Revolution*, 147–8.
[20] Condorcet, *Œuvres*, 'Lettres d'un bourgeois de New-Haven à un citoyen de Virginie', ix, 15–20.

celebrated article, 'On the admission of women to the rights of citizenship', which appeared in July 1790 in the *Journal de la Société de 1789*, he argued that there was no rational case for failing to grant women the vote. He concluded that withholding the vote from women was simply the result of custom and circumstances. 'It is not nature, but education and social conditions' that cause differences between men and women in this regard, he added, a reflection that led him to propose similar schooling for both sexes when educational reform was subsequently considered by the National Assembly.[21]

Few women sought the franchise for members of their sex during the Revolution, as opposed to pressing for equal civil rights, where some significant, albeit temporary, progress was recorded. A recent history of the Revolution that emphasizes women's involvement underscores the point: 'There was no major movement aimed at women's suffrage, let alone female eligibility to public office.'[22] Madame Roland, briefly prominent in government circles, as the wife of a government minister, typifies this reluctance to demand political equality, but Olympe de Gouges did so in 1791, in her ground-breaking pamphlet, *The Declaration of the Rights of Women*, a mirror-image of the Declaration of the Rights of Man.[23] In her often-cited words, 'if women have the right to mount the scaffold, then they should also be able to step up to the rostrum'. In making this comprehensive demand for the female franchise and, in taking the Revolution's universalism at its word, in order to expose its shortcomings, it would become an exemplary document. However, while insisting on the inalienability of rights for women equal to those of men, she envisaged a separate national assembly to represent 'mothers, daughters and sisters', so as to maintain 'the constitution, good morals and the happiness of all'.[24]

There may not have been a concerted campaign for the suffrage, but the Revolution did mark 'the beginnings of the organised participation of women in politics', as historian Barrie Rose has suggested.[25] A female speaker at the Jacobin Club of Saint-Sever (Landes) contended in 1791 that denying women a political voice was unjust, because they were obliged to live under laws passed without their consent. Etta Palm d'Aelders, who hailed from the Netherlands, participated in the *Confédération des Amis de la Vérité* at Paris, which strove to improve conditions for women. On 1 April 1792 she led a female delegation to the Legislative Assembly to protest against 'the state of degradation in which women find themselves regarding their political rights, long denied by oppression', and to demand

---

[21] Condorcet, *Œuvres*, 'Sur l'admission des femmes', ix, 125.

[22] Noah Shusterman, *The French Revolution: Faith, Desire, and Politics* (Abingdon, 2014), 147.

[23] Olympe de Gouges, *Déclaration des droits de la femme* (Paris, 1791).

[24] Scott, *Only Paradoxes to Offer*, 20.

[25] R. B. Rose, 'Feminism, women and the French Revolution', *Australian Journal of Politics and History*, 40 (1994), 173. See also Dominique Godineau, *The Women of Paris and their French Revolution*, trans. Katherine Streip (Berkeley, CA, 1998), 282ff.

raising the status of women via education and employment, so that 'political liberty and equality of rights may be the same for both sexes'.[26] Roughly sixty women's political clubs were created after 1789, mostly in the larger provincial towns and, early in 1793, the *Société des Amis de la Liberté et de l'Égalité* established in Besançon demanded that the new republican constitution should extend the right to vote to women.[27] By the end of that year, such activity had provoked a strident, misogynistic backlash from republican leaders, against 'women engaging in politics'.[28] Their clubs were closed, but this measure was testimony to their achievement in providing a public platform for self-proclaimed *citoyennes* to begin exploring a political role in the new order.

The first year of the Republic represented the apogee of demands for the female franchise, which was finally raised at parliamentary level, when deputies in the Convention commenced the task of drafting a replacement for the now defunct Constitution of 1791. Somewhat surprisingly, the 'Plan de Constitution', on which Condorcet was consulted, presented to the deputies in mid-February 1793 (only to be rejected by them), made no concessions to women and explicitly attributed full citizenship to men only. Yet the committee entrusted with composing the document does seem to have discussed the female franchise, according to the testimony of David Williams, a well-connected Welsh *philosophe*, who had recently been awarded French citizenship and travelled to France to participate in the constitutional debate. When he published his reflections on these proceedings, he condemned the exclusion of women. According to him, although the constraints of the female physique meant that they were not able to fulfil all civic duties, and while husband and wife should be regarded as sharing the same opinions and thus a single franchise, 'it is no less true that when women remain single or become widows, they incontestably have the right to vote, and its refusal...is an injustice...'.[29] It was only after another committee was created to draw up a fresh constitutional draft, in the light of proposals from other deputies, that the question of gender was broached in the Convention itself. Gilbert Romme presented a draft Declaration of Rights on 17 April 1793, which stated, albeit in a contorted fashion, that women should be awarded political rights: 'Any man, of one or the other sex, once he has reached the age of maturity, has the right to consent to his union with the social body, and then he becomes a citizen.'[30]

---

[26] *AP*, 1ere série, XLI, 1 Apr. 1792, 63–4.

[27] Suzanne Desan, '"Constitutional amazons": Jacobin women's clubs in the French Revolution', in Bryant T. Ragan and Elizabeth A. Williams (eds), *Re-Creating Authority in Revolutionary France* (New Brunswick, NJ, 1992), 11 and 24–5.

[28] *AP*, 1ere série, vol. LXXVIII, 9 Brumaire II (30 Oct. 1793), 49.

[29] David Williams, *Observations sur la dernière constitution de la France, avec des vues pour la formation de la nouvelle constitution* (Paris, 1793), 16. See also Witney Jones, *David Williams: The Anvil and the Hammer* (Cardiff, 1986), 127.

[30] *AP*, 1ere série, LXII, 17 Apr. 1793, 267.

Finding an appropriate language certainly posed problems in this debate on gender and politics, exacerbated by the distinctions drawn between the different status of females single, married, or widowed. Some participants rejected 'citoyenne', which was employed by women who were demanding change, while Romme toyed with the gender-neutral 'individu'. Pierre Guyomar, a deputy for the Côtes-du-Nord and an associate of Condorcet, published a contemporary pamphlet which began by asserting that the term 'homme' encompassed both sexes. He went on to argue strongly that the Declaration of the Rights of Man applied to women just as much as it did to all males: 'Is the difference between the sexes any better founded than the colour of black slaves?', he asked.[31] Members of the female sex should thus be entitled to vote, but they should only be eligible for election to local office (to avoid lengthy absences from the household which the role of national deputy entailed), and they should have their own electoral assemblies for legislative polls. Guyomar could not imagine full equality but, he concluded affirmatively: 'I submit that half the individuals in a society have no right to deprive the other half of the imprescriptible right to vote. Let us free ourselves as soon as we can from such sexual prejudice.' 'Defenders of liberty', he continued, 'let us proclaim that of women…and, in face of astonishment across the continent, let us open the doors of the electoral assemblies to them.'[32] Jacques-Marie Rouzet, an obscure deputy for the Haute-Garonne, also supported the female franchise, though he advocated the vote for married women (and widows), while denying it to spinsters. Rouzet's contribution, which was published as part of the constitutional debate in April 1793, included some rather convoluted argument, but the thrust was clear, that women should not de facto be excluded from voting.[33]

In the event, any possibility of including women in the franchise ended when Lanjuinais delivered a further report on constitutional preparations at the end of April, specifically relating to the rights of citizenship, and stated unequivocally that women, like children and minors, could not be full citizens. In justifying his conclusion, he mentioned that there had been opposition to the exclusion of women from the franchise, and not just from Romme and Guyomar, who had presented an 'interesting dissertation' on the matter. Yet he stated that women's 'physique and vocation inhibit them from fulfilling many of the rights and duties of citizenship, while existing customs and the vices of our educational system make their exclusion still more necessary, at least for a few years'. Indeed, he went on to add that 'if the most just and the best institutions are those that conform most closely to nature, then it is difficult to believe that women should be allowed to exercise political rights. It is beyond me to think that, taking everything into

---

[31] *AP*, 1ere série, XLIII, published as annexes to the session of 29 Apr. 1793, 595–9.

[32] *AP*, 1ere série, XLIII, published as annexes to the session of 29 Apr. 1793, 599.

[33] *AP*, 1ere série, XLII, 18 Apr. 1793, 496–7, Jacques-Marie Rouzet, *Projet de Constitution française* (Paris, 1793), annexe to the session.

account, either men or women would gain any advantage from it.'[34] Lanjuinais' exposition hardly amounted to a parliamentary debate, but the female suffrage had at least been raised in committee and aired in pamphlets. Moreover, it remained alive in discussion over the education system, when Lakanal presented a new report on the matter at the end of June 1793 and began by declaring that 'national schools aim to provide children of both sexes with all the instruction necessary for French citizens', but this grand plan did not materialize.[35]

The final version of a new Constitution, which was promulgated at this juncture and put to a popular vote, specifically reserved the franchise to men. Nonetheless, women at Beaumont, in the Dordogne, immediately despatched an address to the Convention in which they asserted the right of 'citoyennes' to ratify it, while others protested about their exclusion from the process.[36] Above all, there are numerous, documented cases of women taking part in the cantonal assemblies where the constitutional vote was taken.[37] Their involvement was facilitated by the nature of the exercise, which allowed a good deal of procedural latitude: electors were 'invited' rather than instructed to comply with existing practice. In some places women's votes were recorded in the formal procès-verbaux, as at Laon or Pontoise, while in others they held their own assemblies, the case at Damazan in the Lot-et-Garonne, perhaps after being refused admission by males in the canton.[38] In yet other instances it was noted that females took part in the general festivities, religious and secular, that concluded the proceedings in many locations. A spectacular celebration occurred at Saint-Nicolas-de-la-Grave in the Haute-Garonne, where some 250 citoyennes shared fraternal embraces with male voters before dancing around the town in a farandole.

Hundreds, perhaps thousands, of women were thus involved in this unprecedented consultation, a striking testimony to their activism in 1793. However, this exceptional episode was rapidly superseded by a severe reaction against any sort of female intervention in politics, while implementation of the new constitution was deferred, and the electoral process was suspended at most levels, with the onset of revolutionary government. Once the emergency was brought under control, it was decided to devise a fresh political settlement and the commission which drafted the Constitution of 1795 received numerous proposals from both deputies and members of the public. These included a slightly amended document from the conventionnel Rouzet, which retained his categories of female voters

---

[34] AP, 1ere série, LXIII, 29 Apr. 1793, 562 and 564.
[35] AP, 1ere série, LXVII, 26 June 1793, 504.
[36] Dominique Godineau, 'Femmes en citoyenneté: pratiques et politique', AhRf, 300 (1995), 201.
[37] AN BII, 1–34, Procès-verbaux (hereafter PV) des assemblées cantonales, 1793 and Serge Aberdam, 'Deux occasions de participation féminine en 1793: le vote sur la Constitution et le partage des biens communaux', AhRf, 339 (2005), 17–34.
[38] AN F1cIII Vendée 5, Acceptation de la Constitution, 5 Pluviôse II (24 Jan. 1794). At Bouin the president of the assembly acceded to a request by 400 women to vote and have their verdicts recorded in the PV.

from 1793, along with some reflections on responses to his earlier publication. Although he was willing to make concessions where female eligibility to office was concerned, he persisted in regarding the denial of the vote to them as an error.[39] Notwithstanding, the agreed constitutional document explicitly stipulated that only men would exercise the more restricted political rights that were to be maintained, and there is no evidence in the record of the accompanying vote to accept it that women were directly involved on this occasion, while even their presence as spectators at electoral assemblies was later banned.

It was some fifty years later before another public challenge to the male monopoly of voting was facilitated by the revolution of 1848 and the advent of the Second Republic. The upheaval resulted in the grand decree issued by the Provisional Government on 5 March, which declared that the suffrage would be 'universal'. This represented a reflex to the restricted franchise prevailing under the constitutional monarchy, rather than a carefully considered innovation which might be interpreted as including all adults, but women themselves quickly seized the initiative. A *Comité des droits de la femme* was created and four delegates were sent to the town hall in Paris to inquire if women would be able to participate in forthcoming elections, only to be told that this was a matter for the Constituent Assembly to decide, later. Jeanne Deroin, a member of the delegation, then launched an appeal to the people in a newly established newspaper, *La Voix des Femmes*: 'Liberty, equality and fraternity have been proclaimed for all. Why should women be left with only obligations to fulfil, without being given the rights of citizens?'[40] Evidently the suffrage was not intended to be truly universal and women were not allowed to register to vote, despite trying to do so.[41] One of their recently founded clubs decided instead to support a female candidature for the National Assembly and proposed the name of George Sand in the press. The writer herself had not been consulted and scotched the suggestion in a somewhat acerbic fashion, though she was more sympathetic to the cause than her refusal might suggest. She felt that women did have a civic contribution to make, and she also believed they would exercise the franchise in future, but only when changes in their social status had prepared the ground for this step to be taken.

There was an alternative way of considering the issue, which was that women would only receive the education required for citizenship once they had acquired legislative leverage through voting and eligibility for office. This was the approach favoured by Deroin, who subsequently attempted to stand for election to the Second Republic's parliament in the spring of 1849, on the basis that: 'A legislative assembly composed entirely of men is as incapable of passing laws to regulate a

[39] Jacques-Marie Rouzet, *Vues civiques sur la Constitution que les Français sont intéressés à se donner* (Paris, 1795).
[40] Jeanne Deroin, 'Aux citoyens français', *La Voix des femmes*, 27 Mar. 1848.
[41] Karen Offen, *The Woman Question in France, 1400–1870* (Cambridge, 2017), 74.

society composed of men and women, just as an assembly confined to the privileged classes would be to discuss the interests of workers...'.[42] She endeavoured in vain to persuade one of the socialist groups in the capital with which she was associated to endorse her candidature (no administrative declaration was required at this point), only to expose herself to a good deal of ribald hostility, in word and image.[43] This earned her notoriety, but the unkindest cut of all was unyielding opposition from the anarchist Pierre-Joseph Proudhon, who strongly denounced the principle of sexual political equality. By contrast, during the preceding period, several socialist groups had been sympathetic to women's rights. Saint-Simonian circles, for instance, were open to females and enabled them to contribute to their newspaper, Le Globe. In fact, various petitions had been submitted to the July Monarchy, demanding the vote for female taxpayers who met the 200-franc criterion set for men, the inclusion of single and widowed women in municipal elections, and the right for women in general to participate in a radically reformed electoral system.[44]

The female suffrage was only briefly raised in the political arena by two left-wing deputies, their voices crying in the wilderness. At the Constitutional Commission, in 1848, Victor Considérant proposed giving women voting rights, arguing that if man-servants and male paupers were given the franchise there was no reason to deny the opposite sex.[45] No discussion of the subject took place in the Constituent Assembly itself, but the Second Republic's Constitution did state that all *Français* over the age of twenty-one could vote. A degree of ambiguity thus persisted in the terminology, which Pierre Leroux attempted to exploit in the Legislative Assembly on 21 November 1851, in the course of a debate over the municipal suffrage, when he declared that women had every right to vote and be elected, just like men. As a start, he demanded female participation at the local level, but his intervention prompted hilarity rather than any serious response.[46] With the republican regime under severe pressure from conservatives and Bonapartists, women's clubs banned, and even their right of petition threatened, there was evidently no immediate prospect of female enfranchisement. Not surprisingly, this would remain the case after Louis-Napoleon seized power and established the Second Empire in 1852. Women might occasionally vote as proxies for husbands or fathers, when allowed to do so by complaisant local authorities, or play some part in electoral activity, but only in the late 1860s did the question of female political rights return to the public domain. Suffragists had at least put the female vote firmly to the fore in 1848, via the creation of newspapers and associations,

[42] Jeanne Deroin, 'Aux électeurs du département de la Seine', 1849.

[43] BNF LB[55] 505, *Campagne électorale de la citoyenne Jeanne Deroin. Pétition des femmes au peuple* (no date).

[44] Michèle Riot-Sarcey, 'Des femmes pétitionnent sous la monarchie de juillet', in Alain Corbin et al. (eds), *Femmes dans la cité* (Grâne, 1997), 395–6.

[45] AN C918, PV of Comité, 13 June 1848.   [46] *Moniteur*, 22 Nov. 1851, 2917–18.

and these provided a platform for reasserting their demands as a more liberal environment re-emerged.

Organizing and Campaigning, 1870–1914

The collapse of the Second Empire in 1870 and the eventual consolidation of a Third Republic initially did little to advance women's suffrage any further than its predecessors. For one thing there was intense debate over the fate of universal *manhood* suffrage, which left little space for considering the female franchise. For another, the violent episode of the Paris Commune in 1871, which had proclaimed its support for women's equality, only served to reinvigorate the myth of the revolutionary female; the *pétroleuse* succeeded the *tricoteuse* and *vesuvienne* as the archetypal disorderly woman who could not be entrusted with political rights. In any case, suffragists subordinated their cause to that of the nascent Third Republic, which was struggling to establish itself in face of the conservative majority elected to the National Assembly, just as others would later sacrifice female demands to the cause of socialism. Yet various associations and a regular press were created to promote women's rights, even if the franchise question scarcely featured on their agenda. Thus, the first feminist organization, *avant la lettre*, the Association pour le droit des femmes, which became the Ligue française pour le droit des femmes in 1882, prioritized civil over political rights.

It was Hubertine Auclert, destined to become the leading French suffragist until her death in 1914, who unambiguously put the vote first in the paper she launched in 1881, entitled *La Citoyenne*. In a speech, later published but denied delivery at the Congrès international du droit des femmes three years earlier, she had asserted: 'The weapon of the vote will be for us, as it is for men, the only means of obtaining the reforms we desire. As long as we remain excluded from political life, men will always attend to their own interests rather than ours.'[47] The women's congress of 1878, the first of its kind, was convened to coincide with an international exhibition in Paris, and a similar event was held in the French capital on the centenary of the French Revolution in 1889.[48] The emergent feminist movement was a transnational one from its inception, with campaigners in different countries seeking cooperation and offering each other inspiration.[49]

---

[47] Hubertine Auclert, *Le Droit politique des femmes: question qui n'est pas traitée au congrès international des femmes* (Paris, 1878), 13 and Steven C. Hause, *Hubertine Auclert: The French Suffragette* (Princeton, NJ, 1987), 42–6.

[48] *Congrès français et international du droit des femmes* (Paris, 1889).

[49] Malcolm Crook, 'L'avènement du suffrage féminin dans une perspective globale (1890–1914)', in Landry Charrier et al. (eds), *Circulations et réseaux transnationaux en Europe (XVIIIᵉ-XXᵉ siècles). Acteurs, pratiques, modèles* (Berne, 2013), 57–68.

The progress of female suffrage at the local level in anglophone countries, from the late 1860s onwards, provided a model that might be emulated in France. Setting the right to vote in a wider context was also a means of shaming opponents: suffragists could argue that France, the much-vaunted leader of democracy, was in danger of losing its vanguard status. The preface to the Dussaussoy bill which, in 1906, proposed giving all French adult women the vote in local polls, accordingly emphasized that 'the extension of the vote to females in these elections is not merely a European but a global development'.[50] It was only right that France should take its place among those parliamentary states that were currently responding to women's demands. When this proposal failed to make any immediate progress, the Commission on Universal Suffrage was prompted to remark that 'opinion all over the world is favourable to altering the status quo. It is not the suffragists who are out of step, but the anti-suffragists. France is falling behind.'[51]

The International Council for Women suggested that feminist organizations in France should federate and affiliate, an invitation reiterated by the International Woman Suffrage Alliance (IWSA), which was founded to focus on the franchise question. Yet, unlike Britain or the United States, it took some time to establish a well-supported suffrage movement in France and it was far from united. Catholic women adhered in far greater numbers than their feminist counterparts to organizations sponsored by the Church that were anti-suffragist, at least until the Pope abandoned his hostility to the female franchise in 1919. Moreover, French society remained overwhelmingly rural and women's rights were scarcely a burning issue in the countryside where most females lived and worked. However, social and economic change was generating more diverse employment opportunities, which better-educated women were not slow to grasp: two suffragist leaders, Madeleine Pelletier and Maria Vérone, were respectively numbered among the first female doctors and lawyers to qualify in France. The turn of the twentieth century thus brought fresh impetus, not least after the Conseil national des femmes françaises, a federation 'more feminine than feminist', was set up in 1901.[52] It was hardly a mass movement, with just 20,000 affiliates at the outset, but this figure grew to over 70,000 five years later, and it fostered greater collaboration among different groups. Yet the reluctance to foreground suffrage demands remained evident; it was only in 1909 that the Union française pour le suffrage des femmes (UFSF) was founded as a specifically suffragist organization, linked to the IWSA, though it claimed only 12,000 adherents among associated groups.[53] Even this was a

[50]   AN C7375, Commission du suffrage universel, Exposé des motifs, 10 July 1906.
[51]   Ferdinand Buisson, Le Vote des femmes (Paris, 1911), 306. This revised version of the report presented to the Chamber of Deputies in 1909 was mostly devoted to documenting developments elsewhere.
[52]   Steven C. Hause with Anne R. Kenney, Women's Suffrage and Social Politics in the French Third Republic (Princeton, NJ, 1984), 38ff.
[53]   Hause, Women's Suffrage, 111–14.

moderate organization, which led militants to secede and create the more radical Ligue nationale pour le vote des femmes (LNVF) in 1914.

The numbers were not great, but other developments contributed to making the decade or so preceding the First World War a *belle époque* for the female suffrage campaign. There was an argument that women should be eligible for election before they could vote, thus enabling women's particular expertise to be brought to bear in parliament or local government without conceding the uncertain element of their vote, especially in view of their superior weight in the population. In fact, in the 1880s the French suffragists had already begun standing for election, a tactic facilitated by the French tradition of 'open' candidatures and ballot papers supplied outside the polling station (both of which will be explored below). Where *scrutin de liste* was concerned, women sought inscription on a party slate, but there was nothing to prevent them from canvassing independently in single-member constituencies, by holding meetings or printing leaflets and *bulletins*. Of course, any votes they obtained would be ruled out of contention, sometimes not even counted, but this was a novel means of publicizing the cause and engaging in electoral practice. Invalid ballot papers, which voters wrote for themselves, do indicate the earlier nomination of certain women, notably the famous *communarde* Louise Michel, though (as a good anarchist) she later refused to stand as an unofficial election candidate when this device became an increasingly salient aspect of suffragist strategy.

In 1881, Maria Deraismes likewise declined to contest a seat in the Chamber of Deputies, though in her case she did not wish to undermine the Republic, a common sentiment among suffragists, who continued to fear for its stability. However, women were attracting votes in some municipal polls in the provinces and one of them was nearly elected in the Nièvre, while in 1884 two female victories in a couple of other departments were duly annulled.[54] By contrast, when Léonie Rouzade had stood in a by-election for the municipal council of Paris, she received a paltry fifty-seven out of 1,122 votes cast.[55] Nonetheless, the ploy was repeated at subsequent elections, legislative as well as local, and the Parisian municipal election of 1908 was especially successful in generating press coverage as well as support from feminist groups, when the *candidate*, Jeanne Laloë, a journalist, may have secured over 20 per cent of the poll in the ninth arrondissement.[56] In the legislative elections of 1910 at Paris, women competed independently (Auclert for the first and only time), as well as under the socialist banner but, despite her especially active campaign, the leading suffragist Madeleine Pelletier failed to

---

[54] Patrick Bidelman, *Pariahs Stand Up! The Founding of the Liberal Feminist Movement in France, 1858–1889* (London, 1982), 137.

[55] Bouglé-Moalic, *Le Vote des Françaises*, 115–16.

[56] Hause, *Women's Suffrage*, 101–3. There is uncertainty over the identity of some invalidated votes and the original PV have not been consulted.

secure more than a meagre 4 per cent of the vote.[57] Conversely, cooperation with provincial socialists, who were sometimes willing to enable females to stand as their parliamentary candidates, could prove more fruitful. 'Citoyenne Elisabeth Renaud', as she appeared on the ballot paper, was the sole opponent of a Radical at Vienne (Isère), in 1910, and she garnered almost 800 (discounted) votes.[58]

Suffragists in France rarely followed those suffragettes (ironically a word with Gallic connotations) across the English Channel in recourse to illegal activities, despite their country's revolutionary tradition. It was only during the course of Laloë's campaign in 1908 that Auclert called for 'direct action' and, having entered a polling station at the *mairie* in the fourth arrondissement of Paris, she knocked over the ballot box and trampled on its scattered contents. This action violated the sanctity of the *urne*, as it was known, which occupied a hallowed place in French electoral ritual (see Chapter 5). Yet Auclert's profane gesture, for which she refused to apologize, was an isolated incident that brought condemnation from feminists as well as the general public. Indeed, the women's newspaper with the biggest circulation, *La Française*, emphasized its complete lack of support for such unruly behaviour:

> We are absolutely opposed to the Englishwomen's method of making their claims. The violent public demonstrations they have organized, which are perhaps justified there, seem to us essentially incompatible with French manners and would be injurious rather than useful to our cause here.[59]

There were certainly some occasions when the law was broken and, in the 1930s, suffragists expressed their frustration by disrupting several sporting events, including horse-racing at Longchamp and the French football cup final.[60] Yet, compared to the violence associated with their British counterparts, or militants in the United States, French women were reluctant to resort to provocation. The contrast has been explained by the predominantly middle-class nature of the suffragist movement in France, though this was not exceptional; members' misgivings about disturbing what they regarded as a delicately balanced republican polity, like the relatively small size of the movement in France, should also be taken into account.[61]

---

[57] Charles Sowerwine, *Sisters or Citizens? Women and Socialism in France since 1876* (Cambridge, 1982), 123–4.

[58] AN C6626, PV de la 2ᵉ circonscription de Vienne, 1910. Sowerwine, *Sisters or Citizens?*, 124–6, wrongly suggests that almost 2,900 *bulletins* were cast for her, when in fact many of these were spoiled papers bearing her opponent's name.

[59] *La Française*, 28 June 1908.

[60] Laurence Klejman, *L'Égalité en marche. Le féminisme sous la Troisième République* (Paris, 1989), 295–9.

[61] Hause, *Women's Suffrage*, 114ff.

Despite these limitations, French suffragists were by no means shrinking violets and they came up with some ingenious, non-violent means of publicizing their cause. In the spring of 1914, the different suffragist organizations (for once working together) were able to demonstrate massive support for their cause among women through a fresh form of action. Besides backing sympathetic candidates in the quadrennial parliamentary elections on 23 April, it was decided to stage a simultaneous mock vote for women, who were asked to cast ballots demanding the franchise.[62] The pro-suffrage *Le Journal*, would publicize the gambit and print 'bulletins fictifs' that could be detached, signed and returned to the newspaper. However, women in Paris and some provincial cities, were able to vote in person, at specially created polling stations (a book shop in Besançon, for instance), using the newly introduced technology of *isoloir* and envelope, thereby generating some striking visual images of female voters.[63] Militants from the LNVF distributed additional ballot papers on election-day in Paris, where nearly 17,000 women voted, making this the most successful suffrage event so far mounted in France. Polling continued all over the country for the next fortnight (until the second round of voting proper), by which point, in person or via postal ballot, over half-a-million French women had taken part, with just 114 votes recorded against the female franchise. This was followed on 5 July 1914 by the 'Condorcet' demonstration, when a march across Seine to the left-bank monument in honour of this early advocate of women's rights not only reflected growing cooperation between suffragists, but also brought an unprecedented crowd of 5,000–6,000 women on to the streets of the capital.

Legislative Expectations

Meanwhile, a parliamentary road to women's suffrage was being opened. A long series of no less than sixty propositions would be presented to the Chamber of Deputies over the next four decades, although a sixth of them only proposed a local vote, and little more than a third eligibility as well as the suffrage, while most of them were never put to parliament. The first, submitted by Jean Gautret in 1901, seeking the franchise in both local and national elections, for adult women who were unmarried, widowed, or divorced (on the grounds that they were potential taxpayers), was quietly buried in committee.[64] A more significant breakthrough was achieved five years later with the Dussaussoy proposal which aimed to give all adult women the vote in local elections, albeit without eligibility. This

---

[62] Hause, *Women's Suffrage*, 179ff.
[63] See http://aetdebesancon.blog.lemonde.fr/2014/04/26/a-besancon-des-femmes-ont-vote-le-26-avril-1914/ (accessed 07/07/19). These 'parallel elections' were repeated in the 1930s.
[64] *JO*, Annexe au PV, no. 31, 1 July 1901.

represented an internationally recognized route towards the full suffrage, offering experience of voting for municipal, arrondissement, and departmental councils, in polls that were deemed 'administrative' rather than 'political' in France, in so far as incumbents did not pass legislation. Women had served an electoral apprenticeship at this level in other countries and French men had done so under the Revolution and July Monarchy. A favourable report was eventually delivered in the Chamber of Deputies by the suffragist Ferdinand Buisson in 1910, on behalf of the Commission on Universal Suffrage. It also proposed female eligibility to local authorities, despite its consequences for the election of the Senate in which female councillors would *ipso facto* be involved.[65] Its sponsor declared that women's suffrage had finally passed from the realm of theory to practice, but implementation remained an extremely vexed question. Further progress was hampered by the priority accorded to contemporary consideration of the wholly secret ballot (see Chapter 5) and, above all, PR.[66] The female franchise accordingly took a back seat, but there was great optimism in the summer of 1914 that a bill awarding women a local franchise and eligibility would succeed in a newly elected Chamber, only for this measure to become an early casualty of the First World War.

In the event, while suffragists suspended their campaign for the duration of hostilities, the role played by women on the home front bolstered their case and offered hope that their efforts would be rewarded as a recompense for their patriotism. As in other countries, there was a groundswell of opinion favourable to the female franchise. Jules Siegfried spoke for many deputies when he stated in the Chamber, in January 1918, that 'the ballot paper should be granted to women on account of their admirable conduct during the conflict'.[67] The nationalist writer, Maurice Barrès, had already proposed a partial award in 1916, via the 'suffrage des morts', according to which wives, mothers, or sisters could take the place of their deceased loved ones on the voting register.[68] Not surprisingly, it was rejected by many feminists, who demanded the vote as an individual right: Nelly Roussel, for example, retorted, 'No, M. Barrès, women of conscience do not want your injurious generosity. We do not want to think via another, or to speak for another...What is due to us...is the suffrage of the living.'[69]

The Chamber of Deputies eventually held its inaugural debate on the female franchise in May 1919, though there was disappointment on the part of suffragists that the pre-war proposition had been watered down by raising the

---

[65] *JO*, Annexe au PV, no. 31, 10 June 1910, pub. as Ferdinand Buisson, *Rapport fait au nom de la Commission du suffrage universel...tendant à accorder le droit de vote aux femmes...*(Paris, 1910).

[66] Chenut, 'Attitudes towards French women's suffrage', 737, points to the contemporary preoccupation with PR, although Buisson remarked that 'women's suffrage is...true proportional representation'.

[67] *JO*, 8 Jan. 1918, 2.   [68] Bouglé-Moalic, *Le Vote des Françaises*, 206–10.

[69] Cited in Karen Offen, *Debating the Woman Question in the French Third Republic, 1870–1920* (Cambridge, 2018), 590.

women's voting age to thirty (in order to limit their numbers in the electorate) and denying them any role in the electoral colleges that chose senators (to render the proposal more palatable in the upper chamber).[70] In the event, the deputies went beyond the limited reform encapsulated in the bill and adopted a counter-proposal for the 'integral suffrage' that conferred a universal vote upon all French adults, at all levels, without any distinction by gender. Passed by 344 votes to 97, it seemed a great victory, yet scepticism was expressed about the sincerity of sup-port for the comprehensive change that had been approved and many predicted that the bill would proceed no further. A report in Le Figaro concluded in satirical fashion that, in order to translate the outcome to the upper house, 'a cortege was formed to follow the mortal remains of political equality between the sexes all the way to the Luxembourg Palace'.[71]

Some deputies do seem to have voted for integral suffrage only to ensure that it would be rejected in the Senate, whereas the local franchise proposal might have been accepted.[72] The most striking example of this apparent politique du pire was offered by the republican-socialist Victor Augagneur, a pronounced anti-suffragist who had opposed even the local vote because, in his view, to admit women into the electoral arena at any level constituted a huge leap in the dark. Yet he proceeded to endorse the conversion of the originally modest measure into full-blown universal suffrage. Other deputies who voted favourably with him were subsequently elevated to the Senate, where they refused to even consider the same bill when it was finally tabled there in 1922. Historian Anne Verjus, however, has queried this interpretation, convincingly arguing instead that the positive vote of 1919 repre-sented an exceptional moment of post-war enthusiasm for change. Widespread misgivings were cast aside and principle triumphed, only to encounter a much more pragmatic response later, in the Senate.[73]

The upper house usually took its time, as befitting a conservative institution designed to act as a counter-weight to the Chamber of Deputies, and it had always dragged its feet over legislation to improve women's civil rights, as well as other voting reforms. It was certainly in no rush to process the female suffrage bill, though a commission was duly appointed to produce a report. Published in October 1919, it has been aptly described as 'a synthesis of 150 years of arguments against political rights for women'.[74] Its author, Alexandre Bérard, began with the familiar allegation that 'the immense majority of French women were politically indifferent' and that demands for the vote emanated from 'the isolated opinions of small groups in Paris'.[75] He went on to make the misogynistic assertion that a woman's place was in the home, because she was not suited to the rough and

[70] Hause, Women's Suffrage, 209.   [71] Le Figaro, 21 May 1919.
[72] Hause, Women's Suffrage, 242–3.
[73] Anne Verjus, 'Entre principes et pragmatisme. Députés et sénateurs dans les premiers débats sur le suffrage des femmes en France (1919–1922), Politix, 51 (2000), 55–80.
[74] Hause, Women's Suffrage, 237.   [75] JO, Annexe 564, 3 Oct. 1919.

tumble of public life, but made to 'seduce men and serve as mothers'. He also highlighted the profound political peril involved in female enfranchisement, since in Catholic France their vote would only encourage clerical meddling and 'doubtless deprive some constituencies of a republican deputy'. Three years passed before the report was finally considered by the Senate, which engaged in a procedural debate, before deciding not to discuss the bill itself. The timing was judged to be inappropriate, since more than doubling the electorate would have, it was frequently said, such unpredictable consequences.[76] Even so, the margin of defeat was a mere twenty-two votes, the closest the upper chamber would come to advancing the suffragist cause. Females would be deprived of the franchise for two more decades, until another international conflagration was drawing to a close.

Suffrage Stalemate, 1922–1939

The Chamber of Deputies continued to pass a variety of proposals in favour of the female franchise during the following decade, culminating in a 'unanimous' vote (there were actually ninety-four abstentions) for integral suffrage in July 1936.[77] Meanwhile, its members made repeated attempts to encourage the Senate to reconsider the issue, but it was 1928 before the subject was broached again at the Luxembourg Palace. On this occasion, presented with another profoundly hostile report, the deputies' bill for a female vote at the local level was decisively rejected without any discussion whatsoever. By contrast there was some preliminary debate in 1932, but it was accompanied by an astounding array of antifeminist and patronizing comments: the *rapporteur*, René Héry, baldly asserted that 'there is a fundamental incompatibility between political activity and feminine nature'.[78] As Christine Bard has suggested, this determination to maintain the gender hierarchy was an admission that the men of the Republic were deeply disturbed by women's increasing independence.[79] Efforts to shore up the existing (masculine) order were exemplified in the speech delivered by Armand Calmel, when he proclaimed: 'We overcame many challenges in the past before we encountered feminism; we surmounted the crisis of Boulangism, like that of nationalism and, each time that the Republic was at risk, it was the Senate that saved it.'[80] On 7 July, over 80 per cent of its members voted against proceeding to scrutinize the proposition, a far heavier defeat than the one inflicted ten years earlier.

---

[76] Verjus, 'Entre principes et pragmatisme', 73–9. See also Bouglé-Moalic, *Le Vote des Françaises*, 220–2.
[77] Paul Smith, *Feminism and the Third Republic: Women's Political and Civil Rights in France 1918–1945* (Oxford, 1996), 112ff., for a chapter entitled 'Women's Suffrage and Parliament'.
[78] *JO*, 7 July 1932, 1030.
[79] Christine Bard, *Les Femmes dans la société française au 20ᵉ siècle* (Paris, 2001), 96–7.
[80] *JO*, 5 July 1932, 1019.

Confirmation of the stalemate was provided the following year when another suffrage proposal was adjourned without discussion and this turned out to be the Senate's final verdict on the matter. The growing preponderance of hostile opinion in the upper chamber must be seen as the major obstacle to the achievement of a female franchise. For the historian Charles Sowerwine 'The Republican project, having constructed citizenship on a gendered basis, never transcended its origins in the exclusion of women', but as his colleague Karen Offen concludes, 'It was not "the Republic" but a particular coterie of resistant senators who blocked the way.'[81] Many of them simply did not see suffrage reform working to their advantage, rather the reverse. A recent examination of the attitudes espoused by the growing contingent of Radicals in the upper house, during the interwar years, endorses Paul Smith's earlier conclusion that unless they changed their views or 'diminished as a political power', suffrage reform would simply not succeed.[82] Another contemporary historian, Geoff Read, adds that in fact 'France's politicians, from right to left, failed French women', with Radicals bearing the brunt of the blame, though socialists and communists must take responsibility for not pressing the issue harder.[83] Successive governments neglected to exert leverage over the Senate, even when the Popular Front was in office and Prime Minister Léon Blum appointed three women to his cabinet. Other organizations were also found wanting: despite its grand declaration of support for the principle of female suffrage, the Ligue des Droits de l'Homme took few practical steps to support the campaign, and earned the opprobrium of a bitterly disappointed UFSF as a result.[84]

Other issues repeatedly took precedence over women's suffrage, notwithstanding the fact that the press, and arguably public opinion, was being won over to the cause.[85] Indeed, the campaign for women's suffrage was complicated by another contemporary aspect of voting reform that attracted numerous adherents during the interwar years, including male suffragists like Buisson: the largely forgotten family franchise.[86] Its origins may be traced to the traditional notion of electoral responsibility belonging to 'heads of household', which was overturned by the individual suffrage proclaimed in the Revolution of 1789, but constantly resurrected. In 1848 there was a proposal for awarding additional votes to married men and those with children, partly as a means of representing women and,

---

[81] Charles Sowerwine, 'Revising the sexual contract: women's citizenship and republicanism in France, 1789–1944', in Christopher E. Forth and Elinor Accampo (eds), *Confronting Modernity in Fin-de-Siècle France: Bodies, Minds and Gender* (Basingstoke, 2010), 37 and Offen, *Debating the Woman Question*, 612.

[82] Smith, *Feminism and the Third Republic*, 162, cited in Teele, *Forging the Franchise*, 173.

[83] Geoff Read, *The Republic of Men: Gender and the Political Parties in Interwar France* (Baton Rouge, LA, 2014), 180–1.

[84] William D. Irvine, 'Women's right and the "rights of man"', in Kenneth Mouré and Martin S. Alexander (eds), *Crisis and Renewal in France, 1918–1962* (Oxford, 2001), 46–65 and *La Française*, 8 June 1935.

[85] Bouglé-Moalic, *Le Vote des Françaises*, 252–6.

[86] Jean-Yves Le Naour, *La Famille doit voter. Le suffrage familial contre le vote individuel* (Paris, 2005).

allegedly, making the suffrage more universal. When the idea re-surfaced in the early 1870s, its rationale was more transparently conservative. Alfred Fouillée thought that women lacked the capacity to exercise the franchise themselves, yet he believed that they might exert a moderating influence if *pères de famille* were given an additional vote.[87] Catholics were naturally attracted to a form of plural voting that boosted family values, but a further dimension was added at the turn of the twentieth century by so-called 'natalists', who saw it as a means of encouraging demographic growth. They regarded increasing the birth rate as more important than expanding the electorate, especially after the problem of a stagnating French population had been exacerbated by the appalling losses sustained in the First World War. Yet natalists were opportunistically prepared to award mothers and widows a vote within the family franchise, to the extent of apportioning additional votes for offspring between partners in what they argued was a fully universal suffrage.[88] They realized that growing support for the right of women to the franchise rendered additional votes for husbands and fathers alone a less attractive proposition, and advocates of the traditional familial vote were inclined to agree with them.[89]

In December 1923, Henri Roulleaux-Dugage proposed an amendment along these lines in the course of a suffrage debate, and it was adopted by the Chamber of Deputies, only to be undone by opponents' procedural objections to the submission of a substantive bill. The cohesion of those deputies who supported the initiative proved to be more apparent than real and divisions soon emerged which ruled out any further progress on plural voting of any sort under the Third Republic. The familial franchise did subsequently achieve some recognition from the Vichy regime and the idea was still being advocated during the early years of the Fourth Republic. Members of Catholic suffrage organizations were naturally sympathetic to the family vote and saw some merit in the Roulleaux-Dugage proposal, but there was a wary response, even outright hostility, from most feminists. Single women would remain excluded, while many deputies who argued that the female franchise would reduce the birth rate had doubtless rallied behind the idea because it detracted from the suffragist campaign.[90] The UFSF had already made a polite but negative response to an earlier proposition from Roulleaux-Dugage. In the words of their general secretary, Cécile Brunschvicg: 'The suffragists' duty is to hold fast to the principle underlying our statutes, that is to say obtaining the vote for women on the same basis as men.'[91] The reaction from readers of *La Française* was that they would rather wait longer for the female suffrage to arrive

[87] Alfred Fouillée, *La Propriété sociale et la démocratie* (Paris, 1884), footnote, 192–3.
[88] Virginie De Luca Barrusse, 'Les femmes et les enfants aussi, ou le droit d'être représenté par le vote familial', *ARSS*, 140 (2001), 51–6.
[89] Le Naour, *La Famille doit voter*, 123ff.   [90] Read, *The Republic of Men*, 205–6.
[91] *La Française*, 22 Jan. 1921, cited in Le Naour, *La Famille doit voter*, 126.

than obtain it via such an undemocratic route.[92] When later approached by partisans of the family vote in 1935 the UFSF reiterated that it was unanimous in rejecting any collaboration, since these were distinct issues which required separate presentation.[93]

While the legislature continued to disappoint suffragists' aspirations, the inter-war years witnessed the election of women to local office and even some limited participation in voting. An isolated instance of the latter had occurred in in 1897, when an extension of the urban garrisons at Fougères and Morlaix (Ille-et-Vilaine) was put to a local referendum. At the former, over two hundred women took part in their capacity as local tax-payers, in an initiative which the centre-left newspaper *Le Temps* hailed as offering an 'education in democracy'.[94] In fact, after 1900 women could vote in a variety of professional elections, reflecting their increasing involvement in different areas of the workforce.[95] More to the point, the resumption of elections after the First World War saw renewed efforts to put up female candidates in municipal elections that continued until the final round of these polls in 1935. The newly created Parti communiste français (PCF) sponsored Marthe Bigot, a school-teacher recently dismissed for her left-wing activities, at a Parisian by-election in 1922, in an effort to demonstrate its commitment to gender equality, as well as publicize her case.[96] In the general municipal elections of 1925, it fielded female candidates on many of its lists, insisting that one of them be positioned towards the top to ensure a good chance of election. The full tally has yet to be established, but communes like Saint-Pierre-des-Corps, an industrial suburb of Tours, or Douarnenez, a Breton fishing port with a large canning factory, were successfully targeted. In these two instances women were actually elected but, as elsewhere, the authorities immediately began proceedings to remove them, though they were able to remain in office until these were completed. The PCF newspaper, *L'Humanité*, trumpeted that 'the Communists have achieved more for women's political rights than any other party in France', but they generally had little respect for the suffragists, whom they regarded as 'bourgeoises', and they lost interest in the female vote when the fight against fascism took priority during the following decade.[97]

There were, however, other practices, which included the co-option or, in some cases, the election of women as 'conseillères adjointes' or 'privées', which meant they could (perfectly legally) participate in local council meetings in a consultative capacity, usually entrusted with a 'feminine' portfolio such as health or charity.[98] A few women had already been appointed to serve in this way in a variety of towns from Auxerre to Aix-en-Provence, when mayors from all over France

[92] *La Française*, 19 Jan. 1924   [93] *La Française*, 13 July 1935.
[94] *Le Temps*, 18 July 1897.   [95] Paul de Poulpiquet, *Le Suffrage des femmes* (Paris, 1912), 245.
[96] Christine Bard, *Les Filles de Marianne. Histoire des féminismes, 1914–1940* (Paris, 1995), 251.
[97] *L'Humanité*, 11 May 1925.
[98] Bouglé-Moalic, *Le Vote des Françaises*, 285–8.

gathered to commemorate the fiftieth anniversary of the municipal electoral law of 1884. They declared their collective support for female suffrage and over forty of them went on to nominate *conseillères* or, in some cases, arrange for their election. In 1935, the socialist mayor of Villeurbanne (Rhône), for example, invited (male) voters to elect four auxiliary female councillors and two-thirds of them took the opportunity to do so. At Dax (Landes) the mayor went further and created a register of women voters who were summoned to choose six *adjointes*, an initiative that attracted the participation of over half the listed *citoyennes*. Louviers (Eure), under mayor Pierre Mendès France, witnessed the most radical experiment of this sort with both men and women voting for six female councillors in 1936, a year after the regular municipal election.[99] At 80 per cent, female turnout was almost double that of men. This was a valuable precedent, which the UFSF welcomed as heralding an eventual change in the law.[100] It revealed widespread provincial support for female voting, although some misgivings were also expressed: as one staunch, socialist sympathizer put it, such limited opportunities for electoral participation 'could be construed as endorsing female inferiority'.[101]

At the opening session of the new legislature in 1936, deputies were presented with forget-me-not buttonholes and a promissory note which read, 'Even after you give us the right to vote, your socks will still be darned.'[102] Suffragists invested great expectations in the left-wing government of the Popular Front, but their hopes of gaining the franchise were soon dashed, and suffragists effectively demobilized for the remainder of the 1930s, in order to assist in defending the Republic against its enemies both inside and outside France. The very real threat from political movements which sought to overturn the system rather than simply reform it must be borne in mind, though such deep-rooted feminist loyalty to the regime was doubtless a liability where their specific objectives were concerned. Having watched the Senate refuse to proceed to discussion of the women's suffrage bill back in 1922, a bitterly disappointed Maria Vérone had intervened from the spectators' gallery, with the defiant declaration, 'Vive la République quand même!', before being unceremoniously ejected.

Whatever the lack of resolve, numbers, or unity, which have been highlighted by some historians as a reason for their lack of success, suffragists were confronted with stubborn opposition that was deeply entrenched in the Third Republic's upper chamber.[103] Yet their apparently futile interwar efforts should not be dismissed when it comes to explaining the eventual triumph of their cause in 1944, when that same, obstinate group of Radicals persisted in seeking to block

---

[99] Pierre Cornu, 'Faire voter les femmes sous la Troisième République: une expérience à Louviers en 1936', *Études normandes* (2005), 43–50.

[100] *La Française*, 18 May 1935.   [101] Cited in Bard, *Les Filles de Marianne*, 352.

[102] William Guéraiche, *Les Femmes et la République. Essai sur la répartition du pouvoir de 1943 à 1979* (Paris, 1999), 35.

[103] Teele, *Forging the Franchise*, 167–71, for a recent example.

the female franchise, but no longer prevailed. Women had demonstrated both their desire and capacity for the vote since the turn of the century. Indeed, their long campaign served to prepare them for an eventual assumption of the franchise which, despite the dire prognostications of die-hard anti-suffragists, they would exercise in great numbers.

The Female Electoral Apprenticeship after 1945

As soon as women had acquired the suffrage, they were presented with the opportunity to vote on no less than seven occasions over the next two years, as the inception of another new regime brought a plethora of consultations (Table 2.1). Significant efforts were made to ensure that women were registered and then cast a ballot, emphasizing their duty to do so, albeit mostly appealing to their maternal and familial interests. The electorate had more than doubled as a result of the enfranchisement of thirteen million *électrices*, producing a preponderance of females that had always worried opponents of the female suffrage, but historians have generally believed that women were initially reluctant to use their hard-earned right. In fact, female participation in the first elections to be held in 1945, for municipal and departmental councils, may have been slightly higher than among men. In the absence of any overall statistics there is impressionistic evidence to suggest that they turned out strongly in the spring, when the first round of municipal elections was held on 29 April.[104] The prefect at Marseille, for example, reported that women had voted 'massively', while in the Hautes-Pyrénées a colleague stated that they 'had taken their electoral duty more seriously

Table 2.1 Voting during the first two years of the Fourth Republic, 1945–1946

Date	Consultation	Electorate	Voters	% Turnout
April 1945*	Municipal	2,215,861	1,713,662	77.3
September 1945**	Cantonal	23,058,214	16,563,447	71.8
October 1945	Referendum/Constituent	24,622,862	19,654,284	79.8
May 1946	Referendum	24,657,128	19,895,411	80.7
June 1946	Constituent	24,696,949	20,215,200	81.8
October 1946	Referendum	25,072,910	17,129,645	68.4
November 1946	Legislative	25,052,233	19,565,697	78.1

Note: * These were two-round elections, but some figures were collected by the ministry of the interior for the first round of voting, and they have been used as a sample here.

** Once again these were two-round elections, but on this occasion a full set of figures was collected for the first round of voting, Paris excluded.

[104] AN F7 15588, Les femmes à la veille des élections, 24 Apr. 1945.

than men'.[105] At cantonal elections held in September 1945, there was similar agreement among prefects that the (as always) relatively lower turnout 'was by no means due to female abstention but, on the contrary, stemmed from the indifference of male electors'.[106] These comments are corroborated by rare data collected in Belfort and Vienne-sur-le-Rhône, two towns where men and women voted separately (on an experimental basis), and the latter participated in greater numbers than the former.[107] It was received wisdom that women would involve themselves more readily in local than national elections and, having just been registered to do so, they were more likely to vote. However, the absence of males serving in the armed forces, or incarcerated as prisoners of war, may also explain this short-lived disparity. In the referendums and national elections that took place later in 1945 and then 1946 any female preponderance seems to have ceased. The persistence of some separate polling stations for women, like opinion polls conducted from 1951 onwards, and the analysis of marked voting registers, all suggest that thereafter female turnout was, on average, between 7 and 10 per cent below participation rates for males.[108] Yet there were exceptions to this general rule, such as Dijon in the Côte-d'Or where, in the legislative elections of late 1946, female abstention was slightly lower (but not in surrounding rural areas), or when only one in eight women, as opposed to one in four men, abstained at Privas in the Ardèche, in the legislative elections of 1951 (though suffragists had waged a special campaign there to mobilize the female vote).[109]

Lancelot's research on electoral abstention shows that it was unusual for married women to vote if their husbands failed to go to the polls, but they were more likely to vote than spinsters or widows, in what he calls 'conjugal conformity'.[110] This was a phenomenon that the prefect at Marseille had noted in 1945, when he wrote that husbands and wives usually came to the polling station together.[111] Elderly people were statistically less likely to vote than middle-aged adults and there were far more senior, single women in the population, so differential gender participation may be partly explained by this factor. There is also evidence to suggest that older women were less likely to value their newfound right to vote,

---

[105] AN F1a 3221, Élections municipales, Apr.–May 1945.

[106] AN F1a 3227, Synthèse des élections cantonales, 28 Sept. 1945.

[107] 'Pour qui votent les femmes?', in François Goguel (ed.), *Nouvelles études de sociologie électorale* (Paris, 1954), 185–98.

[108] AN F1cII 195, L'abstentionnisme, mal français, no date. This memorandum, evidently composed in the mid-1950s, asserted that the enfranchisement of women had increased non-voting, though legislative elections and referendums held during the early years of the Fourth Republic attracted overall turnout of around 80 per cent, so abstention on the part of female electors did not have an especially negative effect. For a more scientific conclusion, based on contemporary opinion polls, see Maurice Duverger, *The Political Role of Women* (Paris, 1955), 140–2.

[109] Raymond Long, *Les Élections législatives en Côte-d'Or depuis 1870* (Paris, 1958), 177, and Mattei Dogan and Jacques Narbonne, 'L'abstentionnisme électoral en France', *Rfsp*, IV (1954), 16.

[110] Lancelot, *L'Abstentionnisme électoral*, 176–8.

[111] AN F1a 3221, Élections municipales, Apr.–May 1945.

while their more junior counterparts were much keener to grasp the unprecedented opportunity.[112]

However, there is a general consensus that this gender gap was of relatively
short duration: from the 1970s onwards women began to vote in roughly the
same proportions as men, while increasing numbers of them were transferring
their electoral allegiance to the left.[113] In other words, their apprenticeship in voting was rapidly accomplished during the 'trente glorieuses', the three post-war
decades of economic development that witnessed a significant evolution in female
social roles, especially in terms of their access to education and employment.
Électrices certainly had to endure continuing prejudice where their political
involvement was concerned, an attitude deeply embedded in a male-dominated
electoral culture that would take considerable time to change.[114] Access to the
public space of the polling station was one thing, but participating more fully in
the practices of canvassing and campaigning quite another. Political sociability
was historically a 'man's business' and women found little place in the parties
which chose candidates, besides confronting the prospect of boisterous electioneering. Men, and in fact some women, long remained averse to voting for female
candidates, whose elected numbers did not rise appreciably, even after women
began turning out as strongly as men.[115] The advent of the vote and eligibility for
women thus posed a series of questions which remained to be answered, particularly in the case of office-holding. Only in the twenty-first century has the law on
parité significantly redressed this imbalance and led to the election of far more
women (see Chapter 3).

Conclusion

There has been much recent discussion over the 'delay' in French women obtaining the vote, though historian Siân Reynolds has rightly queried the notion that
France was quite so exceptional in this regard.[116] The gendering of citizenship
ensured that universal manhood suffrage was not accompanied by women's
right to vote until long after 1848. Yet female exclusion was by no means unique
to France, simply more glaring since a mass franchise for males was such an early
development. In 1919, the French Chamber of Deputies overwhelmingly accepted

---

[112] Laurence William Wylie (ed.), *Chanzeau, a Village in Anjou* (Cambridge, MA, 1966), 272.

[113] Janine Mossuz-Lavau and Mariette Sineau, *Enquête sur les femmes et la politique en France*
(Paris, 1983), 25–8 and Janine Mossuz-Lavau, 'L'évolution du vote des femmes', *Pouvoirs*, 82 (1997), 37–57.

[114] Bruno Denoyelle, 'Des corps en élections. Au rebours des universaux de la citoyenneté: les
premiers votes des femmes (1945–1946)', *Genèses*, 31 (1998), 76–98.

[115] This is not a question to be pursued here but, at both local and national levels, the numbers of
women in office actually declined after the late 1940s. See Siân Reynolds' helpful comments, 'Political
culture: gendered modes of behaviour', in *France between the Wars*, 173ff.

[116] Reynolds, *France between the Wars*, 207–12.

an integral suffrage bill comparable to legislation being adopted elsewhere, only to see it rejected in the upper house, where opposition would only become more deeply entrenched thereafter. Clearly, resistance concentrated in the Senate stymied a measure that was passed with increasing majorities by the lower house, and it would take the downfall of the Third Republic to remove this fundamental obstacle to suffrage reform. Dogged misogyny evidently played its part, but anti-clericals were certainly worried that female voters would allow the Catholic Church to recover the political influence it was in the process of losing. Demographic issues were crucial too, because men would constitute a minority in a universal electorate and it was deemed more important for women to concentrate on reproductive duties rather than involve themselves in politics. Defence of the regime was also paramount in face of mounting internal and external threats in the 1930s. These aspects of the interwar years thus hold the key to explaining French tardiness, but many women had acquired valuable political experience in the course of their lengthy campaign for the suffrage. After 1945 they rapidly adapted to the role of elector, unlike their male counterparts, whose century-long apprenticeship in voting will be examined in Chapter 6.

3

The Voters' Choice

The Question of Candidatures

> The virtuous man always hesitates to put himself forward for election,
> preferring instead to remain calm and restrained; you should vote
> for him.
>
> *Avis aux électeurs*, 27 messidor IV (15 July 1796).[1]

Electors today are confronted by propaganda and ballot papers bearing the names
of individuals who are seeking their vote. These designated candidates have
registered their intention to stand in the contest and completed the necessary
paperwork in order to so. In addition to providing their personal credentials,
sponsorship may be required from members of the electorate or, in the case of
presidential polls in France, from holders of public office. Only votes cast for
these persons, alone or on lists, are deemed valid. Their candidature is thus
'declared', a qualification that will be employed here, because only towards the end
of the nineteenth century was a declaration of this sort required from those pursuing election to the French Chamber of Deputies. Indeed, not until the twenty-
first century was a similar condition applied to those who sought municipal office
in the smallest communes, finally bringing them into line with all other elected
post-holders. During the early modern period, and beyond, the term 'candidate'
was not employed in its contemporary sense.[2] Instead, voters were free to choose
among anyone who was eligible for office and, at a time when mandates were
often employed, the identity of those entrusted with them was not of paramount
importance. It was a different matter under the representative system introduced
after 1789, yet determined French opposition to declared candidatures, despite
the drawbacks of their absence, was more than simply deference to tradition; it
was instead an assertion of the right of the sovereign people to make its own,
unconstrained electoral choices.

---

[1] British Library (hereafter BL) FR99, *Avis aux électeurs*, 27 messidor IV (15 July 1796).
[2] The term 'candidate' was generally employed during the Revolution in a specific sense, to denote
the two persons involved in a *ballottage* (the run-off for election after previous rounds of voting) or,
uniquely, for those nominated on the experimental lists of 1797. Under the First Empire it was used as
a designation for individuals chosen by the electoral assemblies, among whom the regime made the
final choice for office.

How the French Learned to Vote: A History of Electoral Practice in France. Malcolm Crook, Oxford University Press (2021).
© Malcolm Crook. DOI: 10.1093/oso/9780192894786.003.0004

In the past, the 'electoral offer' was not limited in the way it is now (though provision for voters to 'write in' a name of their own choice remains a possibility on ballot papers in the United States). In France, until 1889 at least, the term 'candidate' should not, therefore, be used without qualification, though many historians fail to make the necessary distinction and thus conjure up contemporary connotations. Of course, there were contenders for office long before a declaration was demanded, but they were not publicly registered. Instead, their aspirations for election were communicated personally by those individuals themselves, and through networks of family and friends. There was always a discrepancy between ideal and reality, between *mentalité* and *pratique*, but the subdued sort of electioneering that undoubtedly occurred has left little archival trace. More ostensible activities routinely attracted condemnation as 'brigues' (intrigues) or 'cabales', especially from opponents who had failed in their attempt to gain office.[3] Hence the attraction of sortition as part of the electoral process in many towns during the early modern period, because drawing lots removed the rationale for self-promotion. It would take the sustained practice of mass elections in the nineteenth century, together with the rise of parties and the professionalization of politics, to put paid to such long-standing, informal traditions and overcome the prejudice against declared candidatures.

Voting in a Void?

By means of a careful analysis of protests over alleged infractions of the tacit rules that operated in elections under the *Ancien Régime*, Olivier Christin has demonstrated how disinterest was upheld as a principal value.[4] In the words of another historian, Laurent Coste, 'A person was not a candidate for a post under the *ancien régime*, he was judged worthy of election.'[5] Contemporaries prized vocation rather than ambition, an echo of election as the will of God, rendering an individual who sought office, or revealed an appetite for authority, unworthy of obtaining it. In these circumstances, voting for oneself was especially abhorrent, a reason for the common obligation to sign ballot papers when these were used or, in some cases, issuing ballot papers to voters with a list of names excluding their own. In the absence of declared candidates, the tradition of celebrating mass before polling began, in all kinds of elections, was a means of seeking divine assistance for the choices that would follow. The habitual swearing of oaths to

---

[3] Christin, *Vox populi*, 34–41.
[4] Olivier Christin, 'Disinterest, vocation and elections: two late seventeenth-century affairs', *FH*, 29 (2015), 296–300.
[5] Laurent Coste, 'Être candidat aux élections municipales dans la France d'Ancien Régime', in Philippe Hamon and Catherine Laurent (eds), *Le Pouvoir municipal de la fin du Moyen Âge à 1789* (Rennes, 2012), 210.

leave partiality behind was likewise designed to secure an ideal outcome, another practice that was retained without hesitation at the outset of the Revolution. As one contemporary recalled, 'In those days, candidates did not publish *professions de foi*, circulate propaganda, or display electoral posters as they do now; they did not offer themselves overtly to the voters.'[6]

A pamphlet entitled, *Avis aux citoyens français sur le choix des officiers municipaux*, published in 1790, accordingly avoided naming names, but instead recommended the election of those 'whose probity was universally recognized' and who, 'combining talent, reason and strength of character', did not 'seek out positions, but waited to be awarded them in modest silence'.[7] Another anonymous author concurred: 'True patriots shy away from the electoral limelight; they do not refuse any honours bestowed upon them, but nor do they seek to obtain them.'[8] When, in the summer of that year, a colleague of Bailly publicly proclaimed that his fellow academician should be re-elected as mayor of Paris, his comment was widely circulated in the capital. Citizens in the Cordeliers district indignantly remarked that 'however commendable a citizen was, whatever service he had rendered to the common weal, and notwithstanding his virtues and abilities, it is contrary to electoral liberty to suggest that the assemblies should make a particular choice', adding that 'the voters should decide according to their consciences'. Political clubs like the Jacobins of Paris were torn over this issue in 1791, when some members began organizing to elect certain individuals to the municipality of Paris, while others resolutely invoked 'la "liberté des suffrages"', which they described as the most precious of all the citizens' rights.[9] There was similar reticence about putting forward specific names in the rapidly expanding press, which did not venture beyond reiterating that the election of 'well-qualified' individuals was a matter of the utmost importance, while simultaneously denouncing intrigues and cabals.

This was all well and good, but exactly how were voters to exercise their judgement? As one group of Parisians protested, the recent reorganization of their city into *sections* (electoral divisions) had placed them in 'unfamiliar territory', where they did not even know the names of fellow citizens; they would thus be obliged to vote haphazardly. Likewise in 1790, rural second-degree electors at the departmental assembly in the Eure-et-Loir complained that they had no idea how to choose members of their new *conseil général*, because they were unacquainted with most of their peers.[10] Now, there had been a means of limiting the electoral

---

[6] Adolphe Rochas, *Journal d'un bourgeois de Valence, du 1er janvier 1789 au 9 novembre 1799 (18 brumaire an VIII)* (Grenoble, 1891), 189.

[7] Cited in Maurice Genty, 'Du refus des candidatures ouvertes à la préparation des élections: l'exemple de Paris au début de la Révolution française (1790–1791)', *The Chuo Law Review*, 104 (1997), 3ff.

[8] BL FR99, *Le catéchisme des électeurs* (no place, no date), 12.

[9] Genty, 'Du refus des candidatures ouvertes', 16.

[10] AN C118, PV, Eure-et-Loir, May 1790.

offer before 1789 by remitting to individuals or boards the task of proposing particular names to the relatively small assemblies that made the final decision, a procedure adopted by many eighteenth-century urban oligarchies. In the case of Nantes, for example, serving and former mayors and aldermen made proposals for their successors among which voters were obliged to choose.[11] Choices might also be circumscribed by a series of strict rules for eligibility, based on criteria such as occupation, property ownership, age, or confessional affiliation. After 1789, a fiscal threshold was retained, but there was still a huge pool from which national and local office-holders could be drawn and a vast number of posts to be filled.

The absence of declared candidatures may not have proved problematic in the early modern period, but translated into the context of the Revolution it certainly generated a wide dispersal of votes.[12] At Le Puy-en-Velay in the Haute-Loire, in 1790 for instance, 568 different individuals were proposed to fill eleven posts as municipal councillors and not one of them was elected until the third and final round of polling, all of them having previously failed to achieve the absolute majority that was required at rounds one and two.[13] Such a scattering of preferences was less marked in the second-degree assemblies, but still in evidence: at Paris, in the first round of voting for its twenty-four deputies to the Legislative Assembly of 1791, 282 individuals received at least two votes, while single nominations were simply ignored.[14] The pursuit of absolute majorities did eventually work effectively in the case of separately elected posts like that of mayor when, in the third and final round, there was a run-off (ballottage) between the two, named individuals who had attracted the most votes at the second round. Yet until that point there was no detailed communication of the outcome, simply a report from scrutineers that no one had succeeded in obtaining an absolute majority. In the case of elections by list, for municipal councillors or second-degree electors, where a relative majority eventually sufficed, participants proceeded to the third and final round of voting, at which most elections were decided, bereft of any guidance whatsoever. At Paris, in June 1791, almost 80 per cent of second-degree electors emerged from this round of polling, and few of them had many votes to their credit, because choices were still broadly dispersed and the assemblies were becoming deserted.[15]

Another difficulty that soon became apparent was the refusal of those elected to take up an unsolicited post, with the consequence that voters had to repeat the exercise. As one weary second-degree elector reported from the departmental

[11] Guy Saupin, *Nantes au XVIIe siècle. Vie politique et société urbaine* (Rennes, 1996), 75–8.

[12] Malcolm Crook, 'Le candidat imaginaire, ou l'offre et le choix dans les élections de la Révolution française', *AhRf* (2000), 91–101 for what follows, unless otherwise indicated.

[13] Jacqueline Bayon-Tollet, *Le Puy-en-Velay et la Révolution française (1789–1799)* (Saint-Étienne, 1982), 269–70.

[14] Gueniffey, *Le Nombre et la raison*, 328–9.   [15] Gueniffey, *Le Nombre et la raison*, 328.

assembly of the Seine-Inférieure, which was convened in 1792 to send deputies to the National Convention: 'Yesterday was a complete waste of time. We chose two deputies, both of whom immediately resigned.' In the village of Aigre in the Charente, two years earlier, though the newly elected mayor initially refused to accept the honour he was not allowed to desist: 'the whole community descended on his house and, with a single voice, implored him to stay, which he duly did to appease his fellow citizens.'[16] Mitigating circumstances were simply ignored: the person elected as mayor of Montgazin in the Haute-Garonne, in 1790, protested in vain that he had publicly ruled himself out of contention on account of pressing business interests, poor health, and the recent loss of his wife. Under the *Ancien Régime* it was expected that anyone who was chosen would accept the office and, in Picardy and Burgundy, this was set down as a binding duty. The Laverdy reform of municipal government likewise stipulated in 1765 that 'no inhabitant is allowed to refuse the places to which they have been elected', though no sanction was indicated for non-compliance.[17] In 1790, overwhelmed by the task of filling a vast number of posts, the Constitutional Committee proposed that those who defaulted on 'their patriotic obligation' to accept elective responsibility should literally pay a price for doing so.[18]

The Emergence of Public Candidatures

In his study of elections in the French Revolution, Patrice Gueniffey considers that the reluctance to accept declared candidatures was a major flaw in the system, because unlimited choice rendered a random rather than a rational outcome extremely likely. He rightly regards the lack of any regulation as an inheritance from the past but also, more controversially, as a refusal to endorse pluralistic politics.[19] We should be wary of imposing contemporary liberal values upon elections in the 1790s and, in any event, 'unofficial' candidates were often in evidence, before as well as after 1789. Practice was often at variance with principle, despite grand statements to the contrary and the examples of condemnation that Gueniffey cites. Evidence can be teased out of electoral proceedings in some of the bigger cities to demonstrate a strong concentration of votes around particular individuals, especially in mayoral contests in the early 1790s, which can only have stemmed from the informal promotion of particular candidates.[20] Moreover,

---

[16] Crook, *Elections*, 70.   [17] Bordes, *La Réforme municipale*, 310.
[18] *AP*, 1ere série, XI, 3 Feb. 1790, 422.   [19] Gueniffey, *Le Nombre et la raison*, 315–21.
[20] Christine Lamarre, '"Poser les fondements de la régénération de l'empire": l'élection de la municipalité de Dijon (janvier–février 1790)', in Annie Bleton-Ruget and Serge Wolikov (eds), *Voter et élire à l'époque contemporaine* (Dijon, 1999), 28–30, for instance.

during the Revolution, a series of proposals were put forward in favour of formal-izing candidatures.

Elections to the Estates General of 1789 had already prompted some interest-ing suggestions in this regard. One pamphlet sought to facilitate an informed choice of deputies by permitting an 'open rather than clandestine market' for can-didates, by creating a list of nominated individuals, on whom the electorate would subsequently vote after an intervening period of public discussion.[21] The follow-ing year, radical journalist Jacques-Pierre Brissot announced that 'sound choices' would stem from open debate about those who were in contention for office, while the novelist Choderlos de Laclos made a similar suggestion at the Jacobin Club of Paris in 1791, and deputy François de Neufchâteau did likewise at the Legislative Assembly.[22] The necessity for a new constitution after the overthrow of Louis XVI in 1792 led Condorcet to suggest turning the first round of voting into an explicit opportunity to create a set of candidates for the second and definitive poll. He proposed that, 'Elections will be conducted by means of two votes. The first, purely preparatory, will serve to establish *une liste de présentation*; the sec-ond, based on these nominees, will then determine the outcome and conclude the proceedings.' Voters were to indicate putative candidates and a provisional list of the leading individuals (set at three times the number of posts to be filled) would then be published, inviting them to endorse their selection, in order to avoid a later refusal to serve; if they declined, they were replaced. The election proper was to follow on this basis, after an interval for public discussion of the qualities of those listed. This was, to say the least, a cumbersome procedure, but it did give members of the electorate a role in the selection of candidates.[23]

Nothing came of these propositions until 1795, when a law on candidatures was finally introduced on 25 fructidor III (11 September): 'During the month of nivôse (December–January), every citizen has the right register himself, or those whom he regards as suitable, on a list of candidates…for one or more of the posts to be filled in germinal (March–April)', at the annual round of elections. The municipal authorities which received these names, simply checked them for eligi-bility, and then publicly advertised them for a period of two months, before they were posted and read out at the electoral assemblies. A complementary instruc-tion proclaimed that 'this open manner of offering oneself to the electorate is most worthy of a republican and is certainly preferable to the secret cabals and obscure manoeuvres of ambitious schemers.' It should be stressed, however, that unlike Condorcet's proposal, this legislation was purely permissive; there was nothing to prevent voters naming whomsoever they wished on their ballot papers.

---

[21] BL F292, Anon., *Trois mots aux Parisiens sur la nécessité de publier les noms de leurs candi-dats…*(Apr. 1789).

[22] Jacques-Pierre Brissot, *Réflexions sur l'état de la Société des électeurs patriotiques* (Paris, 1790), 1 and *AP*, 1ère série, XL, 19 Mar. 1792, 140.

[23] Duguit et al., *Les Constitutions*, p. 38ff.

Moreover, as might be expected, an innovation of this sort, implemented in 1797, which contested the dominant mentality where candidatures were concerned, encountered a mixed response that varied from department to department. When registers were opened to receive names, they often remained blank, though large towns generally responded more readily and at Paris it seems that over one thousand names were proposed to the departmental assembly, listing a number of prominent legislators and including a general named Napoleon Bonaparte.

The conservative Quatremère de Quincy, who was personally recommended by several right-wing newspapers and subsequently elected at Paris, remained unconvinced. 'The real candidature', he wrote, 'emanates from public opinion... It should consist, not in a list of a names subject to criticism, but in a reasoned set of principles upon which a proper judgement can be made.'[24] Despite such widely shared misgivings, what really damned the experiment with declared candidatures was the outcome of the legislative elections of the Year V (1797). The republican government attributed its loss of seats to the innovation, which offered a convenient scapegoat, though there is little evidence to suggest that opponents of the Directory effectively exploited the opportunity to put themselves forward. Nonetheless, the law on candidatures was summarily repealed. Pons de Verdun, presenting the parliamentary report which sought its suppression, in January 1798, began by reiterating the traditional belief that 'a serious man will always be shocked by the idea of soliciting votes from his fellow citizens'. Roch-Pierre-François Lebreton concurred, adding that candidatures had brought down the Roman Republic and they would indubitably have the same effect on its French successor. Moreover, Jean-Jacques Rousseau himself had stated that 'voters need only consult their consciences'. Both deputies exhorted their colleagues to 'restore liberty to the electoral assemblies' and Pons concluded with the extraordinary argument that 'the mysterious moral electricity' generated by voters gathered in assemblies was a much surer guide to a sound electoral outcome than the recent experiment.

The issue of legislating for declared candidatures became less urgent as 'public candidatures' (a term first used in 1816) gradually emerged in the following century, not to mention the 'official candidatures' that will be treated below. In 1819, for example, liberals created a central committee at Paris to coordinate their electoral efforts, and establish contact with sympathetic electors in departments where elections were to be held, urging them to form their own local committees and put forward candidates.[25] Indeed, in 1828 two liberals were competing to stand at a by-election at Lyon but, following the intervention of deputies and a meeting of local supporters, the less popular protagonist withdrew. The pioneering historian

[24] Antoine-Chrysostome Quatremère de Quincy, *La Véritable liste de candidats* (Paris, an V), 17–19.
[25] Raymond Huard, *La Naissance du parti politique en France* (Paris, 1996), 49.

of voting, Alexandre Pilenco, suggests that by the end of the Restoration public candidatures had become part and parcel of political *moeurs* in France.[26]

Under the July Monarchy those eligible to be elected to the Chamber of Deputies might announce their intention to stand in the local press (which was itself becoming increasingly important in this regard), assemble an electoral committee (in which former deputies often played a leading role) and then issue a *profession de foi*, or manifesto. Local notables could play a decisive role in deciding who was to stand: Corsica, with its extremely small electoral college (a veritable 'rotten borough', to employ a term the French borrowed from across the Channel) was perhaps not typical, but under the constitutional monarchy candidates required the support of dominant clans in order to stake their claim.[27] Voters might remain free to nominate whoever they wished from among the higher tax-payers eligible to serve as national deputies, yet any real choice, as opposed to a wasted vote, was clearly circumscribed. Before, and especially after 1830, most parliamentary elections were being decided at the first round, as particular 'candidates' swept the board. In 1846, 76 out of 459 seats were effectively uncontested and the winner received almost the entirety of the votes cast (Guizot at Lisieux, for example, with 523 out of 561 preferences).[28]

The unexpected advent of the Second Republic in 1848, by contrast, vastly inflated not just the electorate, but also the number of those eligible for the 900-seat Constituent Assembly, since the only additional requirement was to be aged at least twenty-five (as opposed to twenty-one to vote). Electors were presented with a huge choice: it has been estimated that two thousand individuals put themselves forward at Paris alone, while some seven thousand *professions de foi* were produced overall: 'whether they were drafted by an individual or by an electoral committee, hand-written or more often printed, they became the declaration of candidature *par excellence*', writes Yves Déloye.[29] Nonetheless, a degree of reticence remained common among these individuals, many of whom continued to protest that they were only standing as a result of entreaties from fellow citizens. The press might proclaim that 'no-one has the right to make himself a candidate', in deference to customary misgivings about individual ambition, but local *comités* and political clubs, as well as newspapers, were not slow to suggest names.[30] These organs were responsible for 'la fabrication des listes' for the new departmental constituencies, prior to publishing and printing them for use as ballot

---

[26] Pilenco, *Les Moeurs électorales en France*, 115.

[27] André-Jean Tudesq, 'Les comportements électoraux sous le régime censitaire', in Daniel Gaxie (ed.), *Explication du vote. Un bilan des études électorales en France* (Paris, 1985), 111.

[28] AN C*II 383, Tableau comparatif des élections, 1842.

[29] Yves Déloye, 'Se présenter pour représenter. Enquête sur les professions de foi électorales de 1848', in Michel Offerlé (ed.), *La Profession politique, XIXe–XXe siècles* (Paris, 1999), 233.

[30] Jeremy D. Popkin, 'Press and elections in the French revolution of 1848: the case of Lyon', *FHS*, 36 (2013), 89.

papers, though voters were free to compose their own.[31] Lists were not closed and the outcome was decided by adding up preferences for individuals, with a low threshold for election set at just two thousand votes.

In these confusing circumstances, a veritable 'foire aux candidats' according to one observer, the attraction of the mass electorate to familiar names, and indeed notables in general, can be readily understood. Many of those who had served as deputies under the preceding regime thus succeeded in emerging successfully from these polls. Equally, countless *voix perdues* were cast, in the form of a few votes mustered by a whole host of anonymous individuals who were probably unaware of their nomination and were habitually ignored by the electoral *bureaux* in the compilation of their *procès-verbaux*.[32] Many electors had sought advice from their 'betters' so as to vote more meaningfully and a primary school teacher in the Haute-Vienne urged the republican *commissaire* to send him a list of those he should recommend, because rural voters needed to be 'enlightened and directed' in making their choices.[33] At Bauduen, in the Var, anxious villagers addressed their *commissaire*: 'Here we are on the eve of the election and we do not know who to vote for...we urge you to indicate the candidates to whom we should entrust our votes...'.[34] In 1857, in the same department, a substantial property-owner asked the prefect for ballot papers to pass on to local inhabitants who were struggling to arrive at a choice. Granting universal manhood suffrage did not immediately or automatically confer electoral independence on the newly enfranchised masses and, under the Second Empire, the government was not simply willing to satisfy the demand for suggestions, but provided clear instructions.

Official Candidatures

'Administrative', 'ministerial', or 'official' candidatures emerged alongside the development of public candidatures in the nineteenth century, though this ter-minology was employed by critics rather than exponents of the practice.[35] It was only under the Second Empire that the government openly sponsored particular

---

[31] Christophe Voilliot, *Le Département de l'Yonne en 1848. Analyse d'une séquence électorale* (Vulaines-sur-Seine, 2017), 37ff.

[32] Voilliot, *Le Département de l'Yonne*, 89–97. See also Thomas Stockinger, 'Le lien parlementaire en 1848. Analyse comparée des candidatures aux élections en Seine-et-Oise et en Basse-Autriche', *Rh19*, 43 (2011), 74.

[33] Alain Corbin, *Archaïsme et modernité en Limousin au XIXᵉ siècle, 1845–1880*, 2 vols (Paris, 1975), ii, 795.

[34] Archives départementales (hereafter AD) Var 2M3-13, Conseil municipal au commissaire, 1 Apr. 1848.

[35] Jules Ferry, *La Lutte électorale en 1863* (Paris, 1863), 24, employs the term 'administrative' candi-date in his contemporary critique of the practice, though the more widely used denominations were 'candidat de l'empereur' or 'candidat du gouvernement'.

candidates, but it would be wrong to associate the recommendation and support of designated individuals solely with the regime of Louis-Napoleon. To be sure, government intervention was absent when the Estates General was elected in 1789, but it soon began to feature during the Revolution. Roland, minister of the interior when elections were held for a National Convention in 1792, had sought to influence the result by disbursing public funds to secure certain nominations, while the obligatory re-election of members of the Convention to the two legislative councils created by the Constitution of 1795 (the notorious, and extremely unpopular, law of 'two-thirds'), reflected a blatant attempt by those in power to ensure that the Republic would be placed in safe hands by limiting the voters' choice.[36]

Under the Directory, winning elections became a major preoccupation for the government, and centrally appointed *commissaires*, attached to the elected local authorities, offered unprecedented opportunities to influence the outcome of the annual polls. In 1797, in the Aube for example, the *commissaire du département* drew up a list of 'candidates' and urged cantonal colleagues to support his nominees, albeit with scant success.[37] The following year efforts were redoubled as these local officials were instructed to rally sympathizers, stand for election themselves and, if all else failed, encourage a breakaway assembly (*scission*) to frustrate opponents. In the Haute-Loire, for instance, the *commissaire central* effectively became a 'campaign manager', issuing clear advice and urging fellow commissioners to 'ensure the triumph of the republican cause'.[38] In the Corrèze, another *commissaire* was alleged to have said that 'whatever the choice of the people', the government would only accept those deputies designated by a special commissioner despatched to the department.[39] The executive Directory went still further and employed customs officials, ostensibly establishing toll-booths to pay for road improvements, as covert election agents, who supplied intelligence to the regime and offered financial incentives to voters. In 1799, the government mounted an equally determined electoral effort, this time despatching surveyors of waterways as special emissaries, while exhorting commissioners to 'use all means at your disposal (and) exploit every one of your personal contacts', in order to secure a favourable result.

The Napoleonic regime had little to fear from voters, since it made the final choice of legislators, local councillors, and justices of the peace from shortlists submitted by the electoral assemblies. It was the restored monarchy that effectively invented the practice of 'official candidatures', after the shock of the so-called *Chambre introuvable*, elected in August 1815 in the full flush of reaction against

[36]   Gueniffey, *Le Nombre et la raison*, 33–4.
[37]   Jeff Horn, *Qui parle pour la nation? Les élections en Champagne 1765–1830*, (Paris, 2004), 111–18.
[38]   Crook, *Elections*, 148ff.
[39]   AN F1cIII Corrèze, Commissaire au directoire exécutif, 7 germinal VII (27 Mar. 1799).

Napoleon's Hundred Days, when a majority of the deputies returned was more royalist than the king. After dissolution of the chamber the following year, in order to produce a more pliable parliament, the government initiated a series of measures that would be employed, to a greater or lesser extent, for the rest of the nineteenth century and even beyond. Christophe Voilliot has written a comprehensive history of this 'pratique d'État', by means of which the government, relying on its administrative machinery, routinely supported certain individuals, working behind the scenes to promote designated candidates, while also seeking to hinder aspiring opponents.[40] Prefects played a key role in the process, not least, as Élie Decazes put it when he was minister of the interior, 'by preventing enemies of the throne on the one hand, and ultra-royalists on the other', from determining the choice of personnel.[41] Prime Minister Villèle subsequently issued a circular in 1822 indicating that if they wished to remain in post, all members of the administration should actively contribute to 'the election of deputies sincerely committed to the government'.[42]

The institution of direct election to parliament in 1817 has usually been regarded as a liberal measure, but in practice it facilitated governmental interference, by simplifying the electoral mechanism. Joseph Lainé, the author of the law, openly stated that the monarch was quite entitled to present candidates he deemed worthy of election for his subjects' approval.[43] One means to this end was to nominate such individuals as presidents of the electoral colleges, a practice which originated under Napoleon (whereas during the 1790s they had been elected by the assemblies themselves).[44] The king was thereby indicating that such persons bore the seal of government favour, besides putting increasing amounts of central funding at their disposal to entertain electors and amass votes.[45] After 1830 the selection of its president reverted to the assembly, but the government of the day could still rely on the strong influence it exerted among the electors who were also *fonctionnaires* and who were expected to support particular candidates, or face sanctions, such as denial of promotion. Indeed, they were elected as deputies in increasing numbers, in order to create ministerial majorities: during the July Monarchy between a third and a half of all deputies were civil servants.[46] This had been equally true under the Restoration, but liberals who had objected to the

---

[40] Christophe Voilliot, *La Candidature officielle. Une pratique d'État de la Restauration à la Troisième République* (Rennes, 2005). The dossiers in AN F7 4348–50, Correspondance sur les élections de 1816, reveal the rich repertoire of intervention that was initiated at these elections.

[41] Cited in Louis Puech, *Essai sur la candidature officielle en France depuis 1851* (Mende, 1922), 12.

[42] Sébastien Charléty, *La Restauration (1815–1830)* (Paris, 1911), 183.

[43] *AP*, 2e série, XVIII, 2 Jan. 1817, 8.

[44] In fact, the presidency was often a stepping stone to election during the Revolution and the same was true of *bailliage* and *sénéchaussée* assemblies in 1789.

[45] Georges-Denis Weil, *Les Élections législatives depuis 1789. Histoire de la législation et des mœurs* (Paris, 1895), 125.

[46] François Julien-Laferrière, *Les Députés fonctionnaires sous la Monarchie de Juillet* (Paris, 1970), 177–80.

practice then, were willing to condone it when they subsequently entered office. It was only on the very eve of the Revolution of 1848 that a clear proposal was made to render *fonctionnaires* ineligible as candidates.[47]

When elections for departmental and arrondissement councils were re-introduced in 1833, similar administrative intervention was applied to the process. In the Haute-Loire, for example, the prefect wrote to his sub-prefects concerning the need to 'inform' voters of their 'best interests' and to combat efforts by the 'factions' to elect men who were 'hostile to the government', using all means at their disposal.[48] No less than later regimes, the July Monarchy pro-claimed its respect for electoral liberty, but was soon defending its right, even duty, to make its preferences known.[49] In 1831, Casimir Perier informed prefects that there was no question of the government remaining neutral, since it wished to elect citizens who shared its opinions and supported the national interest.[50] Likewise, in 1848, the arrival in government of critics of official candidatures did little to curb the practice, though the advent of universal male suffrage was a game-changer in so far as small, single-member constituencies were replaced by huge multi-member departmental ones and *scrutin de liste*. Still, on the pretext of 'enlightening' millions of untried voters, the Second Republic promoted 'candi-dates' in numerous departments. As the minister of the interior wrote to his sub-ordinates, 'Ought the government to participate in the elections or simply confine itself to ensuring their orderly conduct?', before answering his own question, 'I have no hesitation in replying that it would be guilty of abdication or even treason if it confined itself to counting votes and publicizing the results.'[51] Republican *commissaires* despatched into the provinces were not in a position to 'prepare' these elections to the extent that prefects had under the preceding regime, but they were able to nominate individuals for some departmental lists and frequently stood as candidates themselves, with considerable success.[52] Nor did minister of the interior Léon Faucher refrain from intervention in the legislative polls of 1849, going well beyond simple advice to support moderate candidates, while prefects did likewise in their departments and removed staunch republicans from local office, notably those who occupied influential positions as mayors.[53] As

---

[47] Julien-Laferrière, *Les Députés fonctionnaires*, 152–3 and 168–9.
[48] Auguste Rivet, *La Vie politique dans la Haute-Loire, 1815–1974* (Le Puy, 1979), 199.
[49] Sherman Kent, 'Two official candidates of the July Monarchy', *American Historical Review*, 43 (1937), 66.
[50] Weil, *Les Élections législatives*, 155.
[51] Cited in Theodore Zeldin, *The Political System of Napoleon III* (London, 1958), 79.
[52] Laurent Quéro and Christophe Voilliot, 'Du suffrage censitaire au suffrage universel. Évolution ou révolution des pratiques électorales?', *ARSS*, 140, 39. No less than 67 *commissaires* were elected out of 110.
[53] Theodore Zeldin, 'Government policy in the French general election of 1849', *English Historical Review*, LXXIV (1959), 240–8 and François Igersheim, *Politique et administration dans le Bas-Rhin (1848–1870)* (Strasbourg, 1993), 184.

Raymond Huard has commented, the way was being paved for the infamous candidatures of the Second Empire.[54]

It was under Louis-Napoleon that the practice of fielding official candidates became systematic and indeed quite transparent.[55] The name of the 'candidate of the government' was publicized on the *affiches blanches*, placards used for government communications, and it was sometimes displayed on the walls of polling stations and even on ballot papers. In an announcement about forthcoming legislative elections that was printed in the *Moniteur* on 20 January 1852, the minister of the interior, Charles de Morny, stressed the importance of these first legislative elections in consolidating the new order, declaring that the regime 'would not hesitate to openly recommend candidates to the electorate'. He had already written confidentially to prefects seeking their proposals so that such candidates could be nominated. On 11 February 1852, his successor, Victor de Persigny, began his electoral proclamation by making ritual obeisance to electoral liberty, but immediately added that it was not to be exercised in the absence of government advice. He went on to argue that inexperienced voters required guidance, not simply to help them choose the 'best candidates', endorsed by the administration, but also to reject those who refused to accept the new regime.[56] He was less restrained in a confidential circular to prefects a week later, when opposition candidates were assimilated to enemies of the regime, to be combated by all available means. These included the arrest of their agents and instructions to replace recalcitrant local officials. Determined opponents could still 'present themselves for election', but they faced a whole range of obstacles in doing so. Until 1858 (when a declaration of loyalty to the regime was required of those seeking office) electors could still cast a valid vote by naming almost any citizen of their choice on their ballot papers. However, during that decade, 'official' candidatures were effectively 'unique' candidatures in more than a third of the 260-odd parliamentary seats.[57]

The system of official candidatures operated at the local as well as the legislative level: in the cantonal elections held in the Basses-Alpes in 1852, for example, the prefect claimed that almost every vote had been cast for what he called 'candidates of the administration', who were mostly elected unopposed. Three years later it was estimated that 80 per cent of the votes delivered for general councillors in seven departments in the northern half of the country were for

---

[54] Raymond Huard, 'Le suffrage universel sous la Seconde République', *Rh19*, 14 (1997), 60.

[55] Patrick Lagouyete, 'Candidature officielle et pratiques électorales sous le Second Empire (1852-1870)', Thèse de doctorat, 5 vols, Université de Paris I, 1990, i, 12 et seq. This comprehensive study has not been published, but there is a useful summary, 'Candidature officielle', in Tulard (ed.), *Dictionnaire du Second Empire*, 226-8.

[56] *Moniteur*, 20 Jan. and 12 Feb. 1852, 103 and 230.

[57] Éric Anceau, 'Les irrégularités et les incidents lors des élections législatives de 1852 à 1870 ou le difficile apprentissage du suffrage universel sous le Second Empire', in Philippe Bourdin et al. (eds), *L'Incident électoral de la Révolution française à la Ve République* (Clermont-Ferrand, 2002), 124-7.

'government' nominees.[58] The administration did not intervene in every canton, however. As the prefect of the Aude put it, he did not become involved where the choice was straightforward, in other words in the absence of real opposition (often the case in the 1850s) but, confronted with 'candidates who expressed party spirit and were protesting against the new institutions', he would fight them tooth and nail.[59] In the neighbouring Hérault, a local newspaper carried a complete list of 'candidates designated and recommended by the government for the department' and, in subsequent municipal elections declared that 'the administration is championing just one list for the municipality of Montpellier'.[60] However, it was always easier to ensure the election of official candidates in the countryside as opposed to towns. Thus, in the legislative elections of 1857, in the Haute-Garonne, the recommended candidate received less than half of the votes cast in urban areas, whereas in nearly all communes with an electorate of less than one hundred there was unanimity in his favour.[61]

The justification for official candidatures was elaborated at successive elections. Not just the fate of deputies but also the head of state, and indeed the political system itself, were alleged to be at stake. Unlike Britain, opponents in France were seeking to change the regime rather than merely the government, which was thus entitled to defend itself.[62] Morny had encouraged the formation of Bonapartist associations after the coup of December 1851, in order to ensure success in the plebiscite that followed hard on its heels, but early the following year he wrote to prefects: 'Until now, the custom in France has been to form electoral committees...that system was useful when men voted for a list...Today this is no longer the case since single-member constituencies have been created...Please dissuade partisans of the government from organizing them.'[63] The former secretary of the (now dissolved) National Electoral Association was in fact passed over as a candidate, much to his chagrin, and he stood unsuccessfully as an independent Bonapartist. In the absence of a governing party, prefects were instructed to seek out worthy candidates devoted to the regime who were not associated with any faction. Thus the prefect of the Var stated that he alone would make the choice of candidates in his department, while the government would endorse them and ensure their success.[64] Billault, another minister of the interior, underscored this approach in 1856, when he informed prefects: 'You will give these candidates your patronage openly and unhesitatingly oppose all others, not only those who

---

[58] AN BB18 1543, Rapports des procureurs généraux, 1855 and AN F1cIII Basses-Alpes 4, Préfet au ministre de l'intérieur, 1 Aug. 1852.

[59] AN F1cIII, Aude 4, Préfet au ministre de l'intérieur, 23 July 1852.

[60] Puech, *Essai*, 82–4 and 98–9.   [61] Lagoueyte, 'Candidature officielle', 227.

[62] *Moniteur*, 13 Jan. 1864, 53. A similar defence of government candidates had been made under the July Monarchy, see *Moniteur*, 5 May 1843, 1008.

[63] Morny, circular, 8 Jan. 1852, cited in Zeldin, *The Political System of Napoleon III*, 25.

[64] AN F1cII 103, Préfet au ministre, 20 Jan. 1852.

are evidently hostile, but even those who claim they are devoted to the regime…you will give candidates of the regime every possible assistance….'[65]

According to the prefect of the Morbihan, there was a subtle distinction to be drawn between 'guiding voters towards the government's objectives' and 'imposing a choice', which he denied was the case.[66] Yet, as the pamphleteer Heulhard de Montigny later pointed out, 'Your deputies are not a product of the electorate, but are nominated by the administration.'[67] The system of official candidatures was, above all, a means of managing universal male suffrage. Opponents, who welcomed the fact that *fonctionnaires* were no longer able to stand for parliament under the Second Empire, did not object to official candidates per se, but vehemently condemned the assistance accorded to them and the impediments placed in the path of their rivals. In a debate in the Corps législatif in 1864, following unprecedented administrative pressure in the previous year's legislative elections, Adolphe Thiers did not deny the right of the government to indicate its electoral preferences, but asserted that it should stop there. Jules Simon likewise lambasted the regime's efforts to campaign on a particular individual's behalf, which made a mockery of electoral competition and deterred any opposition.[68] Precisely what was considered to be an unacceptable abuse of public authority, or 'pression administrative', will be considered in some detail in Chapter 4.

Despite having declined somewhat in 1857, opposition votes increased to almost two million in the legislative elections of 1863 and over three million in 1869. Growing criticism, facilitated by a relaxation of press laws, helped undermine official candidatures, but it was also becoming more difficult to make nominations, as divisions grew within the regime and opponents were emboldened. In 1869 there were no 'government' candidates in roughly a quarter of constituencies, as the practice was partially abandoned, and ministers promised further disengagement in future. Many of those who were officially endorsed actually preferred to highlight personal or political attributes in their *professions de foi*, rather than simply depend on official approval. There was also less reliance on mayors to distribute ballot papers and more emphasis on propaganda conducted by the candidates themselves. In other words, elections became more competitive as politics became more autonomous; committees re-emerged to choose candidates and organize campaigns, a development that foreshadowed their key role in the electoral process under the Third Republic, prior to the advent of full-blown political parties. Indeed, opponents, like the increasingly independent official candidates (as novices in 1852, they may have required assistance, but they

---

[65] Cited in Zeldin, *The Political System of Napoleon III*, 69.

[66] AN F1cIII Morbihan 5, Préfet aux maires, 16 Feb. 1852 and F1cIII Aude 4, Prefectoral proclamation, 22 July 1852.

[67] Charles-Gilbert Heulhard de Montigny, *Un Dernier mot sur le suffrage universel et les candidatures officielles* (Paris, 1869), 46.

[68] *Moniteur*, 12 Jan. 1864, 48ff.

gradually learned to stand on their own two feet), were able to pursue an apprenticeship in appealing to a mass electorate, which was itself becoming more adept at making its own choices.

The trend towards free-standing candidatures continued under the Third Republic, though not without some anomalies. In a period of transitional chaos, with defeat and disorganization accompanying the collapse of the Second Empire, the minister of the interior was recognizing a fait accompli when he declared that the government had no candidates to recommend in snap elections to the National Assembly of 1871. Thiers claimed that these 'hastily improvised elections' were the freest he had ever experienced.[69] In these exceptional circumstances many notables were returned as deputies without even seeking election but, in order to repeat their unexpected triumph, conservatives subsequently resurrected the well-worn practice of official candidatures. In the legislative elections called after the dissolution of the Chamber of Deputies in 1877, voters were presented with 'candidates of the president', or 'the government', half of whom had held office under Napoleon III. As head of state, the reactionary marshal MacMahon publicly proclaimed on 12 October, without apparent irony: 'You will freely vote for those names that I am recommending to you.'[70] There was a preceding purge of the administration to remove unsympathetic prefectoral and municipal personnel, the employment of affiches blanches for electoral purposes, and the wholesale distribution of ballot papers by local officials. Under the ministerial guidance of Oscar de Fourtou, a staunch supporter of the Bonapartist system, it was declared that '(The government) not only has the right, but the duty to say to the people, there is the candidate who does not share our ideas, whereas here, by contrast, is the one who incarnates our outlook and programme.'[71]

Despite the concerted administrative campaign waged against them, republicans emerged victorious in 1877. Would they adopt a disinterested electoral stance now that official candidatures had been thoroughly discredited once more? Their proclamations certainly suggested that this would be the case. In 1878, with a number of by-elections pending, the minister of the interior informed prefects that 'the government utterly dissociates itself from the doctrine of official candidatures', adding that, 'we have in electoral matters just a single duty to fulfil: the strict and equitable application of the law.'[72] Yet he also stated that it was both natural and legitimate that the government wanted voters to express their attachment to the Republic via the choices they made. In the event, 'candidatures officieuses' (unofficial candidatures), that is to say more discreet recommendations

---

[69] Jules Clère, Histoire du suffrage universel (Paris, 1873), 200.
[70] Félix Challeton, Cent ans d'élections. Histoire électorale et parlementaire de la France de 1789 à 1890, 3 vols (Paris, 1891), ii, 264.
[71] Challeton, Cent ans d'élections, ii, 262–3.
[72] Cited in Voilliot, La Candidature officielle, 231.

and a less overt deployment of state resources, would remain in evidence even after the Third Republic was consolidated in the 1880s.

One commentator actually declared in 1907 that 'the official candidate has merely shed his label'.[73] This was especially true of areas where there was strong Catholic opposition to the republican regime, for example in the Lozère, where the prefect both encouraged a candidate to oppose the sitting conservative deputy in 1893 and applied 'thinly disguised administrative pressure' to secure his election.[74] André Siegfried, seeking election in the Basses-Alpes in 1902, met his electoral committee at the prefecture, in the presence of the prefect: he was effectively a government candidate (albeit an unsuccessful one, who subsequently turned his hand to pioneering the study of electoral geography).[75] Prefects continued to work closely with certain deputies whom they accompanied on election tours in their departments and, as late as 1914, the sub-prefect of Chalon-sur-Saône compiled a list of non-voters from first round so they might be persuaded to turn out for a government supporter in the second.[76] Indeed, one former prefect has claimed that tacit forms of intervention are still occurring under the Fifth Republic.[77] Local *fonctionnaires* and the police in France have certainly continued to monitor candidates and anticipate results but, by the turn of the twentieth century, party politics was coming to predominate and a growing profusion of candidates was no longer so susceptible to 'travail électoral' on the part of the prefectoral administration. However, at exactly this point the electorate's unfettered choice was decisively infringed from a different direction when declarations of candidature became obligatory, at least where legislative elections were concerned.

The Imposition of Declared Candidatures

One reason for resistance to declared candidatures was the long history of government interference in elections and, above all, the employment of official candidatures, but their enduring absence had one particular drawback that eventually produced legislation to impose them. Until that point was reached, in 1889, it was possible for the same individual to be named to the national legislature by any number of different assemblies, especially under the system of *scrutin de liste*. Thus, in 1792, twenty deputies were elected to the National Convention by more

---

[73] Marcel Perrier, La République démocratique. Étude critique et historique de la législation électorale de la République en France (Paris, 1907), 121.

[74] Yves Pourcher, Les Maîtres de granit: les notables de Lozère du XVIIIᵉ siècle à nos jours (Paris, 1987), 205.

[75] Alain Garrigou, 'L'initiation d'un initiateur: André Siegfried et le "Tableau politique de la France de l'Ouest"', ARSS, 106–7 (1995), 28.

[76] Pierre Goujon, Le Vigneron citoyen, Mâconnais et Chalonnais (1848–1914) (Paris, 1993), 284.

[77] Charles Rickard, Vérités sur les élections (Paris, 1991), 11–13.

than one department, with the well-known journalist Jean-Louis Carra chosen in no less than eight. In these circumstances, it was necessary to opt for just one of the seats obtained, but the resulting vacancies were filled by simultaneously elected *suppléants*, reserve deputies whose availability obviated the need for by-elections. *Suppléants*, who could also step up in the event of subsequent death, indisposition, or resignation, had been nominated at elections to the Estates General of 1789. They were maintained for parliamentary purposes throughout the 1790s and have recently been revived under the Fifth Republic. However, they were abandoned in the nineteenth century, with the consequence that by-elections for deputies became legion and the political consequences were often significant.

Indeed, in April 1848 a number of leading republicans, among them the writer Alphonse de Lamartine, had been positioned at the head of numerous departmental lists, in order to make them more recognizable and attractive to voters. When they were elected to the Constituent Assembly several times over, they were obliged to opt for just one seat and a vacancy was created in the others. At the subsequent by-elections, Louis-Napoleon's collaborators cleverly exploited the opportunity to publicize his ambitions for office. Although he had been exiled from France since the end of his uncle's regime, and was therefore technically ineligible for election, in June and September 1848 he was returned by no less than five different departments, including the Seine (Paris) twice, besides attracting a substantial vote elsewhere.[78] These by-election campaigns, which involved whole departments electing a small number of deputies, usually on a modest turnout, effectively prepared the ground for Louis-Napoleon's election to the presidency of the Second Republic in December 1848, after he was permitted to stand for that supreme position and then swept the board with over three-quarters of the votes cast. This so-called 'plebiscitary' tactic was in evidence again in 1871, facilitated by the return of departmental *scrutin de liste*, when the seasoned politician Thiers was elected in no less than twenty-six departments, with over two million votes, while his arch-opponent Gambetta was chosen in nine. On this occasion it was the republicans who benefited from the slew of by-elections that followed over the next year or so. They gradually built up their parliamentary presence and eventually secured a Third Republic that had looked destined to disappear after a monarchist majority was returned to the National Assembly following the fall of the Second Empire.

Yet the republican penchant for election by departmental list once more proved toxic after it had been re-established for the legislative elections of 1885. The populist General Boulanger (a bellicose minister of war who promised revenge against Germany to compensate for the crushing defeat of 1870) sought to set

---

[78] Bernard Ménager, *Les Napoléon du peuple* (Paris, 1988), 92–8.

a fresh plebiscitary bandwagon rolling in subsequent by-elections.[79] First nominated in 1887, though as a serving soldier he was ineligible for election, he stood repeatedly, in local as well as legislative elections, a 'permanent candidate' to use the expression coined by historian Odile Rudelle, then promptly resigned if he was successful, thereby generating another round of voting.[80] A series of by-election victories culminated in his topping the poll at Paris in January 1889, at which point measures were belatedly taken to deal with the threat he posed. The following month *scrutin d'arrondissement* was reinstated, and a group of staunch republicans proposed the law of July 1889, 'to thwart a plebiscite on behalf of one man', before general elections were held in the autumn.[81] The socialist Jean Jaurès argued that the measure betrayed a lack of confidence in the electorate, while conservatives protested that liberty was being denied to voters and universal male suffrage 'muzzled'.

In fact, the new law was comfortably passed in the Chamber:

> Each citizen who presents himself, or is presented, in general or by-elections, must indicate in which constituency he wishes to stand, by making a signed declaration, duly certified (at least five days before the date of the election). Any additional declaration will be null and void and subject to a fine of 10,000 francs levied on the candidate, while his ballot papers and election literature will be seized and destroyed.

It now became a matter for invalidation if a vote was cast for other than declared parliamentary candidates, though many voters continued to produce or employ illicit ballot papers bearing now-ineligible names. It also provided a means of ensuring that ineligible individuals would be deterred from putting their names forward in future.

Despite the minimal requirement for a declaration, the law of 1889 on candidatures encountered persistent opposition, which was reflected in several attempts at repeal, on the basis that the elector's sovereignty was being violated. This was only to be expected. Under the Second Empire, in 1858, an oath of loyalty had been imposed on all who stood for parliament, in order to prevent republicans or royalists being elected then refusing to take their seats. It did not prevent multiple candidatures—the republican Jules Favre stood in twelve constituencies in 1869—but, in restricting the voters' freedom of choice, it was widely regarded as a fundamental infringement of their autonomy. As an electoral guide put it in 1861: 'This represents an enormous limitation on voting rights; it is

---

[79] William D. Irvine, *The Boulanger Affair Reconsidered: Royalism, Boulangism and the Origins of the Radical Right in France* (New York, 1989), 76 ff.

[80] Odile Rudelle, *La République absolue: aux origines de l'instabilité constitutionnelle de la France républicaine 1870–1889* (Paris, 1982), 205.

[81] *JO*, 17 July 1889, 2002–9.

longer possible to select a citizen who has not put himself forward.'[82] The remark is reminiscent of the traditional attitude that a true candidate was reluctant to bid for attention.

Not surprisingly then, an initial proposal for the abrogation of declared candidatures was tabled in 1892. Denouncing the law of 1889 as an ill-considered panic measure that negated the ideals of universal suffrage, its authors proceeded to argue that this 'severe blow to the fundamental principle of popular sovereignty' imposed an arbitrary restriction of the right 'to freely choose one's representative'; it should be removed from the statute book without delay.[83] Further demands for repeal to restore 'free candidatures' and the right of voters to 'spontaneously express their sovereign will' soon followed. According to one academic critic, the French people had been deprived of their 'precious right to open candidatures.'[84] Yet the law persisted under the Third Republic, was extended to other elections after the Second World War, and remains in being today; aside from those who serve on selection committees, French voters are now denied any role in choosing the candidates on whom they are invited to pronounce.

Still Spoiled for Choice

Although this electoral liberty was lost, for national deputies at least, the twentieth-century voter was presented with an ever-longer list of names at the polls. Notwithstanding fears that the law would reduce electoral choice, one significant feature of French legislative elections ever since has been the sheer number of declared candidates they have attracted. Indeed, even after 1889, a contest was still held, despite the receipt of only a single declaration, unlike contemporary Britain where still-numerous, solitary contenders were elected without a vote. Thus, in France, Louis Barthou was a 'candidat unique' on four occasions out of seven down to 1914, but he was still obliged to present himself to the electorate and, if nothing else, dissenters were able to cast a protest vote (see Chapter 7). However, uncontested elections diminished dramatically at the end of the nineteenth century with the rise of competition generated by organized political parties, and the number of candidates rose steadily. In the department of the Seine (Paris) there were 333 contestants for just forty-five seats in 1893 and an average of more than two across the whole country.[85] By the eve of the First World War

---

[82] Jean-Jules Clamageran et al., *Manuel électoral. Guide pratique pour les élections...*(Paris, 1861), 22.

[83] AN C5470, Proposition de loi, 25 Oct. 1892.

[84] Francis Bernard, *La Liberté des candidatures aux assemblées législatives en France et à l'étranger* (Paris, 1925), 166.

[85] John (J. E. C.) Bodley, *France*, 2 vols (London, 1898), ii, 83–4.

there were almost two thousand candidates overall, for some five hundred seats in the Chamber of Deputies.[86]

As the preamble to a proposal for compulsory voting observed in 1936, there was no excuse for voters who allegedly abstained because they could not find a suitable candidate; on the contrary, by this time the number of candidates presented the electorate with a veritable *embarras de choix*.[87] In 1928, when a two-ballot majority system was re-introduced, and the electoral outcome became more uncertain as a result, the number of parliamentary candidates rose higher than on any previous occasion, with over three thousand in all, roughly six per seat, while the total rose to almost five thousand in the last general elections of the Third Republic eight years later.[88] No wonder there were proposals for the addition of some further requirements to declarations of candidature, including signed support from a number of electors, as well as the suggestion that no fresh names should appear at the second round of voting.[89] Yet the eagerness to obtain a parliamentary mandate does not show any sign of slackening today: in 2017 there were 7,352 candidates seeking election to become one of 539 deputies in the metropole, an average of more than thirteen candidates per constituency, and no less than twenty-seven in some instances. By way of comparison, in the British parliamentary elections held in the same year, there were little more than three thousand candidates for 639 seats.

Those seeking election at the local level in France long remained free of the obligation to declare their candidature, while voters continued to enjoy the liberty to nominate any eligible individuals (aged twenty-five plus), as members of departmental, arrondissement and municipal councils. Indeed, in the municipal elections of 1929 there were apparently over one million nominations, roughly one for every ten registered voters (though there were many offices to fill).[90] The use of such polls as a vehicle for political protest in the early 1920s, did prompt a proposal for an extension of pre-emptive declarations of candidature to all elections, save in the case of municipal polls in communes with fewer than ten thousand inhabitants, but to no avail.[91] A decade later the prefect of the Var flagged up the need for regulation so that space for electoral advertising on public hoardings could be allocated well in advance of polling day, but there was no legislative response.[92] Only after the Second World War was a declaration finally demanded

---

[86] Georges Lachapelle, *Élections législatives des 26 avril et 10 mai 1914* (Paris, 1914).
[87] AN F1cII 195, Proposition de loi, 5 June 1936.
[88] Campbell and Cole, *French Electoral Systems*, 71.
[89] Georges Lachapelle, *Élections législatives, 26 avril et 3 mai 1936. Résultats officiels* (Paris, 1936), viii.
[90] Gosnell, *Why Europe Votes*, 153.
[91] *JO*, 18 Oct. 1921, annexe 3196, 39–40. An alternative, proposed on 12 June 1923, *JO* annexe 6135, 1197–8, was to simply treat votes cast for ineligible individuals as null and void, but this also proved unacceptable.
[92] AD Var 3M 511, Préfet aux maires, 15 Sept. 1934.

from candidates for local office, although communes with less than 3,500 inhabitants (the great majority) remained excluded from this provision until 2013. Yet these eventual changes in the law do not seem to have reduced the widespread desire to be nominated for election in the localities, where thousands of posts are still being hotly contested.

It is worth emphasizing that the question of voter choice remained at the heart of debates about the electoral process, even under *scrutin de liste*, which was used at the legislative level in 1848, 1849, 1871, and 1885. For these were 'plurinominal' schemes, not closed lists, which individuals were free to amend as they wished, and the result was decided by adding up the votes cast for each candidate. The deputy Charles Benoist, a staunch proponent of PR, acknowledged that the *liste bloquée* would constrain choice and he felt that the French voter would never accept being reduced to the 'role of a puppet', beholden to the electoral committees that decided the composition of party lists. He was, therefore, a strong advocate of *panachage*, which enabled voters to mix and match names from different lists by altering printed ballot papers.[93] The PR introduced in 1919 and 1924 was actually a hybrid which permitted *panachage* and effectively constituted a complex majority system. Full PR with closed lists was finally adopted under the Fourth Republic in 1946, but this system was modified five years later for the following legislative elections, by the inclusion of *panachage*, and also *préférence*, which allowed voters to re-order listed candidates (though only 7 per cent of them subsequently made use of this facility).

The debate over the precise configuration of PR continued until it was abolished for parliamentary elections under the Fifth Republic and the two-ballot majoritarian regime was reinstated. Meanwhile, a plurinominal system for municipal elections, enshrined in the landmark 1884 legislation, had remained in being for all communes (save the biggest, like Paris) until the advent of the Fourth Republic. After 1947 an experiment with genuine list systems was only applied to the minority of municipalities (some five hundred of them) with over nine thousand inhabitants but, even then, legislators were anxious to preserve a measure of electoral choice by allowing *panachage*. The prefect of the Rhône, among others, would complain bitterly that at Lyon allowing voters the right to *panacher* was posing huge problems in counting the votes.[94] Almost 20 per cent of voters had used the opportunity in 1953 and the count took fifty-five hours to complete since, in extreme cases, *bulletins* with names drawn from four or five lists, among 464 candidates, were taking half-an-hour each to process. When PR was restored in 1982, it was on the basis of closed lists, though the permissive plurinominal system was retained in communes of less than 3,500 inhabitants, before being restricted to those with less than one thousand in 2013.

---

[93] Charles Benoist, *Pour la réforme électorale* (Paris, 1908), 120.
[94] AN F1cII 185, Préfet du Rhône au ministre, 9 May 1953.

Since 2001 French voters have faced a different constraint, obliged to opt in most elections for equal numbers of male and female candidates, following the passage of a constitutional amendment and legislation on gender 'parity', that has gradually won general approval.[95] Confronted by the continuing, and significant, under-representation of women in elective office, measures were eventually taken to redress the imbalance by insisting on equal, alternately listed, numbers of both sexes on the ballot paper, a formula first applied to municipal lists in communes with over 3,500 inhabitants, then subsequently employed in regional, European, and some Senate elections.[96] This system works effectively with PR, since only so-called 'zippered' lists are acceptable, but single-seat constituencies have proved more resistant. A law passed was thus passed in 2013 which created two-seat ('binomial') constituencies in departmental (formerly cantonal) elections and stipulated that each party nominate one woman and one man for each of them. State financial assistance is substantially reduced for parties which persist in fielding a preponderance of candidates of a single sex when it comes to legislative polls. In 2017, female *candidates* still comprised fewer than 50 per cent of the total who stood for election to the National Assembly, but the number is rising sharply.

Presidential elections have not been subjected to parity law, but a justification for the recent experiments with presidential 'primaries' in France is that they represent a means of involving more citizens in the process of selecting candidates for this supreme office. There were eleven individuals in contention for the presidential elections of 2017, despite the particular conditions applied to candidatures for this key post, which currently require '500 signatures' to be obtained from among some forty thousand holders of public office, most of them mayors. Roger-Gérard Schwartzenberg, a left-of-centre deputy, aired the idea of primaries in 2004 before submitting a formal proposal to parliament two years later (which was not adopted).[97] One of his stated objectives was to 'democratize the manner of nominating a presidential candidate', by involving supporters of different parties as well as their members, and providing some state financial assistance as an encouragement to organize primary contests of this sort. He suggested regional elections to a national convention, on the American model, in his abortive draft bill.

In fact, the Socialist Party had already begun to stage 'primaries' via direct election among its adherents and the conservative Republicans soon followed suit, though both regarded such involvement as a way of strengthening a candidature

[95] Catherine Achin, 'The French parity law: a successful gender equality measure or a "conservative revolution"?', in Diana Auth et al. (eds), *Gender and Family in European Economic Policy: Developments in the New Millennium* (Cham, 2017), 179–96.

[96] Catherine Achin and Marion Paoletti, 'Le "salto" du stigmata. Genre et construction des listes aux municipales de 2001', *Politix*, 60 (2002), 33–54.

[97] JO, Proposition de loi relative à l'organisation d'élections primaires, no. 2915, 28 Feb. 2006.

and building momentum for the electoral campaign, rather than as a means of enhancing voter participation. However, these initiatives have prompted further debate over the process of nomination necessary for presidential candidates. In 2012, a Commission for the Renewal of Public Life proposed 'citizen sponsorship', which would enable every elector to propose a candidate to occupy the Élysée Palace. Those individuals who passed a threshold set at 150,000 nominations would proceed to polling proper, on the principle that: 'it is to the citizens themselves that the right of authorizing candidatures for the presidency belongs'.[98] The authors of this report may not have realized it, but their suggestion was reminiscent of Condorcet's proposal for a preliminary round of voting to establish a list of candidates for the legislature in 1793.

Conclusion

Paradoxically, the French voter's freedom to nominate an individual of his or her own choice has been progressively eroded as the franchise has been widened and eligibility requirements removed. From 1789 to 1848 the prevailing electoral legislation invariably restricted the scope for personal selection to those of greater wealth, but unrestricted choice was exercised within these limits. This period was followed by a brief interlude of relatively open, democratic competition, quickly curtailed by the imposition of official candidatures under the Second Empire. The subsequent restoration of greater liberty for nominations on the ballot paper survived little more than a decade where legislative elections were concerned. The advent of declared candidatures in 1889, like the increasingly routine involvement of electoral committees, effectively ended a right once jealously guarded by the electorate as a whole. The process was consummated when the leaders and active members of political parties assumed responsibility for selecting the great majority of candidates at both legislative and local levels. It can thus be argued that voters have lost their sovereignty over the choice of candidatures, which is now largely in the grip of party machines. Nonetheless, competition between opponents in the French multi-party system is extremely fierce, and the electoral outcome remains in the hands of voters who must be persuaded to choose among large numbers of candidates. The conduct of this crucial contest will be examined in the following chapter.

---

[98] Commission de rénovation et de déontologie de la vie publique, *Pour un renouveau démocratique*, 2012, 10.

4

A Matter of Persuasion

Campaigning and Corruption

> Unfortunately, in this part of France it is a customary expectation
> that voters are plied with cider and handed cigars. They regard it as
> their right to receive such largesse, and as the candidate's duty to
> provide it.
>
> Procureur de Saint-Brieuc, 26 January 1878.[1]

Canvassing for votes and using corrupt practices to secure them often went hand
in hand in nineteenth-century France, which was not alone in confronting this
relationship as the number of electors increased, elections were held more frequently, and electioneering became more competitive. For while soliciting votes
and offering inducements to voters was anathema to early modern minds, it had
always taken place on an informal basis, and it simply became more evident as
the conduct of elections became more open and campaigns were organized in a
professional manner, with the involvement of paid agents. Press and propaganda
played their part in this process as the electoral space expanded beyond the polling station and into society over the weeks preceding the vote. However, attitudes
towards corruption began to alter and expectations of integrity were growing.
Voting was long regarded as a transaction of favours between superiors and their
subjects, by both parties; indeed, it was considered a natural state of affairs. Yet
the manipulation of the electorate vitiated the quality of representation, while
democratic choice depended upon persuasion not constraint. Legislation to
suppress electoral malpractice and the adoption of procedures to avoid it thus
indicated a greater willingness to tackle a recognized problem as much as an
escalation of its incidence. The ideal of the voter as an independent individual,
participating in free and fair elections, was coming closer to realization in the
twentieth century as a result. However, if fraud was reduced, it was not entirely
eliminated and technological developments today pose a significant threat to
electoral probity.

---

[1] AN BB30 491, Rapport du procureur de Saint-Brieuc, 26 Jan. 1878, cited in Nathalie Dompnier,
'La Clef des urnes', Thèse de doctorat de science politique, Université de Grenoble II, 2002, 176.

How the French Learned to Vote: A History of Electoral Practice in France. Malcolm Crook, Oxford University Press (2021).
© Malcolm Crook. DOI: 10.1093/oso/9780192894786.003.0005

Hidden Agendas under the *Ancien Régime* and Revolution

The election campaign that precedes voting is an accepted activity in liberal democracies today, but this has not always been the case. In the past it was reckoned that virtue and merit should speak for themselves in the electoral contest, allowing the voter make up his own mind without being subject to external pressure. Yet the element of competition inevitably encouraged practices of persuasion that losing candidates were prone to denounce as unacceptable intrigue. Elections were traditionally conducted in assemblies, so personal inter-action and discussion among voters was unavoidable. Hence, in answer to questions raised about the manipulation of eighteenth-century municipal polls at Nantes, the intendant of Brittany could simply reply, 'when was there an election *sans brigues?*', an argument frequently employed by royal administrators to justify their interference in urban affairs.[2] At Troyes, rival groups exploited provisions in the Laverdy law of 1764, which reshaped the town's electoral system, in order to oust merchants who had hitherto dominated the municipality. This was achieved by holding preparatory meetings at which tactics were discussed and ballot papers distributed, leading the former incumbents to protest about the 'man-oeuvres employed to constrain and subjugate the freedom of the vote'.[3] Laverdy subsequently sought to prohibit 'any kind of cabal or activities aimed at capturing votes', explicitly forbidding participants to canvass for support on pain of penal-ties to be decided in court, though sanctions were not specified.[4]

In 1789 deputies were not representatives but mandatories, entrusted with a *cahier*, but a good deal of persuasion, even pressure, was exerted as individuals vied for the honour of election to the Estates General.[5] At Le Puy-en-Velay one person was apparently so keen to secure a nomination that he posted agents on roads into the town to accost members of the *sénéchaussée* assembly and foist handbills on them, which sang his praises while denigrating others likely to be chosen. The presiding official was delighted to report that this disgraceful behav-iour had completely backfired. A political element might be involved: in Burgundy, youthful barristers were accused of making 'crude overtures to the electors at Semur', where they visited taverns 'to grab the attention of peasant delegates and distribute lists of those patriots whose election they wished to ensure'. Even the incorruptible Robespierre was later accused of suborning dele-gates so as to be chosen as a representative by the Estates of Artois, though the graduated process of election afforded ample publicity for aspiring individuals like him to make their mark. Evidence from other locations suggests that

---

[2] Guy Saupin, 'La réforme des élections municipales en France au XVIIIᵉ siècle. Réflexions à partir de l'exemple de Nantes', *Rhmc*, 46 (1999), 649–50.

[3] Horn, *Qui parle pour la nation?*, 33–5. [4] Bordes, *La Réforme municipale*, 315–16.

[5] Crook, *Elections*, 26–8.

rural-dwellers were quite capable of making their own minds up and organizing themselves. It was rare for contests to go the full distance of three rounds in order to achieve an absolute majority, which indicates a concentration of votes, often involving delegates from different areas agreeing to share the deputation on a mutual basis.

Under the representative system established during the Revolution competition grew fiercer and became more partisan. Yet electioneering was not simply stigmatized but actually banned in an instruction from the National Assembly in 1790, which stated that elections were to be annulled if canvassing occurred and the perpetrators were to be punished.[6] When a retailer at Le Havre distributed handwritten ballot papers that year, he was accordingly denounced for inhibiting 'freedom of choice', his *bulletins* were burned and he was taken into custody for the duration of the polls.[7] Political clubs were certainly organizing election campaigns as early as 1790, when a central committee at Lyon asked each *quartier* to provide suggestions from which a list of the most popular nominations would be composed and circulated. The ploy bore fruit in the elevated proportion of votes these 'candidates' amassed, but not without attracting a good deal of adverse comment. There were similar accusations of foul play at Marseille, at the beginning of 1793, when Jacobins compiled a slate of names for the election of municipal councillors. As historian Paul Hanson comments, 'these are electoral tactics we take for granted today...but for many Marseillais in 1792–93, in the midst of inventing a political culture...(this practice) seemed decidedly undemocratic and threatening.'[8]

For all its new-found freedom, the press had been more concerned with promoting ideas than individuals, and editors showed a remarkable reluctance to declare personal preferences at the outset of the Revolution. It was only in 1791 that journalist Jean-Paul Marat, showing a characteristic lack of restraint, chose to excoriate certain aspirants for office in the capital, and a year later he did the same in response to a list of names for election to the National Convention that was published by Jean-Baptiste Louvet in his newssheet, the *Sentinelle*.[9] However, these were isolated exceptions to the general rule of not naming names. In 1795 the leading Marseillais journalist, Ferréol Beaugeard offered Ten Commandments for members of the electoral assemblies who were selecting personnel for the directorial legislative councils, in which he proclaimed: 'Only choose those who do not seek elevation' and 'Those who canvass for places are not worthy of them',

---

[6] Edelstein, *The French Revolution*, 168–9.

[7] Victor Flour de Saint-Genis, *La Révolution en province, d'après des documents inédits... L'esprit public et les élections au Havre de 1787 à 1790* (Le Havre, 1889), 73–4.

[8] Paul Hanson, 'The Federalist Revolt: an affirmation or denial of popular sovereignty?', *FH*, 6 (1992), 339–40.

[9] Malcolm Crook, 'La plume et l'urne: la presse et les élections sous le Directoire', in Philippe Bourdin and Bernard Gainot (eds), *La République directoriale*, 2 vols (Paris, 1998), i, 298–300ff.

pointedly refusing to nominate a single individual himself. It was only in 1797, following fleeting legislation on declared candidatures, that the press really began to engage in personal promotion, no longer simply urging participation but also offering *ad hominem* advice on the choices to be made. At this point *La Quotidienne* on the right, like the *Journal des hommes libres de tous les pays* on the left, began proposing specific names. The press in the provinces followed suit and did so again for the elections of 1798 and 1799.

Annual polling under the Directory was accompanied by unprecedented levels of canvassing on both sides of the deep political divide that separated republicans and their opponents, who were both playing the same electioneering game. In 1797, for instance, it was reported that royalist agents were touring the country-side in Lower Normandy, 'their pockets stuffed full of lists', bearing the names of those whom they were seeking to elect to departmental assemblies.[10] In the Côtes-du-Nord too, these 'Messieurs' were closely following proceedings in each canton and writing out fresh ballot papers for each round of voting, as the complexion of the contest altered.[11] As a result, republicans redoubled their own efforts the following year, with latter-day Jacobin clubs, the newly created constitutional circles, spearheading their campaign. At Moulins, *chef-lieu* of the Allier, a manifesto demanded that club members focus their choices on the same persons: 'Yes, on the same names! Because if we disperse our votes, we will fail to win a majority...We will indicate below those whom we are planning to name to the *bureaux*, as second-degree electors, as municipal administrators, and as justices of the peace and their assistants.'[12]

Members of the departmental assemblies had always been inclined to engage more openly in the quest for votes, though not without attracting criticism. Generally speaking, second-degree electors were more experienced and better-educated citizens, aware of their vital role in nominating important local officials and national deputies. The electoral college of Paris had set a precedent at the end of 1790, when a Society of Patriotic Electors was created in order to 'enlighten' colleagues who had assembled to choose their departmental administrators.[13] The following summer, when elections were held for the Legislative Assembly, the fears of critics who predicted divisive consequences were realized when two societies of this sort emerged. Conservative electors seceded from the re-convened Patriots to form a separate group that secured more places on the capital's deputation than its rival.[14] This episode turned into a celebrated affair, which stimulated an unresolved debate over the issue of canvassing, as opinions

---

[10] Crook, *Elections*, 142.
[11] Hervé Pommeret, *L'Esprit public dans le département des Côtes-du-Nord pendant la Révolution 1789–1799* (Saint-Brieuc, 1921), 385.
[12] Isser Woloch, *Jacobin Legacy: The Democratic Movement under the Directory* (Princeton, NJ, 1970), 268–71.
[13] Crook, *Elections*, 179–80.   [14] Gueniffey, *Le Nombre et la raison*, 366–73.

continued to differ. In 1792, for instance, a member of the departmental college in the Var was taken to task for the way he had 'caballed' in favour of Dubois-Crancé becoming a member of the National Convention. His response, that such partisan action was justified by the patriotic outcome, failed to satisfy the editors of a local newspaper who had condemned his unwarranted interference with the voters' electoral liberty.[15]

The Gradual Emergence of Open Electioneering

The life membership of relatively small, second-degree electoral colleges under Napoleon, populated by notables, ushered in a period of more genteel election-eering, which generally characterized the constitutional monarchies after 1814. Canvassing was mostly conducted on an informal, personal basis, facilitated by the extremely limited electorate, which mostly assembled in arrondissement electoral colleges before 1830, then wholly in those circumscriptions thereafter. Only half of these assemblies numbered more than 500 registered voters under the Restoration, while under the July Monarchy three-quarters of them had less than 600 members.[16] Indeed, in 1846, the overwhelming majority of deputies were elected with less than 400 votes. It was thus easy for participants to obtain first-hand knowledge of the candidates likely to win the contest and even to have been introduced to them, especially if they had already stood and served as a deputy. No wonder Balzac could state in his unfinished contemporary novel, Le Député d'Arcis, that the victor had entertained every single voter at his residence. For what was at stake in most cases was the election of an individual who could represent their personal as well as local interests at Paris.

Pierre-Vincent Benoist, a staunch royalist deputy who served in all but one parliament during the Restoration, offers a good example of this sort of election-eering in his final 'campaign' in 1824. He arrived at Saumur (Maine-et-Loire), which he had represented since 1815, several days before the arrondissement assembly was due to open in order to ensure that he retained the seat. He then spent the intervening period, assisted by his son, wining and dining potential supporters, before concluding that he could muster sufficient votes to achieve a first-round majority. In the event, Benoist took just over 80 per cent of the initial ballot, though his nomination as president and the delivery of an opening address had undoubtedly helped his cause. Family, like friends, played a vital role in the electoral process at this point: in the Lozère, for instance, on the eve of the elec-tions of 1834, the comte de Morangiès wrote to a cousin, 'You gave me your vote in 1830 and I hope that I can count on you again now...I am sorry to put you to

---

[15] Crook, *Elections*, 183.   [16] Tudesq, 'Les comportements électoraux', 107–8.

the trouble of going to the assembly... but please exercise your influence on my behalf... by courting your acquaintances there.'[17]

The idea of openly soliciting votes continued to attract opprobrium in the early nineteenth century. One would-be Restoration deputy had caught rural voters unawares by visiting their hostelries as they arrived for polling in a provincial constituency. This 'English manner of electioneering' discomfited another of the electors, the comte de Maisonfort but, as he reflected, 'when you are influenced by another country's laws, you inevitably acquire their *moeurs*.'[18] In 1818, the journalist Alphonse Martainville wrote in the *Conservateur* that 'a candidate would prostitute himself in search of votes... lobbing circulars into cafes, shops and gaming houses.'[19] When members of the liberal opposition went further and held meetings, which resembled 'hustings of the sort used in England', on the Champs-Elysées in Paris prior to parliamentary by-elections in 1828, they prompted an extremely hostile response. The minister of the interior, Martignac, ridiculed those who criticized what they called 'government tyranny', yet proceeded to attempt to influence the outcome of elections by 'the strangest of means', which involved forming committees, discussing candidates, and distributing propaganda.[20] Such practices were allegedly contrary to the constitutional Charter and there was an unsuccessful proposal for them to be banned, since they recalled political clubs in the bad old days of 1789.[21]

Such overt electioneering evidently remained contentious, but under the July Monarchy the approach of elections led to the publication of accounts of their activities on the part of serving deputies, as well as the circulation of electoral manifestos on the part of those seeking to take their places. These *professions de foi* even extended to polling for departmental councils when they were recreated in 1833.[22] To be sure, they were pretty bland for the most part, mentioning only general aspirations for law and order, the development of agriculture and commerce, or a reduction in taxes, together with details of the candidate's status and a list of the offices he had held. Nonetheless, there were occasions when a political note was struck, as in the case of Descoutures, a magistrate in the Haute-Vienne, who made his pitch on the basis of electoral reform, albeit in modest terms: 'a greater number of citizens should be involved in the choice of their representatives, especially among those endowed with intellectual capacity', he stated.[23]

Paris and some large towns, like departments deeply divided by the Revolution, were witnessing the injection of a more ideological element into electioneering,

---

[17] Pourcher, *Les Maîtres de granit*, 201.
[18] Antoine-François-Philippe de La Maisonfort, *Mémoires d'un agent royaliste sous la Révolution, l'Empire et la Restauration, 1763–1827*, ed. Hugues de Changy (Paris, 1998), 284–6.
[19] Weil, *Les Élections législatives*, 133.   [20] *AP*, 2e série, LIII, 29 Apr. 1828, 517.
[21] *Moniteur*, 11 May 1828, 615–16.
[22] AN F1cIII Aude 4, Aux électeurs d'Alzonne, 10 Nov. 1833, for example.
[23] AD Haute-Vienne, 3M 5, À Messieurs les électeurs de l'arrondissement de Saint-Yrieux, 28 Aug. 1837.

even if the politics of local interest prevailed. Liberals had revived the tradition of forming caucuses as early as 1817, when they met separately at the departmental electoral assembly in the Côte-d'Or, though they beat a hasty retreat when threatened with legal action.[24] Despite efforts to deter them, election committees would become commonplace, often linked to the press and frequently meeting in print shops, where propaganda was prepared. Newspapers were once again enjoying greater latitude and they were playing an increasingly important role in electoral publicity. At Paris there were fourteen titles with a circulation of over 3,000 towards the end of the July Monarchy and, as the radical deputy Cormenin suggested in 1842, their premises offered the location where 'the formulae for all kinds of elections' were devised.[25] The republican deputy François Arago, who represented the Pyrénées-Orientales for the duration of Louis-Philippe's regime, created a local newspaper specifically designed to wage the continuing battle to retain his seat.

Arago led a spectacular campaign, worthy of the military term which was commonly applied to elections later in the century, in 1846. It involved a visit to every *chef-lieu de canton*, holding banquets and speaking at public meetings to audiences that reached well beyond the limited electorate.[26] Alexis de Tocqueville, who had refused to become a ministerial candidate and was initially frustrated in his bid to become a deputy, might decry such 'roving candidates, who peddled their wares from one platform to another'. Yet, while he saw no need to tour the constituency himself at election-time, in addition to his network of family and friends, he had already begun to employ agents who would later prove invaluable in securing his subsequent electoral success.[27] Indeed, in some towns, members of election committees were beginning to engage in activities at the grassroots, delivering circulars and knocking on doors to encourage voters to turn out, in the ways they did at Lyon during the last days of the July Monarchy.[28]

Without warning, the sudden arrival of a mass franchise in 1848, and the concomitant multiplication of cantonal polling stations, made electioneering much more demanding for aspiring national deputies. There was also the challenge, under the Second Republic at least, of *scrutin de liste* rather than single-member constituencies, the end of electoral assemblies, and the advent of printed ballot papers, all of which profoundly altered the rules of the electoral game. The press played a key role in formulating departmental lists, but there were many newspapers, both long-established and newly founded, with competing agendas which

---

[24] Simone Fizaine, *La Vie politique en Côte-d'Or sous Louis XVIII. Les élections et la presse* (Paris, 1931), 142–9.

[25] Tudesq, 'Les comportements électoraux', 116.

[26] Horace Chauvet, *Histoire du parti républicain dans les Pyrénées-Orientales (1830-1877)* (Perpignan, 1909), 38–40.

[27] Alexis de Tocqueville, *Œuvres complètes*, Vol. X, Correspondance et écrits locaux (Paris, 1995), 394–5.

[28] *Le Journal d'un bourgeois de Lyon en 1848*, ed. Justin Godart (Paris, 1924), 6.

were hard to reconcile.[29] In the absence of political parties, local electoral committees and clubs also acquired additional importance in selecting and supporting candidates, not only in 1848 but likewise the following year. Yet while they became more partisan and popular in composition, *comités* struggled to overcome the domination of notables in this somewhat chaotic process, as the example of the Yonne suggests.[30] Tocqueville quickly grasped the imperatives of this unprecedented situation, confident that existing deputies like himself could maintain their positions, provided they adapted effectively to the novel circumstances. Writing to his leading agent, after a new electoral law was issued on 5 March, he recommended the rapid formation of coordinated committees in every canton of the Manche, where he was standing, so as to arrive at an agreed departmental list of fifteen deputies for circulation 'to the lower classes'.[31]

The Professionalization of Electoral Contests

The well-documented example of Tocqueville demonstrates that the notables were quite capable of survival in the dawning era of universal male suffrage; their demise was by no means inevitable. To be sure, the Second Empire closed down the space for electoral competition, imposing restrictions on the press, banning public gatherings, obliging electoral committees to disband (including those sympathetic to the new regime) and arresting opponents. The problem of managing democratic elections was to be sought instead in the endorsement of official candidatures and administrative assistance for electioneering. Indeed, for those so favoured by the new regime, it was essentially a case of allowing prefects to organize their campaigns—a term which came into currency during this period—then meekly following them around the constituency and exchanging greetings with local dignitaries. However, opportunities for canvassing and greater publicity were restored as the regime liberalized during the 1860s and opponents began to exploit them at election-time, most notably by holding 'meetings', a word borrowed from across the Channel, which were permitted under certain conditions after 1868.[32] The immediate example of this practice is furnished by Léon Gambetta's republican crusade in Belleville (Paris) on the eve of legislative polls the following year, when he was delivering five or six speeches every day, in workshops and warehouses. Such public gatherings, which later grew in scope, allowed candidates to display their oratorical skills and would become the highpoint of campaigning in future.

---

[29] Popkin, 'Press and elections', 89–97.   [30] Voilliot, *Le Département de l'Yonne*, 37–84.
[31] Tocqueville, *Œuvres complètes*, X, 451.
[32] Paula Cossart, *Le Meeting politique. De la délibération à la manifestation (1868–1939)* (Rennes, 2010).

The development of electioneering was thus resuming just before the Second Empire abruptly collapsed amidst humiliating military defeat. Yet royalists, who triumphed in the exceptional circumstances in which the legislative elections of 1871 were held, without apparently campaigning too hard, if at all, subsequently failed to capitalize on their unanticipated victory. The argument that this constituted a foreseeable outcome should be treated with some caution, because it is all too easy to caricature their uneasiness in coping with a mass electorate. Supporters of monarchy certainly found it difficult to 'press the flesh' by mixing with ordinary voters in markets and bars, describing universal suffrage as a 'system of hawking and bartering' and refusing 'to lower themselves into the electoral pit'.[33] Their naivety is nicely captured in the memoirs of a Breton peasant, who recalled how he had duped his local *châtelain* in the elections of 1876. Monsieur le comte had supplied a great quantity of food and drink to his tenant farmers the night before the poll, then distributed ballot papers among them the following morning. Yet Déguignet, a wily rustic, recounted that he had already handed out competing *bulletins* for the republican candidate, which villagers concealed about their person and cast instead of those they had been rewarded for accepting.[34] However, William Irvine's assertion that royalists' fundamental contempt for political democracy...rendered ineffective any attempts to create a political machine comparable to that of their opponents', must be questioned.[35]

An outstanding case study of the royalist deputy Armand, baron Mackau, offers a useful corrective to the famous thesis of an electoral 'fin des notables' in the late nineteenth century; his biographer has actually dubbed his career 'the invention of the modern politician'.[36] First elected for Argentan in the Orne, as an official candidate under the Second Empire, Mackau continued to prosper in the adverse environment of the Third Republic, when competition for votes became keener and the administration was working against him. Professionalizing his activities, in order to become a 'political entrepreneur' in the burgeoning electoral market, he employed a set of agents, built up a huge database on his electorate and became the proprietor of a newspaper. As a result, he was able to remain a deputy, virtually uninterrupted, until his death in 1918. Evidently the allure of the 'natural leader' had not completely disappeared, but it was allied with the sort of *savoir faire* that all candidates were obliged to develop, besides possessing the

---

[33] Cited in Robert R. Locke, *French Legitimists and the Politics of Moral Order in the Early Third Republic* (Princeton, NJ, 1974), 239–42.

[34] Jean-Marie Déguignet, *Mémoires d'un paysan bas-breton*, ed. Bernez Rouz (Ergué-Gabéric, 2000), 336–43.

[35] Irvine, *The Boulanger Affair*, 71–2.

[36] Éric Phélippeau, *L'Invention de l'homme politique moderne. Mackau, l'Orne et la République* (Paris, 2002) and Éric Phélippeau, 'La fin des notables revisitée', in Michel Offerlé (ed.), *La Profession politique, XIXe–XXe siècles* (Paris, 1999), 79–108. Jean Joana has proposed deeper roots for the process of professionalization: 'L'invention du député. Réunions parlementaires et spécialisation de l'activité politique au XIXe siècle', *Politix*, 35 (1996), 23–42.

ability to procure benefits for their constituents. Such behaviour was also exempli-fied by the baron Eschassériaux, who served as a deputy for the Charente-Inférieure from 1849 until 1893. He had simply been advised to rely on his own social con-tacts when he embarked on his quest for public office yet, under the Third Republic, he mastered the mass electorate by systematically recording canvass returns, and noting the inclination to vote for him as 'doubtful, good and very good'.[37] The marquis de Solages, who defeated Jean Jaurès in a celebrated electoral contest at Albi (Tarn) in 1898, was following in these barons' footsteps when he compiled a list of those who had failed to vote in recent local elections so as to make a particular point of contacting them for the legislative poll.

A more professional approach meant a less personal one as candidates were routinely assisted by electoral agents. Their historian first refers to them working for Eschassériaux in 1863, while another baron, Soubeyran, was later credited with employing no less than 300 individuals of this kind, who were being paid 50 francs a day to tour the countryside in the Loudun constituency (in the Vienne) in 1881.[38] By the end of the nineteenth century, agents were identified in cam-paign accounts: the marquis de Solages spent half of his budget on them in 1898, chiefly on account of their bar bills. Such expenditure explains why such individ-uals were constantly accused of corruption and their employment remained a bone of contention.[39] In fact, it is not easy to determine precisely when remuner-ated assistance was instituted, as opposed to the earlier, documented use by de Tocqueville, among others, of trusted 'intermediaries' under the July Monarchy or Second Republic. Agents of that sort were often personal acquaintances of the candidate, local notables and office-holders who regarded their role as an honour rather than a source of income; they had tended to confine their activities to their own neighbourhoods and were more discreet about their political objectives.

Under the Third Republic, agents might also put up posters and serve as dis-tributors of ballot papers, though these became separate tasks as the business of electioneering became more sophisticated. Such personnel performed a particu-larly crucial role if the candidate had been 'parachuted' into the constituency and lacked the local connexions that were so often highlighted in *professions de foi*. Indeed, voters were strongly attached to incumbents, at all levels of the electoral process, something the French call the 'prime du sortant'. A study of deputies' longevity under the Third Republic suggests that two-thirds of those who stood for re-election were returned to the Chamber of Deputies, while only 20 per cent of mayoral careers ended in electoral defeat (as opposed to death, retirement, or resignation), and departmental and arrondissement councillors seem to have

---

[37] François Miquet-Marty, 'Les agents électoraux. La naissance d'un rôle politique dans la deux-ième moitié du XIXe siècle', *Politix*, 38 (1997), 58–62.

[38] Miquet-Marty, 'Les agents électoraux', 50–1.

[39] Roland Trempé, 'Une campagne électorale étudiée d'après les archives privées', *Actes du 82e con-grès national des sociétés savantes* (Paris, 1958), 484–6.

been solidly ensconced too.[40] To launch a career was thus far from easy and demanded a great deal of initial effort, but the prospect of success was greatly enhanced by sponsorship from a political organization. Less wealthy republican candidates relied especially heavily on regional congresses or local committees, first to nominate and then to support them.

Louis Barthou, who became the long-serving deputy for the Oloron constituency in the Basses-Pyrénées, was first selected as a candidate in 1889 by a typical republican caucus, or *comité électoral*, which comprised departmental and municipal office-holders, plus sympathizers of more modest means. Such committees had no fixed membership, unlike the political parties which began to assume the role in the following century and insisted on reserving the nomination to their paid-up adherents. In seats which their candidates could expect to win by a comfortable majority this was tantamount to deciding the electoral outcome, so *comités* were condemned for usurping the right of the people to select and censure representatives. Members were dubbed *comitards*, a derogatory term, and denounced as self-serving hacks. As early as 1848, for example, an inhabitant of the Somme had protested that electoral committees were imposing candidates for the Second Republic's Constituent Assembly and making a mockery of voters' freedom of choice.[41] However, as Barthou wrote in his notebook, 'No doubt these much-maligned *comités* are often guilty of an excess of zeal, but their existence is essential for the progress of democracy because they offer the only means of combating wealthy adversaries.'[42]

Committees played an essential role in electoral campaigns under the Third Republic, by providing financial resources and offering a network of (often unpaid) volunteers for the distribution of ballot papers and publicity material. On the basis of such support, Barthou set out to visit all communes in his constituency and deliver speeches whenever the opportunity arose, a routine later facilitated by the motor car which he first used during the election campaign of 1906.[43] Strong lungs and an iron stomach were necessary to survive a punishing schedule of orations and refreshments. Turn-of-the-century professionalism of this sort was duly castigated by conservatives, who likewise decried the rise of 'career politicians' (the neologism *politicien* was coined as a term of abuse), who represented an unwanted import from across the Atlantic. Another phrase in the expanding lexicon of denigration was 'machine politics', a form of electioneering memorably described 'as a mechanical manipulation of democracy, aimed at the industrial

---

[40] Mattei Dogan, 'Longévité des carrières politiques. Une biographie collective', in Jean-Marie Mayeur et al. (eds), *Les Parlementaires de la Troisième République* (Paris, 2003), 296–9 and Yves Billard, *Le Métier de la politique sous la IIIe République* (Perpignan, 2003), 85–6.

[41] AN F1cIII Somme 4, Protestation d'un citoyen de Franvillers, 30 Apr. 1848.

[42] Jean Bousquet-Mélou, *Louis Barthou et la circonscription d'Oloron, 1889–1914* (Paris, 1972), 215.

[43] Bousquet-Mélou, *Louis Barthou*, 69 and 227.

production of favourable opinions for the benefit of the engineer'.[44] Public hostility was particularly apparent in the furore over an increase in deputies' salaries from 9,000 to 15,000 francs per annum in 1906, such that they were disparagingly referred to as 'les quinzemillistes'.[45]

The professional politician was regarded by conservative opinion as a vulgar version of his more gentlemanly, amateur predecessor. A splendid illustration of the contrast is afforded by the respective electoral campaigns of the Leroy-Beaulieus, *père et fils*, the former a repeatedly unsuccessful candidate, the latter an elected deputy, before and after 1900.[46] Leroy-Beaulieu senior encountered a series of defeats at Lodève, in the Hérault, from 1878 onwards, yet he never embraced, rather despised, the more elaborate type of campaigning that electoral competition now demanded. Academic and aloof, he was profoundly averse to personal contact with the electorate. By contrast, his son excelled at such interaction, expressing admiration for American practice, which he had observed first hand, before employing the attendant techniques to win a different seat in the same department. Leroy-Beaulieu junior achieved victory by specifically focusing his efforts on key cantons in the suburbs of Montpellier and by tailoring his propaganda accordingly, not to mention using some dubious, disruptive tactics against his republican opponent.

It has been suggested that *scrutin d'arrondissement* encouraged a concentration on personalities and local issues, as opposed to the broader programme required to win an electoral contest with *scrutin de liste*. The description 'uninominal' is especially apt in the former case, since it signified voting for a single name on the individual ballot paper. An inheritance from the era of domination by the notables, who insisted on its re-establishment under the Third Republic in 1875, it involved a personalization of the vote, rather than the invocation of political ideas or party platforms. As a result, contemporary campaigning in France tended not to accord too much time to national issues. John Bodley, a sharp-eyed English observer, was particularly struck by the lack of reference to government policies. 'Biographical studies of the candidates take the place which altruistic praise of parties, programmes and statesmen has in our (British) electoral literature', he wrote of the French general election of 1893.[47] Instead, candidates stressed their local roots, as *enfants du pays*, family background and previous career. Polemic focused on character as much as political differences, and *questions de clocher* such as the sort of services a deputy could supply. Bodley may have overstated his

[44] Charles Benoist, 'Comment on capte le suffrage et le pouvoir: la "Machine"', *Revue des Deux Mondes*, 21 (1904), 906.

[45] Alain Garrigou, 'Vivre de la politique. Les "quinze mille", le mandat et le métier', *Politix*, 20 (1992), 7–10.

[46] Philippe Secondy, 'Pierre Leroy-Beaulieu: un importateur des méthodes électorales américaines en France', *Rh*, 634 (2005), 309–17.

[47] Bodley, *France*, ii, 135–6.

case, but he reckoned that the absence of matters of wider importance from debate in the constituencies was also a reflection of weak political parties, a situation that would gradually change in the twentieth century.

The Cost of Campaigning

One reason that intimate contact between candidate and voters remained vital was because many of the latter were illiterate and thus impervious to printed material (though songs, a neglected, ephemeral aspect of nineteenth-century elections, could make up for this deficiency).[48] Yet, with the rise of mass education and the expansion of the provincial press, which devoted so many column inches to politics and elections, the means of electoral communication were rapidly evolving. Great store was set on lengthy texts, not only in *professions de foi*, but also on posters, as countless, vibrantly coloured examples in bulging archival dossiers confirm. Posters only started to include photographic material as a matter of course on the eve of the First World War, while the electoral *affiche* as an art form was a development of the interwar period, no doubt influenced by earlier patriotic propaganda. The landmark law of 29 July 1881 on freedom of the press contained a section on election posters, which permitted them to be pasted on public buildings, save those serving as administrative offices and churches, or situated next to polling stations. A 'battle to plaster the walls' rapidly ensued the moment campaigning commenced and it produced 'a great multi-coloured tapestry' of competing slogans according to one observer.[49] Excessive placarding prompted proposals to restrict the practice that came to fruition in the law of 20 March 1914.[50] This stipulated that, in future, election material would only be permitted on hoardings that were specially erected for the purpose, with the number of sites determined by the size of the commune. It has proved an enduring reform, a distinctive aspect of the street décor of French election campaigns (Figure 4.1).

The law was policed and there were fines for fly-posting, for the legislation was also intended as a means of equalizing competition; each candidate or list was to receive the same amount of space, in the same locations. While most campaigns only produced a few different posters, an intensely fought electoral contest sometimes hugely inflated this total. The celebrated duel between Barodet and Rémusat at Paris, for a seat in the National Assembly in 1873, produced a flood of material that was a foretaste of the future.[51] General Boulanger later commissioned more than thirty different posters when he bid to become a deputy for the capital in

---

[48] Georges Le Bail, *Une Élection en 1906. Miettes électorales* (Paris, 1908), 203–13, for some splendid examples, as late as 1906 in Brittany, and Huard, *Le Suffrage universel*, 278–81.
[49] Antonin Lefèvre-Pontalis, *Les Élections en Europe à la fin du XIXᵉ siècle* (Paris, 1902), vii and 30.
[50] AN C5651, Commission du Suffrage universel, 13 June 1898 for an initial proposal.
[51] Wartelle, 'L'élection Barodet', 601.

Figure 4.1 Election hoardings, 2007

In 1914 it was decided that public electoral advertising would be restricted to official hoardings which allocated the same space to each candidate or list of candidates. This example, from the town of Vichy, shows some of the twelve candidates in the presidential election of 2007.

Source: Copyright, Alamy AC455J.

1889, and half as many were designed for his opponent; a staggering total of perhaps two million copies were printed altogether. Some unprecedented and wholly exceptional expenditure was incurred as a result, bankrolled in Boulanger's case by the wealth of the duchesse d'Uzès and the pretender to the throne of France. To be sure, a Parisian campaign was always more costly to stage, but it seems that the average, overall amount spent by a contender in the 1860s was already some 10,000 francs, a sum which had risen to around 20,000 francs by the end of the century.[52] Clearly, the professional approach to electioneering was a costly one, especially as the number of contestants increased, and the personal resources mustered by the candidate remained paramount, despite the funding offered by emergent political parties. It raised the question of how more modestly endowed candidates were to compete and one radical proposal, made in 1902, was simply to prevent the wealthiest individuals from standing for the legislature.[53]

Money had become the nerve of election campaigns under the Third Republic and an unsuccessful proposal was made in 1892 that, as in Britain since 1883

---

[52] *Moniteur*, 13 Jan. 1864, 56 and Billard, *Le Métier de la politique*, 107–12.
[53] AN C7375, Modification à la loi sur la répression des fraudes, 22 Oct. 1903.

(where it proved an effective measure in curbing corruption), all candidates should be responsible for submitting accounts of electoral expenses, within pre-scribed limits.[54] The pioneering historian of electoral culture, Pilenco, bemoaned the continuing absence of any regulation in 1930, describing it as 'one of the worst scourges of the French parliamentary system'.[55] The amount of funding offered by individuals and industry had become a growing concern, with the Union des intérêts économiques, for example, financing candidates who were willing to defend private enterprise.[56] A parliamentary commission was created in 1924 to investigate the issue of campaign expenditure, but businesses proved uncoopera-tive and the inquiry was inconclusive. There was a surprising lack of regulation until as late as 1988, when a series of laws, passed during 'a bout of legislative incontinence', imposed a ceiling on expenses, which were calculated per regis-tered voter. At the same time individual donations were severely restricted and corporate funding was eventually banned, with political parties left to fund them-selves. However, a percentage of election expenses were to be reimbursed by the state, pro rata to the percentage of votes obtained, on receipt of satisfactory accounts by a Commission nationale des comptes de campagne et des finance-ments politiques.[57] This has gone a long way to creating a more level playing field between candidates, as well as reducing the influence of wealthy individuals or organizations.

The authorities in France have always covered the administrative cost of a poll, unlike their British counterparts, but they were slow to accept responsibility for candidates' basic expenses. It was only in 1945, faced with a post-war dearth of paper, that they finally agreed to foot the bill for printing and distributing ballot papers, plus two circulars for each candidate or list, and the production of three different posters for the public election hoardings. However, a deposit of 20,000 francs was required in return, which was only reimbursed if a threshold set at 5 per cent of the votes cast was met.[58] Of course, the nature of political communica-tion was constantly evolving and, while they were immensely proud of their mas-tery of the written word, French politicians were slow to grasp the opportunities offered by radio and television, which initially benefited those in government. The subsequent allocation of broadcasting time to political parties during elec-tions proved relatively easy to organize on an equitable basis, whereas regulating use of the Internet today is proving altogether more troublesome. Dubbed by some a 'cyber-democracy', because it empowers citizens to circulate ideas freely, and readily engage in political networking, the provenance and funding of much

---

[54] JO Annexe 2452, 12 Dec. 1892, 2529–30.
[55] Pilenco, Les Moeurs électorales du suffrage universel, 215 and 299.
[56] Jean-Noël Jeanneney, François de Wendel en République. L'argent et le pouvoir, 1914–1940 (Paris, 2004), 440 et seq.
[57] Abel François and Éric Phélippeau, Le Financement de la vie politique (Paris, 2015).
[58] JO, 19 Aug. 1945, 5156.

digital publicity actually raises serious questions of hidden influence and minimal accountability. The circulation of huge amounts of material at election time, at relatively little cost, has in fact produced a deluge of propaganda, targeted at specific groups and individuals. Since its origins are difficult to identify, and its content hard to verify, this recent, unregulated development is much less conducive to more informed electoral choice than its producers like to pretend. It also raises the vexed issue of corruption.

Electoral Fraud

Trompe qui peut! Playing the system is inseparable from any set of regulations, which are frequently at odds with ingrained habits, and there was never a shortage of guidance on how to engage in electoral malpractice. As early as the Revolution of 1789, advice was published on the seduction of rural voters, who were depicted as especially gullible and easily led, to be intercepted en route to the electoral assemblies, or entertained at hostelries, where they could be 'treated' with food and drink.[59] The tricks of the trade were also revealed by Benjamin Constant, a deputy under the Restoration, who described the 'fake news' that was concocted to damage rival candidates, suggesting that they were withdrawing from the contest (a claim always made on the eve of polling, so the opponent would find it hard to riposte), or that they were so lacking in support that a vote for them would be wasted.[60] Reasoning that the devil should not monopolize the best ruses, one Catholic publishing house produced a comprehensive manual for bending the rules at the turn of the twentieth century, when the Church was deeply embroiled in electoral conflict. Suggested ploys included declaring candidatures at the last minute, so as to wrong-foot opponents, demanding the invalidation of hostile ballot papers on a variety of trivial grounds, and making a series of objections regarding irregularities which might overturn an unfavourable outcome.[61]

Of course, the boundaries between legitimate and illegitimate practices were decidedly porous when it came to the development of *la cuisine électorale*, in France as elsewhere. Norms were always shifting and can only be understood within their particular context, because definitions of fraud are historically constructed, while corruption and custom are often intertwined. In the nineteenth century there was frequent collusion between candidates and voters, who were eager to take the inducements on offer, even anticipating them, since the vote was

---

[59] BNF Lb^{39} 10166, *Petit traité de la cabale, ou l'art d'accaparer les suffrages* (no place, 1791).
[60] Benjamin Constant, 'L'entretien d'un électeur avec lui-même', in *Choix de textes politiques*, ed. Olivier Pozzo di Borgo (Utrecht, 1965), 89–90.
[61] Anon., *Trucs électoraux* (Paris, 1897).

regarded as a transaction. Conversely, much of the electioneering analysed above was considered improper during the initial experiment with mass voting, not to mention under the *Ancien Régime*. Yet such behaviour is quite acceptable today, when electoral malpractice is wrongly thought to be a thing of the past. In fact, stuffing the ballot box, or personation, may still occur, and French deputies were outraged by the 'massive' fraud of this sort uncovered in the municipal elections of 1983, for example.[62] Yet its extent is notoriously hard to measure, because protests against corrupt practices may simply reflect the willingness or ability to complain. What has been called the 'moralization' of voting paradoxically resulted in more evidence of transgression as it became less tolerable and more contestable, while corruption was deemed an inadmissible vice in a virtuous democratic context.

The tradition of voting in a public assembly, which lasted until 1848, was in fact quite an effective means of deterring the falsification of electoral returns. It posed other problems, notably those of physical intimidation, while the various receptacles employed as ballot boxes were notoriously insecure, but the collective dimension did make blatantly rigging the polls more difficult. The absence of the glare of publicity certainly allowed the first Napoleonic regime to inflate the figures in at least three of its four 'plebiscites'. This is not to call the overall result into question in 1799, 1802 and 1804, since there were few negative votes, simply to query the magnitude of the positive majority. Individual voting on a register kept by mayors or other officials, over several days, was wide open to abuse, since there was nothing to prevent the addition of the names of illiterate voters without their knowledge and, when this produced a turnout of over 100 per cent, there is good reason to be more than suspicious. Indeed, in 1804 the prefect of the Deux-Sèvres decided that insufficient numbers had voted, and supplementary registers were opened across the department so that more votes could be collected, but they contained many names which had already appeared in the course of the original exercise; signatures were simply aggregated, regardless.[63] The counting of votes to create lists of notables, in 1801 and 1802, when individuals submitted their ballot papers to a public official, was similarly open to malfeasance, in the absence of any monitoring of the delivery and processing of *bulletins*. Apart from numerous protests surrounding the outcome, it is significant that little documentation has survived from this short-lived experiment which dispensed with the assembly mechanism.

However, fraud did not stop at the locality, and it is more demonstrable at departmental and ministerial levels as returns from Napoleonic 'plebiscites' were collated and declared. In an effort to show solid endorsement of the Constitution of the Year VIII (1799), in the wake of the coup d'état of Brumaire, the ministry of

[62] *JO*, 24 Nov. 1988, 2734.
[63] AN BII 834A and 834B, Registres de vote des Deux-Sèvres, an XII.

the interior hugely inflated the returns. Painstaking research by Claude Langlois almost two centuries later demonstrated that real turnout was little more than half of what was claimed.[64] Since then I have uncovered evidence of falsification of the votes taken in the Year X (1802) and in the Year XII (1804). The former genuinely yielded a substantial increase in turnout 1799, while the latter indicated a slight decline in enthusiasm when Napoleon became hereditary emperor two years later, something that servants of the regime were clearly anxious to hide.[65] I lacked the stamina to conduct an overall verification of millions of votes, but the prefect of the Seine-Inférieure was a serial offender, while other colleagues imitated his manipulation of the figures in 1804 before they dispatched them to Paris. A glance at the crude alterations made in the Pyrénées-Orientales, where eight votes on one register became 508 and seven votes on another 715, would have immediately revealed the deception, but the parliamentary commission which collated the results either overlooked or ignored it.

The return to voting in assemblies after 1802, aside from a further, apparently more reliable plebiscite return in 1815, rendered fraudulent practice of this sort far less feasible in future. The restored Bourbon monarchy thus turned instead to manipulating voter registration as a means of influencing the outcome. Numbers eligible to vote at the electoral colleges actually fell after 1817, since prefects were encouraged to obstruct the inscription of potential liberal voters. Copious fiscal documentation was required, and electors were given little time to present their credentials, while the accompanying duty of jury service was deliberately allocated to likely opponents of the government in order to put others off registering. The administration did its best to make the process as difficult as possible, by refusing to acknowledge the age of white-haired citizens who failed to produce a birth certificate, for instance. Another tactic was to delay posting the register in public, where individuals were obliged to check their inclusion by reading a miniscule type-face on placards pasted high on walls (prompting a famous caricature of an aspiring voter climbing a ladder armed with a magnifying glass).[66] It was only as a result of determined campaigning by a society called Aide-toi et le ciel t'aidera, founded by liberals, that steps were taken towards making more reliable lists in 1828, which immediately yielded 15,000 additional electors.[67] Progress was consolidated under the July Monarchy and the English observer, Bodley, later commended the system of registration by the authorities in France as 'so simple and so inexpensive as to compel the admiration and envy of the

---

[64] Claude Langlois, 'Le plébiscite de l'an VIII ou le coup d'État du 18 pluviôse an VIII', *AhRf* (1972), 43–65, 231–46, and 390–415.

[65] Malcolm Crook, 'Confiance d'en bas, manipulation d'en haut: la pratique plébiscitaire sous Napoléon (1799–1815)', in Bourdin et al. (eds), *L'Incident électoral*, 82–3.

[66] Charléty, *La Restauration*, 106, 'Ah ! Je n'y suis pas!'

[67] Jean-Paul Charnay, *Les Scrutins politiques en France de 1815 à 1962. Contestations et invalidations* (Paris, 1964), 17 and Kent, *The Election of 1827*, 26–32.

inhabitants of the United Kingdom'.[68] However, he did cite a scandalous case of lists being falsified at Toulouse in 1894, by the inclusion of nomadic canal workers; dealing with mobile elements in the population would remain a perennial problem.[69]

Treating and Bribery

Following the advent of a mass franchise in 1848, the main focus of corrupt practices shifted from manipulating the outcome of the ballot, or electoral registration, to influencing the choices voters made. At Nantes in the eighteenth century there were already allegations that lower-class voters were given money or drink in return for their support.[70] The revolutionary leader Barnave might claim in 1791 that across the Channel 'elections were decided by gallons of beer', but the French had little need of British encouragement to adopt what was described as 'treating' by the latter, and commonly called a *rastel* by the former, after a dialect word for eating and drinking freely.[71] 'Soaking' the electorate was a widespread feature of societies where hospitality remained an important obligation and thus it became part of the pathology of democracy. As comments from the south-western department of the Tarn suggested in 1898, 'Sad to say, the use of alcohol has long characterized electoral practice. For many voters it is the sine qua non for obtaining their vote.' Another agent added: 'if there is plenty to drink, then all is well', for what was regarded as a 'dry' election would surely lead to abstention.[72] Bars served as campaign headquarters, so it was only to be expected that *bulletins* should be accepted in return for a beverage. Moreover, these practices were tolerated up to a certain level, especially when all sides were involved, or they appeared to have made little difference to the outcome. Such complicity resulted in a relativist as opposed to normative perspective, and by no means all cases of treating were contested.

Nineteenth-century, mass elections were thus vibrant festive occasions when it was difficult to distinguish between sociability and corruption. They were also habitually regarded as involving a trade-off between voters and those seeking their support, with the latter expected to display generosity, outside as well as during the polling period.[73] After all, largesse was routinely offered by notables to members of their communities, with no obvious electoral strings attached, though always implying a sense of authority and reciprocity. Baron Mackau, like

---

[68] Bodley, *France*, ii, 63.
[69] Bodley, *France*, ii, 126–9; Challeton, *Cent ans d'élections*, iii, 340–1; and Paul Leroy-Beaulieu, *Un Chapitre des moeurs électorales en France, dans les années 1889 et 1890* (Paris, 1890).
[70] Saupin, 'La réforme des élections municipales', 654.
[71] *AP*, 1ere série, XXIX, 367, 11 Aug. 1791.   [72] Cited in Huard, *Le Suffrage universel*, 290.
[73] Pourcher, *Les Maîtres de granit*, 233.

his wife, was routinely involved in almsgiving, sponsoring school prize-giving, and supporting village fetes.[74] The marquis de Solages could plausibly claim that he was only responding to frequent inquiries from constituents when he offered them jobs with his mining company.[75] Promises of administrative posts, decorations, and favours were also made according to this transactional view of voting. As conservatives feared, the entry into the electoral arena of moneyed contenders, who lacked any social capital but wielded big wallets, only exacerbated the tendency: the banker who stood for election at Langres in 1842 was accordingly disqualified for reimbursing electors' travel expenses. By the end of the nineteenth century bribery had become less discriminating: Déguignet, that insubordinate Breton peasant, claimed that royalist agents were touring the countryside at election-time, 'their pockets stuffed full of hundred-sous coins', which they dispensed along with 'cigars and *guin-ardent* (brandy)'.[76] Money might well be exchanged surreptitiously with a handshake, following the receipt of a ballot paper.[77] Only with the advent of party programmes did the competition became more a matter of ideology and less a question of material goods yet, as late as 1924, drawing on his substantial fortune, the *candidat porte-monnaie*, baron Rothschild, was still staging a free-spending 'potlatch' campaign in the Hautes-Alpes.[78]

There were also bribes aimed at whole communities rather than individuals, most famously in the so-called 'railway elections', which were a source of particular controversy under the July Monarchy. An especially celebrated case involved the banker, Jacques Laffitte, who offered to link Louviers, the seat of the constituency he was contesting, to the line from Paris to Rouen, entirely at his own expense. Laffitte claimed he was merely trying to stimulate the local economy and did not regard the large sums he was promising to spend in 1843 as tantamount to corruption. Many deputies thought exactly the opposite, regarding such behaviour as an abuse of his fortune; just as the British had invented railways, so they were exporting their 'shameful electoral habits' along with them. The issue was cast in moral terms and, with the honour of the chamber allegedly at stake, Laffitte's victory was annulled without an inquiry; the electoral assembly at Louviers had, after all, operated in a regular fashion.[79]

Ministerial candidates were equally well-placed to exploit such possibilities. According to the *procureur général* at Montpellier, the electors of Pézenas informed the prefect of the Hérault that he could propose whomsoever he liked for election in 1846, even his horse if he wished, provided the railway passed through their town.[80] The rewards in question were not always so exalted: under

[74] Phélippeau, *L'Invention de l'homme politique moderne*, 49.
[75] Trempé, 'Une campagne électorale', 487.   [76] Déguignet, *Mémoires*, 336.
[77] AN C7305, Enquête sur l'élection de la 1ère circonscription de Guingamp, 27 Apr. 1902.
[78] Dompnier, 'La clef des urnes', 251–2.   [79] *Moniteur*, 21 Jan. 1844, 117–19.
[80] Tudesq, 'Les comportements électoraux', 117.

the Second Empire, a mayor in the Loir-et-Cher urged inhabitants not to forget government aid to the poor, the parish church and, above all, the installation of a fire hydrant, when it came to voting.[81] What the Americans called 'pork-barrel politics' remained much in evidence under the Third Republic too, as a new set of incumbents exploited the fruits of office and 'electoral manna' continued to rain down. As one mayor in the conservative Lozère confessed in 1889, 'This commune cannot but be republican, first of all because it is very poor and secondly because it has constant recourse to the generosity of the State when flooding occurs on its uneven terrain.'[82] Democracy had to come to terms with grassroots realities.

Intimidation

As late as 1906 it was claimed by a French jurist that the number of electors who could cast their vote freely remained extremely small.[83] This was doubtless an exaggeration, but the departmental council in the Vienne would write to the Chamber of Deputies the following year complaining about the unseemly pressure applied to many voters who risked their livelihoods if they failed to use a particular ballot paper.[84] There were longstanding constraints on electoral liberty which took a variety of forms, most of them derived from social circumstances. In Corsica, the republican *commissaire* echoed his prefectoral predecessor when, in 1848, he bemoaned the fact that communal pressure rather than political preferences had determined voters' choices. The island does indeed remain a byword for electoral corruption, yet this was to misunderstand how French society as a whole functioned in the nineteenth century.[85] Voting on the mainland was also as much a social as a political act, not least in rural communities, where unanimous, collective voting was equally the norm at this time, and the expression of individual opinion was as much inconceivable as impractical. As Alain Garrigou repeatedly emphasizes in his key text, *Le Vote et la vertu*, electoral behaviour could not be divorced from the wider web of day-to-day relationships; the voter was a flesh-and-blood inhabitant, not an abstract individual.[86] The influence exerted by notables in elections was regarded on all sides as both natural and unavoidable, and deference should not be simply equated with abject dependence, since voters expected to be rewarded for the electoral services they rendered.

---

[81] Georges Dupeux, *Aspects de l'histoire sociale et politique du Loir-et-Cher 1848–1914* (Paris, 1962), 390.
[82] Jones, 'An improbable democracy', 556.   [83] Cited in Huard, *Le Suffrage universel*, 286.
[84] AN C7375, Conseil général de la Vienne, 24 Sept. 1907.
[85] AN F1cIII Corse 5, Commissaire au ministre, 1 May 1848.
[86] Garrigou, *Histoire sociale*, 80ff.

However, as Nathalie Dompnier suggests in her comprehensive doctoral study of electoral fraud, as the nineteenth century wore on many notables were no longer able to rely on their traditional authority to obtain the electoral outcome they desired.[87] They were obliged instead to employ threats to livelihood, alongside treating and bribery, adopting practices which reflected their waning hegemony and were also mirrored in rising numbers of electoral protests. Rural tenants and labourers might, therefore, face eviction or loss of employment if they failed to vote for designated candidates, while owners of enterprises were equally prone to intimidate members of their workforce. Marching voters to the polls in serried ranks, so-called 'brigading', may have been declining by the turn of the twentieth century but, at Roubaix in the Nord in 1898, textile workers were still being summoned to bars, where they were issued with a ballot paper then taken to vote in small groups by foremen. Industrialists like the Schneiders, at their Le Creusot steel works in the Saône-et-Loire, exerted similar authority. Ballot papers for their chosen parliamentary representative—a member of the family for many years between 1842 and 1914—were to be collected at the bureau de vote, under the watchful eye of a company official, and disobedience could lead to dismissal. One employee denounced 'a powerfully organized tyranny', while others were quite willing to support candidates who would uphold the interests of the company and thus secure jobs. Nonetheless, socialists were making converts among the labour force after 1900 and in the election of 1914 the arms-manufacturer Schneider was defeated by an anti-militarist.[88]

Physical intimidation, evident during the Revolution of 1789, when voters might be 'dissuaded' from attending an electoral assembly, or in 1848 when arrival at the chef-lieu de canton could be met by a reception committee demanding presentation of a ballot paper for its approval, was also generally declining towards the twentieth century. Yet it had not completely disappeared: in 1893, for instance, at Brive in the Limousin, a group of local thugs called the Mamelouks were allegedly threatening individuals outside the polling-station and deterring them from entry if they revealed the 'wrong' voting intentions.[89] Yet by that point violent behaviour had generally shifted from the voting space itself to the public meetings that preceded election-day, where affrays or even fatalities might occur.[90] Such incidents were especially common at times of crisis, such as the Dreyfus affair in 1898, or the worsening economic and political situation in 1936. In that sense elections could still encourage rather than inhibit political violence,

---

[87] Dompnier, 'La Clef des urnes', 227–32.

[88] Michel Offerlé, 'Les Schneider en politique', in Les Schneider. Le Creusot. Une famille, une entreprise, une ville (1836–1960) (Paris, 1995), 289–305.

[89] AN C5573, Enquête sur l'élection dans la première circonscription de Brive (Corrèze), 20 Apr. 1893.

[90] Yves Déloye and Olivier Ihl, 'La civilité électorale; vote et forclusion de la violence en France', in Déloye and Ihl, L'Acte de vote, 371–3.

contrary to one of the main justifications for the vote. Celebrating the electoral outcome, like protesting against it, was equally a source of tension that might spill over into disorder. Under the constitutional monarchies, during the first half of the nineteenth century, for example, liberal successes were often accompanied by the illumination of houses, firework displays, and cavalcades around the town which put the authorities on edge. Indeed, a legitimist victory at Nantes in 1846 led to assaults on some of the winner's associates, two of whom had to seek refuge in a private house in order to escape an even worse fate.[91] In 1869, the announcement of the defeat of the radical candidate, Henri Rochefort, at Paris, actually led to wholesale rioting which ended in the pillage of shops and the destruction of property over the next four days.

A more metaphysical form of intimidation was constituted by clerical *ingérence*, or meddling in elections, frequently highlighted in official reports, as well as in subsequent complaints. The elector in the Finistère who allegedly cast his vote with the words, 'here is a mortal sin', was evidently mocking the clergy, but faithful Catholics were generally loath to disobey priestly instructions when they went to the polls.[92] In April 1848, travelling to vote in the *chef-lieu de canton* had turned into something of a pilgrimage following Easter mass and there were inevitably accusations of *curés* foisting ballot papers onto members of their flocks.[93] For his part, the *commissaire* in the Hérault claimed that pulpits were being turned into political rostrums from which priests recommended particular candidates. The text defining the status of members of the clergy in the Organic Articles attached to the Concordat of 1801 was bitterly disputed: those sympathetic to the Church argued that members of the clergy were citizens entitled to engage in political activity, while republicans maintained that, paid by the state, they were civil servants who should remain strictly neutral. Ministers for religious affairs adhered to the latter interpretation and, in 1885 for instance, just prior to legislative elections, the current post-holder reminded bishops that their parish priests were entitled to liberty of opinion and the vote but, on account of the public authority they had been granted, they should desist from involvement in any electioneering.[94] The minister subsequently asked for feedback on clerical machinations, but *ingérence* was always difficult to prove and officials struggled to come up with much convincing evidence. The prefect in the Haute-Garonne was thus obliged to conclude that priests must be engaged in secret manoeuvres which had escaped their detection.

The republican press was rather less restrained, like the *Petit Nord*, which suggested that the clergy had an insatiable appetite for interference, issuing threats to withdraw poor relief, urging wives to desert the marital bed, and using the

---

[91] Tudesq, 'Les comportements électoraux', 118.   [92] Le Bail, *Une Élection en 1906*, 119.
[93] AN F19 5604, for a dossier on the spring elections of 1848.
[94] AN F19 5617, Ministre des cultes aux évêques, 1 Sept. 1885.

confessional to threaten damnation if parishioners failed to vote for 'bons candi-dats'. Around the turn of the twentieth century rising tension between Church and state was turning priestly intervention in the electoral process into an obses-sion among some politicians. It was a major issue in the general election of 1902 and prompted an inquiry into the matter between the two rounds of voting.[95] The ensuing report revealed that *ingérence* was both more limited and less effective than anti-clericals liked to believe, its alleged incidence reflecting the religious geography of France, more evident in 'faithful' areas and vice-versa in those of weaker practice. The overwhelming prejudice of members of the prefectoral corps towards the Church in areas where it remained strong was laid bare when one of them responded: 'What strikes me above all is the enormous and irresistible influence of the clergy, which is allied with the native coarseness and brutality of the Lozériens, who are the wildest of fanatics...'.[96] Protests would continue unabated; in a cantonal election in 1907 the *curé* of Solignac (Haute-Loire) was accused of openly declaring from the pulpit that 'If you vote for the republican candidate you are committing a deadly sin for which there is no absolution.'[97] The controversy gradually subsided as passions cooled and Catholicism continued to lose ground in society. Nevertheless, even after the Second World War, prefects were still anxiously perusing diocesan publications for signs of priestly electoral injunctions.

Administrative pressure undoubtedly constituted the major form of electoral intimidation in nineteenth-century France. As Chapter 3 has demonstrated, the right of the regime to indicate its preferred candidates was generally conceded, but intervention in the election to support them, through various forms of 'pres-sion' (like material incentives), was certainly not. Government and prefects were keen to stress that they were merely acting to 'enlighten voters without curtailing their liberty'. However, they were constantly accused of overstepping the mark and it was frequently asserted that their electoral intervention had deeply dis-torted the will of the electorate in a supposedly representative system.[98] During an important debate on the matter under the July Monarchy, in 1843, the minister of the interior was upbraided for allegedly informing a prefect that he had carte blanche to combat an opposing candidate and that 50,000 francs were being placed at his disposal for this purpose.[99] Official candidatures were easily assimi-lated to corruption by critics because, as Ernest Picard eloquently argued in 1864, the administration mobilized its resources on their behalf and gave public

[95] Bertrand Joly, 'L'ingérence cléricale et les élections législatives de 1902', in Bourdin et al. (eds), *L'Incident électoral*, 205–36.
[96] Cited by Joly in Bourdin et al. (eds), *L'Incident électoral*, 219.
[97] Rivet, *La Vie politique*, 317.
[98] Louis de Cormenin (under the pseudonym Timon), *Ordre du jour sur la corruption électorale et parlementaire* (Paris, 1846), 12.
[99] *Moniteur*, 5 May 1843, 1008.

servants little option but to engineer a profoundly unequal contest.[100] Prefects financed and organized the official candidate's campaign, but still more objectionable were the measures they and their subordinates took to discredit or inhibit opponents' campaigns. In 1852, for example, it was publicly announced at Nantua, in the Ain, that the official candidate was personally endorsed by Louis-Napoleon, who had accordingly rejected the other contenders.[101] Administrators also made it difficult for opposition candidates to find a printer for their ballot papers, while innkeepers were threatened with the loss of their liquor licences if they allowed them to use their premises. Moreover, while official candidates enjoyed exclusive use of the *affiche blanche*, normally reserved for government proclamations, their opponents would find posters torn down, agents arrested, and circulars censored.[102]

Jules Ferry claimed that growing dissent goaded the government to take administrative pressure to unprecedented heights in the parliamentary elections of 1863 and he produced an extensively documented inventory of its manifold interventions.[103] It might be dubiously claimed that ordinary electors were exercising a free vote, but absolutely no latitude was allowed for public servants. Now that all voting was taking place in the commune, appointed mayors played a crucial role, especially in rural areas; as a justice of the peace in the Haute-Garonne wrote: 'The mayor holds the electors in his hands.' It was he who oversaw the distribution of ballot papers for official candidates, along with voters' identity cards, as well as presiding at the polling station where further influence could be deployed. Mayors were instructed to make official candidates' ballot papers available in the polling station, but no others, and to ensure a high turnout: 'Exert every effort, M. le maire, to ensure that all your electors, without exception, cast their votes…Everything depends on your activity and resolve', wrote the sub-prefect of Sarreguemines (Moselle).[104] Abstention was equated with opposition and voters were instructed to ratify the government's choice: as the mayor of Chaufailles (Saône-et-Loire) implored his *administrés*: 'Do not stay at home; come and use the ballot paper for the candidate that I have recommended in your best interests.'[105] Magistrates themselves were intimidated by threats of dismissal if they proved reluctant to toe the line; purges of personnel always preceded and succeeded the electoral campaign, and a veritable 'massacre des maires' occurred in 1863.

---

[100] *Moniteur*, 12 Jan. 1864, 80–1.

[101] AN C1336, Sous-préfet de Nantua (Ain), 28 Feb. 1852.

[102] Bernard Leclère and Vincent Wright, *Les Préfets du Second Empire* (Paris, 1973), 65.

[103] Ferry, *La Lutte électorale, passim*.

[104] Philippe Hamman, 'La notabilité dans tous ses états? Alexandre de Geiger à Sarreguemines, un patron en politique sous le Second Empire', *Rh*, 622 (2002), 331.

[105] AN F1cII 98, Prefectoral circulars, Basses-Alpes, 19 Feb. and Hautes-Alpes, 22 Feb. 1852, and Ferry, *La Lutte électorale*, 146.

Mayors were in turn aided by a series of local personnel who were also expected to influence polling in the government's favour, from school-teachers to postmen, *garde-champêtres* and even road-menders. An internal memorandum, apparently written for the minister of the interior in 1864, estimated that there were over 100,000 'minor civil servants', whose attachment to the government could be used to its electoral advantage.[106] More than one critical commentator used the image of an army of public employees marching into the electoral battle in serried ranks behind the official candidate.[107] Under the Second Empire there was some debate over the dragooning of teachers, whom opponents argued should not be turned into electoral agents, but the rector of the Academy in the Charente-Inférieure insisted that, as *fonctionnaires*, they were obliged to use their influence on behalf of the government's chosen individual.[108] As the inspector of the Academy in the Côte-d'Or, responsible for education staff, stated: 'Not to support the emperor is to abandon him, while hostility would be a grave error...'.[109] At the inception of the regime, the academic rector at Blois informed teachers that it was insufficient 'to insert a positive vote in the ballot box'; educators also needed to exert their influence to persuade others to vote in the same manner.[110] In fact, by no means all teachers were the republican sympathizers that conservatives liked to imagine and there are some striking examples of *instituteurs* urging parents of their pupils to support the official candidates, or decking out schools used as polling stations in imperial regalia.[111] In May 1870, the rector of the Academy of Strasbourg publicly congratulated university professors and school teachers on the assistance they had given the Emperor in obtaining the favourable outcome of that year's plebiscite.

Combating Corruption

The catalogue of corrupt practices in nineteenth-century France was revealed by a well-worn process of contestation, which commenced with a parliamentary inquiry and might conclude with the annulment of an elected deputy's mandate. This means of exposing corruption has been employed to measure the extent of malpractice but, while shining a light on the variety of forms it assumed, this course of action more accurately reflects the willingness to protest. Early in 1852, for example, the newly installed regime of Louis-Napoleon ensured the election of official candidates for the *Corps législatif* by employing punitive measures

---

[106]   Price, *The French Second Empire*, 107.
[107]   Cyprien de Bellissen, *Le Suffrage universel dans le département de l'Ariège* (Paris, 1869), 11.
[108]   F17 2682, *L'Opinion nationale*, press cutting, 20 Jan. 1865 (dossier on the teaching profession and elections under the Second Empire).
[109]   Charnay, *Les Scrutins politiques*, 50.   [110]   Price, *The French Second Empire*, 108.
[111]   Zeldin, *The Political System of Napoleon III*, 86–7.

against its opponents, but demoralized republicans were in no position to object and just one poll was investigated. By contrast, challenges rose sharply as resistance at the polls mounted and, in 1863, roughly a third of the results were contested.[112] Moreover, the incidence of invalidation was the result of a highly politicized procedure, rather than an objective evaluation of electoral misconduct. For in keeping with long-established custom, dating back to the *Ancien Régime*, it was the legislature which vetted its members' credentials, before the incumbent majority delivered its verdict. Deputies were not acting as a tribunal to determine whether or not grave infractions had occurred, but deciding in partisan fashion if certain colleagues should be allowed to keep their seats or not.

In fact, the elected individual remained in post until the matter was decided, and ineligibility was not a consequence of annulment for the individual concerned. Under the two-round ballot system, the ensuing re-run of the election became known as the 'troisième tour', and the disqualified deputy could immediately stand again, though legislation was frequently, but unsuccessfully, proposed to prevent this happening.[113] Indeed, apart from exceptional cases like that of 1877, when very few of the seventy-six deputies who were deprived of their seats were re-elected, it was not at all unusual for voters to confirm their original choice.[114] The election of Laffitte at Louviers in the 1840s, mentioned above, was invalidated no less than four times on account of his 'railway bribe', but he finally took his seat when he was re-elected on a fifth occasion: those who had been corrupted stuck with their corrupter, as the historian Jean-Paul Charnay puts it.[115] Another egregious example is furnished by Daniel Wilson, who was indicted for the sale of honours, a scandal which forced the resignation of his father-in-law, President Jules Grévy. Wilson was eventually acquitted, only for his return to the Chamber in 1893 to be invalidated for bribery on a grand scale, yet he was subsequently re-elected for the same constituency. Commenting on the continuation of this phenomenon in the twentieth century, *Le Monde* suggested that 'it was only confirming a well-established fact, namely that the electorate is not usually inclined to welcome invalidations, even when these are justified, and it rarely alters its verdict.'[116] Apart from dogged loyalty to a particular candidate, such resolve also stems from voters' sense of their own sovereignty, so firmly entrenched in French electoral culture. Although numerous proposals had been made to remove the power of disqualification from deputies in the past, only

[112] Anceau, 'Les irrégularités', 121–40.
[113] AN 7305, Proposition sur l'inéligibilité des députés invalidés, 7 Apr. 1903 and Benoist, *Pour la réforme électorale*, 293–4.
[114] Jacqueline Lalouette, 'Une vague exceptionnelle d'invalidations: l'épilogue des élections législatives de 1877', in Bourdin et al. (eds), *L'Incident électoral*, 159–64.
[115] Charnay, *Les Scrutins politiques*, 117–18.   [116] *Le Monde*, 24 Feb. 1959.

under the Fifth Republic was the task of adjudicating contested results remitted to judges in the Constitutional Council.[117]

A similar solution was eventually agreed for what Americans baptized gerry-mandering, but which in France is described in culinary terms as 'charcutage électoral'. The allocation of parliamentary seats on a departmental basis, accord-ing to population, caused little dispute during the Revolution but, under the Bourbon Restoration, constituencies were carved out below this level.[118] By 1820 the ideal of rough parity between them was yielding to political advantage, with revision the responsibility of the ministry of the interior. In the Moselle, for example, one of four electoral arrondissements was 'sacrificed' to the opposition, in order that the other three would remain firmly in government hands. The Second Empire was rather less constrained. In 1869, boundaries were altered in thirty-six departments, but demographic developments only justified changes in a quarter of them, and vigorous protests were made about 'chopping up the (gen-erally hostile) urban electorate'.[119] Morny had already declared his views on the subject in 1852, when single-member constituencies were once again installed in place of *scrutin de liste*: 'You must understand the extent to which a more or less ingenious division influences the outcome of an election.'[120] Topography clearly had to be taken into account in shaping boundaries, not least in thinly populated mountainous departments, but apparently technical decisions were always coloured by political calculation. It was 1986 before the task of defining uninomi-nal constituencies, re-established under the Fifth Republic, was finally entrusted to the more impartial Conseil constitutionnel.[121]

Legislation was the major means of combating electoral corruption, by pre-scribing codes of conduct and imposing precise penalties for malpractice. Whereas sanctions had remained vague under the *Ancien Régime*, the advent of a mass franchise in the Revolution prompted the first steps in this direction. In 1790, voters were required to take the following oath as they cast their ballot papers: 'I swear to name only those whom I have consciously chosen as the most worthy of public office, without having been influenced by gifts, promises, requests or threats.'[122] The price for contravention was immediate expulsion from the electoral assembly. In the Constitution of 1795 the consequences escalated: article 32 stated that 'Any citizen convicted of having bought or sold a vote will be excluded from both primary and communal assemblies (likewise the departmen-tal colleges, article 40), and from all public offices for a period of twenty years; if a

[117] AN C7305, Proposition sur la vérification des pouvoirs, 18 June 1903 and Antonin Lefèvre-Pontalis, *La Validation des élections* (Paris, 1894).
[118] Kent, *The Election of 1827*, 68–72. Though called arrondissements they no longer coincided with the administrative divisions of that name.
[119] Charnay, *Les Scrutins politiques*, 49 and *Moniteur*, 3 Apr. 1869, 450–1.
[120] Lagouyete, 'Candidature officielle', ii, 381.   [121] Offerlé, *Un Homme, une voix?*, 46–7.
[122] Décret sur la forme du scrutin, 28 May 1790.

repeat offence is committed, he will be banned in perpetuity.' Following the introduction of universal male suffrage, the electoral law of 1849 stipulated a prison
sentence as well as a fine for electoral bribery or intimidation, as well as criminal-
izing false registration and repeated voting, or tampering with ballot papers.
These categories were reiterated and reinforced by an act of 1914, 'for the repression of corrupt practices in the course of elections', which added the offence of
suborning a community by offering collective benefits and administrative favours,
besides indicating that if the offender was a public official, then the penalty would
be doubled.

Regulation also served to define corrupt practices and, by the end of the nineteenth century, there was a competing narrative of electoral integrity at work. The
consolidation of universal male suffrage inculcated a reverence for democracy
that equated fraud with sacrilege, because it was negating the sovereign will of the
people. A secular moralization of politics was occurring which stressed not just
the citizen's duty to vote, but also to observe and uphold the purity of the process,
summed up perfectly in the title of one brochure: *Électeurs, surveillez les urnes!*[123]
It was also addressed by civic education for a democratic political system, con-
veyed in the electoral guides that proliferated around the turn of the twentieth
century and, above all, in the school textbooks written to cater for the advent of
compulsory primary education in the 1880s. As one author, Paul Bert, put it,
'There is nothing more shameful than to purchase votes, apart from selling one's
own.'[124] Or as Alfred Mézières intoned, 'the voter must not yield to any attempt
whatsoever to intimidate or corrupt him.'[125] The ideal citizen-elector, nurtured by
a society that was developing a culture of personal dignity and independence, was
constituted by an autonomous individual who made his own, disinterested political choices, in the orderly setting of the polling station.[126]

Conclusion

Technologies, such as the envelope and the *isoloir*, have also played their part in
making elections freer and fairer, as Chapter 5 will suggest. Violence, intimidation, and treating have become rare following the imposition of a fully secret ballot in France in 1914, while the falsification of polling returns has been rendered
more difficult by the provision of secure ballot boxes. Prevention has proved more
effective than punishment, though if legislation imposed severe penalties for
fraud, it also helped to outline acceptable conduct. In turn, civic education has

---

[123] *Électeurs, surveillez les urnes* (Villefranche-de-Rouergue, 1902).
[124] Paul Bert, *L'Instruction civique à l'école. Notions fondamentales* (Paris, 1882), 72.
[125] Alfred Mézières, *Éducation morale et instruction civique à l'usage des Écoles primaires* (Paris,
1883), 129.
[126] 'La civilité électorale', in Déloye and Ihl, *L'Acte de vote*, 349–75.

helped to instil them by stressing the integrity of electoral behaviour. To corrupt the voter in an age of mass franchise and individual autonomy was to undermine freedom of choice and distort the electoral outcome, turning the contest into a travesty. Nonetheless, the promises made by candidates and parties today might be equated with the bribery of old, though the goods on offer are less personal than they used to be. What might have particularly alarmed citizens who voted in the past is the current extent of partisan electoral communication, bombarding the electorate at both a public and a private level; in many ways, the digital media have re-introduced the hidden persuasion of the past. However, the torrent of pre-election campaigning, like opinion polling, does halt in France on a Friday evening, to allow a day of quiet reflection before Sunday's *acte de vote*, which is now conducted calmly according to the austere ritual of the polling station. This will be the subject of the following chapter.

5

Open Secrets

From Public to Private Polling

> Each citizen will go into a private room, divided into several com-
> partments, where he can write without being seen...He will then fold
> the paper, stamp it with the national seal, and deposit his ballot in a
> closed box.
>
> Jacques-Victor Delacroix, 1795.[1]

The history of voting over the past two centuries has been marked by a general
shift from public to private polling. Indeed, the secret ballot, most famously pre-
scribed by the Universal Declaration of Human Rights in 1948, is now taken for
granted and has been adopted almost everywhere.[2] The journalist Delacroix's
proposal for a fully secure vote of this sort is a remarkable antecedent, but a fully
secure system of this sort was not implemented in France until the eve of the First
World War. To be sure, the French had led the way after 1789 by insisting on the
employment of a hand-written ballot paper, and they gradually regulated the conditions under which it was cast. However, the revolutionaries were unable to
make it wholly secret on account of widespread illiteracy and the fact that it had
to be composed under the watchful eye of officials, in a traditional assembly
where voters met to conduct their electoral business together. The resulting procedure, which endured until 1848, has been called a 'private ballot cast in public'.
Even after the advent of individual voting, following the abolition of assemblies,
and the acceptance of printed *bulletins*, the elector's choice remained something
of an 'open secret' until 1914. This chapter will examine the hotly contested issue
of casting the vote in France, which eventually culminated in a private act employing a piece of paper, inserted into an envelope in a polling booth, and then
dropped into a ballot box. Despite the invention of mechanical and then electronic voting, the great majority of French communes continue to utilize a paper
bulletin today.

---

[1] Jacques-Victor Delacroix, *Le Spectateur français pendant le gouvernement révolutionnaire* (Paris,
an IV), 232–8.
[2] Section 3, article 21.

How the French Learned to Vote: A History of Electoral Practice in France. Malcolm Crook, Oxford University Press (2021).
© Malcolm Crook. DOI: 10.1093/oso/9780192894786.003.0006

The Birth of the Ballot Paper

Before 1789, voting in elections of all sorts was characterized by enormous diversity and frequent change, but it was invariably conducted in public, in an assembly. The raising of hands was widespread and, like standing up, removing hats, and moving to one side or other of the meeting place, it was a collective gesture which often produced a highly visible degree of unanimity.[3] Oral voting, which has survived in the French habit of referring to votes as 'voix', might be expressed as an acclamation, but it could be delivered individually, out loud (à haute voix) or with a whisper. Casting balls or beans of different colours afforded greater anonymity, and there was some limited use of a written ballot. Clerics, especially those in monasteries or chapter houses, were well-versed in the latter.[4] Members of the nobility might also use a *bulletin*: in elections to the Estates General of 1614, nobles in the Auvergne submitted one, though at Meaux this customary procedure was curtailed, while at Angers a request to this effect was refused.[5] Yet even this practice was not wholly secret, because it was quite easy to determine how an individual had voted, and papers were often signed.[6] What was especially significant about this method was that, unlike the most common forms of voting, participants recorded their decisions without any direct knowledge of the choice their peers were making.

Open polling was employed for the great majority of elections in rural areas, where they continued to be held despite some reduction in the number of persons entitled to take part.[7] The classic village assembly usually eventuated in a show of hands or acclamation, with no attempt to record any figures for the generally unanimous outcome. In larger towns, on the other hand, more formal and often more complex systems were employed in order to manage competition and distribute offices by means of rotation. In the case of Poitiers, for example, oral voting was used to choose members of the town council, unless opinions were narrowly divided, in which case there was recourse to a vote by ballot.[8] At Nantes, electors quietly communicated their choices to secretaries, who entered them in a poll book, called the *piquet*, where literate participants could check that their options had been correctly inscribed.[9] At Arras, the list on which voters crossed

---

[3] Christine Guionnet, 'Vote à main levée', in Perrineau and Reynié (eds), *Dictionnaire du vote*, 942–4.

[4] Léo Moulin, 'Les origines religieuses des techniques électorales et délibératives modernes', *Politix*, 43 (1998), 113–62.

[5] Roger Chartier and Denis Richet, *Représentation et vouloir politiques. Autour des États généraux de 1614* (Paris, 1982), 132 and Yves Durand (ed.), *Cahiers de doléances des paroisses du bailliage de Troyes pour les États généraux de 1614* (Paris, 1966), 46–7.

[6] Christin, 'Disinterest, vocation and elections', 290–1.   [7] Christin, *Vox populi*, 55–65.

[8] Hilary J. Bernstein, 'The benefit of the ballot? Elections and influence in sixteenth-century Poitiers', *FHS*, 24 (2001), 621–3.

[9] *Lettres patentes de la ville de Toulon*, 1776 and Saupin, *Nantes*, 84–5.

out names of those they did not wish to see elected to municipal office was known as the *tapis*, located in the middle of the assembly. Elections at Toulon and in other Mediterranean towns were based on a combination of sortition, nomination, and the use of ballots, though not to the elaborate extent of Venice.

During the latter part of the eighteenth century, there was an effort by the French government to encourage the adoption of the 'scrutin', or vote by written ballot, and with it a greater degree of electoral uniformity across the kingdom. This procedure offered greater numerical precision, in the light of increasing prominence given to the majority principle, and it also prompted the first efforts to apply mathematics to the process of voting.[10] Yet, as so often under the *Ancien Régime*, such legislation was strongly resisted at the local level and only created further variety in a municipal system already plagued by the sale of offices and the disappearance of an electoral element altogether. Such was the sorry fate of the Laverdy reform of the larger municipalities in the mid-1760s, which had stipulated that 'ballot papers (*billets*) must be employed' at the later stages of annual elections.[11]

Nonetheless, a precedent had been set and, when fresh municipal assemblies were created by the crown at the end of the 1780s, to oversee the levy of taxes in smaller communities, the use of a written ballot was required if a majority of those present were able to read and write.[12] This experience served as a basis for debate over the question of voting for deputies to sit in the revived Estates General of 1789. Of course, the key question was whether voting there should be by order or by head, but the manner in which votes would be recorded at the preparatory elections was also discussed. When an Assembly of Notables (which had been consulted the previous year on the question of fiscal and administrative reform) was re-convened at the end of 1788 to advise on this matter, a range of opinions was expressed on the *acte de vote*. However, there was general agreement on oral voting or a show of hands at the preliminary stages—in the parishes, corporations, and urban assemblies of the third estate—then voting by written ballot at the level of the *bailliages* and *sénéchaussées*, for all three orders, when deputies were chosen to go to Versailles.[13] This was the solution inscribed in the regulatory statute of 24 January 1789, which sought, with a considerable degree of success, to impose a uniform electoral system across the kingdom.[14]

[10] Olivier Christin, 'Le lent triomphe du nombre. Les progrès de la décision majoritaire à l'époque moderne', http://www.laviedesidees.fr/Le-lent-triomphe-du-nombre.html (accessed 07/08/19). For the application of mathematics to voting in the eighteenth century, see 'Borda (Méthode de)' and 'Condorcet (Paradoxe de)', in Perrineau and Reynié (eds), *Dictionnaire du vote*, 111–12 and 226–30.
[11] *Règlement pour l'administration des principaux bourgs du royaume*, 1764, in Bordes, *La Réforme municipal*, 291.
[12] Bordes, *L'Administration provinciale*, 336.
[13] AP, 1ère série, I, 28 Nov. 1788, 430, 449, and 472.
[14] *Règlement pour l'exécution des lettres de convocation*, 24 Jan. 1789, in Armand Brette (ed.), *Recueil de documents relatifs à la convocation des États généraux de 1789*, 4 vols (Paris, 1894), i, 85.

The distinction between oral and written voting at different levels for the Estates General made practical sense since, unlike most of the delegates who gathered at the final stage, many of those attending preliminary assemblies of the third estate were illiterate. Such a solution was still being propounded, after the transformation of the Estates into a National Assembly, when Jean-Joseph Mounier set out some initial proposals for the organization of elections under the new regime.[15] Yet caution was soon swept aside and it was decided that the broad franchise adopted for future polling would be conducted entirely by means of a paper ballot, in all types of election, a commitment that marked a global turning point. Only a solitary deputy objected to its use across the board, on the eminently sensible grounds that few peasants would be able to complete their own papers.[16] The matter was re-opened when the first municipal elections were held in February 1790 and the idea that voice-voting should be permitted when more than half of those present were illiterate was reiterated.[17] Yet most deputies were determined to press ahead with the uniform system of written ballot papers, because the principle of equal citizenship was at stake, and Barnave declared there was no other way to combat the influence that habitual forms of voting would give to local notables. Under the new dispensation, electors were summoned to compose their *bulletins* in strict alphabetical order, to avoid any hint of social precedence at the polls. Scrutineers, elected by the assemblies, were made responsible for confidentially recording the preferences of those who could not complete their own.

However, it was not simply a question of writing a single name on a small piece of paper but, in many cases, compiling a whole list of names where municipal councillors or second-degree electors were concerned, not to mention the preliminary election of presiding officials. Indeed, to compound the challenge—in a bizarre, but vain endeavour to avoid cabals—these first elections involved a 'double list', in which twice as many names were to be submitted by the voter as places to be filled.[18] It is not hard to imagine the difficulty experienced by all participants in trying to recall their preferences, especially since many individuals shared the same or similar family names, let alone the problems posed when illiterate or semi-literate electors attempted to submit their ballot papers, albeit with assistance. To make matters worse, the tradition of exhaustive balloting was also retained from the past: up to three rounds of balloting in search of an absolute majority, before a relative majority sufficed at the third, or there was a run-off between the two leading contenders from round two. This lengthy and cumbersome procedure, together with the absence of declared candidatures, rendered the utilization of printed ballot papers impractical. Yet there is no indication that

---

[15] *AP*, 1ere série, VIII, 31 Aug. 1789, 524.   [16] *AP*, 1ere série, X, 25 Nov. 1789, 254.

[17] *AP*, 1ere série, XI, 2 Feb. 1790, 416.

[18] Aberdam et al. (eds), *Voter, élire pendant la Révolution française*, 153–63 for the texts.

they were seriously considered at this point; indeed, pre-written papers were strictly forbidden, though they inevitably circulated, if only to serve as *aides-mémoires* at the assemblies, where the practice was frequently denounced.

The profusion of names on every ballot paper presented further problems. In the cantonal elections of June 1790, at the rural assembly held at Parizot (Aveyron) in the southern massif central, scrutineers apologized for taking most of the day to count first-round ballot papers, which contained 'a huge variety of names, each one in a different combination'.[19] As Brissot commented, the scrutineers were made into martyrs but, even in the light of such experience and severe misgivings, the only adjustment that legislators made was to abolish the double list the following year, though one suspects that many illiterate electors were still deterred from voting by this less demanding procedure. Many *bulletins* were disqualified because the nominations inscribed on them were unclear, even in the departmental colleges, where literacy rates were much higher. Gueniffey, for example, suggests that in seven such assemblies in 1791 up to 12 per cent of ballot papers were invalidated on these grounds.[20] Small wonder that the officials presiding over the departmental assembly of the Gironde firmly instructed electors to designate their choices with names, surnames, profession, domicile, and other distinctive characteristics, albeit without great success.[21] The question of accelerating the electoral process was raised again in 1792 and, when it came to rapidly creating a National Convention in August and September, some changes were made out of necessity. The assemblies' presidents, secretaries, and scrutineers would be elected *en bloc*, and by relative majority, while the number of rounds for the personnel to be chosen was reduced from three to two. These amendments were retained for all subsequent polls, until a reversion to the status quo ante in 1798.

The Resurgence of Open Voting

However, the process of casting and counting votes remained protracted. There is thus a strong suspicion that the renewed popularity of raising hands, oral voting and even acclamation, in 1792 and 1793, at least partly stemmed from the difficulties just outlined. They were potentially inflated after the adoption of a broader franchise threatened to magnify the problems—in terms of numbers and illiteracy—though declining turnout in 1791 had ironically offered some relief from the onerous burden of administering the act of voting. Of course, there were other reasons for the partial return to voice-voting, because belief in the virtues of open polling, which would persist in some quarters for another century, had certainly not disappeared. Indeed, previous practices had probably not altogether

---

[19] AD Aveyron, IL582, PV, June 1790.   [20] Gueniffey, *Le Nombre et la raison*, 298–9.
[21] Gueniffey, *Le Nombre et la raison*, 325.

disappeared and when, much later, municipal elections were re-introduced in 1831, at least one rural commune decided to proceed in habitual fashion, because it was quicker and more in keeping with the capacity of the voters.[22] In discussing the proposal for a new constitution in the spring of 1793, Robespierre insisted on the need to expedite the electoral process, making it short and simple in order to attract rather than deter popular participation, before concluding: 'leave dissimulation and the vote by ballot to criminals and slaves: free men welcome the people as their witness...'.[23] A similar sentiment had been expressed by some members of the Assembly of Notables in 1788, who declared that open polling was 'the only honourable way to vote', rendering electors publicly responsible for their choices, which the paper ballot obscured, at least in theory.

Now it was the turn of radicals to embrace the cause, with Jean-Baptiste Louvet proclaiming in his news sheet in 1792 that it was the only means of voting 'worthy of free men'. Indeed, he continued:

> Do you wish to overcome intrigue and purify the electoral process? Then decree that it will no longer take place in mysterious circumstances; decree that voters will no longer write down their choices; decree that each person will say out loud, 'my name is as follows and I am naming such and such.'[24]

Moreover, greater transparency was demanded by participants in the increasingly influential popular movement in Paris, who had a long tradition of voting in this manner in their corporations and *quartiers*. A deputation to the Convention from various sections (electoral districts) in the capital, in October 1792, condemned the vote by ballot as favouring 'intrigue', allowing certain citizens to name on their anonymous *bulletins* individuals whom they would not dare to support openly.[25] In the late summer of 1792, after the overthrow of the constitutional monarchy, it was argued that sovereignty had reverted to the people, who had the right to decide for themselves how they elected deputies to the new constituent assembly. Legislators could, therefore, only 'invite' conformity with the law of 12 August, when they announced elections for the National Convention. A dozen departmental assemblies (out of eighty-three), including Paris, subsequently adopted voice-voting for their choice of deputies. Yet most of them were careful to preserve polling in strict alphabetical order and the number of representatives elected at the first round of voting, like the percentages of the vote they obtained, was not too different from the results of voting exclusively by ballot in 1791. The one outstanding exception to this rule was furnished by the Bouches-du-Rhône,

---

[22] Guionnet, 'Vote à main levée', in Perrineau and Reynié (eds), *Dictionnaire du vote*, 943.
[23] *Moniteur*, 13 May 1793, 584.   [24] *La Sentinelle*, 21 Aug. 1792.
[25] AN C237, Commissaires des sections de Paris à la Convention, 3 Oct. 1792.

where all deputies were elected at the first round, each with over 90 per cent of the votes cast.[26]

Not surprisingly, when a new Constitution was debated in the spring of 1793, open voting remained firmly on the agenda. The document eventually endorsed by the Convention on 24 June left the decision on how to vote up to each individual elector, by ballot paper or out loud, as he wished, adding that 'a primary assembly cannot, in any circumstances, prescribe a uniform means of voting' (article 17). Following this logic, the regulations issued when the Constitution was submitted for approval to the French people the following month left each elector free to decide how to deliver a positive or negative verdict. This was often agreed by the assembly as a whole, which might opt to raise hands or hats, or employ coloured beans as of old, as well as voting out loud, but the decision of those who chose to proceed differently was usually respected, while in a hundred or so cases, unanimous acceptance was proclaimed without any attempt at head-counting. When the exercise was repeated for the Constitution of 1795, instances of acclamation were once again in evidence, while each voter retained the right to choose 'the means of voting that suits him best'.[27]

Although it was approved in a varied fashion, this later document unambiguously stated that 'all voting will be conducted by secret ballot' (the first official use of the term).[28] By that point, the susceptibility of open voting to intimidation had become painfully apparent to many surviving members of the Convention, who tended to equate it with mob rule. Delacroix's proposal for secure, individual voting by ballot paper was formulated in this particular context, as lessons were drawn from the period of revolutionary government; disinterested choices could not be made in the midst of unruly gatherings. His unprecedented suggestion for polling booths and printed papers was not adopted, perhaps not even noticed, and certainly not discussed during the course of constitutional debate. However, it was decided that voters must be able to write in a readable fashion in the near future (see Chapter 1), though this literacy requirement would remain a dead letter because the Constitution of 1795 which prescribed it did not last long enough to allow for implementation.

The narrow, property-owning franchise introduced after 1814 meant that few, if any, electors were illiterate, but the principle of public voting resurfaced under the Restoration. Prime Minister Decazes, for example, insisted during a parliamentary debate about polling in 1820 that 'openness was the very soul of constitutional government' and that the imposition of secrecy inflicted 'a mortal injury'

---

[26] Alison Patrick, *The Men of the First Republic: Political Alignments in the National Convention of 1792* (Baltimore, MD, 1972), 163 and 180–1.

[27] Crook, *Elections*, 110–11 and 125.

[28] Constitution of 1795, article 31, in Godechot (ed.), *Les Constitutions*, 106. This was the first time the word 'secret' had been used in an official text, but the procedure for writing ballot papers was unchanged.

upon the elector; it was, moreover, 'an incentive to betrayal, an inducement to lying, a mask for falsehood and the height of political hypocrisy'.[29] He was implicitly attacking those ultra-royalists who, in 1819, had exploited the anonymity of the ballot paper to elect that infamous republican, the *abbé* Grégoire, to the Chamber, in a defiant gesture of *la politique du pire*. Other deputies were equally attracted to open voting, certainly in an ideal world, but they probably agreed with the royalist deputy Humbert de Sesmaisons that, in the current circumstances, 'upright men...have no better means of resisting undue pressure than the secret ballot.'[30] There was also an argument that those who exercised the restricted suffrage were accountable to wider society and public voting was a means of demonstrating it, but that principle was disputed by the Orleanist deputy Odilon Barrot, when he claimed in 1845 that the elector was in fact answerable only to himself.[31] This was precisely the sort of attitude that Jean-Paul Sartre was condemning when he wrote much later:

> The *isoloir* planted in the middle of the school hall or the council chamber, symbolizes all the acts of treason that an individual can commit against the groups with which he is involved. It says to everyone: 'No one can see you; you are responsible only to yourself; you are making your decision in complete secrecy and, afterwards, you can conceal your verdict or even lie about it.'[32]

During the 1860s, the jurist and politician Antonin Lefèvre-Pontalis had commended the open vote in Britain (on the eve of its disappearance there), on exactly the same grounds, insisting that the secret ballot 'sacrificed the interests of society to egotistical considerations'.[33] However, while public voting might still be advocated in some quarters, the return of a mass suffrage after 1848 had effectively signalled the end of serious debate on the subject.

A Secret Vote Cast in Public

This did not mean that the 'secret vote' was fully secure; quite the contrary. During the early 1790s, polling in an assembly, which inevitably compromised secrecy, was taken for granted. Quite apart from its customary practice, which meant that electors were familiar with this modus operandi, it was also a way of ensuring some transparency, since the casting and counting of votes was conducted in public. It was also regarded as a good means of arriving at a choice in the absence

---

[29] *Moniteur*, 20 Feb. 1820, 209.   [30] *Moniteur*, 1 May 1828, 541.
[31] *Moniteur*, 19 Mar. 1845, 653.
[32] Jean-Paul Sartre, 'Élections, pièges à cons', *Les Temps Modernes*, 318 (1973), 1.
[33] Antonin Lefèvre-Pontalis, *Les Lois et les mœurs électorales en France et en Angleterre* (Paris, 1864), 365.

of declared candidates and overt campaigning to support them. There was wide-spread belief in the alchemy of an assembly, which inclined voters towards making a common decision. Condorcet certainly felt that some discussion among voters was essential and, as Guizot later put it, if the election was not 'in some way the product of debate in an assembly...it would be easy for voters to lose their bearings, or to be forced to rely solely on a passing whim...'.[34] Even after the assembly mechanism was definitively abandoned in 1848 there remained a strong sense that the vote was an interactive as well as an individual act. In justifying a longer period of residence to qualify for the franchise, the deputy Léon Faucher asserted in 1850 that the elector 'should be influenced by the opinions and interests of those among whom he is accustomed to live', rather than just his own personal outlook.[35]

The great drawback lay in the lengthy process that assemblies entailed, exacerbated by the various rituals surrounding their retention after 1789. At the outset of the Revolution, when most elections were held in churches (often the only large meeting places), a mass was usually celebrated as voters gathered, and a *Te Deum* as they dispersed, though by 1792 this practice had become much rarer and it soon disappeared altogether.[36] The actual proceedings then began with the election of a presiding bureau, which might be strongly contested on account of its strategic role in the business that followed, until the Napoleonic regime insisted on nominating presidents; this highly valued and vital right was only restored to electors under the July Monarchy. Other preliminaries included a variety of oaths, imposed on assembly officials—scrutineers had to promise not to reveal the names that illiterate voters vouchsafed to them—while all electors were required to express their loyalty to the current regime and to undertake to formulate their choices in an honest fashion. As under the *Ancien Régime*, exhortatory speeches were often delivered prior to the start of voting proper, when voters came and went as their names were called, engaging in conversation while they waited to step forward, or to learn the outcome of a series of votes. The electoral assembly was thus a noisy, bustling affair, far removed from the respectful calm expected at a polling station today. It was small wonder that priests complained about the profanation of sacred space, when altars were pressed into service as desks and pulpits were used to make announcements or deliver orations.

Indeed, discussion and election were inextricably interwoven, exemplified by the drafting of *cahiers de doléances* in 1789, their inseparability ensuring that the practice persisted during the Revolution. There is little room here to elaborate on its numerous manifestations, which ranged far beyond electoral business and

---

[34] François Guizot, *Discours académiques* (Paris, 1861), 396.
[35] *Moniteur*, 19 May 1850, 1741.
[36] Patrick, *Men of the First Republic*, 166. In 1792, only nineteen departmental colleges out of eighty-three began with a mass. Clergy were usually present at assemblies earlier in the Revolution and were often elected as presiding officials.

might lead to the admission of all sorts of deputations, especially at the departmental colleges. In 1790, there was much argument about the boundaries of the
new local authorities, while in 1792 army volunteers sought moral and financial
support and, in two instances, babies were presented for baptism (one of them
blessed with the name Aluise Hyacinthe Électeur).[37] The right to assemble outside of the electoral timetable was recognized in the municipal regulations of
1789, as well as in the Constitution of 1793, which proposed the examination of
legislation in the cantons if a sufficient number of citizens demanded it. A sense
of sovereignty thus struck deep roots in all electoral assemblies, which was most
visibly demonstrated in the sections of Paris, but extensively replicated elsewhere.
However, just as the Constitution of 1795 proscribed the open vote, so it also pro-
hibited any consideration of extraneous issues. Yet infractions continued to occur,
and the constantly reiterated reminder that assemblies must concern themselves
solely with the election for which they had been convened is testimony to a firmly
established tradition of considering other business. Even under the Restoration,
electors could not desist from drafting congratulatory addresses to the king or
requesting changes to the electoral system.

The maintenance of order was naturally a major preoccupation for assemblies.
It was not easy to manage the personal, political, and communal tensions that
might arise out of a series of ballots, taken in a confined space over any number of
days. As the Revolution became polarized, so these conflicts acquired an increasingly ideological hue and the secession of one faction or another, to create a separate assembly of its own, became endemic under the Directory. For example, at
Blain in the Loire-Inférieure in the Year V (1797), one of the primary assemblies
was assailed by a host of would-be voters, who insisted that their registration had
been unfairly denied. When they were admitted, the republican minority left to
meet separately at the *hôtel de ville*, taking ink, pens, and paper with them. It was
argued that republicans had the right, indeed the duty, to secede in this fashion
'whenever the Constitution was violated'.[38] Presented with a choice between rival
delegations or deputies, the departmental colleges or legislative councils could
decide which one to validate, though in doing so they only encouraged more
secession. The principal historian of elections during this period, Jean-René
Suratteau, has calculated that in the Year VI (1798), at least six hundred cantonal
assemblies split, more than one in ten, while the phenomenon was replicated in
the departmental colleges, with one third of them divided.[39] Some recourse to
this practice had been made before, usually arising from disputes over communal
status or the location of a cantonal *chef-lieu*, like the rivalry between Cabasse and
Carcès, in 1792, which led to the despatch of two delegations to the departmental

---

[37] Patrick, *Men of the First Republic*, 167.   [38] Crook, *Elections*, 146.
[39] Jean-René Suratteau, *Les Élections de l'an VI et le coup d'état du 22 floréal (11 mai 1798)* (Paris,
1971), 227–31.

college of the Var, but it had never occurred to the extent it assumed in the late 1790s.

The problems inherent in the assembly method help explain the proposal made by Delacroix, cited above, which sought to dispense with it altogether. During debate over the Constitution of 1795, the deputy Garran de Coulon was equally convinced that it was 'in the solitude of one's conscience, disengaged from surrounding activity, that one finds the optimum circumstances for making pure and non-partisan choices'.[40] His conviction also pointed to the abolition of assemblies, while others merely wanted to leave electors freer to vote when they wished, rather than subject them to a strict roll-call. Polls had sometimes been left open for a few days during the constitutional consultations of 1793 and 1795, though not without raising suspicions of the same citizens voting more than once. The possibility of fraud probably scuppered the proposal made in 1795 that voters gather briefly to elect a bureau, before returning at their personal convenience for polling proper over the following days.[41] Indeed, his colleague Rouzet was so convinced that the 'excessive length and tedium' of assemblies, not to mention their 'tumultuous nature', both deterred participation and inhibited liberty of opinion, that he suggested voters simply submit their ballot papers to a local official.[42]

These alternatives bore no immediate fruit, but the idea of a wholly individual vote was introduced after Bonaparte came to the helm in the coup d'état of Brumaire (November 1799). Unlike the consultations of 1793 and 1795, the vote on the rapidly issued Constitution of the Year VIII, which was held in February 1800, completely abandoned assemblies. Indeed, in a further departure from established electoral procedure, 'registers' (in reality loose sheets of paper) were introduced and opened for signature, for and against the new constitution, at the mayor's residence and various administrative offices.[43] The seasoned politician Roederer, who seems to have originated the idea, was delighted: 'The Constitution was presented to the calm and personal meditation of solitary citizens. The greatest freedom and the most perfect security were established for the casting of these votes.' However, the employment of this system, which was repeated for the constitutional consultations of 1802, 1804, and 1815, presented a familiar problem of inscription for the high proportion of voters who were unable to write. It also opened the door to a significant level of fraud, in so far as public scrutiny of the casting and counting of votes disappeared; there was no way of knowing whether or not the illiterate voters whose names appeared on the registers—always expressing an affirmative verdict—had actually offered an opinion of any sort.

---

[40] *Moniteur*, 3 thermidor III (21 July 1795), 1220.
[41] Jean-Philippe Garran de Coulon, *Opinion… sur le mode des élections* (Paris, an III), 78–9.
[42] Rouzet, *Vues civiques*.
[43] Crook, 'Un scrutin secret', in Belmonte and Peyrard (eds), *Peuples en Révolution*, 66–7.

It was especially suspicious when they represented almost the entirety of the community's adult males, their names entered by the same official hand.

Sieyès, the architect of a new constitution that was drafted in 1799 without any public consultation, had envisaged that his system of lists, from which all local and national office-holders were in future to be chosen by the government, would be compiled in the usual electoral assemblies. In the event, the law of 1801 which determined their formation was similar to Roederer's recent innovation. It divided the electorate into 'centuries' of one hundred citizens and then invited them to vote at the private addresses of designated scrutineers, over a period of two weeks. The freshly installed prefect of Paris was delighted to inform inhabitants of the capital that the new procedure would enable them to avoid the 'crowded assemblies of the past, where their choices were often unduly influenced by other people', because they could now compose their ballot papers in the tranquillity of their own homes, before taking them to a local polling station.[44] His colleague in the Mont-Blanc also reported his great satisfaction with the innovation: 'the establishment of the communal lists was conducted with none of the upheaval that accompanied the preceding elections and which, during the Revolution, contributed a great deal to discrediting the representative regime and dividing society…'. Another prefect, in the Charente, concurred and pointed to the convenience factor of voting in one's neighbourhood at the time of one's choice: 'the law requires that you devote no more than an hour to this important exercise of your rights.'[45]

However, fraudulent practice was widespread in the compilation of these lists of notables in 1801, which besides exacerbating the problem of deciphering long, handwritten lists, also prompted a great number of complaints. While they accepted that the electoral assemblies of the 1790s had all too often become 'gladiatorial arena', several individuals elected in the Ariège were concerned that the process was conducted in camera, in the absence of any public supervision. As one deputy put it, during debate over a new electoral law under the Restoration, few had been unaware of the abuses that occurred when citizens 'were obliged to vote separately' and, though very few people had participated, 'the ballot boxes were frequently stuffed full of papers inserted by officials.'[46] Indeed, when he became Consul for Life, in 1802, Bonaparte decided to restore electoral assemblies, in cantons and colleges, at which voters would be summoned in turn to compose written ballots, as they had during the preceding decade, albeit in more closely regulated and carefully managed circumstances. Registers continued to be used for the ensuing constitutional votes and, when his nephew Louis-Napoleon

[44] *Moniteur*, 22 thermidor IX (10 Aug. 1801), 1329.
[45] Malcolm Crook, 'Un scrutin secret émis en public. L'acte de vote sous la Révolution française (1789–1802)', in Cyril Belmonte and Christine Peyrard (eds), *Peuples en révolution. D'aujourd'hui à 1789* (Aix-en-Provence, 2014), 66–9.
[46] *Moniteur*, 21 Dec. 1816, 1424.

came to power in 1851, he initially announced that the plebiscite to confirm the authority he had just seized would be held on the same basis as his uncle's. Yet he rapidly rescinded the decision, after fears for the freedom of voting prompted a hostile public reaction, and he ordained the use of ballot papers instead.[47]

After the restoration of the Bourbon monarchy in 1814 the problem of illiterate voters struggling with a *bulletin* had been temporarily resolved, on account of the drastic reduction of the electorate and the abolition of elections below the legislative level. The rules surrounding electoral assemblies had been refined under preceding regimes, so that printed lists of electors were now available, together with *cartes d'électeur* to control entry. Compared to contemporary Britain, French elections had become more orderly affairs, but that is not to say the vote was completely secure, since it still had to be composed, by individual voters in turn, in the presence of their peers and presiding officials. When, in 1835, Tocqueville appeared before a British parliamentary commission which was investigating the alternatives to public voting, he confirmed that secrecy was compromised under the current French electoral law of 1820 because choices had to be written down 'in front of the president, who had been appointed by the crown'.[48] In some assemblies hats or boxes were used to shield voters from his inquisitive gaze but, in the quest for secrecy, the voter was suggesting he had something to hide.[49] After 1831 a separate table was provided for penning papers, but pressure was still brought to bear on voters by their peers, while public officials who were also electors often made little pretence of keeping their choices to themselves. Although legislative elections remained the preserve of wealthier citizens until 1848, the earlier problems associated with illiterate citizens composing a ballot paper re-emerged in the early 1830s, when the franchise was significantly extended for the election of municipal councillors and national-guard officers. In these circumstances, assistance in completing the *bulletin* remained essential for many voters.

Open Secrets

It was the unexpected advent of universal male suffrage in 1848 which finally brought voting in assemblies to an end, for there were naturally concerns about facilitating the participation of millions of new voters—the great majority of whom did initially turn out—in this time-honoured fashion. The decision was made on purely practical grounds and, in fact, the term 'assemblée électorale' was

---

[47] *Moniteur*, 4 and 7 Dec. 1851, 3023 and 3055.
[48] Malcolm Crook and Tom Crook, 'The advent of the secret ballot in Britain and France: from public assembly to private compartment', *History*, 92 (2007), 453–4.
[49] *Moniteur*, 1 May 1828, 541.

long retained in the official *procès-verbaux*. Nonetheless, in future the act of voting in France would approximate more closely to the one with which we are familiar today: a brief procedure, rapidly transacted, with each elector simply presenting a ballot paper at a polling station—a system already widespread in the United States and employed for some local elections in Britain.[50] There was provision for a second round of voting if the winners failed to achieve a quorum of votes, or in the absence of an absolute majority, but that would be held a week or two later in the same manner. A single vote (either for a list or an individual) was cast on each occasion, which meant that the use of printed papers now became feasible. Indeed, in view of the numbers involved, French voters were required to report to a *bureau de vote*, staffed by local officials, already armed with a *bulletin*, which might be provided by candidates and committees, or detached from newspapers and pamphlets, but could still be hand-written, by the elector himself or a third party.

The secrecy of the vote was proclaimed afresh in 1848, yet its security was profoundly compromised for many participants, since they might be obliged to reveal the contents of their *bulletins* as they made their way to cast them. A splendid example of the pressures to which voters were exposed in elections to the Second Republic's Constituent Assembly is captured in a report from Vabres, in the Tarn:

> I was crossing the floor of the polling station...when I encountered M. Barthès, a voter from the commune of Saint-Pierre. I asked to see his ballot paper and he replied that his parish priest, the abbé Bousquet, had forbidden him from showing it to anyone. I pointed out to him that he should not keep any secret from me, so he gave me the paper...He then said to me, 'our priest is much too attached to this list to allow it to be completely altered, but cross out the name at the bottom and replace it with one of your own choice', something which I did immediately. I had only just given the amended paper back to Barthès, who had not had time to put it back into his pocket, when the priest returned and took it from him, tore it up and said, 'what are you up to, you wretched man?' Barthès was then handed another ballot paper and I was berated for behaving so badly.[51]

Whereas, in the past, attention had focused on persuading electors to name particular individuals when they wrote down their choices in an assembly, now those anxious to be elected, along with their supporters, sought instead to ensure that voters were in possession of a particular ballot paper when they entered the

---

[50] *Moniteur*, 1 May 1828, 541. However, until voting was entirely conducted in the communes, after 1852, there was a roll-call by commune at the cantons, so individuals could not choose when to vote.
[51] AN C1329, Percepteur de Vabres, 26 Apr. 1848.

polling station. In fact, they were also exposed to great pressure during the period preceding the election, because agents and officials might call at their homes, or accost them at markets, urging them to accept a *bulletin*, often bearing a name they could not read. The space occupied by electioneering thus extended beyond the *bureau de vote* and its immediate environs where, on polling day, there was a final attempt to distribute papers and check that rivals had not succeeded in making substitutions. The situation was described by parliamentarian Lefèvre-Pontalis in his account of legislative elections in 1902 as a 'veritable fairground', with voters manhandled and interrogated as they sought to make their way through the *mêlée*.[52] A candidate in the Finistère in 1906 claimed there was one distributor of ballot papers for every six or seven electors, some of whom were deterred by having to run the gauntlet in order to vote, especially since they could end up being frog-marched into the polling station.[53] Scenes like this only disappeared in 1919, when the distribution of *bulletins* was banned on polling day and ballot papers were subsequently circulated by post, besides being made available inside the polling station.

In the spring of 1848, voting had proved more disorderly than contemporaries or historians have generally acknowledged, extending far beyond some well-documented disturbances in one or two towns.[54] In the Ardèche, for example, peasants were often waylaid as they arrived to vote in the *chef-lieu de canton*, asked to show their ballot paper and, if it was not to their interceptors' liking, they were obliged to hand it over in exchange for another one. The resumption of cantonal polling for legislative elections also reawakened the communal tensions that had frequently erupted during the 1790s: in the Aveyron, in 1848, gunshots were fired by the inhabitants of rival villages as they came to vote. The much-reproduced contemporary image of the ballot replacing the bullet should not be taken too literally.[55] The relocation of voting to the commune for all types of election would subsequently remove the opportunity for such confrontations, but the justification of elector convenience and comfort masked the fact that surveillance would be much easier to conduct as a result. For most French citizens continued to reside in 'dwarf' communes with less than 100 registered voters, and their *bulletins* would be counted as well as cast at tiny *bureaux*, where choices were hard to hide and abstention all too evident. Thus, a parish priest was identified as the author of ballot papers employed by peasants in 1848, when his handwriting was recognized. Only urban voters enjoyed the benefits of both neighbourhood polling and a greater degree of anonymity in deciding whether or not to vote and whom to support.

---

[52] Lefèvre-Pontalis, *Les Élections en Europe*, vii.   [53] Le Bail, *Une Élection en 1906*, 147–8.

[54] Malcolm Crook, 'Universal suffrage as counter-revolution? Electoral mobilisation under the Second Republic in France, 1848–1851', *Journal of Historical Sociology*, 28 (2015), 53ff.

[55] Olivier Ihl, 'L'urne et le fusil: sur les violences électorales lors du scrutin du 23 avril 1848', *Rfsp*, 60 (2010), 9–35.

Figure 5.1   Voting in the late nineteenth century

Alfred-Henri Bramtot was commissioned to paint 'Le Suffrage universel', which he completed in 1891. It is a celebration of the (male) vote that had become an established ritual under the Third Republic. It repays detailed attention but, in the absence of the *isoloir* later introduced in 1914, note that the voter hands the ballot paper to the presiding official for insertion into the *urne*.

Source: Copyright, Diomedia C8817.

It was not, therefore, unusual for voters to conceal the paper they really wanted to use about their person, in order to avoid being forced to employ an alternative. Yet a final hurdle remained to be crossed inside the *bureau de vote* when they presented their folded ballot paper to the presiding official, usually the mayor in smaller communes, who was responsible for inserting it into the ballot box. Under the pretext of verifying that it was a single *bulletin*, this official had an opportunity to inspect it, and might even reject it, or spoil it with a grease stain, if he deemed it politically objectionable. Although it was stipulated in 1848 that all ballot papers must be white, this was absolutely no guarantee of uniformity: size, shade, and texture could all indicate which candidate(s) the voter was supporting, while the impression left by bold lettering in a particular font was often visible to an alert observer. Some candidates went to enormous lengths to try to ensure that their papers bore exactly the same outward appearance as their opponents', in order to protect those using them, while in 1869 one competitor in the Haute-Garonne issued an entirely fresh set of *bulletins* on the very eve of the poll, precisely in order to prevent imitation.[56] Crossing-out a printed name and replacing it with a different

---

[56]   Cited in Lagoueyte, 'Candidature officielle', iii, 872–3.

one, like the use of thin strips of gummed paper bearing an alternative denomination, was a common means used by voters to mask their real choices and, generally speaking, papers amended in this fashion were accepted as legitimate ballots. Conversely, voting 'à bulletin ouvert' to placate monitoring patrons was frequently tolerated, though officially banned.

One obvious solution was the provision of an official ballot paper at the polling station, to be marked by the voter, like the ones adopted later in the nineteenth-century in Britain or Belgium. Yet, as so often where voting technology is concerned, what is acceptable in one culture may go firmly against the grain of another. The French continue to eschew a single paper listing all candidates, or containing the two, simple alternatives demanded in a referendum, a practice which is common currency in the anglophone world, though there is the question of size when numerous individuals are in contention.[57] Evidently the issue of papers for 'official' candidates by Louis-Napoleon's government, like the regime's provision of favourable *bulletins* for plebiscites, served as a negative example in this regard.[58] Taine pointed to rural misgivings where all administrative paper-work was concerned and printed ballot papers were initially viewed with similar suspicion.[59] Indeed, Daniel Stern (the *femme de lettres* Marie d'Agoult) recounted how in the elections of 1848, confronted with printed lists of names, some peasants exclaimed, 'since the government has already made up its mind, why are we being asked to vote?'[60]

In fact, until declared candidatures became mandatory for legislative elections in 1889 it was simply not feasible to produce a single *bulletin*. To this day, French electors retain the right to compose their own ballot papers, which some commentators once considered 'the only procedure worthy of a free people'.[61] There was an element of elitism here but, at root, this dogged resistance was another reflection of the widely held belief in the sovereignty of the voter and his right to produce a *bulletin* as he wished. As some dissenters on the Commission for Universal Suffrage argued, 'on the pretext of guaranteeing it, the obligation to employ an official ballot paper will actually infringe the voter's freedom'.[62] After 1890 several recommendations were made for uniform ballot papers furnished by the authorities, including one ingenious proposal for a single, perforated sheet, from which the preferred option could be detached. It was only in 1919 that legislation was eventually passed requiring the authorities to print a separate *bulletin*

[57] The listing of candidates on a single ballot paper was part of Delacroix's proposal for voting in 1795, though it had already been suggested in 1793.
[58] AN C7305, Proposition sur la sincérité du suffrage, 1 July 1902.
[59] Taine, *Du Suffrage universel*, 26–7.
[60] Daniel Stern (Marie d'Agout), *Histoire de la revolution de 1848*, 3 vols (Paris, 1850–3), ii, 358.
[61] Lucien-Anatole Prévost-Paradol, *La France nouvelle* (Paris, 1868), 55 and Edgar Zevort, *La France sous le régime du suffrage universel* (Paris, 1894), 256–7.
[62] AN C7447, Rapport, 6 Feb. 1914.

for each parliamentary candidate (at the latter's expense), for dispatch to voters in the post and availability at polling stations.[63]

The Technology of the *Urne* and the *Isoloir*

Uniform ballot papers were part of an electoral tool-kit, painstakingly assembled across the Western world in the late nineteenth century, which also included a secure ballot-box, to ensure that papers were correctly managed. The *urne*, as the French would 'poetically' call it, while graphically depicting it in classical style (though in reality it was merely a wooden or metal box), had emerged gradually amidst little controversy. Electoral legislation from the 1790s onwards simply pre-scribed the use of *vases* and *boîtes du scrutin*, but the varieties of receptacle that had traditionally been employed, from hats, to basins, jars, soup tureens, and drawers, would survive until the ballot box was subject to stricter regulation fol-lowing the re-establishment of a mass suffrage in the mid-nineteenth century.[64] With the inception of the Second Republic there was great concern that such primitive technology would allow tampering with the contents, especially over-night when the polls were open for two days.[65] Under the Second Empire attempts were finally made to standardize this vital and emblematic piece of equipment by stipulating that ballot boxes must have a double lock and a particular type, called the 'Inviolable' by its manufacturer, was recommended for general use.[66] The pro-cess culminated in 1913, with clear instructions that keys for the two locks on the *urne* must be held separately by the president of the polling station and his senior assistant. In 1973 boxes made of glass instead of metal, and baptized the 'Voltaire' model, were introduced as a symbol of transparency. Well before then, it had become commonplace to invite electors to vote by summoning them 'aux urnes'.

The advent of the *isoloir*, as the voting booth became known in France, was by contrast bitterly resisted and eventually arrived in a more complex form than many of its counterparts elsewhere.[67] Indeed, when it was finally adopted in 1913, complete with curtain, it was also accompanied by the use of an envelope for the ballot paper (a combination that had been recently introduced in Germany). In an era when the transnational comparison of voting practice was becoming rou-tine, the French were clearly no longer at the cutting edge of this electoral tech-nology, much to the dismay of deputies like Joseph Ruau who, at the turn of the twentieth century, declared it was a national disgrace that France was the only

[63] Loi du 20 Oct. 1919, concernant l'envoi et la distribution des bulletins de vote.

[64] Olivier Ihl, 'L'urne électorale. Formes et usages d'une technique de vote', *Rfsp*, 43 (1993), 30–60.

[65] Vincent Villette, 'The urn and the rumour: false information about electoral fraud as a means of discrediting mass suffrage in the department of the Seine, 1848–49', *FH*, 29 (2015), 328–48.

[66] AN F1cII 59, Circulaire du ministre de l'intérieur, 12 Apr. 1869.

[67] Alain Garrigou, 'Le secret de l'isoloir', *ARSS*, 71–2 (1988), 22–45.

country in Europe not doing more 'to safeguard polling secrecy'.[68] In fact, the use of an envelope to afford the voter greater security for his ballot paper had been proposed as early as 1865 by one of the handful of republican deputies in the imperial *Corps législatif*. There was little possibility of the idea being pursued at that point, but it was revived in the 1870s, under the Third Republic, sometimes coupled with the provision of a voting 'compartment', where a ballot paper would be inserted into the envelope. The already controversial issue of voter protection thus grew more complicated and much harder to resolve. Opponents were able to exploit differing levels of support for these two components, as well as emphasizing how expensive they were, since in France the cost of elections had always been borne by the public purse.

In the end no less than fifteen propositions were tabled, over a period of more than thirty years, before the requisite legislation was finally passed. There was a good deal of toing and froing between Chamber of Deputies and Senate, the so-called *navette* that characterized the subsequent, similarly lengthy campaign for the female suffrage. There were of course those who stubbornly insisted that the ballot was already sufficiently secret (though for a few others there was still no reason why it should be) and thus any change would prove detrimental—deterring voters by insisting they perform a more complex task and putting participation at risk. As so often, partisan interests were also in play: consistent opponents of greater security emanated overwhelmingly from rural constituencies where the influence of notables was the underlying issue. Charles Ferry, an arch-conservative, claimed that peasants would struggle mightily 'to insert a ballot paper that requires folding four times, into a small envelope, using bloated fingers calloused by work in the fields'.[69] Concerns were also raised that 'cabins', as the compartments were called during debate, might be occupied for too long: 'What if an inebriated voter – it is not unusual – spends thirty minutes in there?', inquired one deputy, evoking the frustration of those obliged to wait. Cases of claustrophobia were raised by one or two speakers and, if voters were to be 'isolated and shut up in a tiny cabin', they might 'lose their heads as well as their *bulletins*'.[70] For anti-clericals the *isoloir* represented a sort of secular confessional, perhaps not so unreasonably, since the elector was being invited to calmly contemplate how he should vote. The ensuing debates were conducted with hilarity as well as hostility, for others could not resist an allusion to the 'cabinet' as a toilet, while another deputy suggested that seaside towns like Dieppe or Trouville could economize by borrowing bathing huts to serve as booths.[71] Gustave Quilbeuf even speculated

---

[68] Crook and Crook, 'Reforming voting practices in a global age', 199–237.

[69] Crook and Crook, 'The advent of the secret ballot', 460–1 and Garrigou, 'Le secret de l'isoloir', 22–45.

[70] Patrick Lehingue, *Le Vote. Approches sociologiques de l'institution et des comportements électoraux* (Paris, 2011), 31–4.

[71] Pilenco, *Les Mœurs électorales du suffrage universel*, 271–2.

about the need for separate male and female facilities should women ever be enfranchised since, if members of the opposite sex happened to encounter one another in the *isoloir*, 'who knows what might happen!' (Figure 5.2)

In the event, once the act had passed onto the statute book, few problems were reported in trials conducted at by-elections, with particular interest focused on Ivry, a suburb of Paris, where delegations from several large towns arrived to observe the legislative by-election of November 1913. The only significant, recorded mishap emanated from a municipal contest at a rural commune in the Finistère, where one voter spent half an hour in the *isoloir* awaiting instructions to leave. A few revisions were made before the law was applied for the general legislative elections of April 1914, when the new set of instructions assured voters of their complete security:

> Upon entry to the polling station, the elector, having established his identity...will pick up an envelope. Without leaving the *bureau*, he will then go to that part of the room that has been arranged to hide him from view, while he puts his ballot paper into the envelope. He must then confirm to the presiding officer that he is only bearing a single envelope and, without touching it, the official will ensure that the elector himself inserts the envelope into the ballot box.

The small, but significant detail of the voter himself placing his envelope into the *urne*, so frequently photographed, cannot be emphasized too strongly. For the previous intervention of the presiding official in this regard had seriously compromised the voter's secrecy, and his sovereignty, in conducting this supreme gesture of citizenship.

The *isoloir* was immediately placed in storage for the duration of the First World War, but it was re-installed in 1919 as soon as elections resumed. As one gentle satirist of French electoral *moeurs* rightly suggested, a lasting monument had been erected, deeply symbolic of the private act that voting had become. The accompanying envelope was also re-instated after hostilities ended, though YMCA stock (which had been available to civilians in occupied areas) had to be pressed into service on account of a post-war paper shortage. The election-day ritual described above has endured for the past century, though ballot papers were soon made available at the polling station along with envelopes. The elector's identity is now solemnly announced, 'M. ou Mme Le Tel peut voter', before he or she inserts a folded bulletin into the *urne*, followed by the confirmation, 'M. ou Mme Le Tel a voté'. This dignified, civic liturgy thus retains an important public dimension, as well as incorporating a sequence of actions that is occasionally transgressed by voters who deliberately select just one of the candidates' papers that are available to be collected along with the envelope because they wish to

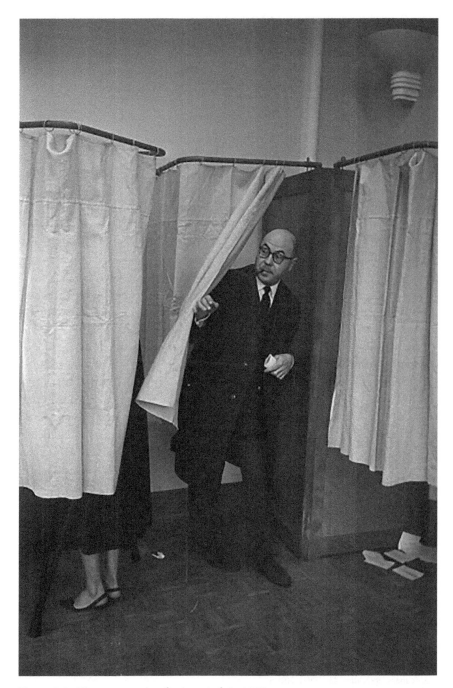

Figure 5.2 Elector emerging from an *isoloir*, 1965

A classic image featuring the curtained polling booth which was introduced in 1914. Discarded ballot papers lie on the floor after the voter has put the chosen bulletin into the envelope, while dispensing with others that have been collected on entry to the polling station. Insertion of the envelope into the ballot box will complete the final stage of the electoral ritual, which is illustrated on the cover of this book.

Source: Copyright, Getty Images, M148061.

reveal their choice, or studiously avoid the *isoloir*, in order to show they can vote without it.[72] A rather more serious threat to the secular ceremony of casting a ballot paper is posed by the reduced ritual that more recent technology involves.

Paperless Polling? Mechanical and Electronic Voting

French politicians were rightly proud of the electoral innovations their country had pioneered, yet a century later, just when paper balloting of the sort inaugurated in France in 1789 seemed to be triumphing everywhere, the invention and utilization of voting machines in the United States began to threaten its hegemony.[73] Indeed, voters in some of the world's largest democracies, such as India and Brazil as well as the United States, are now tapping a screen rather than inserting a piece of paper into a ballot box. Yet, if the global demise of the *bulletin* has been widely predicted, its wholesale replacement is far from imminent in France, where efforts to develop technological support for paper-balloting date from the inception of mass voting. As early as 1791, the departmental college at Paris was shown a device which purported to assist scrutineers with the thankless task of counting votes. Almost a century later the Chamber of Deputies was presented with a ballot box called the 'Scrutateur absolu', which cut the corner off the voter's identity card (to ensure he could not repeat the exercise) and recorded the total, thus helping to verify the (manually) marked-up register of participants.[74] The technology was designed to prevent error and fraud, and thus inspire confidence in the electoral process. This was precisely the argument employed in 1907 by the inventor of the 'Votateur', a machine which counted the cards inserted into separate slots for each candidate or list.[75] Yet, even after a favourable report on a later version of this model from the Commission on Universal Suffrage, there was little enthusiasm from deputies, who hesitated over the financial investment that was required, as well as concerns about the adaptability of the electorate.

There was little further interest in mechanization of the voting process in France until much later in the twentieth century, when what one of its historians, Nathalie Dompnier, has dubbed the 'myth of democratic modernization' began to take hold. Her extensive research into the subject shows that numerous French politicians and much of the press began to subscribe to the idea, which was

---

[72] Yves Déloye, 'L'élection au village. Le geste électoral à l'occasion des scrutins cantonaux et régionaux de mars 1992', *Rfsp*, 43 (1993), 101–5.

[73] Malcolm Crook and Tom Crook, 'Ballot papers and the practice of elections: Britain, France and the United States of America, c. 1500-2000', *Historical Research*, 88 (2015), 557–9 and Roy G. Saltman, *The History and Politics of Voting Technology: In Quest of Integrity and Public Confidence* (New York, 2006), 117–66.

[74] AN BB30 1463, Rapport…, 19 Jan. 1882.

[75] AN C7375, Lettre à la Commission, 13 Nov. 1907 and Nathalie Dompnier, 'Les machines à voter à l'essai. Notes sur le mythe de la "modernisation" démocratique', *Genèses*, 49 (2002), 73–4.

naturally supported by the manufacturers of electronic devices, one of whom famously proclaimed: 'Put the power of technology at the voters' fingertips!' In the course of a debate about electoral fraud, in 1988, a deputy remarked that 'on the eve of the twenty-first century it seems absurd that a nineteenth-century means of counting votes, with the aid of pencils and tally-sticks, is still being employed.'[76] A colleague quickly added that 'voting machines would totally eliminate the possibility of error and malpractice', such as miscounting papers or stuffing the ballot box. Fears of breakdown and breaches of security were raised, but there was great confidence that further technological progress would resolve these issues. It was also argued that an up-to-date means of making electoral choices would attract more young people to vote, though research does not suggest a significant reduction in non-voting as a result.[77] Conversely, concern about negative reactions from elderly people, who have sometimes been invited to familiarization sessions in retirement homes to help overcome any misgivings on their part, appears unfounded. Dompnier's investigation suggests that most of the voters who have used it readily adapt to the new technology. Likewise, officials are pleased with the reduced workload required by paperless voting, both in terms of preparing the polling station and declaring the result.

Yet, these positive attitudes notwithstanding, experimentation with voting machines in France has proved extremely limited. In 1973, twenty-seven communes located in the Île-de-France and Corsica were instructed to use an electronic device, but their singling-out prompted a hostile reaction, since the imposition of this electoral technology was regarded as arising from partisan motives and the implication that these local authorities were incapable of curbing fraud.[78] The political backlash, together with technical problems and the cost of installation, led to the abandonment of the project in 1982, and the Corsican prefect later reported that the redundant machinery had been sold as scrap metal. Only in 2004 were communes with more than 3,500 inhabitants invited to apply to use a new generation of touch-screens and, in the presidential elections of 2007, eighty-one communes, with a combined electorate of 1.5 million voters (roughly 3.5 per cent of the national total), opted to acquire them.[79] However, one third of these pioneers subsequently decided to drop these devices and there has been no subsequent attempt to encourage their adoption. This partial implementation of new technology sits uneasily in the French tradition of electoral uniformity: for the first time since the constitutional consultations of the mid-1790s,

[76] *JO*, 24 Nov. 1988, 2733.
[77] Michel Laflandre, 'Le vote électronique: état des lieux', in Bernard Owen (ed.), *Le Processus électoral: permanences et évolutions* (Paris, 2006), 162.
[78] Dompnier, 'Les machines à voter', 78–82.
[79] Nathalie Dompnier, 'Modernizing the vote and rationalizing the State: computers and the French polling-booth', *FH*, 29 (2015), 371. In fact, another thirty communes acquired screens, but they were not employed due to local objections.

some French voters have been recording their vote differently from others, and there is still no sign that the current experiment will prove to be the forerunner for a thoroughgoing shift in the *acte de vote*.

Conclusion

Once at the forefront of electoral technology, France is now regarded by some as lagging behind. Yet a rich civic ritual has been retained, albeit one that is rapidly accomplished on an individual basis, unlike the time-consuming exercise in a collective assembly that accompanied the initial experience of mass voting at the end of the eighteenth century. The adoption of printed ballot papers in 1848 accelerated and simplified the procedure, but without affording complete secrecy, which was only belatedly secured with envelope and *isoloir* on the eve of the First World War. However, this arrangement is threatened by the introduction of computers, whereby a screen replaces *bulletin*, envelope, and *urne*, with profound implications for all participants in the process, even though it is still conducted at a polling station. Technical personnel from the private enterprises which supply, and indeed market, the necessary devices become integral to a task once wholly entrusted to local authorities and electors, while polling-station officials are restricted to checking a voter's credentials and communicating the outcome. Voters perform the entirety of their electoral duty in the *isoloir*, before receiving a simple on-screen message that they have voted, and members of the public are largely excluded from scrutinizing the casting and counting of votes.[80] French reluctance to embrace the electronic vote has, in fact, preserved a vital civic ritual, which affirms the citizen's electoral role and enhances the affective experience of voting.[81] We shall see next how more and more French people came to engage in elections after 1789, while the long-established, paper-based system prevailed.

---

[80] Dompnier, 'Les machines à voter', 82–8.
[81] Stephen Coleman, *How Voters Feel* (Cambridge, 2013).

6

Getting Out the Vote

Electoral Mobilization

> Citizens! Cast your votes and do not allow any indisposition, any bad
> weather, nor your remoteness from the polling station, nor any press-
> ing business, to prevent you from doing so. Turn out *en masse* for this
> election!
>
> Alfred Naquet, 5 April 1878.[1]

It was not enough to award the franchise, but also a matter of encouraging and
enabling electors to use their vote, for experience soon demonstrated that acquisition of the suffrage did not automatically lead to its employment. Exhortations
often fell on deaf ears. Mobilizing the mass male electorate thus presented an
enormous challenge, during the Revolution and for much of the nineteenth century, but the long apprenticeship in voting finally seemed to have come to com-
pletion around the turn of the twentieth century, after which high levels of
turnout became the norm. It is often forgotten that this had not always been the
case and that the trajectory of electoral participation was a protracted and uneven
one in every respect. This chapter seeks to trace the rather less than linear path
that led to the great majority of French adult males voting regularly prior to the
First World War, then a similarly high percentage of men and women during the
period after the Second World War, besides contextualizing and commenting on
it. A good deal of research on turnout has been conducted over the past quarter of
a century, but it has largely focused on particular periods, like the Revolution, or
types of election, most notably of the legislative variety. Much work remains to be
done, but an attempt will be made here to offer an overall synthesis and analysis,
with the aid of much original data and numerous examples.

A number of important caveats must be entered before presenting any series of
French electoral 'statistics', on account of the specific circumstances in which successive elections took place. The extent of the franchise is a key variable, which
complicates the comparison of turnout from one period to another. Moreover,
voting before 1848 was a lengthy process, involving at least two rounds of polling,

---

[1] Cited in Lancelot, *L'Abstentionnisme electoral*, 268.

How the French Learned to Vote: A History of Electoral Practice in France. Malcolm Crook, Oxford University Press (2021).
© Malcolm Crook. DOI: 10.1093/oso/9780192894786.003.0007

while a second-round runoff, the *ballottage*, remains a feature of most French elections today. It is thus essential to indicate the precise origins of any figures, since fluctuation always occurs and the total of different individuals involved is invariably higher than the number for any single round, though usually impossible to discern. Yet this factor is seldom recognized in the existing literature, still less specified when figures are cited; here, reference is made to the first round of voting, which is mostly better attended, unless indicated to the contrary. A further problem resides in the status of spoiled papers (*blancs et nuls*), which have always constituted a small percentage of votes cast, occasionally a larger one, but have sometimes been assimilated to abstention. In this instance they will be counted as electoral participation, even though they had no direct bearing on the outcome, because those responsible had visited the polling station and submitted a *bulletin*. It should be added that electoral turnout is usually calculated by reference to the registered number of voters, the practice followed here. However, in the general absence of registers before 1789, and the unreliability or unavailability of lists during the Revolution, only rough estimates of eligible electors, and thus turnout, can be made for these elections. Finally, recourse to sampling is unavoidable for the period before national statistics were collected, yet the results may be misleading because levels of participation varied hugely from one area to another, even from one canton or commune to another, to a far greater degree than today. In short, many figures must remain approximate well into the nineteenth century, but they do offer an unprecedented, overall indication of the trajectory of turnout over some 200 years of French electoral history.

Ancien Régime Imponderables

Before 1789, although elections were still held in many rural communes and urban corporations, lists of eligible voters were seldom kept and there was little attempt to record the number of participants. It was a long-established tradition for such polls to involve 'chefs de famille', or group members, based on peer recognition. Nor was it necessary to write down how many votes had been given, provided there was discernible agreement on a particular outcome, as a result of raising hands or voices, or simple endorsement. Indeed, those who had participated were effectively regarded as acting as proxies for others, so turnout (a term invented long afterwards) was not really an issue. Voting was a communal rather than an individual matter, as several testimonies in the Revolution confirm, when handfuls of villagers who had journeyed to distant cantonal assemblies declared they were representing their fellow citizens.[2] One or two historians have suggested

---

[2] AN BII 2, P-V de L'Arche, Basses-Alpes, for example, where voters declared that they were accepting the Constitution of 1793, 'on behalf of those citizens who were absent, as well as those who were present'.

that where a customary electoral regime had survived, perhaps 15 per cent of householders took part in choosing their village *syndic* or *consul* each year. However, figures varied enormously from one place and one election to another and not too much weight should be placed upon them.[3]

During the eighteenth century, with the hesitant adoption of voting by ballot, more accurate accounts began to be kept in the countryside, as in towns. A few historians have calculated turnout in elections to the local councils instituted in 1787 in villages of less than 2,500 inhabitants, according to a fiscal criterion which excluded roughly half of the householders. In some areas close to Paris it seems that, on average, only 10 per cent of those eligible to vote took the opportunity to do so, while in the Rouen area participation reached as high as 35 per cent, and in the particular case of Montreuil-Bellay, in the Touraine, over 50 per cent.[4] Evidently, there was no great rush to the polls. In towns like Nantes, where the suffrage remained relatively wide, with hundreds rather than tens of male inhabitants able to vote, it is unlikely that more than 10 per cent of them usually did so.[5] To be sure, members of narrow urban oligarchies were likely to participate more heavily in annual municipal elections, but there was a particular obligation upon them to do so.

The landmark elections to the Estates General held in the spring of 1789 served as a precursor for those of the Revolution. They were organized with a high degree of uniformity across the kingdom and, while the number of participants remains uncertain, it seems to have been greater than most of the examples just cited. There were still no lists of potential voters, so calculations must be made on the basis of population estimates, tax records, or projected back from the 1790s. Moreover, at the preliminary level for the third estate, it is hard to determine how many individuals actually took part, because only those who could do so added their signatures to the *procès-verbaux*, in order to authenticate the proceedings. Melvin Edelstein has heroically gathered samples from different sorts of communities all over France and estimates that roughly 40 per cent of the putative electorate took some part in the initial round of voting, which would suggest a total in excess of one million individuals.[6] There were some broad geographical patterns in rates of attendance, with the east and north-east generally voting more heavily than elsewhere, but these regional variations were accompanied by great differences between neighbouring communities: in the Île-de-France, for example,

---

[3] Serge Bianchi, *La Révolution et la Première République au village. Pouvoirs, votes et politisation dans les campagnes de l'Île-de-France (Essonne et Val-de-Marne actuels)* (Paris, 2003), 96–7.

[4] Bianchi, *La Révolution et la Première République*, 161; Marc Bouloiseau, 'Notables ruraux et élections municipales dans la région rouennaise en 1787', ChesRf, Mémoires et Documents, XIII (1958), 8–9; and Marc Bouloiseau and Antoine Bouchoux, 'Les municipalités tourangelles de 1787', ChesRf, Mémoires et Documents, XXIII (1969), 35.

[5] Saupin, *Nantes*, 90–2.   [6] Edelstein, *The French Revolution*, 17–20.

turnout ranged from 13 to 75 per cent. Such disparities in the extent of electoral mobilization would persist far into the future and doubtless reside in specific local factors, which are difficult to ascertain without drilling deep down at the communal level.

Mass Voting under the Revolution and Napoleon, 1790–1815

The inaugural elections of the Revolution in 1790 created a new, uniform system of municipal government, in February/March, then the cantonal, or primary assemblies of May/June chose members of the departmental colleges, who in turn elected councils to lead the local authorities at this level. Both polls generated a more enthusiastic response than the formation of the Estates General, with samples suggesting that roughly 50 per cent of the electorate, or around two million male citizens took part on each occasion. Figures for turnout where records have survived can be advanced with a little more confidence from this point onwards, because secretaries elected at the assemblies frequently complied with the regulations issued in December 1789 and recorded totals for each vote that was taken, besides indicating the how many individuals were able to participate. Elections under the Revolution thus appear alluringly modern, with lists of voters and numerical totals for polling, but the specific way in which both were constructed must be taken into account, for they were not like those today.

First, 'electoral registers' (where they exist) were generally derived from tax lists, as a consequence of the fiscal criterion to become a voter (see Chapter 1). Yet, they only indicated *potential* voters, because there were further hurdles to be crossed, notably up-to-date payment of tax and the requirement for civic registration, which also involved signing up for service in the National Guard. It is difficult to gauge how rigorously these provisions were applied in practice, save for Paris, where a few printed lists of *ayant droit de voter* in 1790 suggest a dramatic impact: in the right-bank section of Fontaine-Montmorency, for instance, only half of some one thousand individuals entitled to vote had actually completed the formalities.[7] If this under-registration was replicated across the city it would immediately double the (rather modest) figures for turnout.

Second, when it came to recording the number of participants, there was a series of votes, starting with the election of a presiding bureau, before a succession of polls took place for different categories of office, with up to three rounds of voting each time in pursuit of absolute majorities. There is thus a plethora of figures to be found in those cases where the *procès-verbaux* have survived, but if a single figure is to be retained, then it should be the highest, regardless of when it

---

[7] BL F61* (25), *Liste des citoyens actifs de la section de Fontaine-Montmorency* (no date, but evidently 1790).

was recorded, the course of action adopted for the calculations that follow.[8] Of course, it fails to include those who may have voted at other points in the proceedings. In rare circumstances where nominative lists were made for each successive vote, as in the case of Toulon between 1790 and 1792, the enumeration of individual electors lifts overall turnout by up to 10 per cent.[9] At Auriol, in the neighbouring Bouches-du-Rhône, almost every male head of household voted at least once during the 1790s, but far fewer on a regular basis.[10]

The figures painstakingly exhumed from local archives may tend to overestimate the size of the electorate and underplay the number of participants, but they enable us to plot the broad trajectory of turnout during this initial experiment with mass voting (Table 6.1). The overall level of participation for municipal elections held at the beginning of 1790 may be put at slightly less than 50 per cent, while the first cantonal elections, held in the early summer of 1790, attracted an average of half the electorate, despite the fact that most villagers were obliged to travel to a neighbouring commune to vote.[11] Thereafter, this level of participation were not sustained, especially in the cantons, and when primary elections were repeated, to choose a fresh set of second-degree electors in June 1791, a significant drop was recorded, with turnout averaging below 25 per cent.[12] The extension of the franchise in the summer of 1792, immediately after the

Table 6.1 Turnout at cantonal level during the Revolution, 1790–1799

Year	Purpose	Electorate*	Voters	% Turnout
1790	Primary assemblies	1,531,713	764,483	50.0
1791	Primary assemblies	1,972,320	468,923	23.8
1792	Primary assemblies	1,022,943	171,268	16.7
1793	Constitutional vote	c.6,000,000	c.2,000,000	c.33.3
1795	Constitutional vote	c.6,000,000	c.1,300,000	c.21.7
1795	Primary assemblies	197,644	22,720	11.5
1797	Primary assemblies	169,033	39,600	23.4
1798	Primary assemblies	229,687	45,150	19.7
1799	Primary assemblies	232,016	25,440	11.0

Note: * In the absence of any general returns for primary assemblies, these statistics are based on samples, using the best attended round of voting. In the case of the two constitutional votes, the figures for electorate and voters are approximations.

[8] This was not the procedure I adopted in *Elections in the French Revolution*, but a result of further reflection.
[9] Malcolm Crook, 'The people at the polls; electoral behaviour in revolutionary Toulon, 1789–1799', *FH*, 5 (1991), 169–70.
[10] Cyril Belmonte, 'Voter à Auriol sous la Révolution (1789–1799), *Provence historique*, LVII (2007), 177–87.
[11] Edelstein has collected the most comprehensive sample to date, in *The French Revolution*, 78 and 95–9. His findings broadly correspond to Crook, *Elections*, 57–62.
[12] Edelstein, *The French Revolution*, 211–15.

overthrow of the constitutional monarchy, witnessed further decline in most departments to less than 20 per cent in primary elections to establish a National Convention.[13] There was no time to produce fresh electoral registers, but few formerly 'passive' citizens, either poorer or younger males, seem to have used their newly acquired right to vote.[14] It was a testimony to the durability of the system that these elections were completed so rapidly amidst so much turmoil and, in some cases the absolute number of voters was higher than a year before, though the percentage was lowered by the extended franchise.

By contrast, municipal elections held in December 1792/January 1793 reversed the downward trend, attracting an average turnout of perhaps 40 per cent and, though the evidence is slight, polls held in the commune seem to have drawn a higher level of interest for the remainder of the decade.[15] That said, despite further deterioration in the internal situation, as a result of full-blown rebellion in several parts of the country, the cantonal assemblies convoked the following summer, to vote on the Constitution of 1793, produced a degree of participation in excess of 30 per cent. However, this revival of enthusiasm was not maintained when a further constitution was put to the vote in 1795 and turnout dropped back to around 20 per cent.[16] Thereafter, as annual elections resumed, after the period of revolutionary government, cantonal figures only exceeded that level on one occasion, in 1797.[17] In view of this volatility, it would be incorrect to conclude that there was general decline later in the Revolution for, if average turnout was barely above 10 per cent in the cantons in 1799, it had hit that meagre level in 1795, before more than doubling in 1797. Instead, there was ebb and flow during the revolutionary decade, and no reason to exclude the possibility of renewed upward movement in future, until the coup of Brumaire intervened, in November 1799, and instituted further changes to the electoral system.

The Napoleonic regime maintained a mass franchise, and the published results of the well-known constitutional votes (usually called plebiscites) that were held under the Consulate certainly suggested higher levels of turnout than under the Revolution. However, these consultations were subject to manipulation and fraud (see Chapter 4) and the first of them, in 1799, attracted little more than 20 per cent of the electorate in reality, though this level of participation probably doubled in 1802 and 1804.[18] When he became Consul for Life, in 1802, Napoleon

---

[13] Edelstein, *The French Revolution*, 261–6.   [14] Crook, *Elections*, 82–4.

[15] These elections have yet to receive the same attention as those held in 1790. However, Edelstein, *The French Revolution*, 281, indicates upward movement in big cities, while Bianchi, *La Révolution et la Première République* and Alain Massalsky, 'Élections et politisation dans le département des Hautes-Pyrénées, 1790-1799', Thèse pour le doctorat d'histoire, Université de Paris I, 2006, 189 and 192–6, point in the same direction for two northern and one southern department.

[16] Edelstein, *The French Revolution*, 296–9 and Crook, *Elections*, 121.

[17] Crook, *Elections*, 138–9.

[18] BL R154, *Suite du recueil des pièces et actes relatifs à l'établissement du gouvernement impérial héréditaire* (Paris, an XIII).

reinstated the cantonal assemblies of the 1790s. They met only once every five years, with one of the five designated series of departments convoked in turn each calendar year, but this badly neglected facet of Napoleonic rule kept the practice of voting alive and helped prolong the experiment with a mass suffrage for another decade.[19] Cantonal turnout rarely exceeded more than 25 per cent of the *ayant droit de voter*, differing little in this regard from the Revolution after the initial enthusiasm of 1790 had waned, but the experience should be assessed in more than purely numerical terms. The assembly mechanism ensured that for those who did take part (over one million French citizens in the 'old' departments of the First Empire) the act of voting remained a significant one, which involved rather more than simply casting a ballot.[20]

The Napoleonic prefects were in a good position to collect information on elections and they were required to do so in 1813, providing some valuable clues where electoral mobilization is concerned. Thus, in the Haute-Vienne, only one canton witnessed a relatively high turnout, which the prefect attributed to a battle between rival notables, who drew on their respective clienteles for support.[21] The prefect of the Finistère confirmed the need to motivate the peasantry, with landlords and lawyers on whom they depended playing a decisive role in whether or not they went to vote. Yet their exhortations were not always heeded. Jones cites the example of the mayor who attempted to assemble voters in the hamlet of Rennemoulin (Seine-et-Oise), at 6.00am on the morning of 26 August 1792, in readiness for a trek to the *chef-lieu de canton*. Yet, while half of the electors eventually appeared, only three or four of them eventually accompanied him to the poll.[22] Invitations to vote, even those which stressed the duties of citizenship, rarely bore much fruit, while the level of competition for office would remain a key factor in future turnout. Its obverse, when the outcome was a foregone conclusion, might be termed 'consensual abstention'. Rather than representing an individual choice, voting remained a collective act, deeply rooted in the local context, the reflection of particular circumstances that can only be teased out by means of detailed case studies.

It might, therefore, appear that any attempt to generalize about turnout during the Revolutionary and Napoleonic eras is doomed to failure, especially in the light of different types of vote, constantly changing regulations, and the irregular but frequent incidence of elections, all occurring at a time of tremendous turmoil. At best, only half the electorate was participating, yet the north-eastern quadrant of France, roughly speaking the regions with better communications and higher

---

[19] Coppolani, *Les Élections*.

[20] Malcolm Crook and John Dunne, 'The First European elections? Voting and imperial state-building under Napoleon, 1802–1813', *Historical Journal*, 57 (2014), 661–97.

[21] Malcolm Crook, 'Voter sous Napoléon. L'autopsie de l'expérience électorale du Premier Empire d'après une enquête préfectorale sur les consultations cantonales de 1813', *AhRf*, 382 (2015), 117.

[22] Jones, *Liberty and Locality in the French Revolution*, 132.

rates of literacy, did consistently tend to vote more heavily than elsewhere. The constitutional vote of 1793, for which an almost complete set of departmental figures is available, bears this conclusion out, though there were some salient exceptions in the south-west. This regional pattern of participation is roughly confirmed by a similar analysis of the Napoleonic consultations held between 1800 and 1815.[23] The north-east would remain a bastion of high turnout until more recent decades, when the broad nineteenth-century split between a more strongly polling north, and a south more inclined to abstention, shifted significantly.[24] It was also the case that inhabitants of plains tended to be more assiduous in their attendance at the cantonal assemblies than those from upland areas, but access to polling stations was an obvious factor, a barrier to electoral participation wherever considerable displacement was required.[25]

The urban–rural divide offers a further basis for some general differentiation, which would also prove enduring. Despite the proximity of their electoral assemblies, inhabitants of large towns were especially prone to relatively low turnout, and Paris offers an outstanding example of this characteristic. Despite its celebrated political activism, only 16 per cent of electors voted in polls to choose its first mayor in August 1790 and rates were little higher thereafter.[26] In contrast to urban anonymity, village solidarity was reflected in the greater importance generally accorded to municipal elections in rural areas where, on the whole, the smaller the commune the bigger the turnout.[27] To be sure, in the countryside there was effectively little change from the shape of long-standing village assemblies which had met (regularly in some areas) under the *Ancien Régime* and were convened for preliminary elections to the Estates General of 1789. The impact of the electoral regime established in 1790 was much more disruptive in towns, since it brought to an end to voting in a variety of corporate bodies and, instead, instituted polling by *quartier*, or *section*. However, as the Revolution gathered pace, with the circulation of the revolutionary press and the creation of political clubs, urban turnout in cantonal assemblies began to eclipse those in rural areas.[28] When the level of competition was especially fierce, much higher turnout

---

[23] Malcolm Crook, 'Confidence from below? Collaboration and resistance in the Napoleonic plebiscites', in Michael Rowe (ed.), *Collaboration and Resistance in Napoleonic Europe: State-Formation in an Age of Upheaval, c.1800–1815* (Basingstoke, 2003), 26–8.

[24] Frédéric Salmon, *Atlas électoral de la France 1848–2001* (Paris, 2001), 86–7 and Lancelot, *L'Abstentionnisme électoral*, 54–77.

[25] See, for example, upland areas in the Pyrenees, in Vincent Wright, 'The Basses-Pyrénées from 1848–1870: A Study in Departmental Politics', PhD, University of London, 3 vols, 1965, i, 260–300 and isolated villages in Georges Dupeux, 'Le problème des abstentions dans le département du Loir-et-Cher au début de la Troisième République', *Rfsp*, 2 (1952), 79–84.

[26] Edelstein, *The French Revolution*, 343–5.   [27] Crook, *Elections*, 64–6.

[28] Malcolm Crook, 'Aux urnes citoyens! Urban and rural turnout', in Alan Forrest and Peter Jones (eds), *Reshaping France: Town, Country and Region during the French Revolution* (Manchester, 1991), 152–67.

occurred in cities: for example, 40 per cent at Toulon in 1791 and 70 per cent at Toulouse in 1797.

Yet, in an age when pluralism was not upheld as an ideal, partisan conflict could reduce rather than raise turnout, as voters were deterred from attending the electoral assemblies by threats of violence. Assembling inhabitants from different villages in the same canton was always liable to provoke inter-communal animosity: as one observer of brawling at Villepinte in the Aude put it, in 1790, 'these people end up trading blows every time they encounter one another'.[29] Later in the decade, with the addition of a more pronounced political element, the atmosphere could become still more intimidating: investigating the allegation from one voter, in the elections of 1799 at the canton of Berre (Bouches-du-Rhône), that the earthenware pot employed as a ballot box had been broken over his head, the justice of the peace discovered that the floor of the assembly room was littered with broken chairs, as well as shards of the ill-used *urne*.[30] In these circumstances minorities understandably stayed away and abandoned the field to their rivals. Boycotts also stemmed from a refusal to take oaths of allegiance before a vote could be cast. These tests of loyalty (which accompanied elections down to 1848) certainly stopped many Catholics voting after a schism between Church and Revolution over ecclesiastical reform in 1790.

Nor should the impact of virtually continuous warfare between 1792 and 1815 be ignored when levels of electoral participation are assessed; these days elections are suspended when states of emergency are declared or international hostilities break out. In eastern frontier departments in August 1792, for example, turnout fell sharply as some assemblies were obliged to change location or curtail their business.[31] The unprecedented numbers of adult males engaged in military activity significantly reduced the available electorate everywhere (though members of the armed forces were able to vote on the various constitutions, in their companies). Finally, the government's response to unwelcome electoral results under the Directory was hardly designed to make voting a more attractive proposition. The newly returned deputy for the Dordogne, François Lamarque rightly warned on the eve of the impending purge of deputies in floréal Year VI (May 1798) that 'the people will cease to bother with elections when they cannot be sure that their choices will be respected...'; he was among those whose mandate was subsequently annulled.[32]

Critics have been loath to acknowledge these inhibiting factors when making negative comparisons between turnout during the Revolution and that of later

---

[29] Crook, *Elections*, 75.
[30] AFIII 217, Lettre au commissaire du Directoire exécutif, du juge de paix de Berre, 4 germinal VII (24 Mar. 1799).
[31] Jean-Baptiste Legoff, 'Des élections sous la menace de l'invasion. L'exemple meusien', in Michel Biard et al. (eds), *1792 Entrer en République* (Paris, 2013), 125–30.
[32] BL FR 101, François Lamarque, *Discours*, 11 floréal VI (30 Apr. 1798).

periods, though their strictures have become less persuasive in the light of declining participation in mature democracies during recent years. Extremely adverse circumstances notwithstanding, an unprecedented experiment in mass voting had been conducted in France, for a decade and more. Those who did vote enjoyed, or rather endured, an intensive experience, which constituted a veritable school for citizenship and involved more individuals than the membership of political clubs or the readership of the revolutionary press. Whatever its shortcomings, which were numerous, this initial electoral apprenticeship left a rich legacy.

The Napoleonic extension of voting into the following century actually concluded with two municipal polls of the sort that had been curtailed in 1799. In the summer of 1813, elections took place, by canton, for a partial renewal of councillors in towns with a population in excess of 5,000 inhabitants. Voting occurred at a difficult moment for the regime, but mostly replicated the level of turnout—up to 20 per cent of the electorate—that had typified larger urban authorities since 1790.[33] Then, following the unexpected turn of events which brought Napoleon back to power a year later, during the Hundred Days of 1815, a hastily organized round of local elections took place in communities with a population of less than 5,000 inhabitants (where mayors and councillors had been nominated since 1800). These polls have been almost completely ignored by historians, but John Dunne's recent study of a single department, the Seine-Inférieure, suggests an average turnout of roughly 30 per cent, conducted in an orderly manner at an uncertain moment. These humble elections testify to the success of the past twenty-five years in acculturating the rural population of France to the practice of voting.[34] It would be another sixteen years before ordinary people had the opportunity to participate again.

Turnout in Electoral Colleges, 1790–1848

With mass voting in abeyance after 1815 average turnout was invariably high under the Bourbon Restoration, when only (direct) parliamentary elections remained in being, with involvement restricted to less than 100,000 wealthy taxpayers. The same, elevated degrees of participation remained the rule for legislative polls when the franchise was modestly extended under the July Monarchy after 1830. This outcome should occasion no surprise: from 1790 onwards, it was evident that better-off citizens were much more likely than others to take part in elections at municipal or cantonal level during the Revolution and Empire. They

---

[33] Crook, *Elections*, 114–15.
[34] John Dunne, 'In search of the village and small-town elections of Napoleon's Hundred Days: a departmental study', *FH*, 29 (2015), 304–27.

generally had more time to do so, as well as the incentive of seeking office, not to mention the cultural capital to cope with the demands of complex procedures and composing endless ballot papers.

Equally unsurprising, turnout at the secondary level, in departmental and arrondissement colleges between 1790 and 1815, was usually far stronger than in the primary and local elections that have just been considered. To be sure, those elected by the cantonal assemblies were often serving in some official capacity already and they were expected to participate in the second-degree assemblies, where voting was more of a function than a right. Indeed, in the Year V (1797), these electors were explicitly described as 'fonctionnaires publics', because they were 'undertaking, on its behalf, operations that the people could not perform for itself'.[35] In a few cases they faced sanctions if they failed to discharge this duty, with some Parisian sections asserting the right to recall negligent members of the electoral colleges in 1792. Apologies were certainly required for absence from their Napoleonic successors and the penalty for missing three consecutive sessions without a valid excuse was loss of membership.[36] The level of mobilization for these second-degree elections can be explored together with participation in parliamentary polls during the constitutional monarchies from 1814 to 1848, because they shared a good deal in common.

Despite some democratization during the 1790s, second-degree electors outside of larger towns were mostly drawn from the wealthier elements in society, albeit subject to significant turnover.[37] By contrast, members of the Napoleonic colleges were elected for life and, at the departmental level after 1802, all of them had to be drawn from lists of the 600 highest taxpayers (*les plus imposés*); they were, by definition, well-heeled notables. Attendance at these secondary assemblies was only remunerated between 1792 and 1799, but the cost of travel and maintenance seems to have proved little disincentive before allowances were put in place. At the inaugural departmental assembly in the Loir-et-Cher, in 1790, it was stated, without intentional irony, that 'only' 325 out of 329 electors were present.[38]

In fact, turnout figures at electoral colleges must be subject to the same caveat as those emanating from the primary assemblies, since there was a succession of votes, with a *ballottage* delivering a final verdict if two earlier rounds had failed to deliver an absolute majority. The greatest turnout might be in a tightly contested run-off, although numbers usually diminished the longer the session lasted. In

---

[35] *Moniteur*, 29 Ventôse V (19 Mar. 1797), 718.
[36] Sénatus-consulte organique de la Constitution du 16 thermidor an X (4 Aug. 1802), art. 22. The penalty for non-attendance does not seem to have been imposed.
[37] Malcolm Crook, 'Masses de granit ou grains de sable? Les électeurs des assemblées départementales sous la Révolution française, 1790–1799', in Denise Turrel (ed.), *Regards sur les sociétés modernes XVIe–XVIIIe siècle. Mélanges offerts à Claude Petitfrère* (Tours, 1997), 203–10.
[38] AN F1cIII Loir-et-Cher 1, PV de l'assemblée électorale du Loir-et-Cher, 1 June 1790.

June 1791, the appearance of just two hundred members (out of over nine hundred), to vote for some lesser posts at the electoral assembly of Paris, has been used as evidence of indifference at this level: 'the 40,000 (second-degree electors) did little better than 4,000,000 (primary voters)' according to one historian.[39] Yet this comment completely ignores the fact that members of the departmental college in the capital were summoned on no less than 122 occasions between November 1790 and June 1791: in other words, an average of once every two days. When more important polls had been taken, over three-quarters of the electors were present.[40]

If we retain the highest recorded vote, it was unusual for attendance at the college level to fall below 80 per cent and, when it did so, there were often specific circumstances to explain abstention, such as religious opposition to the Revolution in 1791, or foreign invasion in 1792. Not surprisingly, many Catholic electors, who strongly objected to the changes imposed on their Church, boycotted the election of bishops at specially convened departmental assemblies in 1791.[41] By contrast, mobilization was stimulated by an element of politicization, especially under the Directory, when individuals were often chosen or rejected on account of their previous roles in the Revolution, not least the stance they had adopted during the Terror. To be sure, turnout was more variable under the Napoleonic regime, when the introduction of a quorum of half the membership did sometimes mean that an electoral college might not convene at all, struggled to commence proceedings, or (most likely) concluded with minor business incomplete as individuals drifted away. However, the great majority of both departmental and arrondissement colleges did comfortably meet this threshold and participation levels of over 70 per cent were commonplace.[42] The one salient exception occurred during the Hundred Days, in 1815, when those who did not wish to compromise themselves by association with the returning emperor absented themselves (and the quorum was wisely abandoned). On this particular occasion, in these very specific circumstances, average turnout fell to around 35 per cent.[43]

As an interim measure, the re-restored Bourbon monarchy employed the Napoleonic colleges virtually unchanged; there were no fresh primary elections, though a number of royal nominees were added. These assemblies were used to create a fresh legislature in the summer of 1815, and again in 1816, with notably high turnout on both occasions, before a new electoral regime was introduced in

[39] J. M. Thompson, *The French Revolution*, revised edn (Oxford, 1985), 227.

[40] Étienne Charavay (ed.), *Assemblée électorale de Paris, 18 novembre 1790–15 juin 1791* (Paris, 1890).

[41] Malcolm Crook, 'Citizen bishops: episcopal elections in the French Revolution', *The Historical Journal*, 43 (2000), 964–7.

[42] Crook and Dunne, 'The First European elections?', 689–95.

[43] Malcolm Crook, '"Ma volonté est celle du people": voting in the plebiscite and parliamentary elections during Napoléon's Hundred Days, April–May 1815', *FHS*, 32 (2009), 635–40.

1817. The contingent of less than 100,000 voters, which emerged from the royal charter of 1814, was now charged with directly electing deputies to the legislative Chamber in one fifth of the departments each year.[44] This system only functioned a few times before it was modified in 1820, then abandoned in 1824, but sampling suggests that an average of roughly 70 per cent of this small electorate participated in the process, despite having to travel to the departmental *chef-lieu* to vote. Historians have been misled into thinking turnout was rather lower during this brief period because they have relied on a set of unrepresentative figures, chiefly culled from by-elections, which were published by the writer Chateaubriand, an opponent of the electoral system who was seeking to discredit it.

In the absence of nominal lists for each round of voting, levels of turnout must continue to be calculated according to the best-attended round in the series of votes that the electoral mechanism continued to entail until 1848 (Table 6.2). Of course, participation varied considerably from one to another and, as under the Revolution or Napoleon, when it became obvious that they had absolutely no prospect of winning, some voters simply desisted—the case of the disheartened liberal minority at the arrondissement of Dijon in 1824, for instance.[45] However, as a result of alterations to the electoral process in the 1820s, which added more accessible arrondissement assemblies, plus the impact of fiercer electoral competition arising from a growing liberal challenge to the regime, turnout subsequently rose to an average of over 80 per cent. Indeed, in the political crisis of 1830, it reached almost 90 per cent.

Table 6.2 Electoral participation under the constitutional monarchy, 1815–1846

Year	College	Electorate	Voters	% Turnout
1815	Departments	20,711	15,260	73.7
1816	Departments	20,711	14,316	71.3
1824	Departments and arrondissements	99,125	84,259	85.0
1827	Departments and arrondissements	88,603	74,655	84.3
1830	Departments and arrondissements	94,598	86,515	91.5
1831	Arrondissements	166, 583	125,090	75.1
1834	Arrondissements	171,015	129,211	75.6
1837	Arrondissements	198,836	151,720	76.3
1839	Arrondissements	201,271	164,862	81.9
1842	Arrondissements	220,040	173,694	78.9
1846	Arrondissements	240893	199,827	82.9

Note: Figures for turnout in elections to partially renew the Chamber of Deputies each year between 1817 and 1823 were not collated by the administration.

---

[44] Malcolm Crook, 'Suffrage et citoyenneté sous la Restauration', in Michel Pertué (ed), *Suffrage, citoyenneté et révolutions 1789–1848* (Paris, 2002), 80–2.

[45] Fizaine, *La Vie politique*, 263. Liberals had participated in the initial choice of a presiding bureau, when they realized that rather more numerous royalists would prevail in the substantive votes to follow.

The advent of the July Monarchy may have modestly extended the parliamentary suffrage, but the electoral boycott (the so-called 'internal emigration') by supporters of the fallen Bourbon monarchy, the legitimists, initially reduced the average level of turnout to around 75 per cent.[46] It began to rise again in the 1840s, a result of greater political engagement from both right and left, not to mention pressure from the administrative machine, and it topped the 80 per cent mark in 1846, in what would prove to be the final, general election under this regime. Less than a quarter of a million Frenchmen were learning to vote in parliamentary elections at that point, but it should be stressed that polling under the highly restricted franchise that operated under the constitutional monarchies did attract some popular participation in the towns where it was conducted for up to a week.[47] As in contemporary Britain, where a similar phenomenon of wider involvement was also apparent, despite a limited suffrage, elections created a carnival atmosphere. Ordinary townspeople gathered outside the electors' meeting place, waving placards, singing songs, harassing voters, forming cavalcades, and illuminating windows to celebrate liberal victories (or, in some cases, reactionary ones).[48] According to the prefect of the Côte-d'Or, giant banners were unfurled at Dijon in June 1830, bearing the words 'Vive la Charte' and an 'electoral cantata' was composed to address those able to vote: 'Wealthy citizens of France, do not disappoint our expectations when choosing representatives.'[49]

Moreover, although Louis-Philippe's regime sorely disappointed hopes for a substantially enlarged 'national' electorate, it did offer a fresh opportunity to vote to greater numbers of male citizens at the local level. A slightly more generous franchise was granted to accompany the reintroduction of triennial elections for departmental and arrondissement councils, with the former witnessing rising turnout that exceeded 70 per cent in 1845.[50] Far more significant was the re-establishment of municipal elections, which offered a renewed apprenticeship in mass voting and prompted the regular participation of well over a million Frenchmen, especially in smaller, rural communities where the vote was more widely distributed.[51] The second, triennial round of municipal elections in 1834

---

[46] AN C*II 383, Les élections d'août 1846 et les élections précédentes, tableau comparatif des nombres d'électeurs et de votans depuis l'année 1815. This first indication of comparative turnout reflects growing administrative interest in the subject. On the legitimist boycott, see André-Jean Tudesq, *Les Grands notables en France (1840-1849) Étude historique d'une psychologie sociale*, 2 vols (Paris, 1964), i, 130–3.

[47] Malcolm Crook, 'Citizenship without democracy: the culture of elections in France under the Constitutional Monarchy, 1814-1848', in Silke Hensel et al. (eds), *Constitutional Cultures: On the Concept and Representations of Cultures in the Atlantic World* (Newcastle upon Tyne, 2012), 418–20.

[48] James Vernon, *Politics and the People: A Study in English Political Culture, c.1815-1867* (Cambridge, 1993).

[49] AN F7 6740, Préfet de la Côte-d'Or au ministre de l'intérieur, 26 June 1830.

[50] AN F3 I 16, Tableaux des votants: conseils généraux, 1833-45 and André-Jean Tudesq, *Les Conseils généraux en France au temps de Guizot, 1840-1848* (Paris, 1967), p. 60.

[51] Guionnet, *L'Apprentissage de la politique moderne*, 212–43.

revealed that little more than 50 per cent of the electorate had taken part, but turnout had been higher in 1831, when the system was inaugurated, and it did grow somewhat during the following decade.[52]

Municipal polls, like their departmental and arrondissement counterparts, were regarded by the regime as 'administrative' not 'political' elections, because those elected were not legislators. A series of prefectoral reports in the 1840s accordingly emphasized the predominance of personal over ideological rivalry, especially in the countryside, but there was certainly competition for office, which might involve royalist and republican opponents of the regime, thus enabling some voters to assert their independence by supporting them.[53] Above all, a new generation was being familiarized with the electoral process, via the intensive assembly mechanism, and recent attention to the restoration of elections for officers in the reconstituted militia, the National Guard, underlines this important development.[54] These polls, which offered the vote on a still broader basis, do not seem to have stimulated much enthusiasm in the countryside, but they did attract some remarkable interest in the big cities, and not least at Paris. A manual described them as 'a vital school for electoral instruction', where citizens would learn to exercise their voting rights. During the 1840s, when veritable election campaigns were being conducted in the capital for the choice of colonels and captains, turnout might reach as high as 80 per cent. Further foundations were thus being laid for the massive response to the arrival of direct, universal, male suffrage after another change of regime in 1848.

Establishing the Practice of Universal Male Suffrage, 1848–1880s

The advent of the Second Republic is often regarded as marking the beginning of mass voting in France and it certainly inaugurated direct legislative elections by universal male suffrage. Almost seven million Frenchmen cast a vote in elections to the new regime's Constituent Assembly, held on 23 April 1848, most of them for the first time in their lives, in the biggest electoral operation ever mounted, anywhere in the world. The oft-quoted turnout of over 80 per cent may be a little exaggerated, on account of the debatable calculations made in some departments, but it does compare favourably with the rather lower levels recorded in the Revolution of 1789.[55] However, such a high level of electoral engagement was not

[52] AN F1bI 257, *Compte rendu au Roi sur les élections municipales de 1834* (Paris, 1836).
[53] AN F20 282 (52), Analyse des rapports sur les élections municipales envoyés par les préfets, 30 Jan. 1847.
[54] Larrère, *L'Urne et le fusil*, 269–75.
[55] A rather precise figure of 83.6 per cent is often cited, but there was understandable under-registration and confusion in some departments, including the Var where the turnout was miscalculated, so it would not be wise to go beyond a (still extremely high) figure of 80 per cent. There were

to be sustained. Participation in the numerous polls that followed, between 1848 and 1851, was lower and frequently poor.[56] The presidential election of December 1848, which overwhelmingly returned Louis-Napoleon Bonaparte, did muster some 75 per cent of a (further enlarged) electorate, which actually attracted more voters than in April, but the legislative elections of May 1849 drew less than 70 per cent.

A much more significant decline was evident in polling for local councils and parliamentary by-elections. In the summer of 1848, the suffrage was duly extended to all adult males at municipal, departmental, and arrondissement levels. A survey of municipal polling taken at the time suggests that average participation at the end of July 1848, based on 56 out of 85 departments, was around the 60 per cent mark, and in some cases dropped below 50 per cent. When elections for the departmental and then arrondissement councils were held in the cantons a month later, the departmental average frequently fell below 40 per cent.[57] Meanwhile, numerous by-elections for the Constituent Assembly had been necessary to replace deputies who had been elected in more than one department, but turnout of only 30 per cent was not unusual when a solitary representative was to be chosen, rather than a full slate.

Of course, even a poll that attracted a minority of the mass male electorate meant that far more individuals were now engaging in voting than under the preceding regime. Polling fatigue was undoubtedly a factor in lowering participation during the summer months, when agricultural activity was at its height. It was not an ideal moment to summon country people to vote and similar inconvenience had undoubtedly taken a toll during the 1790s, when polling took place without regard to the rural calendar. Moreover, in 1848, as during the French Revolution, apart from municipal elections, these contests were held in the cantonal *chef-lieu* and usually involved a journey in order to cast a vote. The prefect in the Saône-et-Loire reported that in these circumstances 'rural communes failed to turn up or only despatched a small number of voters', while a mayor in the Vaucluse noted: 'For many of our rural inhabitants universal suffrage is a burden, for it creates the need to travel on a Sunday, when they prefer to be resting from the exertions of the week.'[58] Bemoaning the indifference of rural voters, the

---

actually more than half a million additional voters in December 1848, when the turnout is put at 75 per cent on a significantly expanded electoral register.

[56] Malcolm Crook, 'Getting out the vote: electoral participation in France, 1789–1851', in Ceri Crossley and Martin Cornick (eds), *Problems in French History: Essays in Honour of Douglas Johnson* (Basingstoke, 2000), 50–63.
[57] AN F3 I 16, Rapport sur les élections municipales et cantonales de 1848, 5 Nov. 1849 and Pierre Lévêque, 'Les elections municipales et cantonales en 1848', in Jean-Luc Mayaud (ed.), *1848. Actes du colloque international du cent-cinquantenaire* (Paris, 1998), 85–95.
[58] Lévêque, 'Les élections municipales et cantonales', 95 and Natalie Petiteau, '1848 en Vaucluse, ou l'impossible république bourgeoise', *Cahiers d'Histoire*, 43 (1998), 236.

prefect of the neighbouring Côte-d'Or felt that voting in the commune for all elections was the only answer, otherwise 'the operation of universal suffrage will be distorted...and well-organized minorities will impose their will on the country.'[59] In the event, a large number of subdivisions, or 'sections', were introduced into rural cantons, which reduced the electoral displacement for those voters yet, clearly, the huge turnout recorded on Easter Day 1848 should be set in the wider context of rather variable electoral participation during the Second Republic; the breakthrough was by no means definitive.

It would also be unwise to overstate the unprecedented nature of these mass elections, because they continued to exhibit a strongly collective character, and an element of politicization should not necessarily be inferred from a high level of turnout. Tocqueville's memorable description of voting in April 1848, in Normandy, scarcely requires repeating, but it speaks volumes about the way in which many voters were mobilized:

We were supposed to vote as a body in the town of Saint-Pierre, one league from our village. On the morning of the election, all the voters – the entire male population above the age of twenty – assembled in front of the church. The men lined up double file in alphabetical order. I took the place that corresponded to my name, because I knew that in democratic times and countries one cannot place oneself at the head of the people, but must be placed there by others. Pack horses and carts followed this long procession, bearing the crippled and sick who wished to accompany us. Only the women and children remained behind. We were in all 170 persons...I reminded these good people of the gravity and importance of what they were about to do. I advised them not to allow themselves to be accosted or diverted by people in town, who might try to lead them astray. Instead, we should remain together as a body, each in his place, until everyone had voted...They agreed and obeyed. Everyone voted together and I have reason to believe that nearly all voted for the same candidate.[60]

Once rural citizens like these had arrived in the *chef-lieu*, they were called in turn to cast their votes as a communal group, before returning home in the same way. In this case, a unanimous choice had been made, though Tocqueville was too modest to name himself as one of those elected, taking over 90 per cent of the votes in the department of the Manche as a whole. Ironically, republicans had opted for voting at the *chef-lieu de canton* in an effort to reduce the influence of notables like him but, by allocating each village its own slot at the polling station, they encouraged the collective act that is described here. It was reinforced by the choice of Easter Sunday for this initial election, when practising Catholics were most assiduous in their attendance at mass. Voters often set out together after early-morning communion, accompanied by their priests, in something of a pilgrimage, with clerical influence also playing an important role in these polls.

Mobilization had remained largely in the hands of the notables and this helps to explain the rather conservative complexion of the Constituent Assembly elected in April 1848, as well as the huge success of Louis-Napoleon in the presidential election the following December. Urban turnout was lower on the whole, because there was rarely the same social pressure to vote, and this pattern was repeated in local elections. As in the past, so under the Second Republic, competition between notables was a key factor in turnout in the countryside, when rival candidates, vying on a personal rather than political basis, rallied their respective supporters. An especially dramatic example of this phenomenon emanates from a general council by-election in the Ain, early in 1851, when turnout of almost 95 per cent (100 per cent in some communes) astonished the prefect who commented that he had never witnessed an election that was better supported, nor more hotly disputed.[61] Conversely, in cases where the outcome was a foregone conclusion, in the absence of any real contestation, participation tended to fall sharply.

The legislative elections of 1849 did witness a degree of polarization, which indicated a stirring of politicization, with radical republicans (the *démocrates-socialistes*) and legitimists both making headway with a particular pitch and some concerted campaigning.[62] However, turnout was down compared with the two 'national' elections of the preceding year. A detailed examination of voting statistics suggests that particular communes, or even whole cantons, continued to express distinct preferences for one list rather than another.[63] Indeed, prominent conservative candidates continued to attract near-unanimous votes across some departments and Tocqueville was again returned with almost 90 per cent of the votes cast in his home constituency of the Manche. The development of individual choice, like electoral pluralism, would prove to be a lengthy process and any incipient movement in this direction was quickly interrupted after Louis-Napoleon seized power in his coup d'état of December 1851, overturning the Second Republic before a second cycle of presidential, parliamentary, and local elections could be held in 1852.

Theodore Zeldin suggested long ago that the Second Empire, established under Napoleon III, enabled the practice of universal (male) suffrage 'to become ingrained in the habits of the (French) nation', but at that point Bonapartism was taboo where republican historians were concerned.[64] It took some time before

[61] AN F1bI 230/1, Préfet de l'Ain au ministre, 19 Feb. 1851.
[62] Crook, 'Universal suffrage as counter-revolution?', 61–3.
[63] See, for example, Peter McPhee, *Les Semailles de la République dans les Pyrénées-Orientales 1846–1852* (Perpignan, 1995), 164.
[64] Zeldin, *The Political System of Napoleon III*, 98.

Table 6.3 Plebiscites and legislative elections, 1851–1870

Year	Consultation	Electorate	Voters	% Turnout
1851	Plebiscite	9,980,915	8,152,552	82.3
February 1852	Election	9,836,043	6,222,983	63.3
December 1852	Plebiscite	9,855,238	8,144,926	82.6
1857	Election	9,490,206	6,118,317	64.5
1863	Election	10,004,028	7,290,170	72.9
1869	Election	10,416,666	8,125,017	78.0
1870	Plebiscite	10,939,384	9,044,473	82.7

Guy Hermet's provocative statement that 'an electoral apprenticeship was effected in France under the Second Empire... not under the aegis of democratic government, but through the leadership of an authoritarian regime...', found general acceptance among French historians.[65] The proposition has much to commend it, though it cannot be endorsed without some reservations.

As he had promised, Louis-Napoleon did immediately restore universal male suffrage, undoing most of the severe restrictions imposed on the franchise by conservatives in May 1850. The subsequent plebiscites of 1851 and 1852 both attracted over 80 per cent of an electorate of ten million voters, despite the fact that they were held during winter months (Table 6.3). Of course, tremendous administrative pressure was applied to secure high turnout, like the overwhelmingly positive verdicts. Priests were supportive, while (government-appointed) mayors and other local officials played an even greater role because all voting was now taking place in the commune. In small villages, where the bulk of the population resided, attendance could be easily policed, and some defaulters offered apologies, even though they were not obliged to do so. As the prefect of the Basses-Alpes put it, in a circular to mayors, 'abstention was not permissible', since it would suggest either 'indifference or hostility', neither of which should be tolerated.[66]

By contrast, when it came to both legislative and local elections, the initial impact of renewed Napoleonic rule on participation was a rather negative one. To be sure, as always with the inception of a new regime, these polls took place in rapid succession during 1852, producing some relatively low turnout, with parliamentary elections in February attracting scarcely more than 60 per cent of the electorate (less than in 1849 in fact). The imposition of official candidates, approved and supported by the administration meant there was no real contest in half of the 259 seats, and the incentive to vote in such circumstances was

<hr/>

[65] Guy Hermet, *Le Peuple contre la démocratie* (Paris, 1989), 183–4; Lagouyete, 'Élections', 228; and Sudhir Hazareesingh, *From Subject to Citizen: The Second Empire and the Emergence of Modern French Democracy* (Princeton, NJ, 1998), 312–13.
[66] AN F1cII 98, Préfet des Basses-Alpes aux maires, 19 Feb. 1852.

inevitably diminished. Continuing repression following the coup d'état deterred many republicans, who deliberately boycotted the polls, and some legitimists followed suit. Cantonal elections, held in the summer months of July and August, rarely attracted turnout above 50 per cent, and it was often less. Nor did levels of participation show any improvement at the triennial renewal of one third of departmental and arrondissement councillors in 1855, even in rural areas.[67] In larger towns, in the same year, it was unusual for more than a quarter of the electorate to vote for a complete renewal of municipal councils, repeating the low turnout recorded three years earlier and, evidently, a reflection of political opposition as much as the apathy denounced by administrators.

One or two leading officials were led to query the wisdom of retaining the electoral system as a result. Others were worried about the sheer number of elections being held, to the extent that in 1867, Paul Pamard, a deputy in the Corps législatif, would opine: 'I do not think that any government, whatever its form, can function with a such a frequent electoral regime.'[68] His proposal was to hold a full set of elections, from local to legislative, every six years, in order to minimize the disruption they caused. The Second Empire was indeed holding a regular series of national, departmental, and municipal polls—not to mention numerous by-elections—to the extent that some contests took place each year. On average, every elector was invited to vote every other year, besides being summoned to numerous by-elections. However, under the Second Empire, unlike the First or Second Republics, turnout was to assume an upward trajectory across the board, encouraged by a general process of liberalization after 1860. This development, which culminated in the gradual reduction of official candidatures, first in local and then in legislative polls, was accompanied by a freer press and greater latitude for public meetings, all of which led to greater competition for office and higher levels of electoral participation.

The legislative elections of 1857 had attracted only a slightly bigger turnout than five years earlier, but a more substantial increase occurred in 1863 and, in 1869, it reached almost 80 per cent, in both rounds of voting. Although the subject has never been studied beyond a few localities, the same progression was apparent for cantonal and municipal elections, albeit not to the same degree. In the 1860s, triennial cantonal turnout in a small sample of departments broke the 60 per cent barrier, while the same was true of quinquennial municipal elections, with the exception of urban centres where opposition remained entrenched and republicans counselled abstention.[69] During what would be the final year of the

    [67] AN F1bI 230/1, Listes des membres des conseils généraux, 1852, with voting figures for cantonal elections in six departments, and AN BB18 1543, Analyse des rapports sur les élections cantonales de 1855.
    [68] *Moniteur*, 9 Apr. 1867, 424.
    [69] This conclusion is based on a small sample of departments: AD Côte-d'Or M 306–35, PV des élections cantonales, 1852–70; AD Morbihan M 289–304, PV des élections cantonales, 1852–70;

Empire's existence, from 1869 to 1870, there were two rounds of local elections, as well a general election and a plebiscite, but turnout held up in every case. Indeed, the cantonal elections of June 1870, which involved almost half the seats on departmental and arrondissement councils, attracted a record turnout of over 68 per cent.[70] Moreover, the municipal elections that went ahead in August, despite the fatal declaration of war against Prussia a month earlier, achieved a remarkable average turnout of 64 per cent. Larger towns continued to lag behind, but many of them witnessed their highest levels of participation since 1848.[71]

The 'semi-competitive' elections which the regime had instituted at the outset had become much more competitive by the time it collapsed. This transition is reflected in the growth of 'opposition' votes in legislative elections, which rose from 500,000 in 1852 to over three million (40 per cent of the total cast) in 1869. Just one in ten seats went uncontested in 1869, as opposed to one in four in 1863, when there were just eleven second-round *ballottages*, as opposed to 59 six years later. Equally significant, votes were split in many more cantons and communes than in the past. Unanimity was more rarely recorded at even the smallest of polling stations, and voting was starting to become a matter of individual choice rather than a collective act.[72] According to an observer of a by-election in the Tarn in 1868, 'for the very first time I have witnessed peasants voting independently...with a comprehension of what *la liberté du vote* actually means.'[73] The following year a *commissaire de police* in the Basses-Pyrénées concurred: 'Voters are no longer as easily influenced as they used to be...they are beginning to vote according to their own ideas and opinions.'[74] The legislative polls of 1869 have accordingly been hailed as marking the dawn of the modern electoral era, the first on which a meaningful political analysis can be conducted, with the possible exception of 1849.[75] Yet attachment to personalities or parochial interests would persist long into the future, even though communal political affiliations were beginning to weaken over the course of the Second Empire. The changing character of voting was a complex, uneven process and much more research is required at the grassroots before these contours of politicization can be better understood.

The continuing evolution of the 'liberal' Empire was by no means assured, but its rapid demise, following defeat in the war with Prussia, cut short this expansive apprenticeship in voting and levels of electoral participation subsequently

---

AD Seine-et-Oise (Yvelines) 2M 15/2–2M 16/1, PV des élections cantonales, 1852–70; and AD Puy-de-Dôme M 1840–52, PV des élections cantonales, 1852–70.

[70] Éric Anceau, 'L'Empire libéral: essai d'histoire politique totale', 2 vols, Travail inédit de dossier d'habilitation, Université Paris-Sorbonne, 2014, ii, 678, contradicting the emphasis on abstention in Louis Girard et al., *Les Conseillers généraux en 1870* (Paris, 1967), 134.

[71] Anceau, 'L'Empire libéral', ii, 784–6.   [72] A sample of PV for 1869 from AN série C.

[73] Cited in André Armengaud, *Les Populations de l'est-Aquitain au début de l'époque contemporaine: recherches sur une région moins développée (vers 1845–vers 1871)* (Paris, 1961), 423.

[74] Cited in Wright, 'The Basses-Pyrénées', i, 373.   [75] Girard (ed.), *Les Élections de 1869*, iii.

plummeted amidst the fallout. A Republic was proclaimed in September 1870, but a National Assembly could not be elected on the basis of universal male suffrage until February 1871, following an armistice with the enemy. In circumstances of occupation and displacement, due to civilian flight as well as military service, a relatively low turnout was to be expected. Not surprisingly, no figure for the level of participation was forthcoming at the time, though it may be put at around 60 per cent of the putative electorate.[76] In keeping with republican tradition, polling for deputies reverted to *scrutin de liste*, with votes cast at the cantonal *chefs-lieux*, while poor weather made the necessary travel difficult. Turnout would remain modest in the series of by-elections that followed: one contemporary calculation put the average for all of them, from March 1871 to February 1874, at just under 62 per cent, but the entire departmental electorate was summoned to the polls, even when a solitary deputy was to be returned.[77]

A Third Republic was eventually consolidated, against the odds, but uncertainty about the future, not to mention continuing insecurity in the early 1870s, was also reflected in low turnout at local elections, where the enthusiasm registered at the end of the Second Empire had evaporated. At Paris, for example, a fresh round of municipal polls in the summer of 1871 attracted little more than half the electorate, and the outcome was similar at Dijon.[78] Taine's comment on turnout for cantonal elections that same year was undoubtedly jaundiced, because samples showing an average of around 50 per cent contradict his assertion that more than two-thirds of the electorate abstained, yet this figure still represented a substantial fall compared with the late 1860s.[79]

By contrast, a few years later, the fiercely contested legislative elections of 1877 (a veritable *élection de lutte*, to employ André Siegfried's terminology), prompted turnout slightly in excess of 80 per cent. Polling took place after the monarchist president, marshal MacMahon, had abruptly dissolved the first legislature of the Third Republic, which had been elected the previous year, on the basis of single-member constituencies, with voting once more held in the commune. This upward surge in the number of voters in 1877 demonstrated once again that high levels of participation were produced by determined efforts at mobilization which, in this instance, emanated from all points of the political compass. In the upshot, ill-judged efforts by government officials to influence the outcome only served to alienate many voters and confirm republican dominance. Disillusioned

---

[76] Figure based on data for ten departments in AN série C. The republican leader, Léon Gambetta, reckoned that less than half the electorate participated, but his calculation actually suggests that it was more than 50 per cent: Clère, *Histoire du suffrage universel*, 201–2.

[77] *Moniteur*, 24 Feb. 1874, 305.

[78] Yvan Combeau, *Paris et les élections municipales sous la Troisième République. La scène capitale dans la vie politique française* (Paris, 1998), p. 96 and ADCO 3M 682, PV des élections municipales de Dijon, 1871–2.

[79] Taine, *Du Suffrage universel*, 7, ADCO 3M 338, PV des élections cantonales, 1871 and ADM 3M 344, PV des élections cantonales, 1871.

as well as defeated, royalists subsequently withdrew from the electoral arena and, as a consequence, the legislative elections of 1881 recorded a drop in turnout of over 10 per cent (a so-called *élection d'apaisement*). One sub-prefect commented that such abstention stemmed above all from conservatives' 'fear of being annihilated by the popular vote'.[80]

However, once opponents of the Republic returned to the fray, later in the decade, their involvement helped ensure that higher turnout would become the norm, at all levels of the electoral process. This upward trajectory was by no means completely smooth nor universal, but earlier, violent oscillations were now disappearing. The variation in turnout between neighbouring cantons and communes was also diminishing, even though significant disparities remained, notably between more heavily polling areas located in the north-east and south-west, and other parts of the country. The paradox of low voting in Mediterranean departments, where elections seemed to produce great partisan excitement, has often been noted but never satisfactorily explained. John Bodley, that perceptive British observer, was certainly perplexed by the legislative election of 1893 at Draguignan, in the Var, where the radical republican Georges Clemenceau lost his seat, following an especially hard-fought campaign, on a turnout of just 50 per cent.[81]

Voting Becomes a Habit, 1880s–1980s

After 1881, the overall turnout in French legislative elections only failed to reach 75 per cent of registered voters on one occasion before 1914, despite a contest being held every four years, besides a huge number of by-elections (Figure 6.1).[82] Yet 'contest' is the operative word since, unlike Britain, the electoral process went ahead in France even in the presence of a solitary contender for office. As one commentator put it, 'We do not accept that anyone should be elected without the voters having the opportunity to express their opinion on him.'[83] This tradition inevitably encouraged many voters to 'go on strike', or spoil their paper, often by adding some derogatory comments, but historian Nicolas Rousselier has recently demonstrated how the number of uncontested parliamentary seats practically disappeared during the pre-war Third Republic. He refers to this development as an 'electoral revolution', but it was just one aspect of a wider transformation.[84] In

---

[80] Jean-François Tanguy, 'L' "influence" politique au temps du suffrage universel', in Annie Antoine and Julian Mischi (eds), *Sociabilité et politique en milieu rural* (Rennes, 2008), 289.

[81] Bodley, *France*, ii, 72. This is a subject that I am currently investigating.

[82] There were over eight hundred of these between 1871 and 1914, on account of disqualification, death, and resignation, and by-elections were also numerous at the local level.

[83] Francois Julien-Laferrière, *Manuel de droit constitutionnel*, 2nd edn (Paris, 1947), 583.

[84] Nicolas Rousselier, 'Electoral antipluralism and electoral pluralism in France, from the mid-nineteenth century to 1914', in Julian Wright and H. S. Jones (eds), *Pluralism and the Idea of the Republic in France* (Basingstoke, 2012), 141–60.

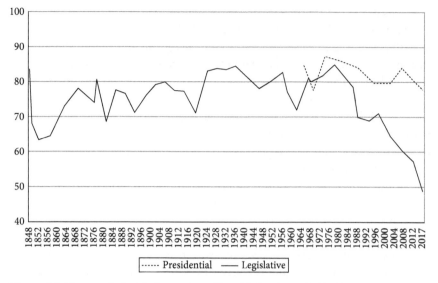

Figure 6.1 Turnout in legislative and presidential elections, 1848–2017

The higher turnout of the two rounds has been selected for both sets of figures, which include blank and null votes.

Sources: Lancelot, *L'Abstentionnisme electoral*, 14 and 16; and *France Politique: le site d'information sur la vie politique française* at https://www.france-politique.fr/elections.

1881, a single candidate was effectively standing in 147 constituencies, a figure which fell to almost one hundred in 1893 (from a total of five hundred), then just thirteen on the eve of the First World War. Not just two-way, but three-way contests were becoming a more regular feature of elections. To cite a specific example, in the Isère in 1881 only one out of eight seats was disputed, whereas in 1914 a record number of thirty-one candidates sought to become one of the department's deputies.[85] The general trend towards greater competition was also reflected in the fact that whereas in 1876 only 20 per cent of seats went to a second-round run-off, by 1914 this proportion had more than doubled.

As the number of electoral 'fiefs' diminished sharply, so higher turnout became the norm, although this is not to imply that consensus, which reflected social solidarity as much as political opinion, was now invariably producing a low turnout. There is evidence to suggest that municipal elections in smaller communes might attract very high levels of participation, despite the presentation of just a single list of candidates. In the arrondissement of Béthune in the Pas-de-Calais, for example, the proportion of *listes uniques* remained virtually unchanged between 1896 and 1912, prompting the sub-prefect to describe consistently high polling in

---

[85] Pierre Barral, *Le Département de l'Isère sous la Troisième République: histoire sociale et politique* (Paris, 1962), 548–61.

religious terms, as 'une communion solennelle'.[86] Series of statistics relating to electoral turnout at this level are extremely rare, but work in progress indicates that rural municipal elections were routinely attracting three-quarters of the electorate by the turn of the twentieth century.[87] Towns were still experiencing higher rates of abstention, yet figures for the municipality of Paris which, under the Third Republic, was once more able to elect its own council (if not a mayor), are indicative of a general increase in urban turnout. In the capital, between 1871 and 1914 there were thirteen 'general elections' (a complete renewal of council-lors every three, then four years), yet the rate of participation never fell beneath 70 per cent after the late 1880s. Formerly poll-shy Parisians were now voting at a level above the average recorded for eighteen of the largest French cities in the municipal elections of 1908 and 1912, which was put at 69 per cent and 67 per cent, respectively.[88]

Few historians have undertaken the equally arduous task of excavating infor-mation from *procès-verbaux* in the archives relating to departmental and arron-dissement elections. These polls were commonly known as *cantonales*, because the canton, though no longer the location of a polling station, survived as the cir-cumscription for elections at this intermediate level. They involved the simultan-eous election of both departmental, or 'general' councillors, and those who served in the arrondissements. Statistics based on three departments suggest that these elections, held every three years to renew a third of their membership, were also attracting higher turnout, though less so than their legislative or municipal coun-terparts, in which all seats were up for grabs every four years. In the Côte-d'Or, for instance, an average of 47 per cent of the electorate took part in the *cantonales* held in 1898, a figure which rose to 56 per cent in 1910.[89] A sample of nine departments compiled by the American political scientist, Harold Gosnell, for 1910 and 1913, confirms this development and suggests that the average turnout had risen to 65 per cent on the eve of the First World War.[90]

Elections resumed in 1919, when a hybrid version of PR was introduced for legislative elections. Proponents of the new system had always argued that its introduction would raise electoral participation still further, since fewer votes would be 'wasted' in one-sided contests, but this did not prove to be the case. Defective registers, from which the missing and displaced had not been removed, doubtless help to explain a relatively low turnout of 70 per cent, the poorest for almost forty years. In 1924, by contrast, the same system attracted over 80 per

---

[86] Yves Le Maner, 'Les maires d'un arrondissement d'un pays minier, Béthune', in Maurice Agulhon (ed.), *Les Maires en France du Consulat à nos jours* (Paris, 1986), 240–2.

[87] Research in progress in AD Var 3M529-606 and AD Yvelines 2M2 29–30.

[88] Gosnell, *Why Europe Votes*, 229. It might be added that these figures were superior to those recorded in nine British cities between 1919 and 1922, Gosnell, *Why Europe Votes*, 225.

[89] ADCO 3M 338, 388, 408 and 420, PV des élections cantonales, 1871–919.

[90] Gosnell, *Why Europe Votes*, 227.

cent of the electorate and this threshold was crossed again after reversion to the familiar second-ballot system in 1928. In fact, the close-fought election of 1936 (the last to be held under the Third Republic), saw a turnout of 84.5 per cent (almost ten million male voters), a figure which remains unequalled for a first-round legislative vote; it was only marginally exceeded by the second-round vote at this level in 1978. Average participation in local elections had likewise fallen in 1919, before rising as high as 80 per cent for a score of larger towns in the municipal elections of 1925.[91]

A series of favourable elements had converged at the turn of the twentieth century to render voting a regular commitment for the great majority of French adult males. The longevity of the Third Republic undoubtedly contributed. Despite conservative efforts to impose renewed restrictions at the outset, the free exercise of universal male suffrage was durably established as the basis for recurrent elections at all levels of government. While monarchists might briefly boycott the system after their brief revival ended in the later 1870s, they soon came to terms with it, as did socialists and later communists, for all their revolutionary rhetoric. Elections were thus endorsed as the acme of political expression, the pivot around which the Republic turned, and voters were encouraged to respond accordingly. Political parties may have been slow to emerge as formal entities in France but, even before the legal recognition of their existence in 1901, they were beginning to mobilize the electorate and challenge the dominance of the traditional notables in this domain. The latter were now forced to compete strongly with them for the vote of rural dwellers, who were becoming more independent-minded, like many of their urban counterparts.

The press was also entering a golden age, disseminating vast quantities of information on politics in general and elections in particular. The growing influence of the printed word reflected an expanding readership provided by the advent of compulsory, secular, primary instruction in the early 1880s. As Rosanvallon suggests, this legislation constituted a milestone for politics as well as society: 'schooling for democracy' was the rallying cry of those who sought to reconcile 'le nombre et la raison', by creating a better informed electorate.[92] Civic instruction would play a key role in the curriculum, inculcating the ideals of republican citizenship. The link between education and the exercise of the suffrage had been forged as early as the Revolution of 1789, but leaders of the First and Second Republics did not dispose of either the time or the resources to implement their plans for the preparation of future citizens and electors. The republican ascendancy after 1880 finally offered an opportunity that its leaders firmly

[91] Gosnell, *Why Europe Votes*, 227–30.
[92] Rosanvallon, *Le Sacre du citoyen*, 369 and Yves Déloye, *École et citoyenneté. L'individualisme républicain de Jules Ferry à Vichy: controverses* (Paris, 1994), 118–21.

grasped, in order to fulfil Gambetta's demand that all voters should understand exactly how the *bulletin*, that 'little square of paper', was to be employed.[93]

Indeed, according to pedagogues like Paul Bert, it was essential 'to instil in (male) children a quasi-religious respect for the great act of voting' from an early age, so that approaching the ballot-box would evoke emotions akin to those of believers as they went to the altar to receive the sacrament.[94] To train pupils in electoral *savoir faire*, Augustine Fouillée (under the pseudonym Bruno) pre-scribed holding mock elections: 'Each child should take a small sheet of paper and write the name of a fellow pupil on it, before proceeding to a count.'[95] In his childhood recollections, Pierre-Jakez Hélias relished recounting an event of this sort, and not least his victory in the classroom poll.[96] Louis Liard, another educa-tionist, was equally convinced that voting was 'the most important act that citi-zens are asked to undertake', and electoral engagement was therefore 'a moral obligation'.[97] He hoped that teachers' injunctions would extend beyond those of school age, for adults also required instruction. The sovereignty of the people demanded that all citizens immerse themselves in public affairs, by reading the press and attending public meetings, besides voting and then assisting at the count. As Alfred Mézières put it in his course-book, every elector needed to con-duct a careful study of the candidates and only make his choice 'having become as knowledgeable as possible about their ideas and capabilities'.[98] This was indeed the heyday of electoral manuals, with more of them published in the 1880s and 1890s than during any other decade of the nineteenth or twentieth centuries.[99]

Yves Déloye has recently demonstrated that the Catholic Church played an unexpected role in raising participation, by seeking to challenge the republicans' political hegemony, even though its electoral involvement was not generally wel-comed by the regime.[100] Clergy had certainly urged their flocks to attend the polls and visibly accompanied them to vote in 1848, but on earlier and later occasions elections had often been boycotted or regarded with indifference. Such ambiva-lence ended with the *ralliement* to the French Republic ordained in the papal encyclical of 1892. The 'expanded' catechisms subsequently issued by several

[93] Arnaud-Dominique Houte, *Le Triomphe de la République 1871-1914* (Paris, 2014), 69.
[94] Paul Bert, *De l'Éducation civique* (Paris, 1883), 15.
[95] G. Bruno (Augustine Fouillée), *Instruction morale et civique pour les petits enfants* (Paris, 1883), 130-1.
[96] Pierre-Jakez Hélias, *The Horse of Pride: Life in a Breton Village*, trans. (New Haven, CT, 1978), 171-2.
[97] Louis Liard, *Morale et enseignement civique à l'usage des écoles primaires (cours moyens et cours supérieurs)* (Paris, 1883), 116-18.
[98] Mézières, *Éducation morale*, 129.
[99] Laurent Quéro, 'Les manuels électoraux français. Objets d'élection (1790-1995)', *Scalpel*, 2-3 (1997), 19.
[100] Yves Déloye, 'Socialisation religieuse et comportement électoral en France', in Déloye and Ihl, *L'Acte de vote*, 412-13. See also Yves Déloye, *Les Voix de Dieu. Pour une autre histoire du suffrage élec-toral: le clergé catholique français et le vote (XIXe-XXe siècles)* (Paris, 2006).

bishops included specific injunctions stressing not simply the duty to vote in elections, but to 'bien voter', in other words to support candidates who were sympathetic to the Church. This objective was also pursued through manuals, tracts, and periodicals published by the Catholic press. In 1945, the bishop of Nancy, like others, would reiterate that electoral abstention was worse than absence from mass: 'to abstain without good cause, such as illness, would be a mortal sin'.[101] The relationship between regular attendance at worship and frequenting the polling station may be exaggerated—'a good parishioner is a good elector', it was said— but evidence from Chanzeau, a village in the west of France, demonstrates a strong, continuing connexion in the 1950s and early 1960s.[102]

In fact, turnout in the immediate post-1945 period remained almost as high as during the interwar years when voting resumed after its abeyance under the Vichy regime. The electorate was now more than doubled to twenty-five million as a result of the addition of électrices, according to the decree of 21 April 1944 which finally enfranchised women. Far from inducing fatigue, the flurry of elections and constitutional referendums accompanying the creation of a Fourth Republic, in 1945 and 1946, attracted record numbers of participants in France, with at least seventeen million voters going to the polls on each occasion. The average turnout of more than 75 per cent was particularly impressive since the country was still adjusting to the demands of reconstruction and also enduring austerity. Although female access to the polls seems to have slightly depressed overall levels of participation in the short run (see Chapter 2), this gender gap was of relatively brief duration: in the 1970s women began to vote in the same proportions as men (Figure 6.2).[103]

By this point, during the second decade of the Fifth Republic, presidential and legislative elections were consistently topping the 80 per cent mark, and municipal elections, like referendums, 70 per cent, while polling for departmental councils was often exceeding the 60 per cent mark, a level matched by the first elections to the European parliament in 1979. There was considerable fluctuation at the local level, but much of this reflected the electoral calendar and the timing of municipales, and especially cantonales, in relation to the national cycle of elections.[104] To be sure, the referendum of 1972 on extending membership of the European Economic Community had failed to arouse significant enthusiasm, and it recorded the lowest score for a constitutional vote since the Revolutionary and Napoleonic periods. There was certainly no room for complacency, as commentators insisted, especially in relatively low polling parts of the country and notably

[101] Cited in Serge Bonnet, *Sociologie politique et religieuse de la Lorraine* (Paris, 1972), 105.
[102] Lancelot, *L'Abstentionnisme électoral*, 205–12 and Wylie (ed.), *Chanzeau*, 274–6.
[103] Mossuz-Lavau and Sineau, *Enquête sur les femmes*, 25–8.
[104] Françoise Épinette, 'L'abstention et les élections locales: le paradoxe de la proximité', in Christophe Boutin and Frédéric Rouvillois (eds), *L'Abstention électorale, apaisement ou épuisement?* (Paris, 2002), 30–40.

Figure 6.2 Turnout in local elections, 1945–2016

The higher turnout of the two rounds has been selected for both these elections. Since 2015 'cantonal elections' have been renamed 'departmental elections'. Both sets of figures include blank and null votes.

Sources: AN F1cII, Ministère de l'intérieur, élections locales depuis 1945; and *France Politique: le site d'information sur la vie politique française* at https://www.france-politique.fr/elections.

the south-east. However, this steady state of at least two-thirds, usually three-quarters or more of the huge electorate regularly turning out to vote, on a more or less annual basis, and with little difference between the two rounds of voting these contests mostly entailed, had now lasted for a century. In 1974 there was a record turnout of over 87 per cent in the second round of presidential elections, which meant that virtually all electors in a position to do so had participated in one round or the other. Four years later, legislative polls reached almost 85 per cent and, in 1981, when the socialist François Mitterrand was elected president on a second-round turnout just shy of 86 per cent, no one could have predicted that the situation was on the cusp of some dramatic change.

Conclusion

Alarmist comments regarding the recent decline in electoral turnout often ignore the fact that it took a century for French males to acquire the habit of voting, though French women later did so far more rapidly. The initial experiment with mass voting during the Revolutionary and Napoleonic decades, which had no contemporary equivalent in terms of the sheer numbers involved, demonstrated that voters would not necessarily turn out, especially if the process was time-consuming and demanded a trip to the *chef-lieu de canton*. What is surprising is not that so few participated in these circumstances, but so many. It is clear that the notables were much more likely to do so than manual workers, a factor reflected in the relatively high levels of attendance at electoral colleges between 1790 and 1847. However, when mass voting resumed in 1848, the costs of participation were lowered, while mobilization increased and voters became better informed. It took some time for rates of participation to rise, but the authoritarian Second Empire unexpectedly facilitated this development as a result of regular polling and, from the Third Republic onwards, 75 to 80 per cent of the electorate were voting in legislative elections. Turnout in local elections might lag behind, but even these polls were also regularly attracting between two-thirds and three-quarters of registered voters. The practice of voting thus appeared to be firmly implanted among French citizens. Yet not everyone who went to the polls cast a valid ballot paper, a hitherto hidden phenomenon that will be considered in the next chapter.

7

Voting as a Subversive Activity

The Ballot Paper as Protest

> A record number of French voters cast their ballots yesterday for nobody.
>
> Journalist Eliza Mackintosh, 8 May 2017.[1]

More than four million French electors invalidated their vote in one way or another in the second round of presidential elections in 2017. The scale was unprecedented, but the practice was not. There is a long tradition of appropriating the ballot paper as a means of protest in France, a particular phenomenon that will be explored in this chapter. These days, when the results are announced by the ministry of the interior, a distinction is drawn between *blancs* and *nuls*, between those papers expressing no choice at all and others which are spoiled in some fashion or other. Yet neither category counts towards the electoral outcome, which is still decided solely on the basis of *bulletins* providing a clear indication of choice, the *suffrages exprimés*. The presence of invalid papers among the total cast, particularly in presidential and legislative elections, as well as referendums, has been rising gradually, sometimes dramatically, over the past three decades, as Table 7.1 and Figure 7.1 demonstrate below. Spoiling is often regarded as involuntary but in France, where it is far more widespread than most other countries, it is evidently deliberate for the most part. It clearly indicates disaffection but, unlike abstention, which has also been growing significantly of late, it still involves the act of voting and, somewhat ironically, spoiled papers are preserved, whereas legitimate ballots are immediately destroyed. This alternative to non-voting, which has been called 'abstentionnisme actif', can be traced back to the growing use of ballot papers in the eighteenth century. The French have learned to subvert as well as support their culture of elections.

---

[1] See https://edition.cnn.com/2017/05/08/europe/french-voters-spoiled-ballots.../index.html (accessed 08/08/19).

How the French Learned to Vote: A History of Electoral Practice in France. Malcolm Crook, Oxford University Press (2021).
© Malcolm Crook. DOI: 10.1093/oso/9780192894786.003.0008

Spoiling: A Historic but Lately Growing Trend

Serious consideration of spoiled papers has been rare among political scientists and is practically non-existent on the part of historians.[2] During the heyday of electoral sociology in the 1950s, Jean Pataut baldly asserted that these *bulletins* traced a similar trajectory to non-voting and since, in his opinion, they mostly resulted from voter error, there was little point in discussing them.[3] He concluded that they should be counted among the abstentions and not as votes cast, though the elector had visited the polling station as opposed to simply staying away. By contrast, a decade later, Alain Lancelot felt that spoiling of any sort was usually deliberate and, in order to separate the two phenomena, he claimed to have established an inverse relationship between abstention and invalid votes during the period 1919–65, a finding that led him to omit further analysis of the latter from his magisterial study of 'abstentionnisme' in France.[4] In fact, some correlation does exist and spoiling is still used as a means of avoiding abstention in the countryside, where (often stigmatized) non-voting is all too apparent at small polling stations. Nonetheless, one result of the disagreement over how to classify spoiled papers is that they may not be indicated in voting statistics at all, or calculated as a percentage of registered voters, which reduces their importance, especially when abstention is high. In this study they have been counted among the votes cast and will be presented as a percentage of that total. Interestingly enough, since the year 2000 the French ministry of the interior has begun reporting them in this way too.

Invalidation stemming from marking the ballot paper so that it could be recognized by candidates or agents, in their efforts to control the voter's choice, has largely ceased, as has spoiling in order to avoid casting a valid paper foisted on the elector by them. Yet the belief that invalidation stems mainly from error remains widely held. This explanation should not be entirely excluded, especially during the electoral apprenticeship of the Revolution, or under the Second Republic, when unfamiliarity and illiteracy posed huge problems for newly enfranchised citizens struggling to produce hand-written *bulletins*. Nor did the advent of printed papers necessarily help: at Dijon, in the 1850s, one elector accidentally submitted an invoice, which was later returned to its addressee by an alert scrutineer, while others confused the ballot paper with their voters' cards.[5] The rise in spoiled papers at the first European elections in 1979, or following the brief reversion to PR for the legislative elections of 1986, might also be partly attributed to their novelty. Yet those nineteenth-century voters who employed an electoral

---

[2] Pierre Bréchon, 'Blanc et nul', in Perrineau and Reynié (eds), *Dictionnaire du vote*, 109.
[3] Jean Pataut, 'Les abstentions aux élections législatives dans la Nièvre (1902–1951)', in François Goguel (ed.), *Nouvelles études de sociologie électorale* (Paris, 1954), 64–6.
[4] Lancelot, *L'Abstentionnisme électoral*, 50–3.   [5] AN C1701, PV Dijon-Est, 1857.

circular, or a *bulletin* they had kept from a previous election, may have been refusing to support any given candidate rather than displaying a lack of *savoir-faire*. Greater familiarity with voting procedures did not reduce the incidence of invalidation, rather the reverse. It increased in the three plebiscites held under Louis-Napoleon, while the level of turnout remained practically identical, rising from less than 40,000 to over 100,000 spoiled papers between 1851 and 1870, a reflection of the growth of dissent rather than an increase in error. The recent presidential election of 2017 provides conclusive evidence of a largely deliberate practice: the number of spoiled papers, cast by a universally educated electorate, summoned to the polls on an annual basis, rose more than fourfold between the two rounds of polling.[6]

Voters clearly feel disenfranchised when presented with the choice of just two candidates in the second round of presidential elections and, since they were given the opportunity to choose the head of state under the Fifth Republic, they have consistently spoiled their papers in greater numbers on this occasion. Moreover, apart from an isolated peak at the second round in 1969, the figures began to rise sharply from 1995 onwards, never subsequently falling below 4 per cent before hitting 11.5 per cent in 2017 (Table 7.1).

Statistics for invalid votes at legislative elections prior to the Fifth Republic relate solely to the first round of the contest, since many were decided at that point and the size of the second-round electorate was consequently much diminished, unlike today when few seats are settled immediately. Spoiled papers averaged around 2 per cent of votes cast in these elections under the Third Republic, with a spike of some 5 per cent in 1898, when over 400,000 *bulletins* were declared void. The proportion remained elevated in 1902 and 1910, but thereafter it rarely

Table 7.1 Spoiled papers in presidential elections, 1965–2017

Year	First Round		Second Round	
	Spoiled papers	% of votes cast	Spoiled papers	% of votes cast
1965	248,360	1.0	668,213	2.7
1969	295,036	1.3	1,303,798	6.4
1974	237,107	0.9	356,788	1.3
1981	477,965	1.6	898,984	2.9
1988	621,934	2.0	1,161,822	3.6
1995	883,161	2.8	1,902,148	6.0
2002	997,262	3.4	1,769,307	5.4
2007	534,846	1.4	1,568,426	4.2
2012	701,190	1.9	2,154,956	5.8
2017	949,334	2.6	4,085,724	11.5

[6] Anne Muxel, 'La mobilization électorale, du décrochage civique à l'abstention record', in Pascal Perrineau (ed.), *Le Vote disruptif. Les élections présidentielle et législatives de 2017* (Paris, 2017), 167–70.

exceeded 2 per cent, though the numbers spoiling their papers had risen, commensurate with an enlarged electorate that later included women. However, invalidated second-round *bulletins* abruptly escalated to over 9 per cent of the votes cast in 1993, then remained at over 3 per cent of the total until 2017, when they reached almost 10 per cent.

The recent, upward trajectory in spoiling contradicts Pierre Bréchon's assertion to the contrary although, as always, the progression has been uneven and the turnout for referendums reveals some spectacular oscillations.[7] These consultations have been accompanied by some huge levels of abstention, in 1972, 1988 and, above all, in 2000, when a reduction in the length of the presidency was at issue. The proportion of spoiled papers has often increased as the level of participation has decreased, yet in the second round of presidential elections in 2017 the practice of invalidation hit a record high, though turnout remained elevated at 75 per cent (Figure 7.1). In the case of local elections, historical series of figures for spoiling are harder to obtain, but recent data suggest no clearly discernible trend, with blank and null votes generally hovering around the 4 per cent mark. The second round of departmental (formerly cantonal) elections did witness a rise to over 8 per cent in 2015, but at this level spoiling is often more pronounced at the first round of voting. Finally, the set of single-round European elections reveals little fluctuation in the casting of *bulletins blancs et nuls*, which has varied from 3 per cent to 5 per cent since these contests began in 1979.

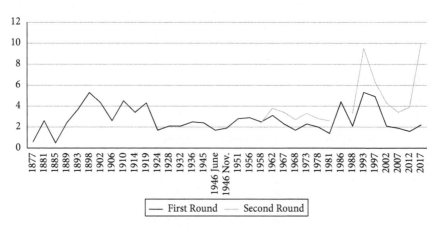

Figure 7.1 Spoiled papers in legislative elections, 1877–2017

Blank and null votes are calculated as a percentage of votes cast.

Sources: Lancelot, *L'Abstentionnisme électoral*, 50; and *France Politique: le site d'information sur la vie politique française* at https://www.france-politique.fr/elections.

---

[7] Pierre Bréchon, *La France aux urnes* (Paris, 2009), 60, though the trend has become clearer over the past decade.

Blank Voting

Beginning with the European polls of May 2014, blank votes have been counted separately from annotated papers, offering solid statistical evidence for their pre-dominance among invalid papers, at a ratio of around 2 to 1, or even 3 to 1 at the second round of presidential polls in 2017, for instance. In fact, from 1848 onwards invalid papers were classified into different categories and polling clerks were instructed to distinguish between the respective totals on the printed *procès-verbaux*. Although this complicated rubric was not always followed, the preponderance of *bulletins blancs* was already quite clear, always amounting to rather more than half the invalidated papers. However, it should be said that literal blanks—unmarked (or 'virgin') pieces of paper—were often fewer than printed *bulletins* where the candidate's name had been crossed out (in some cases obliter-ated), or cut out. Yet, while their totals are now separately published, *bulletins blancs* still do not count as valid votes, as partisans of the right not to vote for any of the declared candidates have regularly demanded since 1967, in over forty pro-posals for a change in the law. Including *blancs* among the *suffrages exprimés* attracts substantial support among members of the public, who regard it as a means of flagging up their dissatisfaction with the choice on offer, but the idea cuts little ice with the political class. As Richard Ferrand, a member of the Commission for Constitutional Legislation, commented on 13 July 2018, in rejecting this reiter-ated request, rather than seeking to undermine those who have come forward as candidates 'we should be encouraging more people to stand for office'.[8]

An Association for the Recognition of Blank Voting was launched in 1994, to be joined in 2010 by the Blank Voting Party, which rather fruitlessly fielded over eighty candidates at the most recent legislative elections in 2017. 'Blancheurs', as they are known, have also been seeking the provision of blank ballot papers at the polling station, a facility accorded in some countries and commonly designated by the acronym NOTA, for 'none of the above'. Somewhat ironically, the voting machines installed in a small number of communes since 1973 do offer a blank option. In the continuing absence of 'official' *bulletins blancs*, guidance on how to prepare such a paper to the standard dimensions, together with an explanation of the rationale behind this option, has been issued by the Association. This paper can be taken to the polling station, put in the regulation envelope, and then inserted in the ballot box.[9] Alternatively, loose *bulletins*, envelopes left empty or stuffed with different ballot papers, may be cast by those who wish to vote blank, a practice adopted by some electors since the introduction of envelopes, along with the *isoloir*, on the eve of the First World War.

---

[8] See http://www.assemblee-nationale.fr/15/cri/2017-2018-extra/20181015.asp (accessed 17/02/19).
[9] An engaging video offering guidance to voters can be found on the Internet: see https://www.parti-du-vote-blanc.fr/fabriquez-votre-bulletin-blanc/ (accessed 16/05/19).

However, blank voting has occurred in France ever since ballot papers were originally employed. The condemnation of so-called *billets blancs* under the *Ancien Régime* attests to its longevity, albeit to an unknown extent. The utmost contempt in which the gesture was once held is splendidly illustrated in the case of a late seventeenth-century ecclesiastical election, when its use was described as 'extraordinary', even 'shocking' behaviour, tantamount to an 'almighty swindle'. Moreover, in a tiny electoral college it was not difficult to identify the culprits and then exclude them from further participation.[10] The regulations governing elections to the Estates General of 1789, at the secondary level where ballot papers were prescribed, simply required that *billets blancs* should be discounted.[11] A sample of *procès-verbaux* from the *bailliage* and *sénéchaussée* assemblies suggests that, when recorded, this was a relatively infrequent infraction involving no more than a handful of voters.[12]

The generalization of voting by *billets*, or *bulletins*, during the Revolution and under Napoleon, does not seem to have increased the recourse to blank voting unduly, even in the run-off round when only two individuals remained in contention. Yet precisely how to deal with these blank votes remained unclear in the absence of any specific instructions. The question of whether blanks should count in the calculation of majorities according to the system of exhaustive balloting was thus repeatedly raised, though the consensus was that they should not.[13] Eventually, in 1807, the Conseil d'État ruled against them and this decision was incorporated into the instructions for those presiding over electoral assemblies. Only 'effective' votes would be taken into account and when, in 1831, this verdict on *bulletins blancs* was reiterated, the phrase 'suffrages exprimés' was introduced to describe valid papers.[14]

Blank voting remained a relatively rare practice under the constitutional monarchies, when invalidation was usually the result of illegibility, or lack of precision in the candidate's appellation on hand-written ballot papers. Cormenin, the jurist instrumental in the adoption of universal male suffrage in 1848, had no doubt that an intentional blank vote signified nothing, for 'it could not create a deputy'.[15] The same is still being said today: according to one political commentator, 'A

---

[10] Christin, 'Disinterest, vocation and elections', 287.

[11] Art. LVII, Règlement 24 Jan. 1789, in *AP*, 1ere série, I, 549.

[12] Jean-Pierre Donnadieu (ed.), *États généraux de 1789. Sénéchaussées de Béziers et Montpellier* (Montpellier, 1989), 438–9.

[13] For an example, see the controversy surrounding elections for justices of the peace in the Year X (1802): AN F1cIII Basses-Pyrénées 2, Préfet au ministre, 27 ventôse 10 (18 Mar. 1802).

[14] AN F1a58, Instructions pour MM les présidents des assemblées, Aug. 1808 and Samuel Zaoui, 'Le vote blanc, approche historique et sociologique d'une déviance électorale', DEA de science politique, Université de Paris I, 1993, 28–9.

[15] Louis-Marie de Cormenin, *Droit administrative* (Paris, 1840), 475, cited in Voilliot, *Le Département de l'Yonne*, 202–3.

bulletin blanc is mute; when you say nothing, how can you achieve anything?'[16] The comprehensive electoral law of 1849 ruled against admissibility and stated unambiguously that: '*bulletins blancs*... will not be taken into account in deciding the outcome of the election.'[17] Although blank votes were now definitively discounted, some deputies subsequently sought their recognition in order to reconcile electors to proposals for compulsory voting: Alfred Letellier, for example, argued in 1889 that 'to use a *bulletin blanc* is tantamount to voting and fulfilling one's civic duty'.[18] This option, which might appear self-defeating, was envisaged as a means of maintaining a degree of liberty for those constrained to vote. It was also a recognition of reality: a voter may be compelled to visit the polling station, but the secrecy of the ballot means it is impossible to enforce the expression of a valid choice.

The anarchist Proudhon recommended that rather than voting for bourgeois candidates, workers should employ the 'stoic veto' of the *bulletin blanc*. As one of his collaborators emphasized, workers who lacked a suitable choice of office-holder should nevertheless demonstrate how much they valued the suffrage by casting a '*vote en blanc*'.[19] The Socialist Federation thus advocated this practice in the elections of 1863 and 1869, as had some republicans after Louis-Napoleon's seizure of power in 1851, while Catholics were sometimes encouraged to use it as a form of protest later in the nineteenth century.[20] In 1914, one voter circulated a flyer to fellow electors in his arrondissement of Paris, urging them to follow his example and vote *blanc* at the first round, because 'it does not mean abstaining, rather it is a way of indicting a group of deputies, more autocratic than their monarchist predecessors, who dare to present themselves once more at the polls; it is a means of communicating your rejection of their dreadful policies...'[21] Aside from a general suggestion aimed at disaffected voters, some political parties may advocate the practice from time to time: for example, the Socialist Party (PSU) urged its supporters to abstain or vote blank so as to indicate their disapproval of extended membership of the European Common Market in the referendum of 1972.[22]

As one recent analysis concludes, 'The blank vote constitutes above all a means of political expression'; unlike abstention, which may stem from apathy, the voter has taken the trouble to attend a polling station and make a point.[23] A particular

[16] Laurent Joffrin, *Libération*, 10 Jan. 2019, cited at http://www.vote-blanc.org/articles (accessed 14/05/19).
[17] Loi du 15 mars 1849, art. 57.   [18] *JO*, Annexe 3520, 7 Feb. 1889, 345.
[19] Pierre-Joseph Proudhon, *De la capacité politique des classes ouvrières* (Paris, 1868), v and 348.
[20] J. Buzon, *Abstention ou vote par bulletin blanc. Fédéraux et socialistes* (Bordeaux, 1869).
[21] AN C7249, PV Paris, 15e arrond. 1914.
[22] Daniel Boy and Jean Chiche, 'Abstention et blancs et nuls au référendum du 24 septembre 2000', *Rfsp*, 51 (2001), 242.
[23] Adélaïde Zulfikarpasic, 'Le vote blanc: abstention civique ou expression politique?', *Rfsp*, 51 (2001), 267.

example of such *abstentionnisme actif* emanates from a by-election in the Allier where, in 1903, a protest against the nomination of a candidate from outside the arrondissement resulted in more than one in ten voters casting their first-round ballot papers as blanks (up to 25 per cent in one canton).[24] Earlier, under the Second Empire, the practice had been prompted by the imposition of official candidates, or later in so-called 'fiefs' where a particular person or party was unassailable. These days the single candidature is a very rare occurrence, but in 2017, in the second round of a legislative election in the Aveyron, only one candidate was left in contention after her remaining opponent withdrew, and over 30 per cent of the ballot papers were subsequently spoiled, most of them as blanks. As part of his postgraduate research into the recent use of *blancs* and *nuls*, Jérémie Moualek has interviewed those who vote in this fashion. He concludes that for the better-educated there is a clear desire to uphold the electoral system and to affirm the civic importance of voting in a way that abstention, which they abhor, does not.[25] Indeed, a tactical choice is made depending on the precise electoral circumstances that obtain, so that this practice, like that of non-voting, is an intermittent one, reflected in the fluctuating statistics.

In the past many papers were defaced rather than being literally left *blanc*, thus shading into annotation, and today they would be classed as *nul*. Indeed, drawing a clear distinction between the two categories has always been problematic, their uses plural. The difficulty is further illustrated by papers where the refusal to make a choice is justified, and the principle of anonymity is accordingly breached. There were always those who helpfully stated 'I am voting blank', or 'I do not wish to vote for anyone', or—a favourite formula to this day—'neither one nor the other', with reference to the two candidates, or plebiscitary verdicts on offer. In the early years of mass voting some frankly acknowledged their inability to choose: 'Lacking the capacity to distinguish the citizen who should govern France, I wish my vote to be counted among the blanks', wrote one voter in the presidential election of 1848, while others admitted, 'I am unable to decide', or declared, 'I am not voting for anyone, for fear of making a mistake.'[26] A familiar device, today as yesterday, was to suggest that all candidates were exactly the same, or both as bad as one another. The classic comment on two conservative contenders (Georges

---

[24] Jean-François Viple, *Sociologie politique de l'Allier. La vie politique et les élections sous la Troisième République* (Paris, 1967), 248.

[25] Jérémie Moualek, 'Des voix (vraiment) pas comme les autres? Les usages pluriels des votes blancs et nuls', *Rfsp*, 67 (2017), 1153–66.

[26] AN BII 977, PV Côte-d'Or, 1848. In the European elections of 1994, one voter referred to the referendum on the Maastricht Treaty in 1992, commenting 'Not being a graduate of ENA or the Sciences Po, I was not capable (like many of my fellow citizens) of pronouncing a verdict', cited in Jérémie Moualek, 'Votes blancs et nuls aux élections européennes de 1994. Des votes "euroconstructifs"?', in Martial Libera et al. (eds), *Abstentionnisme, euroscepticisme et anti-européisme dans les élections européennes de 1979 à nos jours* (Stuttgart, 2016), 88.

Pompidou and Alain Poher) in the second round of the presidential elections of 1969 made by the Communist leader, Jacques Duclos—'c'est bonnet blanc/blanc bonnet'—was frequently reproduced on ballot papers, doubtless cast by party members. It was a justification that could turn into a diatribe: 'I would vote for an honest candidate, but I do not know of one, therefore I am voting blank.'[27]

Annotated Papers

Some of Moualek's contemporary interviewees regard voting blank as quite legitimate, whereas they condemn marking or defacing the ballot as quite objectionable. In the absence of an official blank paper to cast, *bulletins* may be nullified in order to avoid opting for any of the declared candidates, but the deliberate practice of annotation indicates much more than dissatisfaction with the choices on offer. It enables the elector to 'send a message' or make a wide range of comments and, in many cases, to explain the reasons for them, in a personal and sometimes abusive fashion. As Olivier Ihl neatly puts it, 'Secret, the ballot paper is also silent. As the disqualification of *bulletins blancs et nuls* suggests, only opinions devoid of personal comments, that is to say standard and anonymous verdicts, are recognized as valid votes.'[28] There have been few political injunctions to annotate a ballot paper in order to invalidate it, though in the referendum of 1962 which proposed a resolution to the Algerian War, the PSU did distribute 'ready-spoiled ballots reading "yes to peace, no to Gaullist power"'.[29] In fact, there has been precious little public discussion of this particular practice until recently, doubtless in order to 'décourager les autres', because politicians fear it brings the electoral process into disrepute even more than blank voting, by undermining its aura of dignity and civility.

On one of the rare occasions when the matter was debated in the Legislative Assembly, in July 1851, following a by-election in the Seine-et-Marne, there was palpable dismay at the behaviour of 'men who, at the very moment they were summoned to participate in the act of national sovereignty, decided to employ their electoral rights to soil the ballot box with the most perverse utterances and extremely bloodthirsty threats, which were thoroughly cowardly since they were made under the cloak of anonymity.'[30] When the evidence was presented, which included demands for the guillotine to be used against enemies of the Republic, and suggestions that 'vile aristocrats' should either be hanged or burned

[27] AN C6132, PV Lorient, 1902.
[28] Olivier Ihl, 'Vote public et vote privé', in Perrineau and Reynié (eds), *Dictionnaire du vote*, 964.
[29] Philip M. Williams and Martin Harrison, 'The French referendum of April 1962', *Parliamentary Affairs*, XV (1962), 303–4.
[30] *Moniteur*, 17 July 1851, 2034.

alive, some deputies sought immediate action. In the event, their righteous wrath notwithstanding, they had no idea how to identify the authors of these *bulletins*, nor prevent a recurrence.

Nearly a century later, a proposal for obligatory voting rejected allegations that it would encourage offensive comments on ballot papers, by arguing that 'feeble-minded' voters were already indulging in this 'nauseous practice', which should simply be ignored, as it usually was.[31] Public participation in the counting of papers (even if rude remarks were not to be read out) meant that there was some general awareness of such irregular voting, although detailed knowledge of its nature and extent was confined to officials who collated the material at a departmental level. However, the rise in the number of spoiled *bulletins* of late, like separating *nuls* from *blancs* in the published results, has finally prompted some discussion in the press. Above all, much greater visibility has been accorded to disfiguring and annotating ballot papers by the capture of these *bulletins* on mobile phones and then the posting of these 'ballot selfies' on social media. Indeed, after the presidential election of 2017, several websites were offering their selections of the more imaginative instances.[32] This sort of publicity, which arguably violates the secrecy of the vote, can only increase the attraction of such behaviour in future and encourage a competition to produce the most egregious examples.

Hitherto the phenomenon had remained pretty well hidden and only in 1969 was scholarly attention drawn to these papers by Yves-Marie Bercé, writing in the archivists' house journal. In the course of perusing *procès-verbaux* compiled for legislative elections between 1881 and 1909, he came across some striking evidence of annotation.[33] This included anti-clerical stickers affixed to ballot papers, besides a good deal of abuse aimed at candidates, and some frankly bemusing comments which had nothing whatsoever to do with the election. The final category led Bercé to suggest that the electors who produced them clearly required psychiatric help, but he also acknowledged the value of *bulletins nuls* in revealing otherwise unrecorded popular sentiments. It was more than two decades later when the political scientists Déloye and Ihl systematically examined a large sample of spoiled papers cast in the parliamentary elections of 1881, as part of their innovatory research into the act of voting.[34] Since they were primarily concerned with assessing how the universal male electorate was adapting to the suffrage,

---

[31]   AN F1cII 195, Proposition de loi, 5 June 1936.
[32]   See https://www.ladepeche.fr/article/2017/05/08/2570508-top-10-bulletins-nuls-tellement-droles-second-tour.html.
[33]   Yves-Marie Bercé, 'Les bulletins nuls, source de microsociologie électorale', *La Gazette des Archives*, 65 (1969), 82. The author recommended the conservation of spoiled papers but, ironically, the PVs in the particular cartons he consulted have since been stripped of this material.
[34]   Yves Déloye and Olivier Ihl, 'Des voix pas comme les autres. Votes blancs et votes nuls aux élections législatives de 1881', *Rfsp*, 41 (1991), pp. 141–70 and Yves Déloye and Olivier Ihl, 'Légitimité et déviance. L'annulation des votes dans les campagnes de la IIIe République', *Politix*, 15 (1991), pp. 13–24. See also Frédéric Bon and Jean-Paul Cheylan, *La France qui vote* (Paris, 1988), 306–17.

their analysis of annotation did not lead to a broader examination of a practice that was already well established before the advent of the Third Republic, and would persist thereafter. In order to fully grasp this fascinating form of electoral behaviour, an unprecedented, comprehensive exploration will be undertaken here, encompassing different sorts of elections, over the *longue durée*.

Until recently, annotation accounted for the invalidation of less than 1 per cent of ballot papers cast in legislative elections or referendums, and far fewer in local polls. Yet it represents a significant practice that reflects the appropriation of the *bulletin* by a small minority of voters to make more than a simple choice, express their discontent, and call the voting system itself into question. The earliest indication to have come to light dates from 1789 when, in the proceedings of the assembly in the *sénéchaussée* at Béziers, a tantalizing reference was made to comments inscribed on a few ballot papers, none of which has survived.[35] During the Revolution, *bulletins* where the voter's anonymity was compromised by a signature, or which contained 'some statement' on his part, were declared void, but only anecdotal evidence remains to suggest the nomination of fanciful candidates and the addition of derogatory remarks.[36] Such irregularities were certainly denounced in the course of controversial episcopal elections, from the very first instance in the Finistère at the end of 1790, when votes were apparently cast for the mayor of Quimper, two mother superiors, and the seminary dog.[37] Further examples were evident in these polls in 1791, when references to 'the Turk' or 'the Devil' were said to have appeared on the papers of second-degree electors who disapproved of the entire exercise (though dissenters mostly abstained). In the Bas-Rhin it was claimed that five votes were cast for a prominent member of the Jewish community, presumably in another effort to discredit the election.[38] It seems that one voter in the Ardèche nominated the émigré comte d'Artois (a brother of Louis XVI) on his ballot paper in elections to the National Convention in 1792, and he was obliged to flee the rage of fellow electors after his authorship was detected.[39] Thereafter, only one reference has come to light, in the legislative elections of 1816, when the prefect of the Lot-et-Garonne expressed his horror at the comments written on a couple of ballot papers, which 'did not bear repeating'.[40]

[35] Donnadieu (ed.), *États généraux de 1789*, 439.
[36] Loi sur la tenue des assemblées primaires, 18 Ventôse VI (8 Mar. 1798), in Aberdam et al. (eds), *Voter, élire pendant la Révolution française*, 409. In 1808 a prefectoral circular reiterated that such ballot papers should be discounted.
[37] J.-M. Pilven, *Le Premier évêque constitutionnel, Expilly, évêque du Finistère, 1790–1794* (Quimper, 1912), 6.
[38] AN F19 416, PV Corrèze, 20 Feb. 1791 and Rodolphe Reuss, *La Constitution civile du clergé et la crise religieuse en Alsace (1790–1795)*, 2 vols (Paris, 1922), i, 150.
[39] Charles Jolivet, *La Révolution dans l'Ardèche (1788–1795)* (Marseille, 1980), 328–30.
[40] Cited in Pilenco, *Les Moeurs électorales en France*, 144–5.

Not until 1848 was it was laid down that both blank and spoiled papers should be attached to the *procès-verbaux*, in order that departmental electoral commissions could review the material and, if necessary, override the nullification pronounced at the polling station. These papers were thus usually preserved for posterity and the archives contain a veritable treasure trove of such *bulletins*, indicating a rich repertoire of invalidation that awaits further investigation. It is true that some instances may have resulted from an inexperienced voter inadvertently marking, or signing, the paper, such as the enthusiastic supporters of Louis-Napoleon who reinforced their positive plebiscitary votes by adding 'yes, a thousand times yes', wrote the word 'Oui' in huge blue, white, and red letters, or embellished their papers with tricolour flags.[41] Yet most annotation was the deliberate work of voters, fully aware of the consequences of their actions, who sought to use their mastery of the pen or crayon to make a point, or express their anger, as interviews with some of today's non-conformists amply confirm. Indeed, the total of annotated papers has continued to rise with the progress of education and literacy, as more members of the electorate have become capable of making this gesture. It is no surprise that annotation in the past was more pronounced in the northern and eastern parts of France, where the ability to read and write was more widespread in the nineteenth century, while it was also more apparent in town than countryside, and Paris constituted its epicentre.[42] Annotations have often been dismissed as 'merely casting doubt on the virility of the mayor, the virtue of the station-master's wife, or the integrity of the baker', as *Le Monde* put it in 1972 (in the wake of the referendum which elicited a significant number of invalid votes), but this is a gross misrepresentation.[43] In many cases the practice aims to convey serious political criticism and, in some cases, it constitutes a fundamental challenge to the electoral process itself.

The increasing use of printed ballot papers in the twentieth century might have deterred the practice of annotation and the production of graphic images, since fewer voters were likely to produce their own *bulletin*. However, unlike Britain, copies of these papers were delivered to home addresses, where they could be modified, while there was nothing to stop a voter composing his own 'bulletin pirate', taking it to the polling station, and then inserting it into the envelope before proceeding to the ballot box. Moreover, after 1914 there remained the possibility of making briefer remarks on official *bulletins* on polling day, or employing some other form of material such as a flyer or newspaper cutting, in the privacy afforded by the *isoloir*. Unfortunately, the *procès-verbaux* for legislative elections in the wake of the First World War are not currently open to inspection, while documentation for later referendums does not include invalid ballots. However, a few images and annotations have survived from the consultation of

41   AN BII 1244A, PV Côte-d'Or, 1870.   42   Salmon, *Atlas électoral*, 16–17.
43   *Le Monde*, 27 Apr. 1972.

1958, which approved the foundation of a Fifth Republic, while spoiled papers for the first European elections in 1979 have been specially curated at the Archives nationales.[44] In both cases they demonstrate that at least some voters were continuing to draw on a familiar repertoire of remarks, statements, and drawings. Moualek's exploration of spoiling in more recent elections, points to an enduring discourse of justification and exposition, criticism and abuse, albeit expressed in different ways and using a greater variety of materials, to comment on issues and candidates today.

Appropriation

The ballot paper was intended to constitute a standard, anonymous means of achieving a reliable, arithmetic electoral outcome. Yet for this reason it appeared wholly inadequate to many voters who eagerly adapted it to their own purposes, exploiting the opportunity that the act of voting offered to express an opinion, rather than simply endorse an option. Thus, many annotations sought to elaborate upon the laconic verdict that popular consultations required. In the plebiscite of 1870, for instance, one voter glossed his positive response with an element of Bonapartist propaganda: 'Yes, because the Emperor saved France from anarchy in 1848 and since then he has achieved a great deal, for which we must be truly grateful.'[45] Others, of course, adopted an adverse stance on the same constitutional amendments that had been presented to the electorate:

> When, in 1852, a regime emanating from crime and assassination (2 December 1851!!)...submitted a most arbitrary constitution for the approval of the French people, I replied with a firm NO. Today, eighteen years later in 1870, this very authority...employing the same old chicanery, is once more seeking to prolong its existence, and even has the effrontery to wish to place power in perpetuity in the hands of a family of thieves and harlots...to such unparalleled impudence I am replying still more forcefully, NO! NO! NO![46]

In legislative elections an explanation might be offered for the choice of candidate: 'I am voting for citizen Achille Auger, because he is a supporter of free, compulsory and secular education, and I am setting aside M. Paul Le Roux, a proponent of popular ignorance, since he is a partisan of religious teaching orders who feed off the worker's blood.'[47] A century later one voter in the European elections of 1979 listed the reasons why she or he was not adopting any of the lists on offer:

---

[44] AN 19790725, Recensement des votes aux élections européennes, 10 juin 1979.
[45] AN BII 1244, PV Côte-d'Or, 1870.   [46] AN BII 1298A, PV Paris, 6ᵉ arrond. 1870.
[47] Déloye and Ihl, 'Des voix pas comme les autres', 168, Vendée.

'because I am saying no to a Europe of unemployment, nuclear power, repression and uniformity'.[48] Some voters were anxious to amplify their verdict, like this one in 1881: 'I wish this single ballot paper could count for 2,000. Long live de Roux. Long live religion. Down with the Republic'.[49] Others added reservations, such as the one who stated, 'Yes, as long as the Empire really does mean peace', in the plebiscite of 1852.[50]

Elections, like plebiscites, naturally elicited remarks that mirrored campaign issues. In 1871, for instance, many soldiers voted for an immediate end to the Franco-Prussian war and one of them added a touching request to return home as soon as possible.[51] A decade later some voters mentioned primary education, then under discussion in parliament, one of them suggesting that it should be 'non-compulsory', 'because we need our children to work'.[52] In 1898, a whole raft of *bulletins* extolled the virtues of Émile Zola, the writer who famously protested against the notorious miscarriage of justice perpetrated against an innocent Captain Dreyfus. Anti-semitism was also given a thorough airing, via demands for expulsion of the Jews ('les sans patrie') from France, or at least their removal from public office, although commentators of this ilk mostly restricted themselves to 'À bas les Juifs'. Racism has re-emerged with a vengeance of late, with one *bulletin* in the presidential election of 2017 bearing the name of Marine Le Pen declaring: 'I am sick and tired of all these immigrants, who enjoy so many entitlements, while poor French inhabitants receive none.' At the dawning of the twentieth century anti-clericalism had constituted a staple theme as conflict raged between Church and state: 'Down with the people who demolish our wayside crosses and seek to close our churches. Long live a France that is Catholic, Apostolic and Roman', wrote one Breton elector.[53] In 1914, the reduction of military service was often demanded, as numerous *bulletins* proclaimed 'Down with the three years', and made suggestions for Franco-German rapprochement instead.[54] More recently, in the referendum of 1958 some voters welcomed the demise of the Fourth Republic, but reasserted their determination that Algeria remain French, while the author of one annotated ballot paper declaimed: 'Oui à la France, non à de Gaulle'.[55]

Images might be deployed to make a particular point more forcefully, like the ones which drew on published cartoons of Esterhazy, frequently depicting the real traitor in the Dreyfus affair wearing a Prussian helmet (Figure 7.2). Such illustrations inspired another splendid example from 1898, this time a portrait in

---

[48] AN 19790725, Recensement.   [49] Déloye and Olivier Ihl, 'Légitimité et déviance', 18, Gard.

[50] AN BII 1154, PV Côte-d'Or, 1852.

[51] A D Côte-d'Or 3M 263, Élection législative, Feb. 1871.

[52] Déloye and Ihl, 'Des voix pas comme les autres', 164, Nièvre.

[53] AN C6669, PV Morbihan, 1910.

[54] AN C7146, PV d'Argenteuil (Seine-et-Oise), 26 Apr. 1914.

[55] AN BII 1473, Situation d'Algérie, 1958.

Figure 7.2 Annotated ballot papers, 1851–1979

The first, which was cast in the plebiscite of 1851, depicts continuing allegiance to the Republic, overturned by Louis-Napoleon; the second emanates from the legislative election of 1898, which was held at the height of the Dreyfus Affair, hence the allusions to it, along with the anarchist sentiments of its author; the third is a good example of the 'electoral essay', submitted by a voter in the first European elections of 1979.

Source: Used by kind permission of the Archives nationales de France: BII 1065A, PV de Dijon Nord, Dec. 1851; C5103, PV Allier, May 1898; and 19790725, Recensement des votes, June 1979.

colour pencil, emanating from Paris and bearing the legend: 'Feld maréchal Esterhazy, grand cordon de l'aigle noir, major général allemand.' Pictorial annotation had emerged as early as 1848, with a profusion of Napoleonic eagles and bicorne hats on presidential ballot papers, or anti-clerical artwork in the legislative election of 1849.[56] It became more widespread in the plebiscite of 1851, when a striking image of the light of liberty being snuffed out by Louis-Napoleon's coup d'état was composed in the Eure-et-Loir, for instance, while lictors' rods and liberty caps were employed to signify continuing republican commitment (Figure 7.2).[57] The tradition has proved an enduring one as examples from 1979 suggest, when crude drawings were attached to some protests about the loss of national sovereignty to the European Community. In the most recent legislative elections of 2017, the depiction of voters as sheep on one ballot paper would not have been out of place under the Third Republic. However, just as the typewriter began to be pressed into service to replace hand-written annotations at the turn of the twentieth century, so computer graphics are now adorning home-made ballot papers.

Voters have occasionally submitted lengthy diatribes, as extracts like this one, submitted at those European parliamentary polls of 1979, suggests:

> The arguments made in the course of this electoral campaign have generally provided a very dismal idea of the common homeland that Europe ought to represent. All the deep human values that contribute to the creation of a fraternal society have been ignored by candidates...who seem only interested in seeking the comfortable positions on offer...In these circumstances one can only vote in a negative fashion.[58]
>
> (Figure 7.2, bottom image)

However, annotators were not inhibited from pursuing their own agendas, such as demands made in the plebiscite of 1870 that Pierre Bonaparte, a wayward cousin of the emperor, should be punished for killing a republican journalist, Victor Noir, earlier in the year. Voters in the Eure and the Aube used the same opportunity to stake a claim for 'the right to elect our mayors', who were nominated by the government. Opposition to change might be asserted as well as arguments in favour of it: thus, another voter in 1870 lamented the greater freedom granted to the press, which he felt was encouraging dissent. An Alsatian resident in France declared in the election of 1898 that 'if France abandons Alsace-Lorraine, then in turn its inhabitants will abandon France'.[59] Proposals for lowering taxes and complaints about the cost of living were legion, like requests for restrictions on the employment of foreign workers. What Moualek calls 'alter votes', on unrelated issues, were also much in evidence in the European elections of 1994, when a number of voters anticipated the forthcoming contest for the French presidency by castigating President Mitterrand's stewardship during his second term at the

---

[56] AN C1466, PV Ain, 1849.   [57] AN BII 1072, PV Eure-et-Loir, 1851.
[58] AN 19790725, Recensement. Space does not permit the full citation this veritable essay deserves.
[59] AN C5218, Paris, 11ᵉ arrond. 1898.

Élysée.[60] Echoing the sentiment expressed in a popular pamphlet that 'it is up to the people to say what they want, rather than for the government to direct their response', one articulate Parisian concluded his proposals for the extinction of poverty by declaring, 'voilà, mon plébiscite'.[61]

Local issues surfaced too, such as: 'I am voting to have a priest installed at the boys' school', or 'I am selecting this candidate so he can use his authority and good will to open a new road that will give local farmers the opportunity to get to market in winter and sell their produce.'[62] Yet, somewhat surprisingly, local elections themselves attracted relatively few annotations (as opposed to a fair number of blanks), perhaps because they were regarded, by people as well as officials, as 'administrative' rather than 'political' polls. It was extremely unusual to find a remark with broader implications like the one appended to the voter's chosen list at the village of Brissac (Maine-et-Loire) in 1851, which stated: 'We must purge the municipal council of Catholics and Jesuits, because they are the sworn enemies of our infant Republic.'[63] Even in large towns, a municipal voter making reference to a national issue was a rare bird. The Toulonnais who declared that he was voting Socialist despite his opposition to the party's stance on PR, or another who explained that he was not selecting either of the lists in contention because they both contained 'vile freemasons, who have stolen a great deal from the state and passed laws completely at odds with public liberty', were quite exceptional.[64]

Subversion

Personal remarks inevitably abounded in electoral contests and they were rarely complimentary. Yet annotations of this sort were, once again, scarcely apparent in departmental or municipal elections. Scrutineers at Draguignan, in the Var, were so scandalized by the derogatory comments inscribed on one *bulletin* in 1874 that they decided to destroy it immediately, but they were seldom troubled in this fashion at local polls.[65] Perhaps it was unwise to hurl such abuse within the confines of small communities, where authors might be recognized, but voters in larger towns proved equally reluctant to do so. The municipal list cast in 1848 at Dijon, ironically entitled 'Those worthy of entering the town council', was unusual in bearing annotations to each name that ranged from 'drunkard' to 'layabout' and 'tartuffe'.[66] Voters were more distanced from candidates in legislative elections

---

[60] Moualek, 'Votes blancs et nuls aux élections européennes', 81–5.
[61] AN BII 1298B, PV Paris, 13e arrond. 1870.   [62] AN C6669, PV Morbihan, 1910.
[63] Cited in Anne de Bergh, *Les Élections municipales en Maine-et-Loire. Coups de gueule et coups de poing* (Paris, 2008), 68–70.
[64] AD Var 3M 582, PV Toulon, 1912; and AD Var 3M 594, PV Toulon, 1925.
[65] AD Var 3M 529, PV Draguignan, 1874.
[66] AD Côte-d'Or M 3M 682, Dijon, 1848.

and accordingly less constrained, expressing a degree of coarseness, even verbal violence, which was at odds with the intended decorum of the electoral process. A torrent of insults ranging from *fumiste, crapule, voleur, menteur, tricheur,* to *blagueur,* or *pognonniste,* were commonly deployed in the late nineteenth century, when one individual standing for re-election was memorably described as 'a *clocho-député,* much too fond of the bottle'.[67] Elections to the European parliament a century later were no different: 'You are incapable of managing France, so what makes you think that you can run Europe?'[68] The lexicon of abuse has hardly altered in recent years, as a recent investigation of spoiled papers in the presidential and legislative elections of 2007 suggests, though the level of sexual innuendo and profanity has undoubtedly increased in a more permissive era.[69] Conversely, while computer-assisted photomontage, integrating the physical features of rival candidates in an effort to demonstrate their inter-changeability, can be readily accomplished these days, the deputy's head craftily superimposed on a toad's body at the end of the nineteenth century has rarely been surpassed.[70]

Not just individual candidates, but the political class as a whole was subject to disdain and derision. In 1910 national deputies felt the full force of the electorate's displeasure as a result of the 'quinze mille', the 15,000 francs a year to which they had recently raised their salaries.[71] As one rural voter put it, in the Côte-d'Or, 'For 15,000 francs I could raise 150 pigs, which would be much more useful to the Republic.'[72] Another, from the Morbihan, declared: 'Down with all the deputies until they are willing to take their place for the honour alone, like municipal councillors, or paid according to attendance in the Chamber.'[73] The growing professionalization of politics at the turn of the twentieth century encouraged voters to employ the disparaging term *politicien* and to impugn candidates' personal motives: 'When a free people hands itself over to paid politicians, who serve only their own interests or those of their families, then such a people deserves to be subjected to the worst forms of servitude.'[74] With the concurrent emergence of more formal political organizations, anti-partisan sentiment also found its way on to ballot papers: in 1914 a voter at Alger summed this up by declaring: 'Long live a Republic administered by decent deputies who govern in the interests of France and not for a party.'[75] Yet, while the volume of hostility was escalating, it was by no means a novelty; as early as 1848 one voter had written 'Down with the 900 useless deputies (at the Constituent Assembly).'[76] The credibility of politicians has constantly been called into question: 'All the candidates promise the moon,

---

[67] AN C4974, PV Dijon-Est, 1893.   [68] AN 19790725, Recensement des votes.

[69] Jérémie Moualek, 'Tous pourris! Formes et significations des gros mots de l'électeur au prisme des bulletins nuls', *Argotica,* (20), 231–40.

[70] AN C4974, Côte-d'Or, 1893.   [71] Garrigou, 'Vivre de la politique', 7–34.

[72] AN C6576, PV Beaune-Nord, 1910.   [73] AN C6669, PV Morbihan, 1910.

[74] AN C5218, PV Paris, 11ᵉ arrond. 1898.

[75] AN C7170, PV Alger, 1914.   [76] AN BII 1015, Nord, 1848.

but once in office they do as they like', ran a rebuke from 1881 that remains familiar today.[77] An invalidated presidential *bulletin* from 2007, cited by Moualek, may have employed a contemporary environmental metaphor to categorize all twelve contenders as political pollutants, with Jean-Marie Le Pen representing the most toxic variety, but such disenchantment and distrust have a very long history.[78]

In fact, ballot papers might also be appropriated to support candidates who were more to voters' liking, but not permitted to stand for election. Even before the restrictive law of 1889 was passed, requiring a declaration of candidature for the Chamber of Deputies, there had been exceptions to the free range of nomin-ations, which excluded members of the Bourbon and Orleans dynasties under the Second and Third Republics, for instance. Their pretenders attracted numerous votes despite the inevitable annulment, and the same was true of Ledru-Rollin, a republican proscribed for his involvement in protests against Louis-Napoleon's coup of 1851. He received a large number of invalid votes in the subsequent legis-lative elections of 1852, most famously those penned in red ink cast in the Lozère.

After 1889, when a declaration of candidature became mandatory, for legisla-tive elections at least, participants persisted in exercising a liberty which they regarded as part and parcel of their sovereignty, by naming whomsoever they wished on their *bulletins*. General Boulanger, whose simultaneous campaigning in numerous departments in the 1880s had finally prompted the imposition of this constraint, still appeared on thousands of ballot papers in the following elec-tion. Writing down the names of illicit candidates, or producing ballot papers on their behalf, was a popular means of protest and making a political statement. The device was thus widely employed to indicate support for the extension of the franchise to women from the late nineteenth century onwards, by nominating females, and it was also utilized by communists in the early 1920s to publicize the case of André Marty, who had been imprisoned for leading a naval mutiny in the Black Sea in 1919. His name was put forward at no less than forty polls and, in the Var, he was elected to the *conseil général* three times, despite subsequent disquali-fication, before being defeated on the fourth occasion.[79] Angry officials, who felt that such campaigns should be pursued by other means, because an expensive poll had to be retaken, were powerless to prevent a practice they claimed was discrediting the entire electoral process.

The ballot paper might also be employed to challenge the political system per se. In December 1848, for instance, outright hostility was expressed to the estab-lishment of a presidency for the Second Republic, from both left and right. It was the whole point of the socialist Raspail's candidature, which was conceived as an

[77] Déloye and Ihl, 'Des voix pas comme les autres', 165, Hautes-Pyrénées.
[78] Moualek, 'Tous pourris!', 235.
[79] AD Var M 511, PV Hyères, 1922–3; AD Seine-et-Oise 2M19/5, PV Aulnay-sous-Bois, 1926; and Andrew Orr, 'The myth of the Black Sea mutiny: Communist propaganda, Soviet influence and the re-remembering of the mutiny', *FH*, 32 (2018), 86–105.

anti-presidential protest campaign.[80] Monarchists, on the other hand, sought to employ the election to promote a restoration with Henri V (as royalists fancifully called the Bourbon pretender, the comte de Chambord), or via the Orleanist claimant, the prince de Joinville.[81] In the Nord, one voter even asserted that he was 'voting for the government such as it existed before the upheaval of 24 February: Long live Guizot'.[82] The Third Republic would be rejected in a similar fashion, by clericals and royalists, who freely proclaimed their allegiance to God and king. Likewise the Fourth Republic, condemned on ballot papers as corrupt, while Algerian nationalists used their votes to express support 'the struggle for complete independence' from the metropole.[83] By the turn of the twenty-first century the European Union had become a repeated object of the voters' spleen: elections for the European parliament inevitably encouraged repudiation of the overall project, with slogans borrowed from nationalist groups reproduced on some ballot papers and Communist animosity towards what they regarded as a capitalist conspiracy appearing on others. In 1994, in the wake of the divisive Maastricht referendum on greater integration, some voters wrote 'For France, against Europe and foreigners' and, 'If the French are unable to govern themselves, how on earth are they to collaborate with other countries?'[84]

The plebiscites of Louis-Napoleon were denounced as a travesty of democracy, mere ratifications of government policy which sought to dupe voters into believing they were exercising a meaningful choice: 'This vote is not free, in fact it is illegal', wrote one participant in 1852.[85] More probing were the queries raised at a later consultation: 'The question is much too complicated to be answered by a simple yes or no' or, less courteously, 'Are you seriously demanding that I reply with a single word to an insidious question elaborated over five lines? This is simply a political conjuring trick which does not deserve a response.'[86] The whole point of voting was called into question by some annotated *bulletins*, perhaps authored by anarchists, who were staunch opponents of any kind of consultation and proved especially vocal at the turn of the twentieth century. 'Voting is a complete waste of time', declared one Parisian in 1898, while another asserted that 'The inveterate voter (*votard*) who puts all his aspirations into a ballot paper is a complete idiot.'[87] Another inhabitant of the capital recommended the abolition of elections and the formation of a parliament by drawing lots, which he argued was more in keeping with democratic ideals.[88] Universal male suffrage was not

[80] Samuel Hayat, 'Se présenter pour protester. La candidature impossible de François-Vincent Raspail en décembre 1848', *Rfsp*, 64 (2014), 869–903.

[81] AN BII 1028, PV Sarthe, 1848.   [82] AN BII 1015, PV Nord, 1848.

[83] AN BII 1473, Dossier algérien, 1958.

[84] Moualek, 'Votes blancs et nuls aux élections européennes', 85–7.

[85] AN C1602, PV Côte-d'Or, 1852.

[86] AN BII 1298A, PV Paris, 1870 and AN BII 1313, PV Alger, 1870.

[87] AN C7115, PV Paris, 14ᵉ arrond. 1914.   [88] AN C5218, PV Paris, 11ᵉ arrond. 1898.

spared by its opponents, one of whom described it as 'stupid and disastrous', 'the fundamental cause of our innumerable ills'.[89] Ideas of direct democracy were also floated on some *bulletins*: 'I am proposing an imperative mandate to be enforced by penal sanctions', or again, 'We have no need of career politicians since we are quite capable of governing ourselves'.[90] Voters were indeed attempting to take back control; as one Dijonnais put it in 1902, 'By virtue of the authority that has been conferred upon me, I am voting for the suppression of 300 seats in the Chamber of Deputies and 150 in the Senate'.[91]

This persistence of 'anti-representation' sentiment, which had surfaced strongly in the upheavals of the 1790s, 1848, and 1871, also signified an effort to communicate with those elected in a manner which might be interpreted as constructive rather than condemnatory. The point is emphasized by Moualek in his analysis of spoiled papers in the European elections of 1994, where he encountered what he calls a 'euroconstructif' as well as a 'eurosceptique' dimension, with demands for a different sort of Union based on workers rather than elites, and on democracy (via a reformed parliament) instead of technocracy.[92] Yet even these positive aspirations were little more than a 'message in a bottle', cast into a void with little hope of reaching their destination. Other instances demonstrate that, conscious of this shortcoming, the authors of such papers instead addressed those present at the count since, until the advent of mobile phones and social media, they and the departmental electoral commissioners constituted the only audience for their annotated efforts. A salient example emanates from Paris in 1898:

> Kind-hearted scrutineers, in opening this folded paper you will find a fraternal greeting for yourselves and all those citizens who are present. Please read it out loud to the assembled public. My heart cries out 'Long Live Freedom and down with the slaves of all parties'. This message been composed by a liberal-minded citizen.[93]

Of course, such an appropriation of the ballot paper, not least when it was employed to express abuse or insults, might simply indicate a voter letting off steam, like those who tear their *bulletins* to pieces. It could represent anger and political illiteracy, rather than sophistication and engagement, such as the paper simply inscribed 'MERDE', in huge, carefully crafted, capital letters, cast in the plebiscite of 1851.

However, humour has always played a part in this form of protest, employing ridicule to undermine authority and empower opponents. Those who turned 'oui' into 'ouf!', or modified the name Bonaparte to read 'Bon-à-partir', in mid-nineteenth

[89] AN C5233, PV Paris, 14ᵉ arrond. 1898.   [90] AN C5214, PV Paris, 5ᵉ arrond. 1898.
[91] AN C6055, Dijon Ouest, 1902.
[92] Moualek, 'Votes blancs et nuls aux élections européennes', 87–9.
[93] AN C5215, PV Paris, 7ᵉ arrond. 1898.

century plebiscites, were gently mocking a demagogic procedure.[94] Similar *jeux d'esprit* were evident in the constant play on candidates' names in legislative elections: 'I do not love Bienaimé'; 'there is no room for a king in the Republic' (candidate Le Roy), or 'in a Republic we have no need of an emperor' (candidate Lempereur). Under the Third Republic there were votes for Jesus, the Pope, the Tsar, or Bismarck, and wives or mistresses. The extent of this ludic practice was indicated in the first European elections of 1979, when the whole of France was treated as a single constituency and lists of eighty-one candidates were presented to the electorate. Some voters responded with a tongue-in-cheek *panachage*, which produced scores of different nominations across the country.[95] The then Pope, John Paul II, received eight endorsements, while God only got three, but Coluche came top of this unofficial poll with eighty-seven votes. The last-named, a French comedian who dealt in irreverent political satire, subsequently announced his intention to stand as a presidential candidate but, despite attracting 16 per cent support in one opinion poll, he ultimately withdrew from contention.[96] These days some voters ingeniously fold papers in a form of electoral origami, while others insert foreign bodies into their envelopes, which include tissues and toilet paper. In 2017, a 50-euro note was cast as a ballot paper, bearing the inscription 'For Penelope', in reference to the wife of presidential candidate François Fillon, whose spurious employment as his assistant, paid out of parliamentary funds, effectively sank his bid for supreme office.[97]

Such an expensive joke should be regarded as subverting the serious, even sacred aura attached to the exercise of the electoral ritual—Olivier Ihl has invoked the 'fetishization' of the ballot box—which invited desecration of the *bulletin*. The political scientist Philippe Braud has also drawn attention to this playful aspect of delinquent electoral behaviour, going so far as to suggest that electors vote for pleasure much more than in pursuit of self-interest.[98] Many authors of exuberant annotations were evidently sophisticated voters, who sought to puncture the pomposity of the process and expose elements of hypocrisy. A splendid example emanated from the Côte-d'Or, when a plebiscite was held in 1852 to approve bestowing the imperial title on Louis-Napoleon:

Obsequies for the French Republic: Republican sympathizers, whose grief I share…as family members you are invited to be present at the grand funeral cortege organized for your daughter, who has died giving birth to an Emperor. The

[94]   AN BII 1127, PV Vaucluse, 1851.   [95]   AN 19790725, Recensement.
[96]   Bruno Fuligni, *Votez fou. Candidats bizarres, utopistes, chimériques, mystiques, marginaux, farceurs et farfelus* (Paris, 2007), 124–9.
[97]   See   http://www.leparisien.fr/elections/presidentielle/presidentielle-ces-bulletins-farfelus-qui-ont-fait-le-tour-du-web-23-04-2017-6880779.php (accessed 07/08/19).
[98]   Philippe Braud, *Le Comportement électoral en France* (Paris 1973), 39.

indivisible Marianne, who was not supposed to perish, was unable to survive a Caesarian operation. Although the mother has died the infant is thriving...[99]

Nineteenth-century plebiscites or twentieth-century referendums have tended to attract more annotation than elections, perhaps because they are offering a proposition, rather than a simple choice of candidate, and thus encourage the expression of an opinion, while simultaneously restricting the response to a simple yes or no. Yet earlier consultations of this sort, referred to as constitutional votes, did explicitly invite comments and thus helped to create an enduring tradition in France.

Annotation, a Deep-Rooted Practice

Annotation has deep roots in French electoral culture, because it draws on the long-standing, close relationship between voting and discussion that was exemplified by the elections to the Estates General of 1789. This consultation involved drafting the celebrated *cahiers de doléances*, the lists of grievances that were to accompany the elected deputies. The combination of deliberation and vote, conducted in assemblies, was unhesitatingly maintained during the 1790s, and beyond, generating practices of 'direct' or 'participatory democracy' that spread all over France, until they were halted after the period of revolutionary government.[100] Following the abandonment of the assembly mechanism, with the advent of the Second Republic, electoral regulations reiterated that 'all discussion... is strictly forbidden', an indication that the tradition had not been entirely eradicated. In the event, voting on an individual basis after 1848 effectively precluded any collective debate at the polling station, so many voters sought to preserve the oral, deliberative tradition, by translating it into the comments they wrote on their *bulletins*. The practice of discussion surrounding the constitutional votes of 1793 and 1795 was immediately carried over into those held by Napoleon Bonaparte, when thousands of participants entered remarks in the registers, then later into the plebiscites organized by his nephew, Louis-Napoleon. One critic of the consultation held in 1870 actually bemoaned the absence of any formal opportunity for submitting suggestions and, while making specific reference to the *cahiers* of 1789, he argued that those who annotated their ballot papers were justified in seeking to raise issues, rather than simply voting pro or con.[101]

---

[99] AN BII 1154, PV Côte-d'Or, 1852.
[100] The subject deserves much greater attention than it can be accorded here. See Rose, *The Making of the* Sans-Culottes.
[101] M. Boudot de Challaye, *Protestation contre les fausses interprétations du vote du 8 mai 1870. Le gallicanisme et l'ultramontanisme politiques. Les assemblées primaires de 1789; le plébiscite de 1870* (Paris, 1870), 296.

The origins of annotated ballot papers in the earlier plebiscitary exercises in France has not been acknowledged because they were conducted in a rather different fashion, and their content has gone largely unnoticed because attention has focused on the arithmetic outcome, as those in office desired.[102] The Constitutions of 1793 and 1795, like that of 1799, the Life Consulate of 1802, the Hereditary Empire of 1804 and the Acte additionnel aux Constitutions de l'Empire in 1815, were all overwhelmingly endorsed by a virtually universal male electorate. Yet these so-called 'plebiscites' also attracted numerous comments, which ranged from objections and outright opposition to a whole series of extraneous matters. In this way they provided striking precedents for the type of annotation practised after 1848.[103] A tradition of recording opinions on constitutional proposals was thus revived rather than invented in the mid-nineteenth century, when the novelty was the annotation of *bulletins*, not the making and inscription of opinions.

The two consultations held during the Revolution were conducted, like all elections in the 1790s, by means of assemblies, which were convened for this purpose in the cantons, and the practice of discussion flourished there, both with and without official blessing.[104] In 1793 observations that were made in the course of debate on the Constitution were transcribed onto the *procès-verbaux*, which were then taken by deputies to Paris, where the overall outcome of the vote was declared, though no notice seems to have been taken of the comments that were appended. The fact that oral participation was permitted meant that illiterate citizens could contribute and roughly one tenth of the assemblies requested constitutional modifications, with the right to insurrection a widespread object of criticism, while others raised current issues of more general concern. For instance, the status of the Church was frequently mentioned in the west, while in the Midi, on account of its different legal traditions, the recent law on equal testation was roundly condemned.[105]

Although the Constitution of 1793 was overwhelmingly accepted, reservations notwithstanding, it was immediately shelved due to the dire situation facing the First Republic, then later abandoned. When a fresh Constitution was drawn up in 1795 it was also submitted to the mass electorate. On this occasion, discussion was discouraged (and forbidden by the Constitution itself), but when the

---

[102] For an exception, see Vincent Huet, 'Le bulletin nul: une forme de résistance à la normalisation de la vie politique (Paris, 1851–1870)', *Amnis*, 9 (2010), http://amnis.revues.org/312 (accessed 18/04/19) and Malcolm Crook, 'Protest voting: the revolutionary origins of annotated ballot papers cast in French plebiscites, 1851–1870', *FH*, 29 (2015), 349–69, with some illustrations.

[103] Once again, these annotations have attracted little interest from historians, but see Malcolm Crook, 'Les réactions autour de brumaire à travers le plébiscite de l'an VIII', in Jean-Pierre Jessenne et al. (eds), *Du Directoire au Consulat*, 4 vols (Lille, 1999–2001), iii, 325–9; Malcolm Crook, 'The Plebiscite on the Empire', in Philip G. Dwyer and Alan Forrest (eds), *Napoleon and his Empire. Europe, 1804–1814* (Basingstoke, 2007), 23–5; and Crook, '"Ma volonté est celle du peuple"', 631–5.

[104] Crook, *Elections*, 112–14 and 123–5, for an overview of these two consultations.

[105] AN BII 4, PV Finistère, 1793, for example.

assemblies convened to vote on the document substantial debate could not be prevented; indeed, the right to 'deliberation' as well as voting was reasserted in resolutions that declared: 'no administrative body, not even the national assembly, has the authority to withdraw this facility.' There was little reaction to the re-introduction of modest restrictions on the basic franchise, but severe limitations on access to the second tier of indirect elections, which operated above the local level, did prompt some strong comments. Extraneous issues were once again raised in the assemblies of 1795, albeit to a lesser degree than two years earlier. One vital matter was also widely debated: the decree associated with this Constitution, which stipulated that two-thirds of deputies to be elected to the new legislature were to be chosen among existing members of the Convention. Citizens assembled at the Popincourt section in Paris declared that this form of political self-perpetuation was 'contrary to the most precious and sacred rights of the people'.[106]

Napoleon Bonaparte, who naturally served as a role model for his nephew Louis-Napoleon, also employed a series of constitutional votes after he came to power in 1799. However, voters were now invited to record a positive or negative verdict by signing public registers, which were opened for a week or so in every commune.[107] These 'poll books' actually reveal a wide range of fascinating comments, which were in some cases facilitated, even encouraged, by the provision of columns entitled 'observations', where voters could justify or qualify their verdicts. In 1799, many of those who wrote comments described the constitutional text as a sure step towards 'curtailing factionalism' and securing 'the return of public and personal prosperity'.[108] The plebiscite on the Life Consulate in 1802 that soon followed revealed the desire of numerous voters to prolong Napoleonic rule by awarding him hereditary status, which was duly conferred two years later.[109] In 1815, during the Hundred Days, one voter enthusiastically welcomed Napoleon's return, because he was 'convinced by experience that France can only maintain its independence with the aid of a great general'.[110]

Yet such affirmation was far from unanimous. Conditions might be appended, notably in 1799, when there was a good deal of *attentisme*, since the new regime, the Consulate, remained an unknown quantity. Requests for the restoration of Roman Catholicism (hard hit by the Revolution) were especially evident in more conformist areas. The Life Consulate, which extended Bonaparte's authority, prompted some misgivings, like those of a notary in the Aube, who considered it

---

[106] AN BII 61, PV Paris, Section de Popincourt, 22 fructidor III (8 Sept. 1795).

[107] In December 1851, after he had seized power, Louis-Napoleon's initial decree required voting in the same fashion, on public registers, but following protests this was altered to a paper ballot. See Gisela Geywitz, *Das Plebiszit von 1851 in Frankreich* (Tübingen, 1965), 12–14.

[108] AN BII 281B, PV Morbihan, an VIII (1799).

[109] AN BII 615A, PV Paris, Préfecture, an X (1802), for instance.

[110] AN BII 935, PV Paris, 4e arrond. 1815.

a 'danger to public and individual liberty'.[111] Indeed, the establishment of the Napoleonic Empire in 1804 led to some outright opposition: at Marseille, one voter expressed his utter condemnation, adding that 'instructed by the lessons of history and following my own reason, everything suggests that genius and wisdom are not at all hereditary...'.[112] In 1815, when the *Acte additionnel* brought further constitutional amendments, particular hostility was directed at a chamber of peers, for which provision was made alongside a legislative body, and many voters made their support conditional on its removal.[113]

Conclusion

When Louis-Napoleon resurrected the plebiscitary device in 1851, his attempt to re-introduce registers for the reception of voters' verdicts caused outrage and he was obliged to back-track. Yet the use of anonymous *bulletins* actually facilitated the emission of critical comments and, in particular, the composition of visual material. Annotation was already becoming well established in elections after 1848 and it would prove to be an enduring phenomenon. The explosion of spoiled papers in the French presidential and legislative elections of 2017, which has elicited so much recent comment, is thus a matter of degree rather than kind. It stems from a once invisible practice of subverting the act of voting, and appropriating it so as to make one's voice heard, something which contemporary electoral procedure prevents. Annotation may increase as publicity for it increases in the digital age, with images of ballot papers readily posted on the Internet, which offers an ideal platform for attention-seeking as well as political communication. Yet a serious critique of the electoral system underlies the casting of invalid *bulletins*, conveying a series of messages for the political class, as well as symbolic importance for the sovereign voter. As part of a spectrum of electoral behaviour, which starts with *suffrages exprimés*, it should be clearly distinguished from non-voting, which will be addressed in the next and final chapter.

---

[111] Cited in Horn, *Qui parle pour la nation?*, 146.   [112] AN BII 687A, PV Marseille, 1804.
[113] AN BII 880, PV Eure, 1815, for example.

8

Gone Fishing

Non-Voting and the Problem of Abstention

> Abstaining from the vote, that most sacred of all duties, is somewhat
> akin to committing suicide.
>
> Henri Martin, 1848.[1]

By the end of the nineteenth century the political class in France had become so
anxious about abstention that compulsory voting was frequently advocated,
though it would never be adopted. Misgivings about levels of electoral participation had not always been quite so evident, especially during the initial experience
of mass voting during the Revolution and under Napoleon, but non-voting was
perceived as deeply problematic after the principle of one man, one vote was
implemented in 1848. Indeed, a preoccupation with *abstentionnisme* would
endure for the following century or more, notwithstanding the sustained, high
levels of turnout which have been delineated in Chapter 6. Besides conservatives'
conviction that it was their supporters who were abstaining, and thus denying
them a majority, this paradox can also be explained by reference to the French
concepts of citizenship and sovereignty of the people, which demanded a universal response from the electorate as a matter of binding duty. Moreover, failure to
fulfil one's civic responsibility at the polls eroded confidence in the principle of
representation and weakened the legitimacy of those who were elected. Since the
1990s, as participation rates have plummeted, obligation is once more back on the
political agenda. The historical reaction to abstention, together with various
proposals for tackling it, will be considered in this chapter, which explores why
citizens may choose to 'go fishing', as the French picturesquely put it, rather
than voting.

Abstention in the Age of Revolution

Prior to 1789, participation in many electoral or deliberative assemblies was *de
rigueur*. As Christin states, 'without any doubt, the denial of the right to abstain,

---

[1] Henri Martin, *Manuel de l'instituteur pour les élections* (Paris, 1848), 25–6.

How the French Learned to Vote: A History of Electoral Practice in France. Malcolm Crook, Oxford University Press (2021).
© Malcolm Crook. DOI: 10.1093/oso/9780192894786.003.0009

like refusal to accept office, constituted one of key characteristics of elections in the corporations of the *ancien régime*.[2] Members of urban oligarchies and ecclesiastical bodies who failed to fulfil their electoral functions were thus fined, or might have to forfeit their privilege of voting, as at Aix or Aubagne in Provence.[3] As far back as 1340 a statute had been issued at Toulon, which stipulated that 12 *deniers* would be exacted from all those who absented themselves from the annual election of municipal officers.[4] In fourteenth-century Amiens, penalties were likewise imposed on absentees from assemblies convened by the mayor for the purposes of debate as well as election.[5] This obligation was echoed 400 years later in the *cahier de doléances* drawn up at the tiny village of Aurons in Provence, in March 1789, when one article demanded that those who neglected the 'sacred duty' of attending general assemblies of all householders should be fined for absence.[6] It was taken for granted that those chosen as representatives to the *bailliage* or *sénéchaussée* assemblies of that year would make every effort to attend them, and the overwhelming majority duly complied.

After 1789, by contrast, voting at cantonal and municipal elections was emphasized as a right rather than a duty for members of the mass electorate. Yet the fact that some citizens were failing to exercise the franchise was soon attracting attention. Thus, in the Landes in 1790, a motion was passed at the primary assembly in Dax bemoaning the non-attendance of artisans and workers. Its proposer added that 'such indifference on the part of men so long oppressed deeply disturbs my civic conscience'.[7] In the capital, the author of a letter published in the *Moniteur* in June 1791, on the eve of fresh polling, expressed grave concern that so few Parisians had taken part in the municipal elections held the previous year. He proceeded to castigate those individuals who, 'out of sheer idleness', had abandoned the crucial choice of personnel to a small minority of registered voters.[8] The Luxembourg section in the capital later conducted an inquiry into poor turnout in November 1791, when less than 14 per cent of the overall electorate took part in voting for a new mayor. The gross neglect of such a 'precious right', like fears that citizens would relapse into the 'glacial languor of slavery', prompted a demand for urgent remedies.[9] One suggestion was to leave the polls open all day,

---

[2] Christin, *Vox populi*, 121.

[3] Jacqueline Dumoulin, *Le Consulat d'Aix-en-Provence. Enjeux politiques, 1598–1692* (Dijon, 1993), 176.

[4] Octave Teissier, *Le Suffrage universel et le vote obligatoire à Toulon en 1354* (Paris, 1868).

[5] Thierry Dutour, 'Le consensus des bonnes gens. La participation des habitants aux affaires communes dans quelques villes de la langue d'oïl', in Hamon and Laurent (eds), *Le Pouvoir municipal*, 193.

[6] *AP*, Iere série, VI, 258.

[7] AN F1cIII Landes 1, Motion faite aux assemblées primaires de Dax, no date, but evidently June 1790.

[8] *Moniteur*, 17 June 1791, 695.

[9] BNF Lb40 1932, *P-V de l'assemblée générale de la section du Luxembourg* (Paris, 1791).

so that voters could cast their ballot papers when they wished, instead of waiting to be called in alphabetical order (a process that was much easier to police), while another was to publish a list of those who failed attend, or award medals to particularly assiduous participants.

As these examples suggest, and contrary to a view expressed by some historians, notice might be drawn to non-voting, even if calculations of 'turnout'—a hitherto alien notion—were rarely made. Indeed, many assemblies sought to raise levels of participation by adjourning their proceedings so that town criers could redouble their efforts to encourage citizens to come and vote, sometimes successfully.[10] In the Ardèche, in 1790, voters were apparently 'roused from their slumbers and came to vote in their bedclothes'.[11] In Paris, at the Rue de Montreuil section, in June 1791, the president asked those present to shame absent friends and neighbours into joining them. No means were to be spared in achieving this objective and, in this instance at least, almost twice as many citizens appeared for the final round of voting.[12] There was also growing recognition that the electoral procedure introduced in 1790 was too time-consuming. In the spring of 1791, with a fresh round of cantonal elections imminent, Pétion delivered a speech to the National Assembly acknowledging that attendance was not an issue for the ancients—who were supported by the 'odious institution' of slavery—but in revolutionary France at least 90 per cent of citizens were simply unable to spare much of their precious time at the primary assemblies.[13] Yet his fellow deputy, Démeunier, was convinced that, despite 'the demands of the season', rural voters would not begrudge a few moments of inconvenience and he was sure they would 'participate in the forthcoming primary elections with pleasure'.[14] In the event, his optimism proved ill-founded, as turnout fell sharply compared to the previous year.

Eighteen months later, a further Parisian mayoral election witnessed a 50 per cent increase in the number of participants, but this was following the extension of the franchise in August 1792. The Gardes-françaises section still recorded its alarm that 'almost the entirety' of its citizens had abstained from voting for their 'principal magistrate', putting the turnout at barely 10 per cent.[15] By then, Bancal des Issarts, a deputy in the newly established National Convention, had composed a pamphlet on the social order, in which he lamented the fact that so many French electors were failing to vote for public officials and urged members of the new

[10] Gueniffey, Le Nombre et la raison, 197–8.
[11] Cited in Jacques Godechot, Les Institutions de la France sous la Révolution et L'Empire, 2nd edn (Paris, 1968), 111.
[12] AN B1 8, PV de la section de la Rue de Montreuil, 16–20 June 1791.
[13] AP, Iere série, XXVI, 27 May 1791, 509–10.   [14] AP, Iere série, XXVI, 27 May 1791, 501.
[15] BNF Lb40 1844, Délibération de la section des Gardes-Françaises (Paris, 1793).

legislature to seek a remedy.[16] Since the exercise of the franchise was 'a duty as well as a right', Bancal reckoned that a fine should be imposed on all those who neglected to use it, and that three absences without good cause should result in loss of the franchise. The Comité de Constitution sponsored publication of his proposal, but no further action ensued. When a popular vote was taken on a new constitution in the summer of 1793, concern was certainly expressed in the Convention about the level of turnout, though in fact the level of participation was generally higher than it had been since 1790. This prompted a further, equally abortive, suggestion for penalizing non-voters by removing both their right to vote and eligibility for office.[17]

Voting was not included in the declaration of duties (as well as rights) that accompanied the Constitution of 1795, though one proposition submitted to the Convention while the document was being drafted did suggest a 10 per cent tax surcharge for absentees.[18] Centrally appointed *commissaires de canton* subsequently expressed their astonishment, and equally disappointment, that relatively few voters were appearing at the primary assemblies. As the *commissaire* at Légé (Loire-Inférieure) put it: 'I am at a loss to explain such indifference towards the public good and its best interests.' Some of his colleagues consoled themselves with the observation that at least solid republicans were appearing at the polls, while small numbers were not preventing a satisfactory outcome: in 1798, at Saint-Sébastien in the same department, only seventeen out of 344 electors had attended the cantonal assembly but, 'when the result is good, does the inhabitants' insouciance really matter?'[19] This echoed sentiments expressed at the Luxembourg section in Paris, in 1791, where one member had asserted that 'small numbers…bring a purity of intention to the assembly, a unanimity that compensates for poor attendance.'[20] Such comments suggest that some revolutionaries were rather more concerned about the result than the process it involved. Thus, in the case of the constitutional vote of 1793, it was deemed sufficient to proclaim an overwhelming majority in favour of adoption.[21] By contrast, in 1795, statistics for a similar consultation were collected, published, and circulated, broken down by department and canton, but this novel compilation was specifically designed to reassure the population that a clear decision had been made; there was no comment on the level of turnout.[22]

The Napoleonic regime not only seized on the idea of publishing figures for the constitutional votes it conducted in 1799, 1802, and 1804 for propaganda

---

[16] *AP*, Iere série, LV, Annexe, 24 Dec. 1792, 416–17.

[17] *AP*, Iere série, LXXII, 11 Aug. 1793, 32–3.

[18] AN C227, Commission des Onze, 29 Germinal III (18 Apr. 1795).

[19] Yvon Le Gall, 'Les Consultations générales en Loire-Inférieure 1789-an VII', Thèse pour le Doctorat en Droit, 2 vols, Université de Nantes, 1976, ii, 845–6.

[20] BNF Lb[40] 1932, *P-V de l'assemblée générale*.   [21] *AP*, Iere série, LXX, 9 Aug. 1793, 546–8.

[22] AN BII 74, Tableau du dépouillement et recensement, 6 vendémiaire IV (28 Sept. 1795).

purposes (albeit in a fraudulent fashion), but also introduced a comparative dimension, which indicated inferior totals for 1793 and 1795, after details relating to the former had been exhumed from the archives. Above all, unprecedented reference was made to the proportion of the electorate that had voted. In a report to the newly installed Corps législatif, it was asserted that the three million individuals who had endorsed the Constitution of 1799 (it was in fact half this figure, though there were very few negative verdicts), represented 'virtually all those who were in a position to judge and understand the document'.[23] A similarly spurious claim was made by Roederer in 1804, after the vote that vested the heredity of the Empire in the Bonaparte dynasty: 'the number of participants ("scrupulously" verified at 3,500,000 according to him), constitutes the entire political nation, because women, children, domestic servants, the indigent and the sick form more than five-sixths of the overall population.'[24]

Following the installation of prefects in the departments after 1800, there was administrative capacity to monitor electoral turnout more closely. From 1802 onwards, figures for registered voters and the number of participants began to be recorded for both cantonal and college elections, on standard, printed pro forma, with copies despatched to the ministry of the interior in Paris. Yet no use seems to have been made of this material (which has not attracted much interest from historians either). It was only towards the end of the First Empire, in the summer of 1813, that a ministerial circular specifically requested some analysis of 'the eagerness of the voters to attend the assemblies', arising out of polls to elect municipal councillors in towns with a population in excess of five thousand inhabitants.[25] The uncollated replies noted the mostly modest turnout—between 10 per cent and 20 per cent of the electorate—in some cases citing precise figures, and usually seeking to explain them, but without evincing much surprise or dismay. The urban notables, prefects argued, generally took little interest in such elections because of the reduced role for local councillors under Napoleon and, unless there was some competition between them for office, mobilization of other social groups was slight. On the contrary, several prefects regarded abstention as something of a blessing, since it led to peaceful polling, while others, like the incumbent in the Finistère suggested that it was scarcely worthwhile persevering with the electoral process when so few citizens bothered to use the rights that 'his Majesty (Napoleon) has deigned to accord them'. It was left to the acting sub-prefect of Toulon to draw the logical conclusion that 'no one would regret it if the articles in our constitution relating to popular elections were revoked...'.

---

[23] *AP*, 2ᵉ série, I, 21 pluviôse VIII (10 Feb. 1800), 177–8.
[24] BL R154, *Suite du recueil des pièces et actes.*   [25] Crook, 'Voter sous Napoléon', 103–22.

Non-Voting Becomes a Problem

Administrators thus began compiling reports and calculating statistics for elections, thereby inaugurating a lasting practice, while their political masters began to take a closer interest in the subject.[26] Indeed, when they were asked to comment on the turnout in the municipal elections that were re-established in 1831 under the July Monarchy, there was a good deal of criticism of voter apathy. In the wake of the first round of polling, a government official had complained in the Chamber of Deputies that 'far too much indifference was evident when it came to exercising rights that had been so enthusiastically demanded.'[27] Further concern was aroused when an inquiry into the second, triennial round of municipal elections, which took place in 1834, revealed that on average only 50 per cent of the broad electorate had taken part.[28] The minister who was asked to investigate the matter, was forced to admit that the overall level of participation was disappointing: 'in general the electors did not demonstrate the eagerness one might have expected'. Some local officials were much less restrained in their remarks. The prefect of the Basses-Alpes deplored the fact that voters had been 'deaf to his requests' to attend the electoral assemblies and he suggested imposing a quorum of 50 per cent of the electorate in order to validate a result.[29] His colleague in the Deux-Sèvres observed that recently enfranchised citizens were pleased to possess the right to vote but then lacked the energy to exercise it.[30] Perhaps the people were not yet ready to undertake the task with which they had been entrusted?

Massive turnout in the first national elections to be held on the basis of direct, universal male suffrage in 1848 seemed to dispel this gloomy prognostication. However, fresh misgivings soon arose when it became obvious that the initial enthusiasm was not being sustained in the local elections of summer 1848 and, above all, in a series of legislative by-elections. The deputy Théophile Bourbousson drew attention to this worrying trend when, in late September, he declared that the question of where citizens voted was 'a matter of life and death for direct universal suffrage':

> The number of voters is falling to a frightening extent. Today you have discovered that there were many communes in the countryside where not a single

---

[26] This example from 1813 raises a question mark regarding Pierre Karila-Cohen's chronology in *L'Invention de l'enquête politique en France (1814–1848)* (Rennes, 2008). In fact, the first comprehensive investigation of percentage turnout for elections to the Chamber of Deputies, starting in 1815, was undertaken in the mid-1840s, by the ministry of the interior: AN C*383, Les élections d'août 1846 et les élections précédentes. Thereafter the calculation of electoral statistics became increasingly routine, both at official and unofficial levels.

[27] AP, 2ᵉ serie, LXXVIII, le comte d'Argoult, 8 Dec. 1832, 140.

[28] *Compte rendu au Roi sur les élections municipales de 1834* (Paris, 1836).

[29] AN F1bI 258, Préfet des Basses-Alpes au ministre, 25 Nov. 1834.

[30] Guionnet, *L'Apprentissage de la politique moderne*, 218.

elector participated in the recent elections...while in those departments which have just chosen national deputies, the total of rural voters compared to April was hardly a twentieth.[31]

He went on to argue that these electors simply could not afford to travel to the *chef-lieu de canton*:

You are making these people pay for the right to vote, because the poor soul who is obliged make a journey of 20 or 30 kilometres on foot is thereby forced to interrupt his livelihood and condemned to make a sacrifice which, although it might not seem very much to us, is nonetheless significant for both him and his family.

The mayor of one commune in the Gers offered a graphic account of his fellow electors, soaked to the skin and covered in mud after making their trip to vote in April 1848, as a result of which they had contracted colds from which they were still recovering. They were resolved 'to abstain at the next election unless they were granted the facility to vote nearer to home'.[32]

If universal (male) suffrage was to survive, it needed to be more accommodating, allowing voting in the *chef-lieu de commune*, so that rural electors could share the privilege of neighbourhood polling with their urban counterparts. The ensuing debate also called into question the system of *scrutin de liste* which, it was alleged, perplexed rural voters confronted with a slate of deputies, then resulted in abstention when by-elections were held for a single replacement. In the event, the departmental list was retained, but some latitude was allowed for the introduction of 'sections' that reduced electoral displacement for rural inhabitants, though only under the succeeding regime of Louis-Napoleon would all voting take place in the commune. However, it must be said that urban electors, who had ready access to a polling station, were not necessarily more assiduous in voting, often the reverse, as one deputy correctly pointed out.

With presidential elections looming in November 1848, administrators were nervously (but as it turned out needlessly) contemplating how successfully 'the great act of popular sovereignty' would be conducted on this occasion. Hence the minister of the interior's strong advice to government officials:

I am alerting you to an enemy that you must take every measure to combat, namely the insouciance of the electorate. Those who stay away from the polls out of a deadly indifference must understand that they are letting society

---

[31] *Moniteur*, 29 Sept. 1848, 2636.
[32] Cited in Jean Dagnan, *Le Gers sous la Seconde République* (Auch, 1928), 87.

down…and you should also make them realize that they are assuming a terrible responsibility as a consequence.[33]

Early the following year, when debate commenced on an electoral law, an abortive attempt was made to reopen the subject of non-voting, with more evidence to demonstrate that peasants were ill-served by the existing polling system. In fact, reiterating a suggestion originally made in 1795, it was proposed that electors should be able to vote at home, 'in the midst of domestic tranquillity', with ballot papers collected from their doorsteps.[34]

Matters then moved beyond efforts to facilitate greater participation, when a formal proposal for compulsory voting was presented to the Constituent Assembly. On 27 February 1849, taking up an earlier suggestion that absentees should be prosecuted, the conservative deputy Jean-Pierre de L'Espinasse, contended that, since French electors were insufficiently steeped in the electoral habit and inertia was widespread, it was necessary to oblige them to vote.[35] Claiming to speak on behalf of numerous correspondents, he proposed that failure to participate in the polls, without good cause, should incur a set of graduated penalties, proportionate to income. These would range from one to fifteen francs for the first two absences and, on the third occasion, result in the loss of all electoral rights for a period of two to five years. When challenged on the implementation of these punitive measures, he responded that the ordinary courts could deal with non-voters, since he did not expect the number of cases to be enormous, while the proceeds from any fines could be put towards poor relief. No one spoke in support, but the proposal was seconded, then overwhelmingly defeated. On the other hand, a threshold was now set to be elected: it was stipulated that successful candidates needed to attract 12.5 per cent of registered voters, as well as an absolute majority of the votes cast, otherwise a second ballot would be held. This figure was raised to 25 per cent in 1850 and it remains in force today.

A year or so later, when conservatives were seeking to revise the franchise, in the wake of some significant electoral success for radicals in the legislative elections of 1849, de L'Espinasse revived his proposal, albeit to no avail.[36] However, the minister of the interior simultaneously despatched a confidential circular to all prefects on the subject of compelling voters to go the polls, and asked them to comment. No synthesis of their responses seems to have been produced, but a sample of replies from some thirty departments reveals opinion evenly divided between those who felt that compulsion would help the party of order, because it was moderate voters who were abstaining and, conversely, those who thought that constraint would only encourage disaffected electors to heed the siren calls of

---

[33]   AN F1a 58, Circulaire du ministre de l'intérieur, 2 Nov. 1848.
[34]   *Moniteur*, 9 Feb. 1849, 424.   [35]   *Moniteur*, 28 Feb. 1849, 659.
[36]   *Moniteur*, 19 May 1850, 1742.

extremists.[37] Little evidence was offered for either of these opposing views, which presaged a failure to find consensus on the matter in future, though virtually all prefects expressed doubts regarding both the efficacy and practicality of imposing fines for abstention. These reservations would recur in subsequent debate on obligatory voting, and they constituted a major stumbling block for, as the deputy and great advocate of compulsory voting, Joseph Barthélemy, later admitted, 'severe penalties are objectionable, but small ones are ineffective'.[38] After Louis-Napoleon had taken political control, at the end of 1851, the imposition of official candidatures rewrote the rules of the electoral game and officials were instructed to secure high levels of turnout or risk a reprimand. In these circumstances, the issue of compulsory voting disappeared from the legislative agenda, before returning with a vengeance after the collapse of the Second Empire.

Obligation Becomes an Obsession under the Third Republic

Barthélemy would rightly observe in the 1920s that 'the question of obligatory voting has been...constantly submitted to public opinion and parliament'.[39] It was indeed a hardy political annual, or at least a biennial one: over forty propositions were submitted in favour of compulsion under the Third Republic. Yet opinion remained deeply divided, so that notwithstanding the deluge of proposals, which became increasingly repetitive as time went by, voting remained a right rather than a legally binding duty. This inconclusive, century-long debate, which has no parallel in other major democracies, was far more than a question of numbers. Fundamentally, the obsession serves to demonstrate the French commitment to making the sovereignty of the people a meaningful exercise, an aspiration which imposes a significant responsibility upon its citizens.

To be sure, Yves Déloye has recently argued that republicans were generally 'allergic' to the obligatory vote, preferring to stress voting as a duty and to rely on education and exhortation as a means of raising the level of electoral participation.[40] Like the republican schoolteacher, cited at the head of this chapter, they stressed that voting was a moral duty, owed to one's fellow citizens, as well as to

---

[37] AN F1cIII Esprit public et élections, relevant departmental dossiers, préfets au ministre, May 1850, a matter for further investigation.

[38] Joseph Barthélemy, 'Rapport fait au nom de la Commission du Suffrage Universel', 7 July 1922, reprinted as 'Pour le vote obligatoire', *Revue du droit public et de la science politique en France et à l'étranger*, 40 (1923), 101–67.

[39] Barthélemy, 'Pour le vote obligatoire', 101.

[40] Yves Déloye, 'Une allérgie républicaine au vote obligatoire (XIXe–XXe siècles)', in Anissa Amjahad et al. (eds), *Le Vote obligatoire. Débats, enjeux et défis* (Paris, 2011) and Anthoula Malkopoulou, *The History of Compulsory Voting in Europe: Democracy's Duty?* (London, 2014). See fuller detail in Anthoula Malkopoulou, 'Democracy's duty: the history of political debates on compulsory voting' (PhD Thesis, University of Jyväskylä, Finland, 2011).

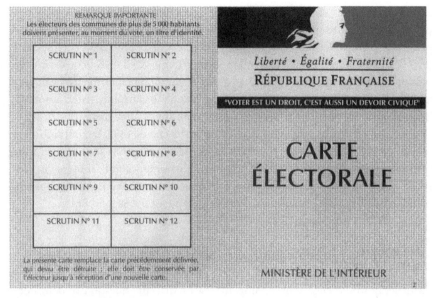

Figure 8.1   A voter's card, 2012

This multi-use voter's card highlights the importance of voting, with the slogan 'Voting is a right, but it is also a duty.' The presentation of an identity card is also required and this has recently been made mandatory for all elections in communes with more than one thousand inhabitants.

Source: Copyright, Alamy M6N25M.

oneself. As a republican electoral manual put it in 1861, 'Every elector has a great duty to fulfil; he must vote. Abstention, when it is caused by indifference or self-ishness, is irresponsible; sometimes the product of noble sentiments, it remains a sterile gesture. Experience condemns it; he who abstains effaces himself.'[41] Another guide declared that 'choosing a deputy is not just a right but also a duty, indeed the most important of duties.'[42] The pedagogical literature that prolifer-ated in the early years of the Third Republic was imbued with the same moraliz-ing message, which is clearly stated on the contemporary voter's card (Figure 8.1).

In fact, a few advocates of a democratic republic did endorse the idea of com-pulsion, notably the lawyer and later deputy Eugène Delattre. Although he did not actually use the term 'vote obligatoire', nor set out any penalties for absten-tion, he clearly regarded the exercise of the franchise as a matter for enforcement:

> Universal suffrage does not constitute a right in the sense that it can be employed, or not, at will; rather it is the most demanding of duties over which there can be no compromise. No one can dissociate himself from participation

[41] Clamageran et al., *Manuel électoral*, 1.
[42] Georges Coulon, *Guide pratique de l'électeur* (Paris, 1868), 6.

in public affairs...which these days we rightly regard as a *social duty*. You do not have the right not to be registered, nor to be absent on polling-day, any more than the member of a jury has the option of not attending a trial.[43]

There were other advocates of recourse to the law among republican deputies, for example Agénor Bardoux who, in 1880, included the obligatory vote in a proposal for restoring departmental *scrutin de liste*. However, the latter proved a rather more popular suggestion than posting the names of non-voters outside the *mairie* and suspending their voting rights after a second offence.[44]

These were relatively isolated instances where committed republicans were concerned. By contrast, the compulsory vote was a constant preoccupation on the part of conservatives, first and foremost because they regarded voting as a function.[45] Not surprisingly, while they dominated the National Assembly after 1871, obligation was frequently advocated. The duc de Broglie had already argued that 'the right to vote is not an exclusively personal right...that the individual is free to exercise or not, even abuse, according to his good pleasure; rather it is a social right, instituted in the interests of the community which must oversee its operation.' As in the case of jury service, absence from the polls should incur a penalty. Underlying this argument was the idea of compulsion as a means of domesticating universal male suffrage, which conservatives deeply distrusted, but felt was irreversible. Its organization or application was of vital importance and the legal requirement to vote had a crucial role to play in drawing its sting, by preventing militant minorities from dominating the polls. According to the marquis de Castellane, for example, 'abstention has caused most of our ills over the past century', damaging French society far more than universal suffrage itself.[46] Right-wing deputies also remained convinced that their own sympathizers were less prone to vote than radicals, hence their progressive loss of seats in low polling by-elections, but it was essentially a matter of speculation.

This partisan argument was never substantiated and the Commission responsible for drafting a new electoral law in 1874 counselled caution: 'It has confidently been asserted that those who are indifferent, if obliged to vote, would be won to the moderate cause', yet 'recent examples of re-election after the result was annulled have shown that such individuals do not always gravitate in that direction.'[47] The decisive drawback for the Commission was, however, the problem of first defining and then imposing a set of penalties. A wide range of escalating sanctions was examined, from naming and shaming absentees, to fines that might be graduated according to income, then eventually loss of the right to vote.

[43] Eugène Delattre, *Devoirs du suffrage universel suivi du texte de la loi électorale* (Paris, 1863), 78–9.
[44] *JO*, 14 July 1880, 8144–5.
[45] Victor de Broglie, *Vues sur le gouvernement de la France* (Paris, 1870), 38.
[46] Antoine de Castellane, *Essai sur l'organisation du suffrage universel en France*, 2nd edn (Paris, 1872), 68.
[47] *JO*, Annexe 2320, 1874.

There was also a suggestion that penalties might fall on the whole community which, in the event of an especially low turnout, would have to pay for a re-scheduled election, an example that, like several others, was borrowed from countries where compulsion was already in operation. Conversely, there were proposals for rewarding voters by offering them a tax reduction, a measure that would effectively penalize absentees, who would have to shoulder a relatively greater burden as a result. Whatever the tariff, there remained the matter of adjudicating abstention, especially when mitigating circumstances were entered. The caseload could be considerable and there were fears that the administrative or judicial authorities might be overwhelmed.

In the upshot, the emergent Third Republic did not include the obligatory vote in legislation for the election of its Chamber of Deputies. Yet, when it came to an indirectly elected Senate, which was intended as a counter-weight to the directly elected deputies, an element of compulsion was introduced that remains in being today.[48] Members of the departmental electoral colleges who chose senators (there were almost 43,000 of them in 1876, then over 76,000 after the reform of 1884), would be fined 50 francs (currently 100 euros) for failure to participate without good cause, or not giving sufficient notice for a substitute to attend in their stead. The argument of 'function' was clearly at work here, with those already chosen by the electorate as deputies, departmental and arrondissement councillors, under an obligation to 'represent' them in the electoral colleges, together with the bulk of college members who were elected by municipal councillors. Compliance for Senate elections has always been extremely high, with rates of abstention never more than 1 per cent, including those unable to attend for legitimate reasons.[49] Yet this is scarcely surprising: the history of departmental assemblies under the Revolution suggests that compulsion is hardly necessary to secure high turnout at this secondary level (see Chapter 6).

Supporters of the obligatory vote were encouraged by arrangements for the Senate and doggedly pursued their campaign for compulsion in other elections. In the wake of the 1881 legislative polls, in which turnout fell just below 70 per cent, a Bonapartist deputy named Jean Edmond Laroche-Joubert tabled a more original proposition. He contended that, since indifference was the root cause of non-voting, adult males should be given the choice as to whether or not they registered as electors but, once they had decided to do so, casting a ballot should become mandatory.[50] This proposal was summarily dismissed by republicans, because they believed that rights could not be abrogated, nor equality infringed, though it led proponents to insist that registration should also be compulsory and

[48] Paul Smith, *A History of the French Senate: The Third Republic 1870–1940*, 2 vols (Lampeter, 2005–6), ii, 57–75.
[49] Bernard Dolez, 'Notables enrôlés. Le vote (obligatoire) des électeurs sénatoriaux', in Amjahad et al. (eds), *Le Vote obligatoire*, 89–106.
[50] *JO*, Annexe, 2 May 1882, 1132.

that defaulters should be fined. Yet, despite the repeated presentation of proposals for obligatory voting, it was 1895 before any formal debate took place in the Chamber of Deputies and, even then, the measure was summarily rejected. Interest in the subject peaked around the turn of the twentieth century when, in addition to parliamentary initiatives, five doctoral theses on the subject were submitted at French universities.[51] By then the debate had acquired an important transnational dimension after Belgium, an influential neighbour where electoral matters were concerned, adopted compulsory voting in 1893 and raised turnout to well in excess of 90 per cent as a result.

This particular aspect of electoral reform reflected a more general debate at the time, by no means restricted to France, as mass voting came of age and efforts were made to improve the integrity of the vote. Indeed, the French Chamber of Deputies established a standing Commission on Universal Suffrage in 1898 to examine the plethora of propositions on topics which included efforts to make voting more secure, combat corruption, and enfranchise women. The impassioned discussion over PR, which will not be considered in any detail here, was part of this wider agenda and was linked to the question of turnout, since it was argued that supporters of minor parties would not necessarily be wasting their votes if it were to be adopted.[52] Although statistics on non-voting, albeit only relating to legislative elections, were now regularly cited as a rationale for making voting obligatory, especially after turnout fell to just over 70 per cent in 1893, the broader issue of majority rule was also thrown into question by its proponents. When roughly one in three electors was abstaining, 'can one still speak of the government of the people, by the people, according to the principle of national sovereignty?', asked Félix Moreau. According to him these words had become 'a fiction, indeed a lie'.[53] Paul Coutant, another jurist, likewise argued that by failing to constitute 'a true mirror of the nation', parliamentary government became both irresponsible and illegitimate.[54] Such authors did not hesitate to demonstrate that the addition of anti-republican votes and abstentions produced a total superior to that garnered by the governing party.[55]

Republican anxieties were exacerbated by the contemporary denigration of representative democracy by syndicalists and nationalists and, above all, by anarchists, who rightly regarded the practice of the vote as an endorsement of the electoral system as much as a choice of candidate. It was the free-thinker Octave

[51] Alain Laquièze, 'L'abstentionnisme dans la doctrine publiciste française du XXᵉ siècle', in Boutin and Rouvillois (eds), L'Abstention électorale, 67–95.
[52] Thomas Marty, Une Histoire sociale de la réforme électorale sous la Troisième République. Mobilisations politique et expertise électorale: la question de la 'représentation proportionnelle' (Paris, 2012).
[53] Félix Moreau, 'Le vote obligatoire. Principe et sanctions', Revue politique et parlementaire, 7 (1896), 38.
[54] Paul Coutant, Le Vote obligatoire (Paris, 1898), 2–3.   [55] Moreau, 'Le vote obligatoire', 39.

Mirbeau who, having advocated a voters' strike in 1888, originated the popular description of *abstentionnistes* as 'anglers' (*pêcheurs à la ligne*), when he wrote in 1902: 'Dear elector, sovereign without a sceptre…(on polling day) you should quietly go fishing…and congratulate yourself on having accomplished a significant political act…'.[56] Frequently reprinted, this advice was echoed in a later pamphlet which declared: 'Voter, when will you realize that when you nominate your deputies you are achieving absolutely nothing?'[57] A 'Manifesto abstentionniste' had expressed the issue metaphorically in 1898: 'Citizens, the electoral circus has opened. The candidates are in the ring, making fine promises…but you have never been rewarded and you never will be. Have done with all these clowns.'[58] Those who engaged in the electoral 'charade' were described by anarchists as 'votards', mere polling fodder, who were all too easily deceived into thinking they could make a difference. Proudhon had once commended 'the silent vote', as he called it, half a century earlier when he argued that a valid vote simply underwrote the status quo: just as republicans refused to attend mass, so workers should shun elections, 'the church of bourgeois politicians.'[59] Whereas the electoral boycotts, demanded by various disaffected groups, from the Revolution onwards did have a discernible impact, the effect of anarchist propaganda is harder to estimate. Their jeremiads were accompanied by some striking caricatures, but sympathizers sometimes stood as candidates and frequently cast spoiled papers in the period preceding the First World War.[60]

After 1919, electoral reform was put firmly back on the agenda, with compulsory voting once more featuring prominently. In 1922 the Commission on Universal Suffrage finally accepted a proposal, which was then presented to parliament by Barthélemy, who was also an expert on the obligation to vote in Belgium.[61] Although his report contained little that was new, it constituted a comprehensive statement of the case for compulsion, yet it still failed to win general approval. Proponents were undeterred and another half a dozen bills were drafted, ultimately to no effect, the last one just prior to the outbreak of the Second World War. The adoption of compulsion elsewhere in the 1920s (Luxemburg, Austria, Czechoslovakia, and Greece among them), plus the growing threat to democracy from the rise of fascism and communism, evidently played a role in sustaining debate about the obligatory vote, despite the extremely high levels of interwar turnout in France. The accent was increasingly laid on the distortion of representation as a result of abstention, restating earlier arguments

---

[56] Octave Mirbeau, *La Grève des électeurs, suivi de Prélude* (Paris, 2002), 12.
[57] Sébastien Faure, *Pour ne pas voter: électeur écoute* (Paris, 1924), 4. For a recent polemic, see Antoine Buéno, *No vote! Manifeste pour l'abstention* (Paris, 2017).
[58] Archives de la Préfecture de Police de Paris, BA 653, Manifeste anarchiste, 1898.
[59] Proudhon, *De la capacité politique*, 441.
[60] Vivien Bouhey, *Les Anarchistes contre la République* (Rennes, 2008), 143–4.
[61] Barthélemy, 'Pour le vote obligatoire', 101–67.

that very few deputies had attracted an absolute majority of registered voters. As a result, governments with only a third to a quarter of the electorate supporting them were struggling to provide the strong direction that the country required. Abstention was allegedly 'putting the nation at risk', and leading conservative deputies continued to make the running in an effort to turn 'a moral obligation to vote into a legal one'.[62] Louis Marin, president of the Fédération républicaine, headed the list of legislative sponsors on three occasions in the 1930s and one of his proposals was actually accepted by the Chamber of Deputies in 1932, but as part of a package containing other reforms that was subsequently rejected in the Senate.

The Quest for Compulsory Voting since the Second World War

Given sustained interest in the subject for more than half a century it was no surprise that the idea of obligatory voting should re-emerge immediately after the Liberation, when it almost entered the statute book. The indefatigable Marin sought its adoption by the Constitutional Commission set up by the Constituent Assembly of 1945, and his suggestion was initially greeted with much approval, only for socialist delegates to change their minds. The following year he failed to secure its inclusion in the Constitution, when his parliamentary amendment in favour of compulsory voting was defeated by just five votes. As he argued, 'In order to ascertain what the people want, you must oblige them to fulfil their binding duty to vote... a verdict expressed by only a fraction of the French people will not enable you to find out.'[63] No fewer than nine parliamentary propositions were submitted during the twelve years' lifespan of the Fourth Republic, yet all to no avail.[64] The outcome was as familiar as the arguments, but the problem of non-voting was becoming much more precisely defined thanks to the efforts of officials and academics (called 'psephologists' in Britain), working with electoral registers that had been 'marked up' during elections and drawing on increasing numbers of public opinion polls.

The Renseignements généraux section at the ministry of the interior, which routinely collected information on elections, chiefly in terms of their political outcome, had recently set up an Office central de sondage et de statistique to support its activities. In 1951, in an effort to understand why individuals had failed to vote in the legislative and cantonal consultations held that year, and 'inspired by the example of Gallup polling', opinion polls were undertaken by officials in a number of departments. The prefect of the Cantal, for instance, reported that slightly more women had failed to vote than men, but there was little difference in

---

[62] *Le Temps*, 23 Apr. 1932, 3.   [63] *JO*, 4 Sept. 1946, 3496.
[64] AN F1cII 195, Note pour Monsieur le Ministre, 18 Sept. 1950.

the incidence of abstention according to occupation or political affiliation. Non-voters claimed there were simply too many elections, too few attractive candidates and that voting would change nothing.[65] The first academic investigations into non-voting followed hard on the heels of this initiative, after François Goguel, the leading exponent of electoral studies in France, had singled the subject out for attention in 1952: 'the problem of abstention, regularly raised by partisans of compulsory voting, has yet to become an object of scholarly study', he declared.[66] Shortly afterwards, two political scientists were given permission to examine the material lately collected by government agents and they conducted a comprehensive analysis which was published two years later.[67]

Far from allaying fears about poor turnout, initiatives like these only exacerbated them, and officials at the ministry of the interior drew some debatable conclusions. The shorter version of a working paper they drafted began with the assertion that: 'The first party in France is that of the non-voter', before continuing 'as the (legislative) elections of 1956 approach, the problem of abstention is seriously worrying both government and political parties'.[68] The document was entitled 'Abstentionnisme, a French disease', though surprisingly the malady in France was not set in an international context, where comparable levels of turnout constituted the norm.[69] Nor did it place the recent French experience in much historical perspective. Accompanying data revealed relatively low rates of electoral participation in recent legislative by-elections: never more than 60 per cent in a single case since 1952, and barely exceeding 50 per cent in the Cantal, for instance. However, this was an established pattern for by-elections in a system of *scrutin de liste* and, as in the past, so under the Fourth Republic, they involved the whole departmental electorate in the choice of a single replacement deputy. Reference was also made to local polls, where an average of only 60 per cent of the electorate had taken part in the cantonal elections of 1951 and 1955.[70] Yet polling for departmental councils was always lower than in legislative or municipal contests, which had recorded participation rates of 80 per cent in 1951 and 1953, respectively. Indeed, turnout at national level had usually hit this mark since the Second World War, the referendum of 1946, boycotted by Gaullists, the only salient exception.

The situation hardly suggested an impending crisis, but a more detailed version of the same document proceeded to assert that this study 'bears witness to the significant extent of abstention in France' and the high degree of 'political

[65] AN F1cII 195, Préfet au ministre de l'intérieur, 23 Oct. 1951.
[66] François Goguel, 'Pour une étude scientifique de l'abstentionnisme électoral', *Rfsp*, 2 (1952), 68.
[67] Dogan and Narbonne, 'L'abstentionnisme électoral', 5–26 and 301–25.
[68] AN F1cII 195, Anonymous memorandum, 15 Sept. 1955.
[69] Pascal Delwit, 'L'introuvable électeur? La participation électorale en Europe (1945–2005)', in Amjahad et al. (eds), *Le Vote obligatoire*, 27.
[70] AN F1cII 195, Anonymous memorandum, 15 Sept. 1955.

disaffection that is afflicting all parts of the electoral body...'[71] An unnecessary note of alarm was being struck, although the long-held and partisan belief that moderates were more likely to abstain, or that the allegedly well-disciplined PCF was especially successful in mobilizing its supporters, was doubtless causing dismay in a pre-electoral period. These nostrums were accompanied by a good deal of prejudice. Much of the abstention was attributed to female enfranchisement and the authors of the memorandum commented that 'having bitterly protested about being denied the right to participate in political life, women have failed to fully embrace it'. At this juncture, females were indeed slightly less likely to vote than men, especially among the older generation, particularly in rural areas. Great astonishment was accordingly expressed that even so, between the ages of twenty-one and twenty-five, young women were turning out more strongly than their male counterparts. It was suggested that this stemmed from parental influence over the former, and indulgence in 'sport and cinema' on the part of the latter.

Other data in the document demonstrated that electoral participation was strongest between the ages of thirty-five and sixty-five for men, while decline set in at sixty for women. Geographical variation was patently evident too, with polling north of the Loire generally stronger: in the municipal elections of 1953, for example, the Nord had turned out most heavily, while Corsica, as always, brought up the rear. Some less controversial comments were also made about voter attitudes, suggesting that 'political confusion, notably ministerial crises, and the struggle to build stable parliamentary majorities', were distancing electors from deputies. Citizens were put off by a succession of 'party political games' in a Fourth Republic that had inherited too many of the faults of its predecessor. Many women still felt that politics was best left to men, while young people clearly required more civic education, and numerous individuals regrettably preferred to devote Sundays to the pursuit of leisure rather than voting, especially during *la belle saison*.

When it came to remedies, rather than proposing compulsory voting, emphasis was placed on combating the fundamental causes of abstention, above all by 'altering behaviour, restoring the authority of the state and improving the standing of parliament', in order to raise esteem for a regime that 'in its current situation, in the opinion of many French men and women, appeared to be afflicted by a state of paralysis'. Changing the day elections were held, and giving people time off work to vote (provided they could prove they had done so), would merely treat the symptoms and not its underlying causes.[72] The obligation to vote was dismissed on the same grounds, a sign of waning official support, despite its popularity with politicians and opinion polls indicating that a majority of the public

---

[71] AN F1cII 195, Anonymous memorandum, 17 Sept. 1955.
[72] AN F1cII 195, Projet de loi, élections un jour ouvrable, 22 July 1955.

was now in favour of it.[73] In the event, the dreaded legislative elections held early in January 1956 confounded all expectations and produced an increased turnout of 83 per cent while, two years later in the spring of 1958, the subsequent round of *cantonales* attracted almost 70 per cent of the electorate. The whole issue was dropped as attention turned to establishing a new republican regime under general de Gaulle, before disappearing from the radar during the early decades of the Fifth Republic.

An alternative to compulsion, as a means of raising turnout, was to offer the possibility of casting a vote *in absentia*, but postal and proxy voting had found little favour during the debate over non-voting at the turn of the twentieth century. A few parliamentary proposals were made regarding the former, notably in 1894, when it was agreed that members of the 'peripatetic professions' were involuntarily abstaining in large numbers, but the matter progressed no further.[74] An essay published a decade later argued that up to 10 per cent of registered electors were prevented from participating by unavoidable absence from their communes, while voting by post was a simple means of securing higher turnout, yet surprisingly little political interest was aroused.[75] There were precedents, because postal voting had been used by military personnel in 1848/9 and 1871, and it was re-established in the wake of the First and Second World Wars to cater for refugees. In fact, the post-Liberation experience seems to have proved decisive: both postal and proxy voting were introduced in 1946, so that citizens unable to vote 'under normal conditions' would have the opportunity to do so in future.[76] Those away from their homes for occupational reasons, such as seamen or railway workers, or prevented from visiting the polling station due to infirmity, could apply for a postal vote. As for proxy voting, sailors, civil servants, and some *militaires* were now able to appoint another elector to cast a ballot on their behalf, provided they completed a rather more complicated procedure involving testimony at a local court.

In the event few electors availed themselves of these facilities. A single set of figures available for the legislative elections of November 1962 show that postal and proxy voting amounted to little more than 1 per cent of the votes cast, the great majority of them in the first category. Lancelot concluded that 'generally speaking the mobile individuals who might benefit from this facility prefer to abstain.'[77] An opinion poll taken in 1965 demonstrated widespread ignorance of the procedures involved: almost 70 per cent of those asked were unaware of the circumstances in which a postal vote could be requested.[78] Evidence from the following decade, however, suggests that the practice was becoming more widespread, with up to 5 per cent voting 'par correspondance' in the Côtes-du-Nord,

[73] Lancelot, *L'Abstentionnisme électoral*, 257–8.   [74] *JO*, Annexe 1026, 29 Nov. 1894, 2008.
[75] André Labussière, 'Le vote par correspondance', *Revue politique et parlementaire*, 45 (1905), 260–9.
[76] Duguit et al. (eds), *Les Constitutions*, 491–5 and 501–7.
[77] Lancelot, *L'Abstentionnisme électoral*, 39–42.
[78] Lancelot, *L'Abstentionnisme électoral*, 252–3.

for instance, but this increase may have led to its demise.[79] The authorities had always been wary of postal voting since it detracted from 'the solemnity of the act of voting' and it was open to the sort of peer pressure that the *isoloir* was designed to deter.[80] Concern that third parties were interfering with the electoral choices of those who were employing it, notably in the case of elderly people, led to the abolition of postal voting in 1975. Parliamentarians somewhat vaguely alleged that it had produced 'a massive level of fraud, which was not being punished and perhaps not even detected'.[81]

Postal voting has proved a popular and effective means of tackling abstention elsewhere; in Britain almost one in five electors are now using it. To be sure, when this option was abolished in France, the scope for proxy voting was significantly extended and subsequent changes to the law have made this alternative still easier to obtain. As a result, proxy voting has recently become much less of a marginal practice, amounting to no less than 1.5 million votes (just over 4 per cent of the total) in the second round of the presidential election of 2012, for instance.[82] Voting this way has increased substantially over the past twenty years, but it has also raised profound suspicions. In 1988 it was said that half of the votes had been cast in this fashion in some Corsican communes, contradicting the deeply held conviction that the vote should be 'a personal and secret act', only exercised by an intermediary in exceptional circumstances.[83] It also raises the question of equality, since the mandatory is voting twice, while secrecy is violated because he or she is evidently aware of the absentee's choice. Moreover, proxy voting is mostly employed by those who are already highly motivated to participate, such as better educated or older townspeople, so the facility is not, on the whole, re-integrating occasional voters into the electoral process, still less those who never vote. Mobilizing these latter categories remains a challenge for which there are no easy solutions, obligatory voting included.

Just three proposals for compulsion were submitted to the French parliament between 1959 and 1971, then not a single one for the next three decades. The tone was set by a memorandum drawn up during constitutional discussions surrounding the foundation of the Fifth Republic in June 1958, which concluded by rejecting the idea: 'Means should be sought to encourage electors to use their right to vote and to accomplish the moral duty it entails, rather than compel them to fulfil an obligation under threat of punishment.'[84] By contrast, the early years of the twenty-first century have seen no less than thirteen fresh submissions, plus a

---

[79] AD Côtes-d'Armor 1308 W47-8, PV de l'élection présidentielle, 1974.

[80] AN F1cII 195, Ministre de l'intérieur au conseil général de la Creuse, which was seeking the extension of postal voting, 19 Oct. 1955.

[81] André Demichel and Francine Demichel, *Droit électoral* (Paris, 1973), 202.

[82] Arthur Charpentier et al., 'Un homme, deux voix: le vote par procuration', http://www.laviedesidees.fr/Un-homme-deux-voix-le-vote-par.html (accessed 08/08/19).

[83] *JO*, Chambre des Députés, 24 Nov. 1988, 2721–4.

[84] AN F1cII 195, Note sur le vote obligatoire, 24 June 1958.

survey of the practice of obligatory voting in other countries, and renewed academic as well as political interest in the subject, not to mention its inclusion in President Macron's *grand débat* on the state of the nation in 2019. It seems that compulsion is regarded by a majority of the electorate as an acceptable, and proven, way of reversing sharply declining turnout, which has rekindled deep-seated fears about the legitimacy of the representative regime. The current campaign has still not achieved success, but it is now attracting more interest from the left. Thus, debate has recently been aired in the online journal of the Fondation Jean-Jaurès, initiated by its director-general.[85] While acknowledging that compulsory voting is no panacea and accepting that it treats the symptoms rather than the causes of abstention, he suggests that such a draconian measure is an appropriate response to the 'spectacular progress of non-voting', pending further research into the underlying problems. An experienced socialist colleague disagrees and has called the obligatory vote a 'fausse bonne idée', precisely because he feels that the real reasons for rapidly falling electoral participation require addressing first: 'It is not by means of coercion that the people of France will return to the polls.'

Conclusion

Compulsory voting is a tried and tested means of raising electoral participation, though evidence from countries where it has been successfully applied, and then abandoned, suggests that it does not have a lasting impact on electoral behaviour.[86] France is exceptional in the amount of time that has been devoted to considering this drastic remedy, without actually adopting it. The explanation for this paradox should be sought not so much in low turnout—on the contrary it was relatively high over a long period of time—but rather more in terms of the sovereignty of the people, which demanded universal turnout from a mass electorate in order for a government to be truly representative. There was general agreement on this point, but the solution of compulsion divided republicans and conservatives who regarded the vote in different ways, the former as a right, the latter as a legally binding function. However allergic they were to the idea of obligation in this regard, republicans were always willing to emphasize the citizen's responsibility to participate in elections. Now that turnout is falling much more sharply than in the past they are being forced to reconsider their response. The concluding part of this book will, among other things, briefly discuss the 'disappearing voter'.

[85] Gilles Finchelstein, 'Pour le vote obligatoire', Fondation Jean-Jaurès, Note 257, March 2015, https://jean-jaures.org/nos-productions/pour-le-vote-obligatoire; and Didier Maus, 'Le vote obligatoire. Une fausse bonne idée', Fondation Jean-Jaurès, Note 258, March 2015, https://jean-jaures.org/nos-productions/le-vote-obligatoire-une-fausse-bonne-idee (both accessed 07/08/19).
[86] Antoine Bilodeau and André Blais, 'Le vote obligatoire exerce-t-il un effet de socialisation politique?', in Amjahad et al. (eds), *Le Vote obligatoire*, 139–56.

Conclusion

Unfinished Business

When, in 2002, Alain Garrigou published a second version of his earlier, land-mark study of voting, under a fresh title, *Histoire sociale du suffrage universel en France 1848–2000*, he was obliged to take the recent drop in turnout into account. Whilst acknowledging that the phenomenon is not confined to France, he wrote, 'For more than a decade this history has been one of declining electoral participation.'[1] Since then, non-voting has become still more pronounced and, though its progress has been less than linear, it is clearly not a temporary trend which might be explained by short-term constraints. Although an upward trajec-tory in the future should not be ruled out, this downward movement calls into question the successful acculturation of the great majority of French citizens to the regular exercise of the franchise, which has constituted the main theme of this book. It does appear that their earlier achievement is now being undermined, but perhaps they are instead learning to vote differently. The frequently employed metaphor of an electoral apprenticeship may be a misleading one, which wrongly posits a process to be completed. Current developments suggest that like democ-racy, to which it is closely if not invariably connected, the practice of voting remains a work in progress.[2]

The 1980s certainly represented a watershed for electoral participation in France, when more or less consistently high turnout, sustained over the previous century, began to break down (see Figures 6.1 and 6.2). Presidential elections have held up pretty well, never falling below 80 per cent in the second round, before suffering a slight dip in 2017, but all the others have experienced secular decline, the degree of participation in some cases dropping below 50 per cent of registered voters, a level not recorded since the mid-nineteenth century. Municipal elections, which have fared better than most, offer a good illustration of this erosion, pro-gressively falling from 78 per cent to 64 per cent at six-yearly intervals, between 1983 and 2014. Legislative elections have collapsed from 78 per cent in 1986 to plumb the depths of 43 per cent in the second round in 2017, recording one or two small upturns along the way (though they now suffer the severe handicap of being

---

[1] Garrigou, *Histoire sociale*, 343.
[2] Keane, *The Life and Death of Democracy*, 867, for some helpful reflections on that subject.

How the French Learned to Vote: A History of Electoral Practice in France. Malcolm Crook, Oxford University Press (2021).
© Malcolm Crook. DOI: 10.1093/oso/9780192894786.003.0010

held immediately in the wake of presidential polls). In other cases, the pattern is more uneven, with regional, departmental, and European elections showing modest improvements in their latest returns, but from a rather lower base. Nonetheless, the increasing incidence of non-voting is clear. Now, a major finding of this book, stemming from its long-term perspective, is that high turnout cannot be taken as the norm, not only on account of current experience, but also in the light of earlier periods of mass voting after 1789. It took a century for the French to learn to vote regularly in huge numbers, across the board, but the 'golden age' of high turnout after the 1880s has proved to be the exception to the rule of weaker participation, to which the practice of electoral participation is now reverting.

Moreover, the initial experience of elections with a broad male suffrage, not least during the French Revolution, reveals a further, familiar feature which characterizes the present situation, in so far as turnout fluctuated considerably from one election to another and between rounds of voting, as well as from one sort of election to another. Research into recent patterns of turnout has demonstrated that in the four rounds of polling that comprised the presidential elections of 2002 and 2007, for example, less than half of those who voted did so on every occasion. Political scientists are calling this development 'the rise of the intermittent voter', but it is by no means a novel phenomenon.[3] During the 1790s and under the Second Republic, overall levels of participation oscillated between 20 per cent and 80 per cent of the electorate. Nor is the fact that only a small proportion of registered voters, rarely, if ever, darkens a polling station door, an unprecedented feature of electoral behaviour either. The slender evidence that can be gleaned from earlier periods also confirms that these habitual abstainers are most likely to be found among the poorer, marginal elements in society, indicating the perennial existence of a *cens caché*, a hidden restriction on the franchise, to borrow the term coined by Daniel Gaxie.[4]

The contrast between town and country has also proved a consistent electoral factor: in 1995, for instance, abstention in both the presidential and municipal elections held that year progressively increased as communes grew in size, though the difference was much less marked for the *présidentielles*.[5] In the *municipales* of 1989 the level of participation in communes with fewer than 3,500 inhabitants had been over 80 per cent on average, twenty points higher than towns with a population of more than 30,000.[6] The same differentiation can be observed in the municipal elections of the revolutionary period and equally when they were restored in the nineteenth century. The citizens of Paris, like those in other big towns, were notoriously prone to non-voting until, towards the end of the nineteenth century, the electoral gap with smaller communes began to narrow,

---

[3] François Héran, 'Voter toujours, parfois...ou jamais', in Bruno Cautrès and Nonna Mayer (eds), *Le Nouveau désordre électoral* (Paris, 2004).

[4] Gaxie, *Le Cens caché*.   [5] Salmon, *Atlas électoral*, 85.

[6] Françoise Subileau and Marie-France Toinet, *Les Chemins de l'abstention. Une comparaison franco-américaine* (Paris, 1993) 128.

though it was never closed. Even though a diminishing proportion of the electorate resides in diminutive municipalities today, as urbanization continues apace, rural solidarity remains a strong mobilizing force, which frowns upon abstention, because voting represents a collective as well as an individual act and it remains highly visible. Humble local elections, so often ignored in studies of voting in favour of legislative contests, albeit not here, were, as many contemporaries recognized, the place where citizenship was practised and learned.

What was simplistically blamed on 'indifference' or insouciance' by those concerned about non-voting in the past can be examined more precisely by contemporary researchers employing interviews and opinion polls. Sociological factors, especially transformations of the environment that the electorate inhabits, are especially conducive to political demobilization. The demise of heavy industry and the declining influence of the Catholic Church have both taken a heavy toll in former bastions of high turnout like the north-east of France. An excellent, in-depth study of an electoral ward in the Parisian suburb of Saint-Denis, where abstention is particularly high, has clearly demonstrated the impact made by the loss of steady employment, since trade unions as well as work colleagues encouraged political engagement, not to mention the downfall of the PCF whose militants played a key role in mobilizing the community for elections.[7] Neighbourhood and family also provided a context in which young people learned to vote in the past, but the increasing instability and diversity of the former, like the fragmentation of the latter, have both contributed strongly to the drop in electoral participation. The crisis in voting is thus a reflection of a deeper crisis in society.

However, the significant numbers of citizens who have become intermittent voters of late are not abandoning the exercise of the franchise altogether and, generally speaking, they are not lacking in civic awareness, which was a factor in abstention during the early decades of mass voting in France. The irregular practice of the vote is in fact most widespread among younger voters who are well educated, politically engaged, and socially integrated, rather than among the unemployed and badly housed, who tend not to vote at all or who are not even registered to do so. There are no easy answers to this conundrum, but one explanation is that these intermittent voters have come to regard voting as a right much more than a duty, to be exercised, or not, as they deem appropriate, depending on the stakes and circumstances.[8] Indeed, according to some surveys, many of these independently minded individuals only decide whether or not to vote shortly before polling day. Such intermittent voting is likely to increase in future, because

---

[7] Céline Braconnier and Jean-Yves Dormagen, *La Démocratie de l'abstention. Aux origines de la démobilisation électorale en milieu populaire* (Paris, 2007), quatrième partie and, for an update, Céline Braconnier and Jean-Yves Dormagen, 'Logiques de mobilisation et inégalités sociales de participation électorale en France, 2002–2012', *French Politics, Culture & Society*, 30 (2012), 20–44.

[8] SPEL (Collectif de sociologie politique des élections), *Les Sens du vote. Une enquête sociologique (France 2011–2014)* (Rennes, 2016), Introduction.

regular voters tend to belong to members of older generations over 60 years old.[9] It was always the case that young people needed time to adopt the habit of voting, but now far fewer of them seem to be acquiring it to the extent they did in the past.[10]

Yet at least one commentator has suggested that intermittent voters should not be seen as heralding the collapse of democratic citizenship, which abstention might imply, but instead as espousing different attitudes towards it, with a more conscious, strategic approach to voting than that of habitual participants in the past.[11] It may, therefore, be regarded as a sign of vitality. The irregular voter's electoral behaviour is equally unpredictable in terms of which candidates receive support, but this too might be regarded as a more discriminating approach than automatically—perhaps somewhat mechanically—turning out on every occasion, without much reflection, to vote for the same candidate or political party. As in other walks of life, conformism has crumbled as social ties have loosened and individual gratification has come to predominate. Yet, opinion polls suggest that the right to vote remains highly valued, a conclusion which is ironically reinforced by the fact that more people claim to have voted than the official figures attest, while other surveys suggest that an overwhelming majority of French citizens still consider that voting in elections is an essential means of making their voices heard.[12]

Instead of denouncing abstention, which the popular press is inclined to ascribe to laziness or irresponsibility, a recent polemic has suggested that French citizens have good reasons for not voting more often.[13] The political class rather than the electorate is blamed for generating disenchantment and thus deterring electoral participation. This scathing analysis lambasts the growing distance between legislators and voters, which has allegedly been created by time-serving career politicians, who fail to deliver their promises of change. In France, as elsewhere, opinion polls have recorded a declining faith in the political elite, whose members are regarded as indistinguishable whatever their particular affiliation, though this study has suggested that such disaffection actually originated with the professionalization of politics at the end of the nineteenth century. The sharp fall in electoral participation of late has certainly been accompanied by a reduction in ideological polarization between governing parties in France, as well as a weakening of partisan loyalties. The prolonged struggle to overthrow conservative dominance of the Fifth Republic in the 1970s produced some spectacularly high levels of turnout before the left finally came to power in the following decade, only to disappoint many of its erstwhile supporters. André Siegfried, the pioneering

---

[9] Pierre Bréchon, 'La signification de l'abstention électorale', *Séminaire doctorale*, ULB, 29 April 2010, https://halshs.archives-ouvertes.fr/halshs-00822289 (accessed 08/08/19).

[10] Vincent Tiberj, *Des Votes et des voix, de Mitterrand à Hollande* (Paris, 2013).

[11] Anne Muxel, 'L'abstention: déficit démocratique ou vitalité politique?', *Pouvoirs*, 120 (2007), 46.

[12] Subileau and Toinet, *Les Chemins de l'abstention*, 74–6. See also, Adam Przeworski, *Why Bother with Elections?* (Cambridge 2018).

[13] Thomas Amadieu and Nicolas Framont, *Les Citoyens ont de bonnes raisons de ne pas voter* (Lormont, 2015).

electoral geographer, famously distinguished between *élections de lutte*, which raised turnout, and *élections d'apaisement*, which lowered it. The absence of political enthusiasm, and a lack of belief that change could be achieved, always discouraged electoral participation in the past. Nonetheless, the current, sustained decline in turnout goes significantly beyond previous, short-lived slumps and does seem to represent a more fundamental shift in contemporary attitudes.[14]

The practice of intermittent voting in France has in fact been associated with a renewed critique of the limitations surrounding polling in a representative system, which is summed up perfectly in the title of one broadside: *Voter et se taire*.[15] Its object, like others, which have been prompted by the recent electoral *débâcle* of 2017, is to censure the restricted role accorded to the elector, who is denied any role in choosing candidates, or setting agendas for reform and then lacks any means of controlling those who are elected.[16] Of course, this is by no means the first time that the idea of representation has been called into question. From its very inception in the 1790s, it was contested by the practice of direct, or participatory, democracy, which periodically resurfaced in the nineteenth century. The Third Republic firmly established the equation of democracy with the majoritarian outcome of periodic elections, and the supreme act of citizenship that was highlighted in school primers was conscientious participation on these occasions. Yet the sovereignty of the people continued to sit uncomfortably within the representative system, which restricted the role of the electorate to the act of voting.

Today, political participation can be expressed in a much wider range of ways, not least via the Internet, which offers a more immediate and accessible means of civic involvement than the relatively infrequent casting of a vote at a polling station. Social networking threatens much of the institutional politics of old, from party membership to public meetings and printed electoral propaganda. There has been much talk of 'e-democracy' and the prospect of using personal computers and phones to facilitate voting on all sorts of issues and occasions, largely unrealized. However, over the past couple of decades, digital technology has facilitated the practice of online petitions which can attract millions of supporters with great rapidity.[17] Very recently, the French Senate has followed the British example, by creating an official website where they may be posted, and it has undertaken to consider their demands should they pass the 100,000-mark.[18]

[14] Nicolas Sauger, 'L'impact de la structure de la compétition politique', in Amjahad et al. (eds), *Le Vote obligatoire*, 64–5.
[15] Alain Garrigou et al., *Voter et se taire. Monopoles politiques, influences médiatiques* (Paris, 2008).
[16] Stéphane Brams, *Pour une démocratie directe! Ou comment mettre en place une démocratie citoyenne et sans élection* (Paris, 2018) and Florent Bussy, *Les Élections contre la démocratie? Au-delà du vote utile* (Paris, 2019).
[17] Matt Qvortrup, *Direct Democracy: A Comparative Study of the Theory and Practice of Government by the People* (Manchester, 2013), 1–3. An academic study of e-petitioning is eagerly awaited.
[18] See https://www.vie-publique.fr/rapport/36643-democratie-representative-participative-paritaire-cooperative (accessed 23/04/20).

Unlike the laborious business of collecting signatures in the past, little more than a click of the mouse is required, but the phenomenon does reveal an appetite for taking part in the political process. It also suggests that received opinion regarding public apathy and citizen passivity may be exaggerated.

Having so brilliantly explored the historical development of democracy in France, Pierre Rosanvallon has more recently turned his attention to its current discontents and, as always, he draws heavily on historical evidence in his analysis, acknowledging that voting has always promised more than it can reasonably deliver. He goes on to argue that besides seeking ways to instil greater confidence in representation through refinements to the electoral process, it is necessary to explore means of responding to the growing distrust of those who are elected. His book *La Contre-démocratie* thus proposes ways in which voters can exercise their role of holding the *élus* to account, apart from taking the opportunity to eject them from office at the next election.[19] Such a 'counter-democracy' provides corrective devices in the form of oversight by the people which extends beyond polling day. It may, for example, involve a recall procedure, which allows voters to decide if deputies should be removed before the expiry of their mandate. John Keane, who has invented the somewhat ungainly term 'monitory democracy' to describe a similar process, argues that the development of 'post-representative' democracy is already underway, as a result of the 'power-scrutinizing' mechanisms that began to be put in place towards the end of the last century.[20]

The euphoria which greeted the collapse of communism at that point, and appeared to signal the triumph of democracy, quickly evaporated. On the contrary, there is a widespread perception at the moment of a serious crisis for liberal democracies across the globe, and one striking symptom is the growth of disengagement from the electoral process.[21] As this study has shown, similar disaffection has been expressed in the past in France, where the threat to democratic procedures has been very real on several occasions, and the sovereignty of the people has sometimes been abused, but the electoral system has not simply survived, but emerged stronger. The recourse to violence which has characterized the protracted protests of the *gilets jaunes*, like the massive demonstrations and strikes opposing reforms of employment rights and pension entitlements introduced since the presidential and legislative elections of 2017, might suggest that the much-vaunted role of elections as a means of overcoming divisions and resolving differences via the ballot box is losing its aura. There is after all a French culture of insurrection dating back to 1789. Yet this study suggests that in the case

---

[19] Pierre Rosanvallon, *La Contre-démocratie. La politique à l'âge de la défiance* (Paris, 2006), 207–13.
[20] Keane, *The Life and Death of Democracy*, 688ff.
[21] Colin Hay, *Why We Hate Politics* (Cambridge, 2007; Peter Mair, *Ruling the Void: The Hollowing of Western Democracy* (London, 2013); and Adam Przeworski, *Crises of Democracy* (Cambridge, 2019).

of France the imminent demise of representative democracy must be subject to some significant qualification.[22]

To begin with, the French continue to vote frequently, and it is rare for a year to pass without any elections occurring, while in most of them two rounds of voting are required. Although turnout has certainly declined, it has done so from a very high base, especially when compared to Britain or the United States. Indeed, French citizens continue to participate relatively strongly when compared to many other countries where the act of voting remains voluntary, most notably in the case of presidential elections. Electoral participation remains far and away the outstanding expression of civic solidarity: no less than 37 million electors turned out in the first round of the *présidentielles* held in 2017. Comparisons with municipal polls in other countries are difficult, on account of the different structures of local government, while data are not easy to obtain. Nonetheless, almost half of the electorate in France still took part in the first round of municipal elections in March 2020, which was (inadvisably) held just as lockdown was imposed to contain the coronavirus pandemic, and many electors voted wearing masks and gloves. By contrast, British turnout for a variety of elections at this level over the past decade has rarely exceeded 40 per cent of registered voters, however favourable the circumstances may have been.

While non-voting has progressed, so the incidence of spoiled papers has increased. Many French electors are making a trip to the polling station in order to indicate their dissatisfaction with the candidates on offer, or with the electoral procedure itself. Research for this book has revealed the deep historical roots of this practice, which has now become more visible as a result of campaigns to have blank votes accepted as a legitimate option, the posting of annotated papers on social media and improved reporting in election returns. Investigation into what might be called 'civic abstention' suggests that those who currently practise it are, for the most part, politically engaged and seeking to register their discontent with the alternatives on offer, or to express an opinion, rather than to make a simple choice. Campaigners for the *vote blanc* have vainly demanded provision of a *bulletin blanc* at the polling station, an option available in some democracies; for the moment they are obliged to make their own. Ironically, touch-screens do allow for a blank vote, but the limited extent to which electronic voting is being deployed in France (unlike many countries) does not represent resistance to new technology, so much as stem from firm attachment to a relatively elaborate and dignified ritual of voting. French participants are verbally identified before and after they drop their envelope (containing the ballot paper) into a transparent box. A public dimension has thus been retained in the essentially private performance of the citizen's electoral duty.

---

[22] Élisabeth Dupoirier, 'Vote', in Perrineau and Reynié (eds), *Dictionnaire du vote*, 940–2, for some cautionary words on this subject.

Finally, though the French may be less willing to experiment in the electoral sphere these days, one salient innovation should be singled out, namely the legislation on *parité*. The precocious achievement of universal manhood suffrage has been overshadowed of late by severe criticism of the failure to enfranchise women before the end of the Second World War and, even after women belatedly began to exercise the vote, their chances of election to office remained extremely slim. However, the legislation on gender parity in elections has transformed this sorry situation over the past couple of decades. In 2000, France was the first country to legislate for equality where candidatures are concerned and it remains one of very few to have done so; most have accepted voluntary measures negotiated with political parties.[23] By insisting that all lists of candidates contain equal numbers of men and women, the proportions of females elected to office have risen dramatically at all levels. In the case of the former *cantonales*, recently renamed as departmental elections, parity has been guaranteed by the creation of two-seat constituencies, which require the presentation of a female and a male candidate. The presidency and parliament have proved less amenable to such reform but, following the legislative elections of 2017, an unprecedented 40 per cent of deputies were women.

A good deal remains to be done in terms of electoral equality in general, and the same is true of other areas such as voter registration, efforts to facilitate participation, and blank voting, but this is hardly surprising. As this study has shown, both the universal franchise and secure voting took a very long time to establish, during the course of uneven processes, which were always strongly contested and never easily achieved. There inevitably remains a good deal of unfinished business on the electoral agenda and the issues are especially challenging in a rapidly changing context, which is characterized by increasing personal mobility, growing individualism, and ever greater complexity. These developments are universal, but the specific responses to them have always been shaped by the society in which they are addressed. This particular study of electoral culture over the *longue durée* thus reveals much about the always enthralling, often explosive history of France, and the values underlying the ways in which it has unfolded. This book began with the bemusement expressed by a child, observing what was happening on election day, at a French polling station located in his school. The final word goes to the outspoken elector who cast an annotated ballot paper in favour of the writer Émile Zola, at Paris in 1898, at the height of the Dreyfus Affair:

> I am employing the sovereignty vested in me to explain why I am voting in this manner. In the name of an outstanding citizen I am declaring my faith in the Republic, my trust in Justice, my contempt for base parliamentary behaviour and my condemnation of the fickle nature of public opinion.[24]

---

[23] Lenoir, 'The representation of women in politics', 235ff.
[24] AN C5214, PV Paris, 5ᵉ arrond, 1898. It should be noted that Zola, though prominent in the Affair, was not a candidate in these elections.

A Chronology of Significant Electoral Legislation and Changes of Regime, 1789–2014

24 January 1789	Ordinance convoking the Estates General.
14 December 1789	Decree constituting directly elected municipalities.
22 December 1789	Decree creating primary assemblies and electoral colleges, for a Legislative Assembly, via departmental *scrutin de liste*.
3 September 1791	Constitution of 1791, enshrining constitutional monarchy and a limited male franchise at all levels of the electoral process.
11 August 1792	Decree convoking a National Convention, on an enlarged franchise, following the overthrow of the monarchy.
24 June 1793	Constitution of 1793, not implemented but incorporating a universal male franchise and direct legislative elections, on the basis of single-member constituencies.
5 Fructidor III	Constitution of the Year III (23 August 1795), reintroducing electoral colleges and a limited franchise at all levels of the electoral process.
25 Fructidor III	Law on candidatures (11 September 1795). Repealed in 1798, after a single outing.
22 Frimaire VIII	Constitution of the Year VIII (13 December 1799), with Bonaparte as first consul, instituting quasi-universal male suffrage and abolishing electoral assemblies.
16 Thermidor X	Constitution of the Year X (4 August 1802), making Bonaparte consul for life, while restoring cantonal assemblies, with electoral colleges in departments and newly created arrondissements.
28 Floréal XII	Proclamation of the Napoleonic Empire (28 May 1804).
4 June 1814	Constitutional Charter, restoring the Bourbon monarchy in the person of Louis XVIII, on the basis of a severely limited male suffrage to a Chamber of Deputies.
22 April 1815	Additional Act to the Constitutions of the Empire, issued during Bonaparte's 100-day return, its minor electoral changes not implemented.
5 February 1817	Law on elections; the so-called Loi Lainé, after the minister of interior, with legislative elections at departmental colleges, based on the heavily restricted franchise of the Restoration.
29 June 1820	Law on elections, the so-called law of the 'double vote', creating arrondissement colleges (distinct from administrative arrondissements, headed by a sub-prefect) and giving a second vote to wealthier electors at departmental level.

26 July 1830 July   Ordinances, issued by Charles X from Saint-Cloud, giving still greater electoral weight to the small elite of wealthier voters in the departmental colleges.

14 August 1830   Revised Constitutional Charter issued under a new monarch, Louis Philippe.

21 March 1831   Municipal law restoring elections at this level, on a much broader male franchise than what followed for the legislature.

22 March 1831   Law reforming the National Guard to include all males aged between 18 and 60 years old, who will elect their officers.

19 April 1831   Law on elections to the Chamber of Deputies slightly extending the Restoration franchise and determining that electors will vote in arrondissement colleges.

5 March 1848   Decree establishing a direct universal male suffrage, subsequently confirmed in the Second Republic's Constitution of 1848, on the basis of *scrutin de liste* for a National Assembly.

15 March 1849   Electoral law sets down a comprehensive set of regulations.

31 May 1850   Law modifying the preceding document, notably by extending residence and criminal record restrictions on the franchise, imposing severe limitations. Rescinded on 2 December 1851, when the Republic was overturned.

14 January 1852   Constitution issued by Louis-Napoleon, who had seized power the previous month, based on universal male suffrage, with a Legislative Body created by *scrutin d'arrondissement* (single-member constituencies).

2 February 1852   Decree on the election of deputies to the legislature, accompanied by a revised set of electoral regulations.

7 November 1852   Constitutional decree creating the Second Empire.

4 September 1870   Downfall of Louis-Napoleon and declaration of a Republic, with a provisional government.

8 February 1871   Elections to a National Assembly via *scrutin de liste*.

27 July 1872   Law removing electoral participation from serving military personnel, eventually revoked in 1945.

30 November 1875   Electoral law for a Chamber of Deputies, on the basis of *scrutin d'arrondissement* congruent with administrative boundaries.

29 July 1881   Law on freedom of the press and electoral advertising.

16 June 1885   Law re-establishing *scrutin de liste*, only to be abandoned again in 1889 (law of 13 February 1889).

17 July 1889   Law forbidding multiple candidatures for members of the Chamber of Deputies, from whom a declaration of candidature is now required.

1 July 1901   Law on freedom of association which brought recognition of political parties.

29 July 1913   Law to ensure the secrecy of voting, by introducing envelope and *isoloir*, slightly modified the following year when generally applied.

20 March 1914   Restriction of electoral advertising to official hoardings.

31 March 1914	Laws to repress electoral corruption.
12 July 1919	Law re-establishing *scrutin de liste* with an element of proportional representation (PR).
8 June 1923	Ballot papers to be made available at polling stations, ending distribution outside them.
20 March 1924	Law making the administration responsible for the distribution of ballot papers, to be delivered to the elector's domicile.
10 July 1927	Law restoring *scrutin d'arrondissement* for the Chamber of Deputies.
10 July 1940	Constitutional law granting the plenitude of power to marshal Pétain as head of the French state, also known as the Vichy regime.
21 April 1944	Ordinance organizing public authority in France after the Liberation and declaring that a Constituent Assembly would be directly elected by both adult men and women.
17 Aug 1945	Ordinance creating a National Assembly based on *scrutin de liste* and PR (a system confirmed in the Constitution of the Fourth Republic in October 1946, which also enshrined universal suffrage).
12 April 1946	Law instituting the postal vote and procuration.
9 May 1951	Law modifying the list system embodied in the electoral law of 1946, by giving voters the power to modify the lists in contention. Electoral registration becomes compulsory, but is not enforced.
13 October 1958	Reversion to single-member *scrutin d'arrondissement* under the newly created Fifth Republic. A new constitution also authorizes the use of referendums.
28 October 1962	Direct election to the presidency approved by referendum.
28 December 1972	Decree introducing electronic voting machines in some communes for the legislative elections of 1973, but no subsequent general adoption of this technology to replace paper balloting.
5 July 1974	Voting age lowered to eighteen.
31 December 1975	Abolition of postal voting, though proxy voting becomes more accessible.
10 July 1985	Law reintroducing PR on a departmental basis for the National Assembly, rapidly abandoned in favour of the status quo ante after its use in the legislative elections of 1986.
11 March 1988	Public funding of political parties, part of a law on 'financial transparency' in public life.
15 January 1990	Law limiting electoral expenses and regulating political advertising.
23 June 1992	Participation in municipal elections opened to citizens of the European Union.
29 January 1993	Further legislation on the financing of political activities.
8 July 1999	Modification of constitutional articles introducing parity for elective office; further change is made in 2008.
6 June 2000	The so-called 'parity law', implementing constitutional reform designed to give equal access for women and men to elective office: all

lists of candidates must contain equal numbers of men and women and political parties will suffer financial penalties if they fail to achieve parity in legislative elections.

17 May 2013   Law on local councils amends and extends parity, so that only municipal councils with less than 1,000 inhabitants are now beyond its purview.

21 February 2014   Law distinguishing blank and spoiled ballots in election returns.

The Size of the Registered, 'Metropolitan' Electorate, 1790–2017

Year		Population	Registered voters	Percentage
1790	Constitutional Monarchy*	28,100,100	4,298,960	15.3
1792	First Republic*	28,100,100	5,000,000	17.8
1793	Constitution of 1793**	28,100,100	6,000,000	21.4
1795	Directory*	28,100,100	5,000,000	17.8
1801	Napoleonic Regime*	29,107,000	6,000,000	20.6
1817	Bourbon Restoration	30,462,000	90,878	0.3
1831	July Monarchy***	32,569,000	166,583	0.5
1848	Second Republic	35,783,000	9,977,452	27.9
1850	Electoral Law of 31 May**	35,783,000	6,600,000	18.4
1852	Second Empire	35,783,000	9,836,043	27.5
1876	Third Republic	36,103,000	9,961,261	27.6
1914	Eve of First World War	39,605,000	11,185,078	28.2
1936	Eve of Second World War	41,524,000	11,768,491	28.3
1945	Female enfranchisement	40,125,230	24,622,862	61.4
1978	Suffrage extended to 18+ (1974)	53,731,387	34,424, 388	64.1
2017	Most recent election	65,188,000	44,430,902	68.2

Notes: * Indirect election to legislature. ** No general elections were held on this basis. *** Legislative elections only; unusually, if not quite uniquely, under the July Monarchy there was a rather larger electorate for municipal elections (see Chapter 1).

A number of caveats must be entered. As the title of this table indicates, the colonial and later overseas electorate has been omitted. Focused on the 'metropole', the figures offer an order of magnitude that makes no pretence at scientific accuracy, as is evident in many of the rounded figures. From 1792 to 1816 the size of the electorate is an approximation, since registers were either non-existent, or no attempt was made to collate them at national level. The same must be said of population, which is based on estimates for the revolutionary decade and then the nearest decennial census from the nineteenth century onwards. Percentages will vary according to the age profile of the population on the one hand, and the vagaries of registration on the other (the figure for the electorate in 1848 is the rather larger one used in the December presidential elections), besides reflecting the electoral legislation that has largely determined the choice of dates in the table.

The Location of Voting Assemblies and Polling Stations since 1789

Revolution	Commune Canton Department
Napoleonic Era	Commune Canton Arrondissement Department
Restoration	Arrondissement Department
July Monarchy	Commune Arrondissement
Second Republic	Commune Canton
1852 onwards	Commune

The notion of an electoral arrondissement can be deceptive. During the Napoleonic era, as under the Third and Fifth Republics, it coincided with the administrative circumscription, with a sub-prefect at its head. This was not the case under the Restoration and July Monarchy, and also under the Second Empire, when electoral arrondissements were carved out separately and offered significant scope for gerrymandering.

Subjects of Consultation in Constitutional Votes, Plebiscites, and Referendums, 1793–2005

1793	The Constitution of 1793.
1795	The Constitution of the Year III (1795) and the decree of the two-thirds (the obligatory re-election of two-thirds of the existing national deputies).
1800	The Constitution of the Year VIII (1799).
1802	A Life Consulate for Bonaparte.
1804	Imperial Heredity to be vested in the family of Napoleon Bonaparte.
1815	The Additional Act to the Constitutions of the Empire.
1851	Confirmation of the authority of Louis-Napoleon as President.
1852	Re-establishment of the imperial heredity in the family of Louis-Napoleon.
1870	The liberal reform of the Second Empire.
1945	Granting of constituent powers to the National Assembly and approval of interim arrangements.
1946 (May)	The Constitution proposed by the Constituent Assembly.
1946 (Oct.)	A further proposed Constitution for the Fourth Republic.
1958	The Constitution for a Fifth Republic.
1961	De Gaulle's policy in Algeria.
1962 (Apr.)	The Évian Accords to end the Algerian War.
1962 (Oct.)	Direct election of the President by the French people.
1969	Reform of the Senate and the introduction of regional government.
1972	Enlargement of the European Economic Community.
1988	The Matignon Accords on the status of New Caledonia.
1992	Ratification of the so-called Treaty of Maastricht on European unification.
2000	Reduction of the presidential term of office from seven years to five years.
2005	The Treaty establishing a European Constitution.

Just three of these twenty-two consultations—in May 1946, 1969, and 2005—failed to elicit an affirmative verdict from a majority of those who voted.

Bibliography

1. Manuscript Sources

Extensive sampling has been conducted in the following archival series, to which detailed reference is made in the footnotes, since much of the material is widely dispersed. For more detail on sources for the Revolution, see the archival sources in my *Elections in the French Revolution*, 197–203.

(i) Archives nationales at Pierrefitte-sur-Seine

AF Archives du pouvoir exécutif.

AFIII 211–67, Rapports des Commissaires du Directoire, including comments on elections, 1798–9.

B Élections et votes.

BII 1–1499, Votes populaires, comprises the *procès-verbaux* (PV), or registers, catalogued chronologically, by department, arrondissement, and commune for the votes (later called plebiscites, then referendums) that were held on constitutions and constitutional changes, from 1793 to 1958. They also include the PV for the direct election of a president in 1848. BII 1–34, Constitution de 1793; 35–74, Constitution de l'an III; 75–471, Constitution de l'an VIII; 472–671, Consulat à Vie an X; 672–853, Hérédité impériale an XII; 853–957, Acte additionnel 1815; 958–1046, Élection du Président 1848; 1047–1134, Plébiscite 1851; 1135–1223, Plébiscite 1852; 1224–1316, Plébiscite 1870; 1317–1338, Référendums 1945–6; 1339–1499, Référendum 1958.

BB Ministèrè de la Justice

BB18, Correspondance générale de la division criminelle et correctionnelle, which contains occasional material relating to nineteenth-century elections.

BB30, Versements divers, notably 367–90, which contain reports from the departmental *procureurs généraux* on the electoral process from 1849 to 1870.

C Assemblées nationales

The key resource, extensively employed for sampling the PV of legislative elections from the Revolution to 1914: this series also contains statistical material, petitions and the papers of committees and commissions, notably the Commission on Universal Suffrage from 1898 onwards, which have also been extensively used here. The PV are catalogued as follows: C118–81, 1790–2; 480–584, 1795–9; 1164–1324, 1814–48; 1325–1584, 1848–51; 1585–2024; 1852–70; 3448–3727, 1871–5; 3728–4100, 4444–5367, and 6011–7254, 1876–1914. C10001–14628, the dossiers relating to elections after 1919 are not currently available for consultation.

F Ministère de l'Intérieur.

F1a, Objets généraux, chiefly ministerial circulars and advice relating to electoral matters in the nineteenth century, notably 22–68, Circulaires et instructions ministérielles, 1789–1869.

F1bI, Personnel administratif, of general relevance to the election of local councillors in the nineteenth century.

F1cII, Élections, which includes ministerial correspondence with prefects on this subject in the nineteenth century, as well as reflections on the outcome, and material on participation relating to the twentieth.

F1cIII, Esprit public et élections, another vital source, catalogued chronologically, by department, which includes some electoral PV, and data for the electorate and turnout but, above all, comments from officials, notably the prefects, on public opinion and elections, from the 1790s to the early Third Republic. Campaign material such as posters, newspaper cuttings and *professions de foi*, is also to be found here.

F3, Ministère de l'intérieur, administration communale, for some statistics on turnout in municipal elections.

F7, Police générale, which can be consulted for reports on activities surrounding elections, not least relating to campaigns, clubs, and the press, from the Revolution to 1830, then again for the late nineteenth and early twentieth centuries.

F19, Cultes, a series which includes a wide variety of material relating to organized religion, beginning in the Revolution, where the dossiers relating to clerical elections are of particular interest, then those regarding clerical involvement in elections down to the twentieth century.

(ii) Archives de la Préfecture de Police de Paris

BA 653–4 Cabinet du Préfet de Police. Reports on the legislative election of 1898 in Paris.

(iii) Archives départementales

Séries L, Révolution, which usually include a sub-series on elections from 1790 to 1799, containing electoral lists, PV, and related issues. For a more detailed guide to this variable, but essential material, see the bibliography in my *Elections in the French Revolution*, 198–203.

Séries M, Administration Générale, from 1800 to 1940, subseries on elections, usually classified as national, departmental, and municipal, on a chronological basis. The PV for general elections and plebiscites/referendums can be consulted at the Archives nationales, but few statistics regarding local elections were collected at the national level until after the Second World War, so consultation of PV held in the *archives départementales* is absolutely essential. The archives principally consulted for the post-revolutionary period were located in the Côte-d'Or at Dijon, the Morbihan at Vannes, the Var at Draguignan, and the Yvelines at Saint-Quentin-en-Yvelines.

Séries W, Archives administratives et judiciaires postérieures à 1940. Most departmental election material in the series M peters out in 1940, and recourse to electoral material thereafter is more difficult, since it is broadly scattered in this series. Fortunately, at this point more statistics become available for local elections in centrally held documentation, so I have conducted little research in this regard at the archives départementales.

2. Printed Sources

(i) Bibliothèque nationale and British Library

Pamphlet collections relating to elections. At the British Library there is an excellent guide for the Revolution: G. K. Fortescue, *French Revolutionary Collections in the British Library*, revised edn, A.C. Brodhurst (London, 1979).

(ii) Official Material

Annales de l'Assemblée nationale. Compte-rendu in extenso des séances, annexes, 46 vols (Paris, 1871–6).

Archives parlementaires de 1787 à 1860. Recueil complet des débats législatifs et politiques des Chambres Françaises, 1ᵉʳᵉ série, 1789–99, eds Jérôme Mavidal, Émile Laurent et al. (Paris, 1867–), still in progress beyond 1794.

Archives parlementaires…, 2ᵉ série, 1800–1860 (Paris, 1862–1913), eds Jérôme Mavidal, Émile Laurent et al., but actually ends in 1839.

Bulletin des Lois, 1789–1931.

Journal Officiel, 1870–.

(iii) Press

Gazette nationale ou le Moniteur universel (*Le Moniteur universel* from 1811 onwards)
Le Figaro
La Française
L'Illustration
Le Monde
Le Temps

(iv) Memoirs

Déguignet, Jean-Marie, *Mémoires d'un paysan bas-breton*, ed. Bernez Rouz (Ergué-Gabéric, 2000).

Guizot, François, *Mémoires pour servir à l'histoire de mon temps*, 2nd edn, 4 vols (Paris, 1858–63).

Hélias, Pierre-Jakez, *The Horse of Pride: Life in a Breton Village*, trans. (New Haven, CT, 1978).

de La Maisonfort, Antoine-François-Philippe, *Mémoires d'un agent royaliste sous la Révolution, l'Empire et la Restauration, 1763–1827*, ed. Hugues de Changy (Paris, 1998).

Le Journal d'un bourgeois de Lyon en 1848, ed. Justin Godart (Paris, 1924).

Rémusat, Charles de, *Mémoires de ma vie*, 5 vols (Paris, 1958–67).

Rochas, Adolphe, *Journal d'un bourgeois de Valence, du 1ᵉʳ janvier 1789 au 9 novembre 1799 (18 brumaire an VIII)* (Grenoble, 1891).

Tocqueville, Alexis de, *Œuvres complètes*, Vol. X, Correspondance et écrits locaux (Paris, 1995).

Tocqueville, Alexis de, *Recollections: The French Revolution of 1848 and its Aftermath*, ed. Olivier Zunz (Charlottesville, VA, 2016).

Vitrolles, Eugène François de, *Mémoires*, 2 vols, ed. Pierre Farel (Paris, 1950–2).

3. Reference

Aberdam, Serge et al. (eds), *Voter, élire pendant la Révolution française 1789–1799, Guide pour la recherche*, 2nd edn (Paris, 2006).

Brette, Armand (ed.), *Recueil de documents relatifs à la convocation des États généraux de 1789*, 4 vols (Paris, 1894).

Charavay, Étienne (ed.), *Assemblée électorale de Paris*, 3 vols (Paris, 1890–1905).

Donnadieu, Jean-Pierre (ed.), *États généraux de 1789. Sénéchaussées de Béziers et Montpellier* (Montpellier, 1989).

Duguit, Léon et al. (eds), *Les Constitutions et les principales lois politiques de la France depuis 1789*, 7th edn (Paris, 1952).

Durand, Yves (ed.), *Cahiers de doléances des paroisses du bailliage de Troyes pour les États généraux de 1614* (Paris, 1966).

Godechot, Jacques, *Les Institutions de la France sous la Révolution et l'Empire*, 2nd edn (Paris, 1968).

Godechot, Jacques (ed.), *Les Constitutions de la France depuis 1789* (Paris, 1970).

Robespierre, Maximilien, *Oeuvres complètes*, eds Marc Bouloiseau et al. (Paris, 1910–2007).

Salmon, Frédéric, *Atlas électoral de la France 1848–2001* (Paris, 2001).

Tanchoux, Philippe, *Les Procédures électorales en France de la fin de l'Ancien Régime à la Première Guerre mondiale* (Paris, 2004).

Wickham-Legg, L.G., *Select Documents Illustrative of the History of the French Revolution*, 2 vols (Oxford, 1905).

Books, Pamphlets, and Articles

Anon., *L'Instruction civique à l'école laïque des sans Dieu expliquée par un homme de bon sens* (Paris, 1883).

Auclert, Hubertine, *Le Droit politique des femmes. Question qui n'est pas traitée au congrès international des femmes* (Paris, 1878).

Barthélemy, Joseph, 'Pour le vote obligatoire', *Revue du droit public et de la science politique en France et à l'étranger*, 40 (1923), 101–67.

Batbie, Anselme, *Rapport fait au nom de la commission chargée d'examiner les lois constitutionnelles sur le projet de loi électorale* (Versailles, 1874).

Bellissen, Cyprien de, *Le Suffrage universel dans le département de l'Ariège* (Paris, 1869).

Benoist, Charles, 'Comment on capte le suffrage et le pouvoir – la "Machine"', *Revue des Deux Mondes*, 21 (1904), 885–918.

Benoist, Charles, *Pour la réforme électorale* (Paris, 1908).

Bernard, Francis, *La Liberté des candidatures aux assemblées législatives en France et à l'étranger* (Paris, 1925).

Bert, Paul, *L'Instruction civique à l'école. Notions fondamentales* (Paris, 1882).

Bert, Paul, *De l'Éducation civique* (Paris, 1883).

Bodley, John (J. E. C.), *France*, 2 vols (London, 1898).

Brams, Stéphane, *Pour une démocratie directe! Ou comment mettre en place une démocratie citoyenne et sans élection* (Paris, 2018).

Brennan, Jason, *Against Democracy* (Princeton, NJ, 2017).

Brissot, Jacques-Pierre, *Réflexions sur l'état de la Société des électeurs patriotiques* (Paris, 1790).

Broglie, Victor de, *Vues sur le gouvernement de la France* (Paris, 1870).

Bruno, G. (Augustine Fouillée), *Instruction morale et civique pour les petits enfants* (Paris, 1883).

Buéno, Antoine, *No vote! Manifeste pour l'abstention* (Paris, 2017).

Buisson, Ferdinand, *Le Vote des femmes* (Paris, 1911).

Burger, Aloïs, *Le Suffrage universel coordonné, vote plural* (Paris, 1893).

Bussy, Florent, *Les Élections contre la démocratie? Au-delà du vote utile* (Paris, 2019).

Castellane, Antoine de, *Essai sur l'organisation du suffrage universel en France*, 2nd edn (Paris, 1872).

Clamageran, J.-J. et al., *Manuel électoral. Guide pratique pour les élections au Corps législatif, aux conseils généraux, aux conseils d'arrondissement et aux conseils municipaux* (Paris, 1861).

Clère, Jules, *Histoire du suffrage universel* (Paris, 1873).

Commission de rénovation et de déontologie de la vie publique, *Pour un renouveau démocratique*, 2012.

Condorcet, Jean-Antoine-Nicolas de, *Oeuvres de Condorcet*, eds A. Condorcet O'Connor and M. F. Arago, 12 vols (Paris, 1847).

Condorcet, Jean-Antoine-Nicolas de, *Sur les élections et autres textes choisis*, ed. Olivier de Bernon (Paris, 1986).

Congrès français et international du droit des femmes (Paris, 1889).

Constant, Benjamin, *Choix de textes politiques*, ed. Olivier Pozzo di Borgo (Utrecht, 1965).

Cormenin, Louis de [under the pseudonym Timon], *Ordre du jour sur la corruption électorale et parlementaire* (Paris, 1846).

Coulon, Georges, *Guide pratique de l'électeur* (Paris, 1868).

Coutant, Paul, *Le Vote obligatoire* (Paris, 1898).

Delacroix, Jacques-Victor, *Le Spectateur français pendant le gouvernement révolutionnaire* (Paris, an IV).

Delattre, Eugène, *Devoirs du suffrage universel suivi du texte de la loi électorale* (Paris, 1863).

Deroin, Jeanne, 'Aux électeurs du département de la Seine', 1849.

Durand, Olivier, *Le Vote blanc. Pour un suffrage vraiment universel* (Paris, 1999).

Duvergier de Hauranne, Prosper, *De la réforme parlementaire et de la réforme électorale* (Paris, 1847).

Électeurs, surveillez les urnes (Villefranche-de-Rouergue, 1902).

Faure, Sébastien, *Pour ne pas voter: électeur écoute* (Paris, 1924).

Ferry, Jules, *La Lutte électorale en 1863* (Paris, 1863).

Fouillée, Alfred, *La Propriété sociale et la démocratie* (Paris, 1884).

Fouillée, Alfred, 'La philosophie du suffrage universel', *Revue des Deux Mondes*, 65 (1884), 103–29.

Fouillée, Alfred, *La Démocratie politique et sociale en France* (Paris, 1910).

Gouges, Olympe de, *Déclaration des droits de la femme* (Paris, 1791).

Guizot, François, *Discours académiques* (Paris, 1861).

Heulhard de Montigny, Charles-Gilbert, *Un Dernier mot sur le suffrage universel et les candidatures officielles* (Paris, 1869).

Jouvenel, Robert, *La République des camarades* (Paris, 1914).

Labussière, André, 'Le vote par correspondance', *Revue politique et parlementaire*, 45 (1905), 260–9.

Lachapelle, Georges, *Élections législatives, des 26 avril et 10 mai 1914* (Paris, 1914).

Lachapelle, Georges, *Élections législatives, 26 avril et 3 mai 1936. Résultats officiels* (Paris, 1936).

Le Bail, Georges, *Une Élection en 1906. Miettes électorales* (Paris, 1908).

Le Goff, Jean-Paul Yves, 'Pourquoi je suis contre le suffrage universel', 23 Jan. 2009. https://blogs.mediapart.fr/jeanpaulyveslegoff/blog/230109/pourquoi-je-suis-contre-le-suffrage-universel,

Lefèvre-Pontalis, Antonin, *Les Lois et les mœurs électorales en France et en Angleterre* (Paris, 1864).

Lefèvre-Pontalis, Antonin, *Les Élections en Europe à la fin du XIXe siècle* (Paris, 1902).

Leroy-Beaulieu, Paul, *Un Chapitre des moeurs électorales en France, dans les années 1889 et 1890* (Paris, 1890).

Liard, Louis, *Morale et enseignement civique à l'usage des écoles primaires (cours moyens et cours supérieurs)* (Paris, 1883).

Mariotte, L., *Des Conséquences de l'établissement du suffrage universel en France* (Paris, 1888).

Mézières, Alfred, *Éducation morale et instruction civique à l'usage des Écoles primaires* (Paris, 1883).

Mirbeau, Octave, *La Grève des électeurs, suivi de Prélude* (Paris, 2002).

Moreau, Félix, 'Le vote obligatoire. Principe et sanctions', *Revue politique et parlementaire*, 7 (1896), 36–69.

Poulpiquet, Paul de, *Le Suffrage des femmes* (Paris, 1912).

Prévost-Paradol, Lucien-Anatole, *La France nouvelle* (Paris, 1868).

Proudhon, Pierre-Joseph, *De la capacité politique des classes ouvrières* (Paris, 1868).

Quatremère de Quincy, Antoine-Chrysostome, *La Véritable liste de candidats* (Paris, an V).

Ribot, Paul, *Du Suffrage universel et de la souveraineté du peuple* (Paris, 1874).

Rickard, Charles, *Vérités sur les élections* (Paris, 1991).

Rouzet, Jacques-Marie, *Vues civiques sur la Constitution que les Français sont intéressés à se donner* (Paris, 1795).

Sartre, Jean-Paul, 'Élections, pièges à cons', *Les Temps Modernes*, 318 (1973).

Scherer, Edmond, *La Démocratie et la France: études* (Paris, 1883).

Stern, Daniel [Marie d'Agout], *Histoire de la révolution de 1848*, 3 vols (Paris, 1850–3).

Taine, Hippolyte, *Du Suffrage universel et de la manière de voter* (Paris, 1872).

Ténot, Eugène, *Le Suffrage universel et les paysans* (Paris, 1865).

Trucs électoraux (Paris, 1897).

Turgeon, Charles, *Le Féminisme français*, 2 vols, 2nd edn (Paris, 1907).

Van Reybrouck, David, *Against Elections: The Case for Democracy* (London, 2016).

Williams, David, *Observations sur la dernière constitution de la France, avec des vues pour la formation de la nouvelle constitution* (Paris, 1793).

Zevort, Edgar, *La France sous le régime du suffrage universel* (Paris, 1894).

4. Secondary Sources

(i) Theses

Anceau, Éric, 'L'Empire libéral: essai d'histoire politique totale', 2 vols, Travail inédit de dossier d'habilitation, Université Paris-Sorbonne, 2014.

Dompnier, Nathalie, 'La Clef des urnes', Thèse de doctorat de science politique, Université de Grenoble II, 2002.

Lagouyete, Patrick, 'Candidature officielle et pratiques électorales sous le Second Empire (1852–1870)', Thèse de doctorat, 5 vols, Université de Paris I, 1990.

Le Gall, Yvon, 'Les Consultations générales en Loire-Inférieure 1789–an VII', Thèse pour le Doctorat en Droit, 2 vols, Université de Nantes, 1976.

Malkopoulou, Anthoula, 'Democracy's duty: the history of political debates on compulsory voting' (PhD Thesis, University of Jyväskylä, Finland, 2011).

Massalsky, Alain, 'Élections et politisation dans le département des Hautes-Pyrénées, 1790–1799', Thèse pour le doctorat d'histoire, Université de Paris I, 2006.

Wright, Vincent, 'The Basses-Pyrénées from 1848–1870: a study in departmental politics', PhD, University of London, 3 vols, 1965.

(ii) Books, Essays, and Articles

Aberdam, Serge, *Démographes et démocrates. L'œuvre du comité de division de la Convention nationale* (Paris, 2004).

Achin, Catherine, 'The French parity law: a successful gender equality measure or a "conservative revolution"?', in Diana Auth et al. (eds), *Gender and Family in European Economic Policy: Developments in the New Millennium* (Cham, 2017), 179–97.

Achin, Catherine and Marion Paoletti, 'Le "salto" du stigmata. Genre et construction des listes aux municipales de 2001', *Politix*, 60 (2002), 33–54.

Agnès, Benoît, *L'Appel au pouvoir. Les pétitions au Parlements en France et au Royaume-Uni (1814–1848)* (Rennes, 2018).

Amadieu, Thomas and Nicolas Framont, *Les Citoyens ont de bonnes raisons de ne pas voter* (Lormont, 2015).

Amjahad, Anissa et al. (eds), *Le Vote obligatoire. Débats, enjeux et défis* (Paris, 2011).

Antoine, Annie and Julian Mischi (eds), *Sociabilité et politique en milieu rural* (Rennes, 2008).

Baczko, Bronislaw, *Comment sortir de la Terreur. Thermidor et la Révolution* (Paris, 1989).

Balland, R., 'De l'organisation à la restriction du suffrage universel en France (1848–1850)', in Jacques Droz (ed.), *Réaction et suffrage universel en France et en Allemagne* (Paris, 1963).

Barbier, Pierre and France Vernillat, *Histoire de France par les chansons*, 8 vols (Paris, 1956–61).

Bard, Christine, *Les Filles de Marianne. Histoire des féminismes, 1914–1940* (Paris, 1995).

Bard, Christine, *Les Femmes dans la société française au 20ᵉ siècle* (Paris, 2001).

Barral, Pierre, *Le Département de l'Isère sous la Troisième République: histoire sociale et politique* (Paris, 1962).

Bastid, Paul, *Les Institutions de la monarchie parlementaire française, 1814–1848* (Paris, 1954).

Bateman, David A., *Disenfranchising Democracy: Constructing the Electorate in the United States, the United Kingdom, and France* (Cambridge, 2018).

Bayon-Tollet, Jacqueline, *Le Puy-en-Velay et la Révolution française (1789–1799)* (Saint-Étienne, 1982).

Belmonte, Cyril, 'Voter à Auriol sous la Révolution (1789–1799), *Provence historique*, LVII (2007), 177–87.

Benessiano, William, 'Le vote obligatoire', *Revue française de droit constitutionnel*, 61 (2005), 73–115.

Bensel, Richard Franklin, *The American Ballot Box in the Mid-Nineteenth Century* (Cambridge, 2004).

Bercé, Yves-Marie, 'Les bulletins nuls, source de microsociologie électorale', *La Gazette des Archives*, 65 (1969), 75–84.

Berger, Suzanne, *Peasants against Politics: Rural Organization in Brittany, 1911–1967* (Cambridge, MA, 1972).

Bernstein, Hilary J., 'The benefit of the ballot? Elections and influence in sixteenth-century Poitiers', *FHS*, 24 (2001), 621–52.

Berstein, Serge and Michel Winock (eds), *L'Invention de la démocratie 1789–1914* (Paris, 2002).

Bertrand, Romain et al. (eds), *Cultures of Voting: The Hidden History of the Secret Ballot* (London, 2007).

Bianchi, Serge, *La Révolution et la Première République au village. Pouvoirs, votes et politisation dans les campagnes de l'Île-de-France (Essonne et Val-de-Marne actuels)* (Paris, 2003).

Bidelman, Patrick, *Pariahs Stand Up! The Founding of the Liberal Feminist Movement in France, 1858–1889* (London, 1982).

Billard, Yves, *Le Métier de la politique sous la IIIᵉ République* (Perpignan, 2003).

Bleton-Ruget, Annie and Serge Wolikow (eds), *Voter et élire à l'époque contemporaine* (Dijon, 1999).

Bodin, Louis and Jean Touchard, 'L'élection partielle de la première circonscription de la Seine', *Rfsp*, 7 (1957), 271–312.

Bon, Frédéric and Jean-Paul Cheylan, *La France qui vote* (Paris, 1988).

Bonnet, Serge, *Sociologie politique et religieuse de la Lorraine* (Paris, 1972).

Bordes, Maurice, *La Réforme municipale du Contrôleur général Laverdy et son application, 1764–1771* (Toulouse, 1968).

Bordes, Maurice, *L'Administration provinciale et municipale au dix-huitième siècle* (Paris, 1973).

Bouglé-Moalic, Anne-Sarah, *Le Vote des Françaises. Cent ans de débats 1848–1944* (Rennes, 2012).

Bouhey, Vivien, *Les Anarchistes contre la République* (Rennes, 2008).

Bourdin, Philippe et al. (eds), *L'Incident électoral de la Révolution française à la Ve République* (Clermont-Ferrand, 2002).

Bousquet-Mélou, Jean, *Louis Barthou et la circonscription d'Oloron, 1889–1914* (Paris, 1972).

Boutin, Christophe and Frédéric Rouvillois (eds), *L'Abstention électorale, apaisement ou épuisement?* (Paris, 2002).

Boy, Daniel and Jean Chiche, 'Abstention et blancs et nuls au référendum du 24 septembre 2000', *Rfsp*, 51 (2001), 241–5.

Braconnier, Céline and Jean-Yves Dormagen, *La Démocratie de l'abstention. Aux origines de la démobilisation électorale en milieu populaire* (Paris, 2007).

Braconnier, Céline and Jean-Yves Dormagen, 'Logiques de mobilisation et inégalités sociales de participation électorale en France, 2002–2012', *French Politics, Culture & Society*, 30 (2012), 20–44.

Braud, Philippe, *Le Comportement électoral en France* (Paris, 1973).

Braud, Philippe, *Le Suffrage universel contre la démocratie* (Paris, 1980).

Bréchon, Pierre, *La France aux urnes* (Paris, 2009).

Bréchon, Pierre, 'La signification de l'abstention électorale', Séminaire doctorale, ULB, 29 April 2010, https://halshs.archives-ouvertes.fr/halshs-00822289.

Buchstein, Hubertus, *Öffentliche und geheime Stimmabgabe. Eine wahlrechtshistorische und ideengeschichtliche Studie* (Baden-Baden, 2000).

Campbell, Peter and Alistair Cole, *French Electoral Systems and Elections since 1789* (Aldershot, 1989).

Cautrès, Bruno and Nonna Mayer (eds), *Le Nouveau désordre électoral* (Paris, 2004).

Challeton, Félix, *Cent ans d'élections. Histoire électorale et parlementaire de la France de 1789 à 1890*, 3 vols (Paris, 1891).

Charléty, Sébastien, *La Restauration (1815–1830)* (Paris, 1911).

Charnay, Jean-Paul, *Les Scrutins politiques en France de 1815 à 1962. Contestations et invalidations* (Paris, 1964).

Charpentier, Arthur et al., 'Un homme, deux voix: le vote par procuration', http://www.laviedesidees.fr/Un-homme-deux-voix-le-vote-par.html.

Chartier, Roger and Denis Richet, *Représentation et vouloir politiques. Autour des États généraux de 1614* (Paris, 1982).

Chauvet, Horace, *Histoire du parti républicain dans les Pyrénées-Orientales (1830–1877)* (Perpignan, 1909).

Chenut, Helen, 'Attitudes towards French women's suffrage on the eve of World War I', *FHS*, 41 (2018), 711–40.

Christin, Olivier, 'À quoi sert de voter aux XVIe–XVIIIe siècles', *ARSS*, 140 (2002), 21–30.

Christin, Olivier, *Vox populi. Une histoire du vote avant le suffrage universel* (Paris, 2014).

Christin, Olivier, 'Disinterest, vocation and elections: two late seventeenth-century affairs', *FH*, 29 (2015), 285–303.

Christin, Olivier, 'Le lent triomphe du nombre. Les progrès de la décision majoritaire à l'époque moderne', http://www.laviedesidees.fr/Le-lent-triomphe-du-nombre.html.

Cointet-Labrousse, Michèle, *Le Conseil national de Vichy: vie politique et réforme de l'État en régime autoritaire (1940–1944)* (Paris, 1989).

Collard, Sue, 'French municipal democracy: cradle of European citizenship?', *Journal of Contemporary European Studies*, 18 (2010), 91–116.

Combeau, Yvan, *Paris et les élections municipales sous la Troisième République. La scène capitale dans la vie politique française* (Paris, 1998).

Coppolani, Jean-Yves, *Les Élections en France à l'époque napoléonienne* (Paris, 1980).

Corbin, Alain, *Archaïsme et modernité en Limousin au XIXe siècle, 1845–1880*, 2 vols (Paris, 1975).

Cornu, Pierre, 'Faire voter les femmes sous la Troisième République: une expérience à Louviers en 1936', *Études normandes*, 54 (2005), 43–50.

Cossart, Paula, *Le Meeting politique. De la délibération à la manifestation (1868–1939)* (Rennes, 2010).

Cotteret, Jean-Marie et al., *Lois électorales et inégalités de représentation en France, 1936–1960* (Paris, 1960).

Crook, Malcolm, 'The people at the polls; electoral behaviour in revolutionary Toulon, 1789–1799', *FH*, 5 (1991), 164–79.

Crook, Malcolm, *Elections in the French Revolution: An Apprenticeship in Democracy, 1789–1799* (Cambridge, 1996).

Crook, Malcolm, 'Masses de granit ou grains de sable? Les électeurs des assemblées départementales sous la Révolution française, 1790–1799', in Denise Turrel (ed.), *Regards sur les sociétés modernes XVIe–XVIIIe siècle. Mélanges offerts à Claude Petitfrère* (Tours, 1997), 203–10.

Crook, Malcolm, 'La plume et l'urne: la presse et les élections sous le Directoire', in Philippe Bourdin and Bernard Gainot (eds), *La République directoriale*, 2 vols (Paris, 1998), i, 295–310.

Crook, Malcolm, 'Les réactions autour de brumaire à travers le plébiscite de l'an VIII', in Jean-Pierre Jessenne et al. (eds), *Du Directoire au Consulat*, 4 vols (Lille, 1999–2001), iii, 323–32.

Crook, Malcolm, 'Citizen bishops: episcopal elections in the French Revolution', *The Historical Journal*, 43 (2000), 955–76.

Crook, Malcolm, 'Getting out the vote: electoral participation in France, 1789–1851', in Ceri Crossley and Martin Cornick (eds), *Problems in French History: Essays in Honour of Douglas Johnson* (Basingstoke, 2000), 50–63.

Crook, Malcolm, 'Le candidat imaginaire, ou l'offre et le choix dans les élections de la Révolution française', *AhRf* (2000), 91–110.

Crook, Malcolm, 'Confidence from below? Collaboration and resistance in the Napoleonic plebiscites', in Michael Rowe (ed.), *Collaboration and Resistance in Napoleonic Europe: State-Formation in an Age of Upheaval, c.1800–1815* (Basingstoke, 2003), 19–36.

Crook, Malcolm, 'The Plebiscite on the Empire', in Philip G. Dwyer and Alan Forrest (eds), *Napoleon and his Empire: Europe, 1804–1814* (Basingstoke, 2007), 16–28.

Crook, Malcolm, '"Ma volonté est celle du peuple": voting in the plebiscite and parliamentary elections during Napoléon's Hundred Days, April–May 1815', *FHS*, 32 (2009), 619–45.

Crook, Malcolm, 'Citizenship without democracy: the culture of elections in France under the Constitutional Monarchy, 1814–1848', in Silke Hensel et al. (eds), *Constitutional Cultures: On the Concept and Representation of Constitutions in the Atlantic World* (Newcastle upon Tyne, 2012), 403–25.

Crook, Malcolm, 'L'avènement du suffrage féminin dans une perspective globale (1890–1914)', in Landry Charrier et al. (eds), *Circulations et réseaux transnationaux en Europe (XVIIIe–XXe siècles). Acteurs, pratiques, modèles* (Berne, 2013), 57–68.

Crook, Malcolm, 'Un scrutin secret émis en public. L'acte de vote sous la Révolution française (1789–1802)', in Cyril Belmonte and Christine Peyrard (eds), *Peuples en révolution. D'aujourd'hui à 1789* (Aix-en-Provence, 2014), 57–69.

Crook, Malcolm, 'Universal suffrage as counter-revolution? Electoral mobilisation under the Second Republic in France, 1848–1851', *Journal of Historical Sociology*, 28 (2015), 49–66.

Crook, Malcolm, 'Voter sous Napoléon. L'autopsie de l'expérience électorale du Premier Empire d'après une enquête préfectorale sur les consultations cantonales de 1813', *AhRf*, 382 (2015), 103–22.

Crook, Malcolm and Tom Crook, 'The advent of the secret ballot in Britain and France: from public assembly to private compartment', *History*, 92 (2007), 449–71.

Crook, Malcolm and Tom Crook, 'Reforming voting practices in a global age: the making and remaking of the modern secret ballot in Britain, France and the United States, c. 1600–c. 1950', *Past & Present*, 212 (2011), 199–237.

Crook, Malcolm and Tom Crook, 'Ballot papers and the practice of elections: Britain, France and the United States of America, c. 1500–2000', *Historical Research*, 88 (2015), 530–61.

Crook, Malcolm and John Dunne, 'The First European elections? Voting and imperial state-building under Napoleon, 1802–1813', *Historical Journal*, 57 (2014), 661–97.

Dagnan, Jean, *Le Gers sous la Seconde République* (Auch, 1928).

De Luca Barrusse, Virginie, 'Les femmes et les enfants aussi, ou le droit d'être représenté par le vote familial', *ARSS*, 140 (2001), 51–6.

Déloye, Yves, 'L'élection au village. Le geste électoral à l'occasion des scrutins cantonaux et régionaux de mars 1992', *Rfsp*, 43 (1993), 101–5.

Déloye, Yves, *École et citoyenneté. L'individualisme républicain de Jules Ferry à Vichy: controverses* (Paris, 1994).

Déloye, Yves, *Les Voix de Dieu. Pour une autre histoire du suffrage électoral: le clergé catholique français et le vote (XIXe–XXe siècles)* (Paris, 2006).

Déloye, Yves and Olivier Ihl, *L'Acte de vote* (Paris, 2008).

Déloye, Yves and Olivier Ihl, 'Des voix pas comme les autres. Votes blancs et votes nuls aux élections législatives de 1881', *Rfsp*, 41 (1991), 141–70.

Déloye, Yves and Olivier Ihl, 'Légitimité et déviance. L'annulation des votes dans les campagnes de la IIIe République', *Politix*, 15 (1991), 13–24.

Deluermoz, Quentin, *Le Crépuscule des révolutions 1848–1871* (Paris, 2012).

Demichel, André and Francine Demichel, *Droit électoral* (Paris, 1973).

Denoyelle, Bruno, 'Des corps en élections. Au rebours des universaux de la citoyenneté: les premiers votes des femmes (1945–1946)', *Genèses*, 31 (1998), 76–98.

Derlange, Michel, *Les Communautés d'habitants en Provence au dernier siècle de l'ancien régime* (Toulouse, 1987).

Desan, Suzanne, '"Constitutional amazons": Jacobin women's clubs in the French Revolution', in Bryant T. Ragan and Elizabeth A. Williams (eds), *Re-Creating Authority in Revolutionary France* (New Brunswick, NJ, 1992), 11–35.

Dogan, Mattei and Jacques Narbonne, 'L'abstentionnisme électoral en France', *Rfsp*, 4 (1954), 5–26 and 301–25.

Dompnier, Nathalie, 'Les machines à voter à l'essai. Notes sur le mythe de la "modernisation" démocratique', *Genèses*, 49 (2002), 69–88.

Dompnier, Nathalie, 'Modernizing the vote and rationalizing the state: computers and the French polling-booth', *FH*, 29 (2015), 370–88.

Duclert, Vincent and Christophe Prochasson (eds), *Dictionnaire critique de la République* (Paris, 2007).

Dumoulin, Jacqueline, *Le Consulat d'Aix-en-Provence. Enjeux politiques, 1598–1692* (Dijon, 1993).

Dunne, John, 'In search of the village and small-town elections of Napoleon's Hundred Days: a departmental study', *FH*, 29 (2015), 304–27.

Dupeux, Georges, 'Le problème des abstentions dans le département du Loir-et-Cher au début de la Troisième République', *Rfsp*, 2 (1952), 71–86.

Dupeux, Georges, *Aspects de l'histoire sociale et politique du Loir-et-Cher 1848–1914* (Paris, 1962).

Duverger, Maurice, *The Political Role of Women* (Paris, 1955).

Edelstein, Melvin, *The French Revolution and the Birth of Electoral Democracy* (Farnham, 2014).

Fauré, Christine, 'Doléances, déclarations et pétitions, trois formes de la parole publique des femmes sous la Révolution', *AhRf*, 344 (2006), 5–25.

Favier, Laurence (ed.), *La Démocratie dématérialisée. Enjeux du vote électronique* (Paris, 2011).

Finchelstein, Gilles, 'Pour le vote obligatoire', Fondation Jean-Jaurès, Note 257, March 2015, https://jean-jaures.org/nos-productions/pour-le-vote-obligatoire.

Fizaine, Simone, *La Vie politique en Côte-d'Or sous Louis XVIII. Les élections et la presse* (Paris, 1931).

Flour de Saint-Genis, Victor, *La Révolution en province, d'après des documents inédits . . . L'esprit public et les élections au Havre de 1787 à 1790* (Le Havre, 1889).

Follain, Antoine, *Le Village sous l'ancien régime* (Paris, 2008).

Forth, Christopher E. and Elinor Accampo (eds), *Confronting Modernity in Fin-de-Siècle France: Bodies, Minds and Gender* (Basingstoke, 2010).

François, Abel and Éric Phélippeau, *Le Financement de la vie politique* (Paris, 2015).

Fuligni, Bruno, *Votez fou. Candidats bizarres, utopistes, chimériques, mystiques, marginaux, farceurs et farfelus* (Paris, 2007).

Gaboriaux, Chloé, *La République en quête de citoyens. Les républicains français face au bonapartisme rural, 1848–1880* (Paris, 2010).

Garrigou, Alain, 'Le secret de l'isoloir', *ARSS*, 71–2 (1988), 22–45.

Garrigou, Alain, *Le Vote et la vertu. Comment les Français sont devenus électeurs* (Paris, 1992).

Garrigou, Alain, 'Vivre de la politique. Les "quinze mille", le mandat et le métier', *Politix*, 20 (1992), 7–34.

Garrigou, Alain, 'L'initiation d'un initiateur: André Siegfried et le "Tableau politique de la France de l'Ouest"', *ARSS*, 106–7 (1995), 27–41.

Garrigou, Alain, *Histoire sociale du suffrage universel en France 1848–2000* (Paris, 2002).

Gauchet, Marcel, *La Révolution des pouvoirs. La souveraineté, le peuple et la représentation 1789–1799* (Paris, 1995).

Gaxie, Daniel, *Le Cens caché. Inégalités sociales et ségrégations politiques* (Paris, 1978).

Gaxie, Daniel (ed.), *Explication du vote. Un bilan des études électorales en France* (Paris, 1985).

Genty, Maurice, *Paris 1789–1795. L'apprentissage de la citoyenneté* (Paris, 1987).

Genty, Maurice, 'Du refus des candidatures ouvertes à la préparation des élections: l'exemple de Paris au début de la Révolution française (1790–1791)', *The Chuo Law Review*, CIV (1997).

Geywitz, Gisela, *Das Plebiszit von 1851 in Frankreich* (Tübingen, 1965).

Girard, Louis (ed.), *Les Élections de 1869* (Paris, 1960).

Girard, Louis et al., *Les Conseillers généraux en 1870* (Paris, 1967).

Godineau, Dominique, 'Femmes en citoyenneté: pratiques et politique', *AhRf*, 300 (1995), 197–207.

Godineau, Dominique, *The Women of Paris and their French Revolution*, trans. Katherine Streip (Berkeley, CA, 1998).

Gouault, Jacques, *Comment la France est devenue républicaine, 1870–1875* (Paris, 1954).

Goguel, François, *Géographie des élections françaises de 1870 à 1951* (Paris, 1951).

Goguel, François, 'Pour une étude scientifique de l'abstentionnisme électoral', *Rfsp*, 2 (1952), 68–70.

Goguel, François (ed.), *Nouvelles études de sociologie électorale* (Paris, 1954).

Gosnell, Harold F., *Why Europe Votes* (Chicago, IL, 1930).

Goujon, Bertrand, *Monarchies postrévolutionnaires, 1814–1848* (Paris, 2012).

Goujon, Pierre, *Le Vigneron citoyen, Mâconnais et Chalonnais (1848–1914)* (Paris, 1993).

Gourvitch, A., 'Le mouvement pour la réforme électorale (1838–1841), *La Révolution de 1848. Bulletin de la Société d'histoire de la Révolution de 1848*, 11–13 (1914–17).

Gueniffey, Patrice, *Le Nombre et la raison. La Révolution française et les élections* (Paris, 1993).

Guéraiche, William, *Les Femmes et la République. Essai sur la répartition du pouvoir de 1943 à 1979* (Paris, 1999).

Guionnet, Christine, *L'Apprentissage de la politique moderne. Les élections municipales sous la monarchie de Juillet* (Paris, 1997).

Hamman, Philippe, 'La notabilité dans tous ses états? Alexandre de Geiger à Sarreguemines, un patron en politique sous le Second Empire', *Rh*, 622 (2002), 317–52.

Hamon, Philippe and Catherine Laurent (eds), *Le Pouvoir municipal de la fin du Moyen Âge à 1789* (Rennes, 2012).

Hanson, Paul, 'The Federalist Revolt: an affirmation or denial of popular sovereignty?', *FH*, 6 (1992), 335–55.

Hanson, Stephen E., 'The founding of the Third Republic', *Comparative Political Studies*, 43 (2010), 1023–58.

Harivel, Maud, *Les Élections politiques dans la République de Venise (XVIe–XVIIIe siècle). Entre justice distributive et corruption* (Paris, 2019).

Harrison, Martin and Philip M. Williams, 'The French referendum of April 1962', *Parliamentary Affairs*, XV (1962), 294–306.

Hause, Steven C., *Hubertine Auclert: The French Suffragette* (Princeton, NJ, 1987).

Hause, Steven C. with Anne R. Kenney, *Women's Suffrage and Social Politics in the French Third Republic* (Princeton, NJ, 1984).

Hayat, Samuel, 'Se présenter pour protester. La candidature impossible de François-Vincent Raspail en décembre 1848', *Rfsp*, 64 (2014), 869–903.

Hazareesingh, Sudhir, *From Subject to Citizen: The Second Empire and the Emergence of Modern French Democracy* (Princeton, NJ, 1998).

Hermet, Guy, *Le Peuple contre la démocratie* (Paris, 1989).

Horn, Jeff, *Qui parle pour la nation? Les élections en Champagne 1765–1830* (Paris, 2004).

Houte, Arnaud-Dominique, *Le Triomphe de la République 1871–1914* (Paris, 2014).

Huard, Raymond, *Le Suffrage universel en France 1848–1946* (Paris, 1991).

Huard, Raymond, 'L'affirmation du suffrage universel masculin 1848–1880', in Serge Berstein and Michel Winock (eds), *L'Invention de la démocratie 1789–1914* (Paris, 2002), 183–220.

Huard, Raymond, *La Naissance du parti politique en France* (Paris, 1996).

Hubble, Nick, *Mass Observation and Everyday Life* (Basingstoke, 2006).

Huet, Vincent, 'Le bulletin nul: une forme de résistance à la normalisation de la vie politique (Paris, 1851–1870)', *Amnis*, 9 (2010), http://amnis.revues.org/312.

Igersheim, François, *Politique et administration dans le Bas-Rhin (1848–1870)* (Strasbourg, 1993).

Ihl, Olivier, 'L'urne électorale. Formes et usages d'une technique de vote', *Rfsp*, 43 (1993), 30–60.

Ihl, Olivier, *Le Vote*, 2nd edn (Paris, 2000).

Ihl, Olivier, 'L'urne et le fusil: sur les violences électorales lors du scrutin du 23 avril 1848', *Rfsp*, 60 (2010), 9–35.

Ihl, Olivier and Gilles J. Guglielmi (eds), *Le Vote électronique* (Paris, 2015).

Irvine, William D., *The Boulanger Affair Reconsidered: Royalism, Boulangism and the Origins of the Radical Right in France* (New York, 1989).

Irvine, William D., 'Women's right and the "rights of man"', in Kenneth Mouré and Martin S. Alexander (eds), *Crisis and Renewal in France, 1918–1962* (Oxford, 2001), 46–65.

Isakhan, Benjamin and Stephen Stockwell (eds), *The Edinburgh Companion to the History of Democracy: From Pre-history to Future Possibilities* (Edinburgh, 2015).

Jarrige, François, 'Une "barricade de papiers": le pétitionnement contre la restriction du suffrage universel masculin en mai 1850', *Rh19*, 29 (2004), 53–70.

Jeanneney, Jean-Noël, *François de Wendel en République. L'argent et le pouvoir, 1914–1940* (Paris, 2004).

Jennings, Jeremy, *Revolution and the Republic: A History of Political Thought in France since the Eighteenth Century* (Oxford, 2010).

Jessen, Ralph and Hedwig Richter (eds), *Voting for Hitler and Stalin: Elections under 20th Century Dictatorships* (Frankfurt, 2011).

Joana, Jean, 'L'invention du député. Réunions parlementaires et spécialisation de l'activité politique au XIXe siècle', *Politix*, 35 (1996), 23–42.

Jolivet, Charles, *La Révolution dans l'Ardèche (1788–1795)* (Marseille, 1980).

Jones, Peter (P.M.), 'An improbable democracy: nineteenth-century elections in the Massif Central', *English Historical Review*, XCVII (1982), 530–57.

Jones, Peter (P.M.), *Liberty and Locality in the French Revolution: Six Villages Compared, 1760–1820* (Cambridge, 2003).

Jones, Witney, *David Williams: The Anvil and the Hammer* (Cardiff, 1986).

Julien-Laferrière, François, *Les Députés fonctionnaires sous la Monarchie de Juillet* (Paris, 1970).

Kahan, Alan S., *Liberalism in Nineteenth-Century Europe: The Political Culture of Limited Suffrage* (Basingstoke, 2003).

Karila-Cohen, Pierre, *L'Invention de l'enquête politique en France (1814–1848)* (Rennes, 2008).

Keane, John, *The Life and Death of Democracy* (London, 2009).

Kent, Sherman, *Electoral Procedure under Louis Philippe* (New Haven, CT, 1937).

Kent, Sherman, 'Two official candidates of the July Monarchy', *American Historical Review*, 43 (1937), 65–73.

Kent, Sherman, *The Election of 1827 in France* (Cambridge, MA, 1975).

Kermoal, Christian, *Les Notables du Trégor: éveil à la culture politique et évolution dans les paroisses rurales, 1770–1850* (Rennes, 2002).

Klejman, Laurence, *L'Égalité en marche. Le féminisme sous la Troisième République* (Paris, 1989).

Lacroix, Bernard, 'Retour sur 1848. Le suffrage universel entre l'illusion de "jamais vu" et l'illusion de "toujours ainsi"', *ARSS*, 140, (2002), 41–50.

Lagoueyte, Patrick, *La Vie politique en France au XIXᵉ siècle* (Gap, 1990).

Lagoueyte, Patrick, 'Élections', in Jean Tulard (ed.), *Dictionnaire du Deuxième Empire* (Paris, 1995), 227–32.

Landes, Joan B., *Women and the Public Sphere in the Age of the French Revolution* (Ithaca, NY, 1988).

Langlois, Claude, 'Le plébiscite de l'an VIII ou le coup d'État du 18 pluviôse an VIII', *AhRf* (1972), 43–65, 231–46, and 390–415.

Larrère, Mathilde, *L'Urne et le fusil. La garde nationale parisienne de 1830 à 1848* (Paris, 2016).

Lawrence, Jon, *Electing our Masters: The Hustings from Hogarth to Blair* (Oxford, 2009).

Lawrence, Jon, 'The culture of elections in modern Britain', *History*, 96 (2011), 459–76.

Le Digol, Christophe et al. (eds), *Histoires d'élections. Représentations et usages du vote de l'Antiquité à nos jours* (Paris, 2018).

Le Gall, Laurent, *L'Électeur en campagnes dans le Finistère. Une Seconde République des Bas-Bretons* (Paris, 2009).

Le Gall, Laurent, *A Voté. Une histoire de l'élection* (Paris, 2017).

Le Maner, Yves, 'Les maires d'un arrondissement d'un pays minier, Béthune', in Maurice Agulhon (ed.), *Les Maires en France du Consulat à nos jours* (Paris, 1986).

Le Naour, Jean-Yves, *La Famille doit voter. Le suffrage familial contre le vote individuel* (Paris, 2005).

Leclère, Bernard and Vincent Wright, *Les Préfets du Second Empire* (Paris, 1973).

Lehingue, Patrick, *Le Vote. Approches sociologiques de l'institution et des comportements électoraux* (Paris, 2011).

Lenoir, Noëlle, 'The representation of women in politics: from quotas to parity', *The International and Comparative Law Quarterly*, 50 (2001), 217–47.

Locke, Robert R., *French Legitimists and the Politics of Moral Order in the Early Third Republic* (Princeton, NJ, 1974).

Long, Raymond, *Les Élections législatives en Côte-d'Or depuis 1870* (Paris, 1958).

McPhee, Peter, *Les Semailles de la République dans les Pyrénées-Orientales 1846–1852* (Perpignan, 1995).

Mair, Peter, *Ruling the Void: The Hollowing of Western Democracy* (London, 2013).

Malkopoulou, Anthoula, *The History of Compulsory Voting in Europe: Democracy's Duty?* (London, 2014).

Manin, Bernard, *The Principles of Representative Government*, trans. (Cambridge, 1997).

Markoff, John, 'From centre to periphery and back again: reflections on the geography of democratic innovation', in Michael P. Hanagan and Charles Tilly (eds), *Extending Citizenship, Reconfiguring States* (Lanham, MD, 1999), 229–46.

Marty, Thomas, *Une Histoire sociale de la réforme électorale sous la Troisième République. Mobilisations politique et expertise électorale: la question de la 'représentation proportionnelle'* (Paris, 2012).

Maus, Didier, 'Le vote obligatoire. Une fausse bonne idée', Fondation Jean-Jaurès, Note 258, March 2015, https://jean-jaures.org/nos-productions/le-vote-obligatoire-une-fausse-bonne-idee.

Mayaud, Jean-Luc (ed.), *1848. Actes du colloque international du cent-cinquantenaire* (Paris, 1998).

Mayeur, Jean-Marie et al. (eds), *Les Parlementaires de la Troisième République* (Paris, 2003).

Ménager, Bernard, *Les Napoléon du peuple* (Paris, 1988).

Merriam, Charles Edward and Harold Foote Gosnell, *Non-Voting: Causes and Methods of Control* (Chicago, IL, 1924).

Miquet-Marty, François, 'Les agents électoraux. La naissance d'un rôle politique dans la deuxième moitié du XIXe siècle', *Politix*, 38 (1997), 47–62.

Monnier, Raymonde (ed.), *Citoyens et citoyenneté sous la Révolution française* (Paris, 2006).

Mossuz-Lavau, Janine, 'L'évolution du vote des femmes', *Pouvoirs*, 82 (1997), 37–57.

Mossuz-Lavau, Janine and Mariette Sineau, *Enquête sur les femmes et la politique en France* (Paris, 1983).

Moualek, Jérémie, 'Tous pourris! Formes et significations des gros mots de l'électeur au prisme des bulletins nuls', *Argotica*, 1 (2013), 231–40.

Moualek, Jérémie, 'Votes blancs et nuls aux élections européennes de 1994. Des votes "euro-constructifs"?', in Martial Libera et al. (eds), *Abstentionnisme, euroscepticisme et anti-européisme dans les élections européennes de 1979 à nos jours* (Stuttgart, 2016), 79–90.

Moualek, Jérémie, 'Des voix (vraiment) pas comme les autres? Les usages pluriels des votes blancs et nuls', *Rfsp*, 67 (2017), 1153–66.

Moulin, Léo, 'Les origines religieuses des techniques électorales et délibératives modernes', *Politix*, 43 (1998), 113–62.

Muxel, Anne, 'L'abstention: déficit démocratique ou vitalité politique?', *Pouvoirs*, 120 (2007), 43–55.

O'Gorman, Frank, *Voters, Patrons and Parties: The Unreformed Electorate of Hanoverian England, 1734–1832* (Oxford, 1989).

Offen, Karen, *The Woman Question in France, 1400–1870* (Cambridge, 2017).

Offen, Karen, *Debating the Woman Question in the French Third Republic, 1870–1920* (Cambridge, 2018).

Offerlé, Michel, *Un Homme, une voix? Histoire du suffrage universel* (Paris, 1993).

Offerlé, Michel, 'Les Schneider en politique', in *Les Schneider. Le Creusot. Une famille, une entreprise, une ville (1836–1960)* (Paris, 1995), 289–305.

Offerlé, Michel (ed.), *La Profession politique, XIXᵉ–XXᵉ siècles* (Paris, 1999).

Offerlé, Michel, 'Les figures du vote. Pour une iconographie du suffrage universel', *Sociétés & Représentations*, 12 (2001/2), 108–30.

Orr, Graeme, *Ritual and Rhythm in Electoral Systems: A Comparative Legal Account* (Abingdon, 2015).

Owen, Bernard (ed.), *Le Processus electoral. Permanences et évolutions* (Paris, 2006).

Palmer, Robert R., *The Age of the Democratic Revolution*, 2 vols (Princeton, NJ, 1959–64).

Patrick, Alison, *The Men of the First Republic: Political Alignments in the National Convention of 1792* (Baltimore, MD, 1972).

Perrier, Marcel, *La République démocratique. Étude critique et historique de la législation électorale de la République en France* (Paris, 1907).

Perrineau, Pascal, 'Les usages contemporains du vote', *Pouvoirs*, 120 (2006), 29–41.

Perrineau, Pascal (ed.), *Le Vote disruptif. Les élections présidentielle et législatives de 2017* (Paris, 2017).

Perrineau, Pascal and Dominique Reynié (eds) *Dictionnaire du vote* (Paris, 2001).

Pertué, Michel, (ed.), *Suffrage, citoyenneté et révolutions 1789–1848* (Paris, 2002).

Petiteau, Natalie, '1848 en Vaucluse, ou l'impossible république bourgeoise', *Cahiers d'Histoire*, 43 (1998), 223–45.

Phélippeau, Éric, *L'Invention de l'homme politique moderne. Mackau, l'Orne et la République* (Paris, 2002).

Pilenco, Alexandre, *Les Moeurs électorales en France: régime censitaire* (Paris, 1928).

Pilenco, Alexandre, *Les Moeurs électorales du suffrage universel en France (1848–1930)* (Paris, 1930).

Pilven, J.-M., *Le Premier évêque constitutionnel, Expilly, évêque du Finistère, 1790–1794* (Quimper, 1912).

Pommeret, Hervé, *L'Esprit public dans le département des Côtes-du-Nord pendant la Révolution 1789–1799* (Saint-Brieuc, 1921).

Popkin, Jeremy D., 'Press and elections in the French revolution of 1848: the case of Lyon', *FHS*, 36 (2013), 83–108.

Pourcher, Yves, *Les Maîtres de granit: les notables de Lozère du XVIIIe siècle à nos jours* (Paris, 1987).

Price, Roger, *The French Second Empire: An Anatomy of Political Power* (Cambridge, 2001).

Puech, Louis, *Essai sur la candidature officielle en France depuis 1851* (Mende, 1922).

Quéro, Laurent, 'Les manuels électoraux français. Objets d'élection (1790–1995)', *Scalpel*, 2–3 (1997), 11–58.

Quéro, Laurent and Christophe Voilliot, 'Du suffrage censitaire au suffrage universel. Évolution ou révolution des pratiques électorales?', *ARSS*, 140 (2002), 34–40.

Qvortrup, Matt, *Direct Democracy: A Comparative Study of the Theory and Practice of Government by the People* (Manchester, 2017).

Read, Geoff, *The Republic of Men: Gender and the Political Parties in Interwar France* (Baton Rouge, LA, 2014).

Reuss, Rodolphe, *La Constitution civile du clergé et la crise religieuse en Alsace (1790–1795)*, 2 vols (Paris, 1922).

Reynolds, Siân, *France between the Wars: Gender and Politics* (London, 1996).

Reynolds, Siân, 'Le sacre de la citoyenne? Réflexions sur le retard français', in Yolande Cohen and Françoise Thébaud (eds), *Féminismes et identités nationales. Les processus d'intégration des femmes au politique* (Lyon, 1998), 71–84.

Reynolds, Siân, 'Lateness, amnesia and unfinished business: gender and democracy in twentieth-century Europe', *European History Quarterly*, 32 (2002), 85–109.

Riot-Sarcey, Michèle, 'Des femmes pétitionnent sous la monarchie de juillet', in Alain Corbin et al. (eds), *Femmes dans la cité* (Grâne, 1997), 389–400.

Rivet, Auguste, *La Vie politique dans la Haute-Loire, 1815–1974* (Le Puy, 1979).

Romanelli, Raffaele (ed.), *How Did They Become Voters? The History of Franchise in Modern European Representation* (The Hague, 1998).

Rosanvallon, Pierre, *Le Sacre du citoyen. Histoire du suffrage universel en France* (Paris, 1992).

Rosanvallon, Pierre, *La Monarchie impossible. Les Chartes de 1814 et de 1830* (Paris, 1994).

Rosanvallon, Pierre, *Le Peuple introuvable. Histoire de la représentation démocratique en France* (Paris, 1998).

Rosanvallon, Pierre, *La Démocratie inachevée. Histoire de la souveraineté du people en France* (Paris, 2000).

Rosanvallon, Pierre, *La Contre-démocratie. La politique à l'âge de la défiance* (Paris, 2006).

Rose, R. B., *The Making of the* Sans-Culottes: *Democratic Ideas and Institutions in Paris, 1789–1792* (Manchester, 1983).

Rose, R. B., 'Feminism, women and the French Revolution', *Australian Journal of Politics and History*, 40 (1994), 173–86.

Roussellier, Nicolas, 'Electoral antipluralism and electoral pluralism in France, from the mid-nineteenth century to 1914', in Julian Wright and H. S. Jones (eds), *Pluralism and the Idea of the Republic in France* (Basingstoke, 2012), 141–60.

Rudelle, Odile, *La République absolue: aux origines de l'instabilité constitutionnelle de la France républicaine 1870–1889* (Paris, 1982).

Saltman, Roy G., *The History and Politics of Voting Technology: In Quest of Integrity and Public Confidence* (New York, 2006).

Saupin, Guy, *Nantes au XVIIe siècle. Vie politique et société urbaine* (Rennes, 1996).

Saupin, Guy, 'La réforme des élections municipales en France au XVIIIe siècle. Réflexions à partir de l'exemple de Nantes', *Rhmc*, 46 (1999), 629–57.

Saupin, Guy, *Les Villes en France à l'époque moderne (XVIe–XVIIIe siècles)* (Paris, 2002).

Scott, Joan, *Only Paradoxes to Offer: French Feminists and the Rights of Man* (Cambridge, MA, 1996).

Secondy, Philippe, 'Pierre Leroy-Beaulieu: un importateur des méthodes électorales américaines en France', *Rh*, 634 (2005), 309–41.

Sewell, William H. Jr, 'Le citoyen/la citoyenne: activity, passivity, and the revolutionary concept of citizenship', in Keith M. Baker et al. (eds), *The French Revolution and the Creation of Modern Political Culture*, 4 vols (Oxford, 1987–94), ii, 105–23.

Sewell, William H. Jr, *A Rhetoric of Bourgeois Revolution: The Abbé Sieyes and What is the Third Estate?* (Durham, NC, 1994).

Seymour, Charles and Donald Paige Frary, *How the World Votes: The Story of Democratic Development in Elections*, 2 vols (Springfield, CA, 1918).

Shusterman, Noah, *The French Revolution: Faith, Desire, and Politics* (Abingdon, 2014).

Siegfried, André, *Tableau politique de la France de l'Ouest sous la Troisième République* (Brussels, 2010).

Smith, Paul, *Feminism and the Third Republic: Women's Political and Civil Rights in France 1918–1945* (Oxford, 1996).

Smith, Paul, *A History of the French Senate: The Third Republic 1870–1940*, 2 vols (Lampeter, 2005–6).

Sowerwine, Charles, *Sisters or Citizens? Women and Socialism in France since 1876* (Cambridge, 1982).

SPEL (Collectif de sociologie politique des élections), *Les Sens du vote. Une enquête sociologique (France 2011–2014)* (Rennes, 2016).

Spitzer, Alan B., 'Restoration political theory and the debate over the law of the double vote', *Journal of Modern History*, 55 (1983), 54–70.

Stockinger, Thomas, 'Le lien parlementaire en 1848. Analyse comparée des candidatures aux élections en Seine-et-Oise et en Basse-Autriche', *Rh19*, 43 (2011), 57–75.

Subileau, Françoise and Marie-France Toinet, *Les Chemins de l'abstention. Une comparaison franco-américaine* (Paris, 1993).

Suratteau, Jean-René, *Les Élections de l'an VI et le coup d'état du 22 floréal (11 mai 1798)* (Paris, 1971).

Teele, Dawn Langan, *Forging the Franchise: The Political Origins of the Women's Vote* (Princeton, NJ, 2018).

Teissier, Octave, *Le Suffrage universel et le vote obligatoire à Toulon en 1354* (Paris, 1868).

Temple, Nora, 'Municipal elections and municipal oligarchies in eighteenth-century France', in J. F. Bosher (ed.), *French Government and Society, 1500–1850: Essays in Honour of Alfred Cobban* (London, 1973), 70–91.

Thompson, J. M., *The French Revolution*, revised edn (Oxford, 1985).

Tiberj, Vincent, *Des Votes et des voix, de Mitterrand à Hollande* (Paris, 2013).

Trempé, Roland, 'Une campagne électorale étudiée d'après les archives privées', *Actes du 82ᵉ congrès national des sociétés savantes* (Paris, 1958), 471–90.

Tudesq, André-Jean, *Les Grands notables en France (1840–1849). Étude historique d'une psychologie sociale*, 2 vols (Paris, 1964).

Tudesq, André-Jean, *Les Conseils généraux en France au temps de Guizot, 1840–1848* (Paris, 1967).

Verdeau, Simone, *L'Accession des femmes aux fonctions publiques* (Toulouse, 1942).

Verjus, Anne, 'Entre principes et pragmatisme. Députés et sénateurs dans les premiers débats sur le suffrage des femmes en France (1919–1922)', *Politix*, 51 (2000), 55–80.

Verjus, Anne, *Le Cens de la famille. Les femmes et le vote, 1789–1848* (Paris, 2002).

Vernon, James, *Politics and the People: A Study in English Political Culture, c.1815–1867* (Cambridge, 1993).

Villette, Vincent, *Apprendre à voter sous la IIᵉ République. Le suffrage de masse dans le département de la Seine (1848–1851)* (Paris, 2013).

Villette, Vincent, 'The urn and the rumour: false information about electoral fraud as a means of discrediting mass suffrage in the department of the Seine, 1848–49', *FH*, 29 (2015), 328–48.

Viple, Jean-François, *Sociologie politique de l'Allier. La vie politique et les élections sous la Troisième République* (Paris, 1967).

Voilliot, Christophe, *La Candidature officielle. Une pratique d'État de la Restauration à la Troisième République* (Rennes, 2005).

Voilliot, Christophe, *Le Département de l'Yonne en 1848. Analyse d'une séquence électorale* (Vulaines-sur-Seine, 2017).

Waresquiel, Emmanuel de and Benoît Yvert, *Histoire de la Restauration 1814–1830* (Paris, 2002).

Wartelle, Jean-Claude, 'L'élection Barodet (avril 1873)', *Rhmc*, 27 (1980), 601–30.

Weil, Georges-Denis, *Les Élections législatives depuis 1789. Histoire de la législation et des mœurs* (Paris, 1895).

Woloch, Isser, *Jacobin Legacy: The History of the Democratic Movement under the Directory* (Princeton, NJ, 1970).

Woloch, Isser, *The New Regime: Transformations of the French Civic Order, 1789–1820s* (New York, 1994).

Wylie, Laurence William (ed.), *Chanzeau, a Village in Anjou* (Cambridge, MA, 1966).

Zeldin, Theodore, *The Political System of Napoleon III* (London, 1958).

Zeldin, Theodore, 'Government policy in the French general election of 1849', *English Historical Review*, LXXIV (1959), 240–8.

Zulfikarpasic, Adélaïde, 'Le vote blanc: abstention civique ou expression politique?', *Rfsp*, 51 (2001), 247–68.

(iii) Digital Resources

A number of primary and secondary sources listed in this bibliography are available online, affording easy access to basic materials like the *Moniteur*, or the *Journal Officiel de la République*. See BNF Gallica for a wide range of titles. Other materials indicated as such in the footnotes only exist in digital form.

The International Institute for Democracy and Electoral Assistance (IDEA) https://www.idea.int/ houses a host of information on different aspects of electoral practice around the world.

France politique: le site d'information sur la vie politique https://www.france-politique.fr/elections provides statistics on recent elections in France.

Index